Introduction to Family Processes

•

Introduction to Family Processes: Diverse Families, Common Ties serves to provide an explanation of the complex workings of inner family life. The text primarily focuses on family processes and dynamics (the "inside" of families) as opposed to sociological trends, political topics, or the individual psychological approach. The text further presents the research underlying these processes and effectively presents ways to increase the positive aspects of family life.

This edition has been updated to include current research and contemporary topics. The text has been divided into four parts: Foundations, Building and Establishing Families, Maintaining Families, and Change/Turbulence/Gains/Losses. While the research methods chapter still provides an introductory examination of family science research, it now includes an expanded discussion on research design, methods, and advances in the area. A new chapter, titled "Forgiveness, Kindness, Hope, and Gratitude" has been incorporated to amplify positive family processes and highlight emerging research. This edition provides added emphasis on diverse families (e.g., race/ethnicity, family structure, LGBTQIA, ability, culture, and family formation), and each chapter includes a new "Discussions in Diversity" section related to that chapter. The authors have consciously included an epilogue as a way of reflecting on what they have learned, along with what they hope to learn in the future.

Aimed at courses related to family studies and family dynamics, this text provides a comprehensive review of family processes. Whether it is used for undergraduate or graduate classes, professional growth, or personal enrichment, the text assists readers in enhancing the positive aspects of family life, avoiding undesirable aspects, and more effectively managing the challenges and obstacles families face that cannot be avoided. Thus, the text holds an appeal for people who live (or will live) in families, as well as those who want to work with families.

Denise Ann Bodman, PhD, has taught family and human development courses at Arizona State University's T. Denny Sanford School of Social and Family Dynamics for over 30 years, garnering numerous teaching and service awards. Her writings (both popular and scientific) and research have focused on cross-cultural parenting and family relationships.

Bethany Bustamante Van Vleet, PhD, is a Senior Lecturer at Arizona State University in the School of Social and Family Dynamics. Her passion lies in engaging students while teaching them about family and human development, measurement, and statistics. With a husband and six kids, *Family Processes* is more than just a textbook to Bethany.

Before his passing, **Randal D. Day, PhD,** was a popular teacher, mentor, researcher, and scholar. He published more than 100 research articles, books, and government documents focusing on family processes, men in families, and social science research.

Introduction to Family Processes

Diverse Families, Common Ties

Sixth Edition

Denise Ann Bodman
Bethany Bustamante Van Vleet
Randal D. Day

Routledge
Taylor & Francis Group

NEW YORK AND LONDON

Cover image: © Getty Images

Sixth edition published 2022
by Routledge
4 Park Square, Milton Park, Abingdon, Oxon OX14 4RN

and by Routledge
605 Third Avenue, New York, NY 10158

Routledge is an imprint of the Taylor & Francis Group, an informa business

First edition published by Brooks/Cole Publishing Company 1993
Fifth edition published by Routledge 2010

Library of Congress Cataloging-in-Publication Data
A catalog record has been requested for this book

ISBN: 9781138312876 (hbk)
ISBN: 9781138312890 (pbk)
ISBN: 9781003128717 (ebk)

DOI: 10.4324/9781003128717

Dedication

This book is dedicated to our families, past, present, and future.

In loving memory of our friend and mentor, Randy Day, and his wife, Larri-Lea.

Their lives touched so many and will continue to be positive forces for good.

Contents

Preface

This text has been a labor of love, not only because it allowed us to work together as mother and daughter (we are both faculty members at the T. Denny Sanford School of Social and Family Dynamics at Arizona State University), but it also allowed us to maintain an enduring connection with our friend and mentor, Randy Day, who died unexpectedly at the outset of this project. Prior to his death, the three of us had discussed the importance of extensively revising and expanding this text to further embrace inclusivity and diversity. We think Randy would have liked the final product and are happy to see his continued contribution to a field he so dearly loved and so heavily influenced.

INTRODUCTION TO THE 6TH EDITION

Families are complicated, and this text attempts to explain the complex workings of inner family life. What began as a working project for introductory undergraduate family classes blossomed into this sixth edition text, with wide classroom (and even personal) applications. The original intent was to create a book that focused primarily on family processes and dynamics rather than sociological trends, political topics, or the individual psychological approach. It is written for undergraduate courses on family processes and family studies, the family, marriage and family interaction and relations, and family diversity, as well as for family dynamics taught in family studies, human development, psychology, sociology, social work, education, consumer sciences, home economics, health, nursing, and medical programs. It is an excellent introduction to or review of family processes for graduate and professional courses, as well. Outside of a classroom setting, this book also appeals to those who want to maximize the positive parts of family life.

This edition tries to stay true to that initial mission, with significant chapter updates to include new research and address modern families and family issues. Each chapter in the book opens with a Preview and concludes with "Discussions in Diversity," a Summary, Study Questions, Key Terms, and Suggested Readings. Principle Boxes highlight key chapter concepts to serve as a study reference.

We have incorporated several exciting changes in this edition. We have updated the chapters, making every attempt has to include current research and contemporary topics. For example, research on the COVID-19 pandemic was just beginning as we were writing this text, so where appropriate, it has been included.

In this edition, we have reorganized chapters, added chapters, and restructured the text. We have divided the text into four parts: Foundations, Building and Establishing Families, Maintaining Families, and Change/Turbulence/Gains/Losses. This new organization resulted in some of the chapters from the previous edition appearing in different locations or being renamed. The research methods chapter that debuted in the last edition and is now *Chapter 3, How We Study Family,* has been significantly changed in depth and focus. While still an introductory examination of how research is done in family science, it now includes advances in the area and an expanded discussion on research design and methods. *Chapter 9, Communicating in Families,* now includes a section on family secrets. *Chapter 12 Families as Units of Change and Transition* expanded to take in genetics and family, as well as gender issues (gender socialization, gendered parenting, division of household labor, power relationships), recognizing that family member change and family system change are tightly linked. Further, we added a new chapter, *Chapter 11 Forgiveness, Kindness, Hope, and Gratitude.* Research in this area is new and expanding, and we liked the idea of adding a chapter on positive family processes. We also added an epilogue in an attempt to reflect on what we learned, what we hope to learn in the future, and applications to policy.

An important objective for this edition was to include more research and information on diverse families (race/ethnicity, family structure, LGBTQIA, ability, culture, family formation). Each chapter includes a new "Discussions in Diversity" topic related to that chapter: E. Franklin Frazier (first African American President of the American Sociological Association), MTurk, Graphing Diversity, Mail Order Brides, Cultural Competence, Indigenous Perspective on Family Resilience, Grieving Rules, Family History and Self-Identity, Mom—I'm Trans, Self-Forgiveness, Adoption and Family Change, and ABC-X Across Contexts. We hope that these topics will lead to fruitful and lively class discussions.

Last, the online resources for this text have been moved to www.routledge. com/9781138312890. The student resources include Chapter Activity Questions that reinforce writing and critical thinking skills, Journal Activities to strengthen students' personal connection to the material, and Web Links to encourage further investigation into the material online. The instructor resources include lecture outlines, small group and in-class exercises, topics for debate, suggested films, PowerPoint presentations, and a test bank with multiple-choice, true–false, matching, and essay questions.

OUR PURPOSE

As this text has been revised over the years, it has become clearer that studying and understanding family life is increasingly important. Families and family life are ever changing, and the study of family life is occasionally fraught with important but controversial issues. As in past editions, this text does not attempt to tackle all the social issues that attend the study of the family. Instead, we have made a conscious decision to speak mostly about how families do the business of family life. This approach might not mesh well with those who want to focus their discussion about family on key cultural issues that typically attend the study of families in today's world. It is not our position that those issues are less important. It is our position, however, that a beginning-level text on family interaction cannot cover everything and understanding these foundational concepts can deepen our examination and conversations about these social issues. Therefore, we have chosen to devote our efforts to examining the *how* of family life instead of the *why.*

A strong and enduring theme of this book is that (to paraphrase a line made famous by Dickens in his epic novel *A Tale of Two Cities*) the family realm is the best of human life and it is the worst of human life. The best parts of family life are experienced as we find deep joy and the greatest pleasure from our interaction with those whom we love and love us the most. Family life is also a crucible that refines and tests and helps us grow and mature in ways that are noble, great, and wonderful. If we are wise in the way we manage this precious part of our lives, family life can provide satisfaction, fulfillment, love, security, a sense of belonging, and other beauties and riches that are difficult to attain outside the family realm.

The undesirable parts of the family realm reflect the worst side of human relationships. More murders are committed in families than anyplace else. Abuse in families, from spousal to child to sibling, is all too common. The privacy that allows intimacy and the deepest of love also allows sexual and emotional abuse. Family life is the source of some of the deepest frustrations, intense misery, immeasurable exploitation, and serious abuse that humans ever experience.

As we wrote this text, it was our hope that ideas assembled here would assist readers in finding ways to increase the positive aspects of family life, avoid the undesirable parts that can be avoided, and more effectively manage the challenges and obstacles that cannot be avoided. Some of the positive things that can come from healthy family life are intimacy that is not stifling, bonds without bondage, meaning and purpose, growth and progress, maturation and beauty, and enough security and stability that we have a sense of being in a wholesome home. On the negative side, our goals are to avoid violence, exploitation, dominance, abuses, tyranny, negligence, and other forms of excess that bring pain, hurt, disappointment, and inhumanity.

The original goal for this book was to help families and those who help families better attain these positive parts of the family realm and avoid the undesirable parts. Thus, this book is written to and for those who live (or will live) in families and, also, for those who want to work professionally or as a volunteer to help families. Each of us can help in many ways. We can help our own families and our friends, and we can help in our professions and avocations.

Many contributions of our families, colleagues, students, and friends have played a key role in the intellectual journey that this book represents. Several have directly impacted this edition with ideas, support, encouragement, reactions, and suggestions. We are grateful for Dr. Scott Brooks for his insight into early sociology; Georgette Enriquez for her editorial support and getting this project together; Dr. Frank Fincham and Dr. Douglas Kelley for their help with forgiveness science; Aubrey Hoffer for contributing her experience with Mturk and collecting data in today's world; Dr. Carol Martin for sharing her expertise on prosocial behavior, as well as gender; Dr. Eva Smidova for her excellent feedback regarding transgender; Tamara Rounds for her global support and caring feedback, and Dr. Sonya Xinyue Xiao, for her input on prosocial behavior.

—*D. Bodman, B. Bustamante Van Vleet, and R. Day (posthumous)*

Part I
Foundations

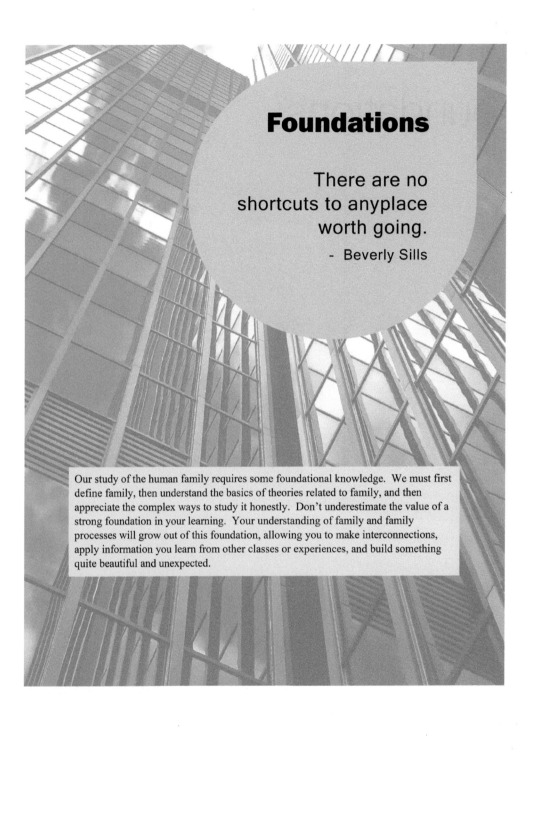

Foundations

There are no
shortcuts to anyplace
worth going.

- Beverly Sills

Our study of the human family requires some foundational knowledge. We must first define family, then understand the basics of theories related to family, and then appreciate the complex ways to study it honestly. Don't underestimate the value of a strong foundation in your learning. Your understanding of family and family processes will grow out of this foundation, allowing you to make interconnections, apply information you learn from other classes or experiences, and build something quite beautiful and unexpected.

CHAPTER 1

"Family" and Family Processes

CHAPTER PREVIEW

In this chapter, you will learn:

- Why families are important, as is the study of family life.
- That defining "family" is difficult and changes across time and culture.
- How the study of family life is different from the study of families using a sociological, psychological, or historical point of view.
- That we bring biases to our study of family life.
- How family processes are the strategies used by family members to maximize family goals.

INTRODUCTION

> Nearly every human being on earth has at least some family ties. Everyone is at least a member of a family of origin, and many people are also currently members of a primary living group. In this way, most of us have multiple family memberships. Therefore, "the family" is without question a very important concept for almost everybody.
>
> (Petzold, 1998, p. 60)

Philosopher George Santayana wrote, "Family is one of nature's masterpieces" (Santayana, 1907). Think of it. Most of us are born into families, and it is in our families where we first encounter the world. Our families may be rich or poor, biological, blended, step, or adopted. They may be headed by a single parent, two parents, or even several parents, parents who may be heterosexual or homosexual, married or unmarried. We may be born in a high rise in NYC or a hogan on the Navajo reservation. Our families may speak Spanish, English, Chinese, Swahili, Hindi. We laugh, we cry, we argue, we support, we touch, we grow close, we distance. We are so similar and simultaneously so different. Borrowing from Charles Dickens, in families, we see the best of times, we see the worst of times. No wonder that despite his difficult childhood, his experience of half-siblings, changes in place, and parents in an unhappy marriage, George Santayana was still able to describe families as "nature's masterpiece!"

People's interest in family has resulted in family life becoming a legitimate field of study. Many universities across the United States have degree programs dedicated to helping students

DOI: 10.4324/9781003128717-2

better understand the complexities of family life. Our study of family life is important for several reasons. For example, information about family life can assist us as we choose to form and build our own **family of procreation**. A family of procreation is the family we create with a partner and refers to that partner agreeing to form a relationship (formal or informal) that may include children (either by birth or adoption). Further, as we learn about family, we can better understand someone's **family of orientation**. One's family of orientation focuses on the family in which a person was raised. In both cases (i.e., reflecting on our families of procreation and families of orientation), when we understand family interaction either from the perspective of procreation or orientation, we have the potential of increasing the quality of those relationships and increasing our chances of attaining the goals and desires that inevitably reside within families.

As we undertake our exploration into family and family processes, we must first define them. Seems simple enough, right? Don't be so quick to answer.

PRINCIPLE 1.1

FAMILIES ARE IMPORTANT

We care about families because of the value they have to us (as individuals), our society, and the economy.

What Is Family?

"When **I** use a word," Humpty Dumpty said, in rather a scornful tone, "it means just what I choose it to mean—neither more nor less."

"The question is," said Alice, "whether you **can** make words mean so many different things."

"The question is," said Humpty Dumpty, "which is to be master—that's all."

Humpty Dumpty—Through the Looking Glass, Lewis Carroll

In Greek mythology, Proteus (Figure 1.1) was a lesser known but important god of the sea. His claim to fame was that he could change his shape into various forms at will. The derivative word, **protean**, describes someone or something that has this same ability. The family seems to fall into this category. Families themselves take on many forms; they are changeable, polymorphous, and versatile. Additionally, the definitions of family life are also protean. Those who think about family life and decide which type of small group is a family and which is not choose from among the many definitions available and select the one that best suits their purposes and ideological orientation, often reflective of their culture.

For example, businesses or governmental agencies define the family in ways that serve a particular purpose and are usually very specific and precise. Billions of dollars are meted out each year in transfer payments to "family members." For instance, insurance companies will cover only the medical expenses of family members that fall within their very restricted family member definition. Some authors (e.g., Cherlin, 2012) suggest that such definitions fall into our notion of a public family.

Those wishing to broaden the definition of the family seek to make private family life (as opposed to public family life) an individual choice in which a variety of styles, configurations,

FIGURE 1.1 Proteus, Greek God of the Sea.

Source: Woodcarving image from iStock

and combinations are acceptable. Those who approach the study of family life from more traditional business or governmental points of view might seek to limit and constrict the definition of the family for economic reasons. In addition, those who view the family as a sacred religious institution will suggest a particular configuration and even gender role assignment within the family based on doctrine and beliefs that support their point of view.

Because of its protean nature, the difficulty in defining family is seen in science, government, business, and the general population (see Table 1.1) and is often conflicting. For example, Article 16 of the UN's Universal Declaration of Human Rights (1948) proclaims, "The family is a natural and fundamental group of society and is entitled to protection by society and the State," yet a more recent UN report (Human Rights Council, 2016) stated, "There is no definition of the family under international human rights law … 'The concept of family may differ in some respects from State to State, and even from region to region within a State, and that it is therefore not possible to give the concept a standard definition.'" In the late 1970s, the then President Jimmy Carter organized what came to be known as the White House Conference on Families. Unfortunately, very little of the original agenda was discussed. Most of the conference energy was spent on the key question of what constitutes a family. For the conference, the battle over this single issue ended the conference with virtually nothing else of any significance to family life being discussed!

How would you define family? Would you only include blood relations and those adopted by law? Perhaps you would include your best and closest friends or even your pets! How much does culture influence your definition? This topic makes for an interesting discussion around the dinner table! Likely, a universal definition of family will never exist; however, functional definitions of family can be used as appropriate to the situation. Such definitions may be based on structure, function, and inclusion.

By Structure

Families come in all shapes and sizes, and some people define family by their type or structure. Varying family structure is often related to varying child outcomes, although not always, and is influenced by culture. What are some family structures?

TABLE 1.1 How Is Family Defined?

Family, Definition(s) of

- "The family is the natural and fundamental group unit of society and is entitled to protection by society and the State" (United Nations, 1948). "Society's definition of 'family' is rapidly expanding and has come to include single parents, biracial couples, blended families, unrelated individuals living cooperatively, and homosexual couples, among others. Unfortunately, family policy has been slow to catch up to changing trends in modern lifestyles" (Crawford, 1999, p. 271).
- "Ultimately, I define 'family' as the smallest, organized, durable network of kin and non-kin who interact daily, providing domestic needs of children and assuring their survival" (Stack, 1996, p. 31).
- "…an employee's spouse and dependent, unmarried children under age 19 (age 23 or 25 if a full-time student and dependent upon the employee for support)" (Abbott, 2002, p. 3).
- "Society's definition of a family has expanded to include 'single parents, biracial couples, blended families, unrelated individuals living cooperatively, and homosexual couples, among others'" (Crawford, 1999; Kenyon et al., 2003, p. 571).
- "Most uses of the word family in research indicate that it was often defined as 'spouse and children' or 'kin in the household'. Thus 'family' as defined in economics, sociology, and psychology often was a combination of the notions of household and kin… An exception to this standard definition of family is in clinical and counseling psychology, where family includes one's family of origin (parents and siblings) in addition to spouse and children" (Patterson, 1996; Rothausen, 1999, p. 818).
- "There are diverse types of families, many of which include people related by marriage or biology, or adoption, as well as people related through affection, obligation, dependence, or cooperation" (Rothausen, 1999, p. 820).
- "We define family as any group of people related either biologically, emotionally, or legally. That is, the group of people that the patient defines as significant for his or her well-being" (McDaniel et al., 2005, p. 2).
- "A family consists of two or more people, one of whom is the householder, related by birth, marriage, or adoption and residing in the same housing unit. A household consists of all people who occupy a housing unit regardless of relationship. A household may consist of a person living alone or multiple unrelated individuals or families living together" (U.S. Census Bureau, 2005).
- "…the National Institute of Mental Health (NIMH) adopted the definition of a 'network of mutual commitment' to connote the new structures that are the reality of families in the 1990s" (Pequengnat & Bray, 1997, p. 3).

From the Work and Family Researchers Network
https://wfrn.org/glossary/family-definitions-of/

From standard and modern dictionaries…

- The basic unit in society traditionally consisting of two parents rearing their children (Merriam-Webster. Family. (n.d.). Retrieved March 9, 2018, from https://www.merriam-webster.com/dictionary/family).
- A group of people, usually of the same blood (but do not have to be), who genuinely love, trust, care about, and look out for each other. Not to be mistaken with relatives sharing the same household who hate each other. REAL family is a bondage that cannot be broken by any means (Urban Dictionary, top definition https://www.urbandictionary.com/define.php?term=family).

- **Nuclear Family.** The **nuclear** family (also referred to as the conjugal family) consists of a household with two parents and their child/ren (Figure 1.2). This is likely the type of family most people think of when they are given the word "family." Indeed, this popular family form can be found across time and across culture. One "subtype" of nuclear family is the **traditional family**. By definition, the traditional family consists of a working father, a stay-at-home mother, and child/ren in the household. Although dominant in the 1950s,

FIGURE 1.2 A nuclear family consists of two parents and their children; however, nuclear families can still be quite different from each other.

Source: https://www.istockphoto.com/photo/multiethnic-parents-giving-children-piggyback-ride-gm1270066890-373151712

it was not the dominant form before or even after that time period. Before and after the 1950s, women worked as well as men to help sustain their families.

- **Extended Family.** The **extended** family is nuclear family + (Figure 1.3). In the household of an extended family, you may find grandparents, aunts/uncles, and cousins. Such multigenerational households can also be found across time and across culture. Often, extended family members live under one roof; however, many families today in the United States are not under one roof yet are **functionally extended**. Grandparents, for example, may not live in the same household, yet they provide support for their adult children and grandchildren and vice versa.
- **Single Parent Family.** Single parent families are households headed by one parent. Many people point to studies of "single parents" but overlook the various ways these parents become single. Some parents may be single due to divorce, others due to death, and still others out of choice. As you can imagine, each type of single parent family can have unique issues, so it is important to avoid lumping all "single parent families" into one category.
- **Stepfamilies.** Stepfamilies are also referred to as reconstituted families. They are usually formed following the death or divorce of one partner and remarriage to another partner. A variant of this family type is the blended family, where each partner brings children into the marriage and may even produce offspring together.
- **Cohabiting Families.** These families may be biological or step and exist without the formality of marriage; they are sometimes referred to as consensual unions. According to the U.S. Census (2021), about 32% of cohabiting couples have children under the age of 18 living in the household. Some of these children may come from previous relationships and others may be born into the household.

FIGURE 1.3 Extended families include grandparents, aunts, uncles, and cousins.

Source: https://www.istockphoto.com/photo/portrait-of-multi-generation-family-group-with-dog-on-winter-beach-vacation-gm1203194266-345709302

- **Same-Sex (Lesbigay) Parent Families.** Most gay and lesbian couples do not have children (Gates, 2012). Children in the household are more likely to come from a previous relationship, although an increasing number of gay and lesbian couples are adopting or utilizing reproductive technology (Figure 1.4). Some same-sex couples choose to marry, while others cohabit. Again, we see great diversity in this group.
- **Polygamous Families.** Polygamous families are families that have more than one partner by marriage. **Polygyny** refers to one man having several wives and has been practiced by more human societies than any other form of marriage. Its opposite, **polyandry**, refers to one woman having several husbands (Figure 1.5). Although rare, this form of family can be found in at least 50 societies around the world (Starkweather & Hames, 2012). **Polygamy** of any type is illegal in the United States but is legal and practiced in many countries around the world (most in Asia, the Middle East, and Africa). Interestingly, the UN currently does not recognize polygynous families as a valid family form and regards it as an attack on the dignity of women.

By Function

Because it would be impossible to capture all idealized notions about family in one definition, it seems reasonable to follow the lead of two prominent family scholars. In their book *Family Systems in America*, Reiss and Lee (1988) suggest that one should define family in terms of what family members *do* rather than its structure. That is, instead of trying to capture all the possibilities of who could be found in a family, it is a more useful approach to ask *what family groups do with each other*. They suggest four central functions of family life: providing sexual intimacy, reproduction, economic cooperation, and the socialization of children.

According to anthropologists, families found in most cultures and subcultures of the world perform these functions. What families do (e.g., have and rear children, solve problems, take care

FIGURE 1.4 Same sex parent families may have children from previous relationships or through various reproductive technologies.

Source: https://www.istockphoto.com/photo/loving-male-same-sex-couple-cuddling-baby-daughter-on-sofa-at-home-together-gm1177244727-328570292

FIGURE 1.5 Fraternal polyandry, where a woman marries the brothers in a family, is a marriage form found in Tibet. Although outlawed in 1981, it can still be found in rural areas.

of each other) has remained relatively unchanged for centuries. However, *how* those activities are performed and who is present (i.e., the composition of family life) is everchanging over time and varies from family to family and culture to culture.

By Inclusion

Many people define family by including people and pets outside biological or legal bonds. For them, their dog and best friends are **"family."** While familial relationships in these situations are not recognized legally (such as automatic inheritance by a dog or best friend, unless specifically spelled out in a will), these people and animals "feel" like family. Anthropologists refer to such non-related "family" members as **fictive kin**. Fictive kin includes godparents, close friends, fellow church members, and others. Many young people are surprised when they grow up and discover that their "Aunt Alicia" or "Tata Cruz" was not biologically related to their family at all!

Inclusive definitions are in response to our increased understanding of diversity and the willingness to accept anyone's perception of family. As a result, we see the word *family* replaced with *families* or **"family."** Rothberg and Weinstein (1996) write, "Families can be defined in many ways. They include persons related by blood, legal ties, friendship, or close emotional bonds … The constellation of family is limited only by the limits of participants' creativity" (p. 57).

Our Definition

In this text, we define family as a group of individuals in which there is a generational connection present (i.e., a parent–child relationship is found). Additionally, family members provide close intimate contact, usually characterized by deeply held commitment, trust, respect, and a sense of long-term obligation. It is assumed that sexual intimacy is an element of the relationship between the parents and that this family group seeks to achieve goals by acquiring, allocating, and distributing resources (i.e., time, money, space, and close personal contact).

It is also assumed that individuals choose to participate and contribute to the core sense of family life with varying degrees of enthusiasm. In some cases, the federation of individuals is loosely connected, and the beliefs, ideologies, goals, and values of the individuals do not overlap as much. In other cases, there is a stronger sense of the family group in which individuals with the family share, subscribe, endorse, and contribute to central family ideals, ideologies, beliefs, and goals.

You should know from the outset that we believe that family and family life are essential, enduring, and critical aspects of the human experience. You could say that we are biased in that regard. In addition, we assume that you, the reader, approach the study of family processes with biases, from how to define family to what family does (or should do). We cannot avoid our personal views of life, but we can acknowledge how those views might influence how we think about family life.

PRINCIPLE 1.2

FAMILIES ARE PROTEAN

The definition of "family" varies; families, themselves, are very adaptable and change structure and even what they do within family life (function) to meet the demands of a changing and volatile world.

What Are Family Processes?

Do you remember the poem about the blind men who encountered an elephant—some felt the tail, others the trunk, and still others the large midsection? Each of the wise men had a different story to tell (Figure 1.6).

Several academic disciplines explore "different parts of the elephant" when studying families. Family researchers in disciplines outside family science focus on the outer view of family life. For example, anthropologists might focus on the differences in marriage patterns across several different cultural groups.

Sociologists typically study marriage as one of many institutions in a complex society. They might have great interest in how families have adapted to a changing society, how divorce rates change in times of national crises, and how family life is impacted by changes in employment availability.

Historians, on the other hand, go to great lengths to discover the historical changes in marriage and how those changes can help explain better who we are. An example of the historical approach to studying the family could be a look at how people chose their mates in medieval Europe.

Psychologists are another group who study family life. For example, a psychologist might study family life by exploring how married relationships impact the psychological well-being of a particular family member. On the other hand, a research psychologist might want to know how family life pushes young women toward anorexia or other eating disorders.

FIGURE 1.6 The parable of the blind men and the elephant crosses centuries and reminds us how we are limited to our own experience as we seek truth.

Source: Creative commons, from Medieval Jain temple.

Demographers, people who study statistics related to human populations, are yet another group of scientists who study family life. They typically are interested in descriptions of how families are changing demographically in our culture. They might, for example, want to know how many families have children, how many live below the poverty level, or how many remarry. Demographers are also interested in the economics of family life, how much money families spend, and the intricacies associated with general resource allocation.

Until relatively recently, most of these ways of studying family dealt with the *outside* of the elephant (family). For family scientists, however, the study of family life is different. Metaphorically, it is about looking *inside* the live elephant and watching how the internal organs interact, how blood flows, where food is processed, and what the elephant is thinking. **Family processes** are the *inner* family life. They are what families do on a daily basis, how they solve life's dilemmas, and how they use various strategies to achieve goals. Family scientists now ask questions about the intricacies of inner, private family life. These are the aspects of life that fall somewhere in between the study of the individual and the study of groups in society. Said differently, family processes are what happens behind closed doors.

It is critical to understand family processes and the strategies used by family members to maximize family goals (Day, Gavazzi, & Acock, 2001). For example, a family goal (derived from a core belief or **ideology**) might focus on education, with the belief that educated family members will have the greatest chance of doing better in life. Therefore, family processes are those strategies used to reach that goal, which could include tactics such as saving money, insisting on certain family habits, and restricting time use. The communication we use, how we solve problems, and how we set and maintain boundaries are all examples of family processes. We realize that most of the goals families have are not very explicit. We also acknowledge that most of the choices we make as family groups are made with a vague notion about why we are doing them. Moreover, in many cases, it might be that not all family members agree on the family's direction, goals, beliefs, or choices. This ambiguity about family life makes it both rich and exciting to study but also makes it very difficult and challenging.

The study of problematic areas of family life (i.e., divorce, death, poverty, violence) is important and has alerted us to the many challenges facing today's children and parents, but there is another side of family life, characterized by the ordinary, mundane, prosaic, everyday events of life. In this book, we spend most of our time talking about the ordinary choices and everyday decisions families make. There is a growing awareness that the ordinary acts of daily living have a special power. It is often the routine acts of daily life that shape who we are and how our lives "turn out." Occasionally, a dramatic event will severely alter a family forever; nevertheless, for most people, lives are filled with the routine acts of daily living that combine to form and shape who we really are.

PRINCIPLE 1.3

FAMILY EMPLOY PROCESSES AND EFFECT GOALS

Family processes are the strategies and daily sequences of behavior employed by family members to achieve goals: Those goals are often implicit, and the goals might or might not be shared by every family member equally.

SUMMARY

Family plays an important role in most of our lives, although defining "family" can be difficult when families are so changeable and polymorphous. There are at least two distinct ways of examining family life. The first way is to examine the family as a definitional unit in which the actual structure of the membership is the focus. By that, we mean we would study family membership (who is there and who is not) and changes in membership (divorce, birth of a child, remarriage, etc.). On the other hand, another legitimate focus of study is the examination of the shared beliefs that family members hold, regardless of who they are, and the strategies families use to achieve goals. This latter focus is on family processes that involve the inner workings of family.

This book is about trying to explore and discover what those beliefs and ideologies might be, how families organize around those ideologies, and how those ideologies are acted out in everyday life. Ultimately, we want to know what strategies families use to reach the goals they have and if there are ways to assist them so that they can more successfully reach those goals.

It goes without saying that most people realize that family life is a double-edged sword; it can be a source of love, compassion, and fulfillment, but it can also be a harbor of destruction, oppression, and violence. Either condition is possible; however, we believe it is the responsibility of each family member to learn how to improve family life. It is assumed that by studying the intricacies of daily life, we can have some chance of assisting individuals as they try to make daily family life better for those involved.

By the numbers....

Statistical Overview of Families in the United States in 2017

Number of families in the United States	82.83m
Average number of people per family	3.14
Number of families with three or more children	6.76m
Number of families with single mother	15.58m
Number of families with single father	6.45m
Number of children under one living with unmarried parents	383,000
Number of children under one living with grandparent couple	268,000
Number of married couples	60.8m
Number of couples cohabiting (2016)	9m
Percent of LGBT adults married to same-sex spouse	10.2%

Sources:

- U.S. Families—Statistics & Facts https://www.statista.com/topics/1484/families/
- Number of U.S. Adults Cohabitating (2017) FactTank http://www.pewresearch.org/fact-tank/2017/04/06/number-of-u-s-adults-cohabiting-with-a-partner-continues-to-rise-especially-among-those-50-and-older/
- Gallup (2017) Social & Policy Issues http://news.gallup.com/poll/212702/lgbt-adults-married-sex-spouse.aspx

STUDY QUESTIONS

1   Why is family so difficult to define?
2   What does the term *protean family* refer to?
3   What is the difference between polygamy, polygyny, and polyandry?
4   Is it possible to study the family without bringing a bias to that endeavor?
5   What do we mean when we say that family life is unique?
6   Define what we mean by *family processes*. Give several examples of different family processes.
7   What is meant by "family" and how is this inclusive?
8   What do we mean when we say that we are defining family in terms of function instead of structure?
9   Explain in your own words what Principle 1.3 means when it says that families employ processes that effect goals.
10   Why do we (the family science scholarly community) care about families?

KEY TERMS

Family of procreation
Family of orientation (or origin)
Protean family
Nuclear family
Traditional family
Extended family
Functionally extended family
Lesbigay family
Polygamy
Polyandry
Polygyny
"Family"
Fictive kin
Family processes
Ideology

SUGGESTED READINGS

Amato, P., Booth, A., Johnson, D., & Rogers, S. (2007). *Alone together*. Cambridge, MA: Harvard University Press.
Brodrick, C. (1993). *Understanding family process: Basics of family systems*. Newbury Park, CA: Sage.
Coltrane, S., & Adams, M. (2008). *Gender and families*. Lanham, MD: Rowman & Littlefield.
Coontz, S. (1992). *The way we never were: American families and the nostalgia trap*. New York, NY: Basic Books.
Kowaleski-Jones, L., & Wolfinger, N. (2006). *Family families and the marriage agenda*. New York, NY: Springer.
Roopnarine, J., & Gielen, U. (2005). *Families in global perspective*. Boston, MA: Allyn & Bacon.
Thornton, A. (2001). *The well-being of children and families*. Ann Arbor, MA: University of Michigan Press.

Just for Kids

- *The Great Big Book of Families* by Mary Hoffman and Ros Asquith, Frances Lincoln Children's Books, 2015.
- *The Family Book* by Todd Parr, Little, Brown Books for Young Readers, Reprint edition (May 1, 2010).

REFERENCES

Cherlin, A. J. (2012). *Public and private families: An introduction* (7th ed.). New York, NY: McGraw-Hill.

Day, R. D., Gavazzi, S., & Acock, A. (2001). Compelling family processes. In A. Thornton (Ed.), *The well-being of children and families: Research and data nees* (pp. 103–126). Ann Arbor, MI: University of Michigan Press.

Gates, G. (Winter 2011). Family formation and raising children among same-sex couples. Family Focus on LGBT Families. *NCFR*, Issue FF51.

Human Rights Council (2016). Protection of the family: Contribution of the family to the realization of the right to an adequate standard of living for its members, particularly through its role in poverty eradication and achieving sustainable development. Advance Unedited Version. http://www.ohchr.org/_layouts/15/WopiFrame.aspx?sourcedoc=/Documents/HRBodies/HRCouncil/ProtectionFamily/A-HRC-31-37_en.doc&action=default&DefaultItemOpen=1

Petzold, M. (1998). The concept of "the family" in family psychology. In L. L'Abate (Ed.), *Family psychopathology: The relational roots of dysfunctional behavior* (pp. 60–74). New York, NY: Guilford Press.

Reiss, I. L., & Lee, G. R. (1988). *Family systems in America*. New York, NY: Holt, Rinehart, & Winston.

Rothberg, B., & Weinstein, D. (1996). A primer on lesbian and gay families. *Journal of Gay & Lesbian Social Services*, *4*(2), 55–68. DOI: 10.1300/J041v04n02_05

Santayana, G. (1907). *The life of reason: Reason in society* (Vol. 2). New York, NY: Dover Publications (1980).

Starkweather, K. E., & Hames, R. (2012). A survey of non-classical polyandry. *Human Nature*, *23*(2), 149–172. DOI: 10.1007/s12110-012-9144-x

CHAPTER 2

Theories About Family Life

CHAPTER PREVIEW

In this chapter, you will learn:

- Why theories are important.
- The difference between facts and theories.
- How various theories have been applied to family and why specific theories related to family have developed.
- Basic concepts related to social learning theory, symbolic interaction theory, social exchange theory, conflict theory, family development theory, and family systems theory.
- About renowned sociologist, E. Franklin Frazier.

INTRODUCTION

> There is nothing as practical as a good theory.
>
> (Kurt Lewin, 1943, p. 116)

Have you ever walked along a beach and seen sandcastles built on the edge of the surf? Some sandcastles are simple "structures" made by dumping a bucket upside down. Others are large and creative, with towering parapets, windows, doors, and courtyards, often put together by several people adding and expanding the structure. Sometimes the ocean waves come and bit-by-bit, the sandcastle dissolves; other times, a large wave levels the entire structure. Not all sandcastles are destroyed by powers outside the builder. Children themselves may be dissatisfied with their work and knock it down, only to rebuild again (Figure 2.1). Each sandcastle "architect" brings a unique view to the use of sand. This metaphor aptly applies to scientists (architects and builders) and their theories (sandcastles). This is the very basis of science.

The theories we use in social science are representations or models for something tangible and real. Empirical and theoretical ideas change and develop over time and are never meant to represent a position of truth, per se. Instead, theories are perspectives that help us understand reality and are merely constructs that we use as tools to approximate our understanding of the "real" world. An important question to ask in response to that last statement could be "Is there a real world?"

As we discuss theories, it is also important to realize that most of the methodological and theoretical ideas and terms presented here did not originate in the young discipline of family science. Instead, these ideas have, for the most part, a long and rich history in other disciplines, including sociology, economics, anthropology, and psychology. In this chapter, we present a

DOI: 10.4324/9781003128717-3

FIGURE 2.1 Children building sandcastles.

Source: CCO Public Domain

quick look at the theories most frequently used to study family. For a "deep dive" into theories, consider taking a theories class. In addition, we provide a list of suggested readings as a starting place for extended study.

FACTS AND THEORIES: ARE THESE IMPORTANT?

> Before I got married I had six theories about bringing up children;
>   now I have six children, and no theories.
>
> Frequently attributed to Lord Rochester

Legal scholar and philosopher Felix Cohen once said, "Generally the theories we believe we call facts, and the facts we disbelieve we call theories." Although many people use the terms "facts" and "theories" interchangeably, in science they are very different. A fact is an observation that most people agree with (Fabes & Martin, 2003). For example, it is a fact that the sun rises in the East. It is also a fact that toddlers seem to prefer being with their mothers. These are observations that most people agree with.

Theories, on the other hand, are proposed explanations of facts. The fact that the sun rises can be explained by several theories, from ancient sun gods carrying the sun across the sky on their backs to the sun moving around the earth to the earth rotating in orbit around the sun. Toddlers preferring their mothers could be explained by mothers being the primary caregivers or Freud's belief in unconscious incestuous desires! These explanations for facts (observable phenomena) are theories.

Students will often tell us that facts are "true" and that theories become facts as they get "proven." These popular misconceptions reflect a lack of understanding of science. Scientists do not try to *prove* theories; rather, they try to *disprove* them. Einstein reportedly said, "No amount of experimentation can ever prove me right; a single experiment can prove me wrong." The mountain of scientific knowledge we have today is precisely because science took on the task of building, changing, and challenging theories. Occasionally, some theories, such as gravity, are so strong that findings seem to consistently support them. This does not mean the theory has been proven; rather, it means the theory has moved from theory to "**law**," with the understanding that one day, a single finding may change the law.

Theories provide a common language for discussion about a topic, as well as direction for research and application. They are *tools* for researchers and serve several important purposes beyond explaining facts (White, 2005). Theories also serve to organize and make sense of facts. Several years ago, scholar Bernard Forscher (1963) wrote an essay titled "Chaos in the Brickyard." He saw researchers "making bricks" (facts) that were thrown into piles rather than being guided by a blueprint (theories) to build edifices. (For a fun graphic presentation of Forsher's essay, do an Internet search on "Matteo Farinella Chaos in the Brickyard.") Just as with sandcastles, walls might be torn down and changed but there is sense in the edifice that cannot be found in a pile of bricks.

Another important purpose of theories is that they can help us plan for the future and provide guidance for interventions. For example, many theories have been proposed for why teenagers may experience an unplanned pregnancy. These theories strongly influence the intervention one might use to decrease such pregnancies. If your theory is that teenagers lack appropriate sex education, then you might choose to change how and when they receive sex education. If your theory is that teenagers lack monitoring by parents or other adults, you may institute after school programs that encourage teen participation under watchful adult eyes. Providing interventions without having an underlying theory can be an exercise in futility, resulting in money and time being wasted. As tools, theories may be utilized in standard ways, but they also can be applied in innovative ways that can lead to new discoveries and new interventions. The most effective practitioners are those who understand theories and are willing to apply them.

Still, theories can have their downsides. They might help us see things we might not see without the theory, but they might result in us overlooking things because of our theory. Family therapy pioneer, Murray Bowen (2004), wrote, "Man can fail to see what is in front of his eyes unless it fits into his theoretical frame of reference" (p. 105). Thus, if you think teens get pregnant because of a lack of sex education, you might overlook other possibilities. Another example? If you are from Texas, you might look at the accompanying map (Figure 2.2) and think it is an accurate representation of the United States; meanwhile, non-Texans see something quite different!

THEORIES AND THE STUDY OF FAMILY

Family and family life have always been topics of discussion, thought, and theory by scholars from various disciplines, including sociology, psychology, anthropology, economics, history, development, and communication. Each discipline has taken a slightly different perspective, used different terms and definitions, and focused on different aspects on the family. It wasn't until the 1950s that theories specifically addressing family began to develop, with some valuable and

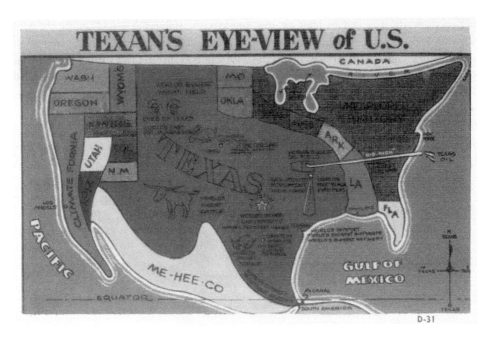

FIGURE 2.2 Our beliefs influence what and how we see the world.

Source: Alamy

insightful family theories developing in the 1970s and 1980s (White, Klein, & Martin, 2015). Family theories assume that families are different from other social groups and therefore require different ways of thinking and conceptualizing. As White (2005) states:

> The family is both a biological unit and a social unit, a unit that has a connection with history and a connection with the future. It is a social group where emotions, such as loyalty, love, devotion, commitment, and sharing are not only finely expressed but even expected. Seldom do work or friendship groups trace those that preceded them in role or position, yet most families are not only aware of their progenitors but consider this as their lineage heritage.
>
> (White, 2005, p. 4)

Families are complex and dynamic. Given the protean nature of family, it makes sense that family scholars utilize several theories to address their complex nature. Each theory provides important and unique insights. Most of the theoretical ideas presented here will sound familiar and you might discover that many of them are rather commonsense notions. However, these collected ideas represent a "language"; in other words, terms and constructs summarize our best thinking about the ways families and individuals in families set out to solve life's problems, build stronger relationships, and make daily decisions.

Social Learning Theory

In the 1960s, psychologist Albert Bandura conducted a series of experiments using a blow-up plastic "Bobo Doll" that would return to a standing position if knocked down. Bandura found that children who watched an adult hit, toss, and kick the Bobo doll would imitate the adult's behavior with the doll when left alone with it. These classic experiments demonstrated that human beings could learn through observation. We can both **model** and **imitate** behavior, and we need not be directly reinforced to learn, marking a major shift in learning theory. Bandura's **social learning theory** introduced a cognitive component to the strictly behaviorist tradition of operant conditioning. It was empirically (research) based, fairly easy to understand and apply in "real life," and allowed scholars to take the family, rather than the individual, as the unit of study (Robinson & Jacobson, 1987). Social learning theory has been productive in several areas, including education, human development, social work, psychotherapy, criminology, business, and media.

Key concepts of social learning theory:

- **Reciprocal Determinism.** This concept refers to the idea that the person (and his or her thinking), the behavior of a person, and the environment are all interconnected and influential. If a person is hostile in his thinking, his behavior may turn hostile, which in turn results in a hostile environment. The hostile environment may result in a person's thinking being hostile and may result in more hostile behavior.
- **Components of Observational Learning.** According to Bandura, we can learn simply by observing the behavior of others. Observational learning involves four underlying processes. The first component is attention; if the individual is not attending to a model, it is unlikely that the individual will learn the behavior. The second component is retention, which is the ability to keep the behavior in one's mind to create at a later time. The third component is motor reproduction and the ability to reproduce the behavior. The final component is motivation, which includes being reinforced for producing the behavior or seeing the model being reinforced for the behavior.
- **Self-Efficacy.** The personal belief that one has the ability to succeed at something or achieve one's goals. This can be highly related to motivation.
- **Expectation.** Expectations are related to self-efficacy. If one has high levels of self-efficacy, then one expects certain outcomes resulting from certain behaviors. We also have expectations of reinforcement (or not).
- **Reinforcement.** Traditionally, reinforcement refers to anything that increases the likelihood of a behavior. Bandura introduced the concept of vicarious reinforcement, which refers to the fact that seeing another person get reinforced (or punished, which decreases a behavior) influences the likelihood of us imitating that behavior. If a child sees her sister get a big hug from mom because the sister helped mom pick up some toys, the child is more likely to help pick up toys, with the expectation of a big hug, as well.

We see social learning at work when children watch the television show "Mr. Rogers" and imitate the kindness behaviors they have seen on the program. We see it when we observe teenagers wearing similar clothes and using similar slang in their speech. We may also be seeing social learning at work when we see children who grow up in families with strong, supportive marriages that handle conflict well go on to create their own strong, supportive marriages.

Social learning theory continues to be utilized and studied; however, recent research has found that couple intervention therapies based on social learning theories may not be as effective as previously thought (Johnson & Bradbury, 2015). So, while the strength of this theory might lie in its practicality and research support, it may be too simplistic and overlook other determinants of behavior.

Symbolic Interaction Theory

Symbolic interaction theory is a widely used perspective in family science. The theory enjoys a long history and was cobbled together by many philosophers and social scientists, including Charles Darwin, John Dewey, psychologist William James, and sociologist George Herbert Mead (Chibucos, Leite, & Weis, 2005; White et al., 2015). According to this perspective, we (as individuals) grow and develop through our everyday interactions with others in our society. As a society and as individuals, we learn and attribute meaning to words, behaviors, and objects, with words, behaviors, and objects becoming symbols that may (or may not) have shared meaning among individuals. When symbols have similar meanings for us, it aids in communication and interaction; when the same symbol has a different meaning, it can lead to problems. For example, "give me a little sugar" in the South may mean to give someone a kiss or to pass the sweetener! According to symbolic interactionism, our behavior is a function of how situations are *perceived* and interpreted, and it is *perception that drives reality*. As social creatures, we tend to align our behaviors with what we believe others are thinking and doing.

Key concepts of symbolic interactionism:

- **Symbols.** Words, gestures, behaviors, and even things are symbols, and we learn the meaning of these symbols through our interaction with others and experience with the environment. The word "mother" carries all sorts of symbolic meaning, including nurturer and supporter. Some people may perceive "mother" to be a warm and caring individual; however, others may perceive "mother" to be cold, distant, and overbearing. Gestures, such as touching, carry symbolic meaning that could be misunderstood. Some families are "touchers" and huggers, while those outside the family may misinterpret such gestures of familiarity. Families exhibit behaviors that are meaningful to the members of the family. Most of you know "the look" that your mother gives you when you "cross the line" in terms of behavior, and you know you will pay for it later. One of your friends might not perceive your mother's look as particularly menacing, but you have learned through your numerous interactions that you are in trouble. When two people from different families meet and begin a relationship, learning the meanings of certain symbols is important.
- **Definition of the Situation.** The definition of the situation refers to the meaning one gives to a behavior or situation. This allows an individual to focus attention on what is important and behave accordingly. According to Thomas and Thomas (1928), "If (people) define situations as real, they are real in their consequences" (p. 572). Suppose a 12-year-old adolescent experiences her first menstruation. An Apache family will perceive this to be an important milestone in their daughter's life, inform members of the community, and arrange for a large communal gathering, with 4 days of rituals, dancing, and teaching. This "Sunrise Ceremony" brings the girl to womanhood. At its conclusion, the young woman is welcomed into adulthood. Conversely, a non-Apache family may perceive their daughter's first menstruation as an indication of a developing adult body with the potential of early pregnancy. This daughter is taught that her period is kept secret, and family fears of pregnancy might result in increased rules related to boyfriends and time away from home. Certainly, the daughter would not expect a community announcement! Both girls experience a physical event at a similar point in life, yet each girl and family perceive (and define) it differently, resulting in different behaviors and outcomes. In a sense, each family has *constructed a different reality* that exists beyond an objective reality.

- **Roles and Role Taking.** In symbolic interactionism, a **role** is a category that carries meaning and expectations that define our behavior. Every role has a counter role (father–child, parent–teacher, boss–employee) with expectations that influence our interactions. **Role taking** refers to the ability to put one's self in another's shoes and perceive a situation through the other's eyes. The ability to take on the role of another assists us in our interactions as we understand their expectations, anticipate their responses, and adjust our own behavior appropriately. Suppose you are a university student who would like your parents to pay for a Spring Break trip to Cozumel, Mexico. You could simply ask your parents for the money but likely you would be turned down post-haste. Instead, you could put yourself in your parents' position, consider what is important to them, practice in your mind your conversation with your parents *(imaginative rehearsal)*, and then say, "I know it's really important to learn Spanish well and I'd like to prepare for my second-year Spanish class by spending a week in Mexico. Would you be willing to help pay for this experience?"

  We all play certain roles within our family. These roles have been constructed through our experience, our culture, and our personal beliefs. "Husband," "wife," "father," "mother," "son," "daughter," "grandmother," "aunt"—each word likely brings up ideas in your mind about what is expected and how these people interact. It is important to note how much consensus there is among family members about the collected idea about how a role is performed (Burr, Leigh, Day, & Constantine, 1979). This is a good example of a family-level idea that is used in the symbolic interaction tradition. The more consensus family and community members have about what should occur in a family role, the less strain a family member will have as he or she enters and performs that role.

  In roles where there is high consensus about what a person should do in the role, we would expect that the person would have much less anxiety as he or she takes on that new role. Conversely, a young father might not have a clear idea of what he should be doing as a father because the people around him (i.e., family and community members) do not have much consensus about what it is he should do in that part of his life. Therefore, this theory would suggest that as a young father enters the fathering role (e.g., at the birth of a child) he might feel anxiety and strain as he considers what he should do and how he should do it.

In summary, symbolic interaction theory helps us understand that humans are thinking, choosing, and deliberate creatures. We humans place meaning on what we see and the events that impact us. Those who study families using this perspective pay attention to those meanings that family members hold. Additionally, family scientists attend to the roles performed in family life and the ease of adopting or exiting roles (e.g., becoming a parent, losing one's parent, changing partners, gaining a partner).

Social Exchange Theory

One of the more frequently used theoretical ideas in family science is called **social exchange** or **rational choice theory**. According to this theory (which is actually a collection of theories), human interaction centers around the exchange of social and material resources (Mitchell, Cropanzano, & Quisenberry, 2012). At the heart of this perspective is the idea that each individual seeks to maximize individual self-interest and minimize costs. This is not to say that all people are necessarily "selfish" per se, but it does assume that each person acts with his or her personal welfare in mind as a primary motivating force (White et al., 2015).

An important aspect of this theory is that decisions related to costs and rewards are rational and deliberate. A good example of this theory at work is when you need to make a decision and write out all the "pros" and "cons" related to your decision, making a choice on what will result in the best outcome for you. The concept of rationality does not suppose that people make good choices all of the time (or even most of the time). Nor does this approach assume that goals that have been consciously or implicitly selected are appropriate or worthy. Instead, it assumes that people weigh their choices, balance the costs and rewards, and try to do the best they can at the time.

Key concepts of social exchange theory:

- **Resources.** Resources are things of value that can be exchanged. Resources can be concrete (money, goods, services), symbolic (a smile or pat on the back), and even abstract (time) (Foa, 1971). According to social exchange theory, a relationship is nothing more than an exchange of resources.
- **Costs and Rewards.** Costs are defined as outcomes that are not beneficial to one's interests and rewards are anything that is "perceived as beneficial to an actor's interests" (Klein & White, 1996, p. 65). Costs and rewards can vary across time, circumstance, and individual. A child might do almost anything for a cookie, but an adult usually requires more (unless it is one awesome cookie).
- **Outcomes.** Outcomes refer to the rewards we receive in a relationship minus the costs. As human beings, we do not want to give up too many resources (costs) and hope to gain resources (rewards). In other words, we want to maximize our profits and minimize our losses. When we make a decision to buy a car, choose a spouse, name a child, or select an occupation, those who subscribe to this point of view suggest that we weigh the costs and rewards and choose what we believe to be in our best interest at the time of the choice. This theory assumes we do not make choices that are deliberately bad for us.
- **Equity.** In social exchange theory, equity refers to maintaining a balance (or perception of balance) between costs and rewards. Stable relationships are associated with equity. When partners in a relationship are more equal with regard to the resources they bring to the relationship (e.g., money, looks, talents), it is more likely the relationship will be stronger and systemic goals will be achieved. Objectively, others may perceive a relationship to be inequitable, but subjectively, the individuals perceive equity. Relationships perceived as inequitable are unlikely to last. It's important to remember that standards of evaluation of equity can change across time. What seemed "enough" to keep a relationship alive early on might not be enough later.

Two important criticisms of this approach need to be mentioned. First, this perspective has a difficult time with the concept of altruism. Altruism reflects the idea that sometimes people seem to act without calculating the cost–reward ratio (e.g., when protecting a child). A perpetual discussion by those who write about social exchange ideas is the struggle to explain behavior that seems to not be "rational," or in other words, behavior that seemingly does not result from a cost–reward calculation. Feminist writers have focused on this notion to show that this approach undervalues the contribution women make in relationships. For example, Sabatelli and Shehan (1993, p. 396) suggested that social exchange theory does not do a good job of considering the part played by family members whose mission in the family might be to create solidarity at the expense of individual gain. This is really an extension of the problem that social exchange theory has explaining seemingly selfless acts of contribution.

A second criticism with this approach relates to the idea that many family scientists are interested in studying the family as an *entity*. That means we want to see the family as a whole unit rather than trying to imagine all of the calculations that apparently occur in each family member's mind. Social exchange theorists have only recently begun to talk about how this theory can move from describing only the behavior of individuals to describing the complex behavior of several people in a close-knit group like a family.

Like all theories, this one falls short of explaining everything we wish it would in family life. However, there are some aspects of family life that are easily explained and understood using the language of social exchanges. For example, we suggest later in this chapter that families, like individuals, have goals and do maximize resources to attain those goals. The language for that construct comes from social exchange theory, and it suggests that a unit, like a family, moves forward with a belief about what they would like to accomplish and, for the most part, they do not deliberately set out to fail.

Conflict Theory

Conflict theory has a long and interesting philosophical history going back to Niccolo Machiavelli (1513) and Thomas Hobbes (1651). From this perspective, conflict is simply part of being human. Despite this basic premise and long theoretical tradition, the theory was not applied specifically to families until 1969, when Jetse Sprey suggested that studying family as "a system in conflict" (1969, p. 699) could be more fruitful for researchers than the conventional perspective of family harmony. The essence of this theoretical approach is to answer one central question: As family members come and go, age, and change, how is order achieved in such seemingly complicated and chaotic situations?

Key concepts of conflict theory:

- **The Natural State of Humans.** At first glance, one might think that **conflict theory** is simply about why people argue and fight. That is too simple and does not capture the intent of this theoretical perspective. Instead, conflict theory is the struggle that we all have (in and out of family groups) to survive. This theory suggests that there is a natural state that humans live in that is rather unruly, nasty, and carnal. All men and women are in competition with each other because, in life, resources (e.g., money, time, space, etc.) are scarce and each person wants to not only survive but also to compete for those resources and have the freedom to choose a personal direction. One person might want to buy a new car, whereas someone else wants to keep the old car and use the extra money to pay off debts.
- **The Process of Struggle.** A key idea in understanding conflict theory comes to us from German philosophers such as Hegel, who viewed the human condition as one of struggle. He suggested that although each of us is primarily self-interested (as in the exchange perspective above), the process of struggling is a good thing. He did not say that fighting or having wars is an effective strategy. However, when we try to solve life's difficult problems (like how to spend family income, who should sleep in what room, or

who should do the dishes) and a family member suggests who should do the dishes, the resulting exchange can either build strength in the family system or it can tear it down. If prolonged conflict ensues and the balance of power is uneven, then families will be less likely to meet their goals. When families struggle together and are successful at reaching a consensus, then they become stronger.

This process idea has the following elements. First is the original idea, and we call this the **thesis** ("Sandra, I would like you to do the dishes tonight"). The thesis or original idea always comes attached to the other side of the coin, the **antithesis**. The antithesis is the opposite point of view in which someone says, "No, I don't think so, it is your turn to do the dishes," or "I think it would be better if we spent the tax refund on tires for the car," or "Our apartment is not as big as you would like. You will have to share your room with your younger brother." In this way, a dialogue or dialectic emerges or, in other words, a struggle arises. When members of a family group struggle together and make decisions that consider both the thesis and antithesis, the hope is that a **synthesis** will emerge. When a synthesis occurs, it is assumed that this creates strength and the family is more effective. When there is no synthesis or consensus and agreement, the family is weakened and is less likely to meet its goals.

- **The Causes of Conflict.** Conflict often results for two reasons. First, different people (or groups) want different things. In the family, conflict can arise because different people want to watch different television programs, disagree on which computer to buy, or desire different meals for dinner. Second, conflict can arise because individuals in the family want the same thing, but there is a limited supply, such as the availability of only one household computer but several family members who want to use it. At the core of this theoretical idea is the notion of scarce resources (Sprey, 1969; White et al., 2015;). Resources are more than just money or things, however (White et al., 2015). Resources can be problem-solving skills, talents, abilities, the ability to control or exercise authority in a family, or even time (e.g., how much time each person in the family can spend with Mom). Thus, according to this theory, most conflict is inevitable because there is almost always an imbalance of resources or power in family relationships. In short, **inequity** creates conflict. Those families who are better able to meet their goals are the ones who share resources more equitably and are better able to experience true consensus and synthesis rather than prolonged conflict when allocating family resources.
- **Harmony in Families.** A basic assumption of conflict theory is that conflict is typical and harmony is problematic. What might appear to be a harmonious family might actually be a family with an imbalance of power and members not able to express their own disagreements. Nickola Overall (2018) suggests that healthy family conflict can actually make families stronger (we will discuss this in a later chapter).

This theory's focus on conflict as being constructive and positive and moving groups forward is a decidedly Western conception, with ties to Marx and Hegel (Huang, 2016). Huang proposed a dynamic model of interpersonal harmony and conflict based on the Chinese conception of yin-yang (a dualistic concept of seeming opposite forces that are interconnected and interdependent) and based in Confucian and Taoist beliefs. For the Chinese, conflict is problematic in all relationships and harmony is valued and deeply rooted. Chinese teens from Hong Kong and their parents identified the absence of conflict and the presence of harmony as important for a happy family (Shek, 2001). Understanding such deep-seated beliefs in culture can be helpful for studying and working with family.

It is important to note that from this intellectual tradition emerged a strong, gender-oriented feminist critique of family life. In this view, social historians, family scientists, and feminist writers illuminate the idea that men have traditionally controlled most of the tangible resources and have typically had more power in family life. Therefore, when the power is unbalanced and the resources are not distributed equally, families are not as effective. This imbalance ensures the privilege of some (usually the males) in the family at the expense of others.

Family Development Theory

In the social sciences, the word "development" refers to a specific type of change. Development is a type of change that is orderly, expected, and better than a previous state. From at least the 18th century, intellectuals have engaged in discussions of how families grow and develop; however, it wasn't until the mid-20th century that a formal theory on family development was created. One of the giants and founders of family science research was Rubin Hill. In 1949, Hill advanced the idea that a family was composed of social roles and that the nature and assignment of these roles changed over time (Hill & Hansen, 1960).

According to family development theory, families go through different stages across time. Not only do individuals within the family grow and develop, but the family itself develops. If you think about it, you likely could identify various stages of a family. For example, a couple at the beginning of a relationship and without children likely is quite different from a couple with very young children, which is different from a couple with teenagers, which is different from a grandparenting couple. Various theorists have outlined different stages of the family life cycle, from four to 24 stages! Evelyn Duvall's (1962) well-known and widely cited eight-stage family development model consists of the following stages: (1) couple without children; (2) childbearing; (3) preschool; (4) school-age; (5) adolescence; (6) launching; (7) middle age; and (8) aging. Each of these stages has its own unique challenges, demands, and expectations. Glick (1989) is credited with including the influence of the social change of these stages and recognition of variant family forms, keeping this theory useful in both research and therapy.

Key concepts of family development theory:

- **Positions and Roles.** As families move through the family life cycle, positions and roles change. Going from the childless couple to childbearing couple changes the role of husband and wife to father and mother. Over time new roles may be added; the wife becomes wife/mother, who later becomes wife/mother/grandmother, who becomes mother/grandmother/widow, each with different statuses and roles within the family. A mother's role for a preschool child is much different from a mother's role for an adult child living away from home. Members of the family are expected to fulfill the responsibilities (developmental tasks) of their roles.
- **Developmental Tasks.** Each stage of the life cycle presents the family with unique responsibilities that must be addressed and achieved for healthy development. These tasks encompass all aspects of human development, including physical, social, emotional, and cognitive areas. Tasks of families with school-aged children include helping children succeed in school and get along with peers. Failure to do this could have negative consequences later in the cycle, not only for the child but for the family as a whole; conversely, success

brings satisfaction and the potential for increased success at later stages. Many developmental tasks are universal (such as attachment of infant to parents); others are prescribed by culture (such as puberty ceremonies) (Goldenberg & Goldenberg, 2008).

- **Norms and Normative Events. Norms** are accepted standards of behaviors or patterns of behavior, values, understandings, actions, and rules that govern the family and individuals within the family. **Normative events** are those events that most families typically experience. Puberty, for example, is a normative event for children that often changes family functioning. In family development theory, the timing of events can be normative ("**on time**") or non-normative ("**off time**") and influence the functioning of the family. For example, the launching stage in family development refers to the time when young adult children "leave the nest." Most of you have an age frame in mind when you think children "should" be on their own (in other words, a norm). You may not be aware that this time frame varies by culture, so what is considered the norm in one group is not in another. Eurostat (2019) found that the average age children left home in Sweden was 18.5; the average age for children in Croatia was 31.8. Norms and family response to normative and non-normative events in the family life cycle may be utilized by family therapists as they assist families experiencing a disruption or seeking assistance with improving family functioning, so understanding cultural differences can be useful.
- **Transitions.** Transitions occur in families as they change and try to adapt to the events that happen over time (Klein & White, 1996, p. 128). The central idea is simply that the transitions we make in family life, such as getting married, having and raising children, and divorcing and remarrying, create a path of possible events. Depending on the paths one chooses, other events are more or less likely to result. For example, once a child is born into a family, family members find a new set of paths that were of little concern before the child was born. In a few short years, the child might be attending preschool, and parents might begin thinking ahead about other school plans, the child's future, and how their family will be a part of the child's future. Smooth transitions are likely to occur when developmental tasks are accomplished and the timing of normative events is not out of the ordinary, thus allowing families to achieve their goals.
- **Epigenesis.** Epigenesis, a simple idea provided by psychologist Erik Erikson, is useful and powerful in understanding everyday family life. Epigenesis is a process of development, with stages unfolding in sequence and influenced by the environment. What we do in life early on has a significant impact in our lives later. The choices we make early in our lives affect who we are, the type of family we raise, and the life we will lead later. This does not mean we cannot overcome the choices we make in times of family transitions, but those choices have the power to strongly influence our futures. For example, if a young couple decides to have several children early in their marriage, for better or worse, it will not only have an economic effect on future choices available to them, but can influence the resources available to their children, choice of family activities, where they can and cannot live, and even the educational pursuits of the parents.

Throughout this text, two of the most powerful ideas from family development theory are referred to frequently: First, family life has a course and that course can have many paths. Second, as family members make transitions, the choices they make within those transitional times can (and usually do) influence future opportunities and choices available to each family member. While every human being and family is unique, we also follow common patterns.

Understanding these common patterns can help in anticipating and addressing common challenges most families face. On the other hand, with the recognition of more diverse family forms, family development theory comes up short, especially in the development of couple-only families (Crapo, 2020). To address these shortcomings, Crapo has modified the theory and reconceptualized it as the multidimensional family development theory. In sum, the family developmental theory provides several ideas that help us understand important family processes. It is a useful perspective that continues to grow.

Family Systems Theory

One way to understand family life is to think of families as an interactive system. Systems are often defined as a group of interacting parts (Broderick, 1993; White et al., 2015). This idea simply means that when describing any **entity** (a football team, a habitat in the forest, or a complex factory), it is assumed that all of the parts are somehow connected and interrelated and those relationships make up that entity (Figure 2.3). Many different types of system theories have been applied to human development, including Bronfenbrenner's bioecological theory and dynamic systems theory.

In the case of family science, family systems theory has developed out of recognition of the unique and complex properties of family. Noted family therapist and author Virginia Satir (1972) used a metaphor of an infant mobile to describe the family system, its interconnections, and the influence of the individual on the whole:

> In the mobile, all pieces (family members) no matter what size or shape can be grouped together and balanced by shortening or lengthening the strings attached or rearranging

FIGURE 2.3 Sometimes, people use the metaphor of a factory to try and explain family systems theory. This approach does not capture what systems theorists had in mind. A family system is more organic than mechanistic; that is, it is like a small ecosystem.

the distance between the pieces. So it is with a family. None of the family members are identical to any other; they are all different and at different levels of growth. As in a mobile, you can't arrange one without thinking of the other.

(pp. 119–120)

Key concepts of family system theory:

- **The Family as a Whole.** A basic notion proposed by systems researchers and family intervention workers is that it is impossible to understand family life without viewing the family as a whole (Broderick, 1993; Hall & Fagen, 1956; White et al., 2015). In Freudian psychology and other general social science approaches, the unit of analysis is almost always an individual, with other family members playing a supporting role in the story. In a systemic view of family life, the primary story centers on what the whole family is doing and the focus on a particular individual (even if she or he is the person with the most obvious "problem") is secondary to understanding how family life works. Indeed, solving an individual's "problem" often involves changing patterns that involve other family members. In short, the whole is greater than the sum of its parts.

  A common analogy used to talk about family systems theory is baking a cake. Eggs, flour, sugar, and butter somehow combine to make something so much (deliciously) more than these basic elements. We have attended events that included food baked by the participants using the same recipes. It is always amusing to see how DIFFERENT each dish is from each other, despite all using the same ingredients and instructions. The same idea applies to families. We may find similar families in terms of number of children, age of parents, even socioeconomic status, yet, these families as a whole are still quite different from each other. Okun and Rapport (1980) summarized this idea as follows:

  > The system in an integrated coherent entity is more than the mere composite of independent elements. This wholeness transcends the sum of the system's component elements … a change in one part of the system may cause a change in many parts (subsystems) of the larger system and in the larger system itself.
  >
  > (pp. 8–9)

  Given this perspective, we cannot understand a particular family simply by understanding *each individual member* of the family. We must also understand (i.e., we must observe, take note of, and record) the *relationships and interactions* that occur within this family entity (or systemic unit).

- **Systems and Subsystems.** A family system exists within the context of a larger social system, such as neighborhoods and communities. Within the family, systems are smaller systems, known as **subsystems,** that form **hierarchies** (London, 2019). Possible subsystems include the spousal or executive subsystem, the parent–child subsystem, the sibling subsystem, and the parental subsystem (in which the husband and wife relate to each other with regard to a parenting role).

  A key task of subsystems is boundary maintenance. Family therapists have long known that a sure sign of a family in difficulty is when the family's subsystems are not kept separate and distinct (Minuchin, 1981, 1996). For example, when family members build coalitions across subsystems, the family's ability to achieve goals is weakened. If a mother builds a stronger relationship with a child than she does with her spouse, then the family system is weakened. If a parent (in this case, often the father) blurs the boundaries between himself and a child emotionally and sexually, the entire family system is weakened and can even be destroyed, as is often the case with incest.

The concept of the subsystem helps us understand that the primary "parts" of the system are not the individuals but instead are the *interactions between and among* the various subsystems within a family group. The father influences his partner, and in turn, the response of those two people influences how they allocate resources, make decisions, and monitor their children. The great American playwright Arthur Miller once said "all human interaction is 98% historical," referring to the simple idea that the patterns of previous interactions and decisions live on and direct the next thing we say to a family member in the next situation. The study of those patterns of interaction is a characteristic of the study of the family using a systems approach.

- **Boundaries.** The idea of boundaries is a key to understanding systems thinking. System boundaries occur where two or more systems or subsystems interface, interact, or come together. They are the borders of a system. Sauber, L'Abate, Weeks, and Buchanan (1993) define family boundaries as "invisible lines drawn within and among family members that form subsystems—for example, the lines within the individual self, the marital coalition, and the children" (p. 38). Sometimes these boundaries can be very solid and rigid, and other times they are very permeable, allowing for sharing of resources and information. Family systems with rigid boundaries are referred to as **closed**. These families tend to keep outside information (and sometimes prying eyes) out of the family system. Families with secrets, such as abuse or alcoholism, tend to be closed. Families with more permeable boundaries that allow for interactions with outside influences are referred to as **open**. Open family systems tend to be more adaptable and subject to change. Generally (but not always), open family systems are healthier.

Boundaries occur at every level in the system and between systems. Often, we understand where a boundary is by listening to the rules families construct about where people can and cannot go, what they can and cannot do, and who is allowed in the family and who is not allowed to leave. For example, families with a very open system might allow family members to come and go without much restriction. Boss (1998) researched the idea of boundaries in many settings and applied her work to the problem of families who have a member with Alzheimer's disease. In her book, she shows how the physical and mental awareness of family members can greatly influence our ideas about family membership and responsibility.

- **Underlying Structures.** Systems theory assumes that every system has an "underlying structure." This idea has been used by many theorists and is at the heart of the writings of Sigmund Freud. In the Freudian approach to understanding the human psyche, the notion is that the skilled observer can detect hidden patterns or undiscovered, unresolved conflicts deep within the subconscious of the individual. By finding, identifying, and revealing those hidden conflicts, one can attain a higher level of mental health. Similarly, in describing the cognitive abilities of children, Piaget suggested that hidden, internal schemata or mental structures direct our ability to solve problems and make sense out of life's puzzles.

Similarly, family theorists have suggested that within family life are underlying structures or patterns of interactions that direct what occurs in the family, and one role of the family therapist or family science researcher is to discover these underlying, hidden structures. By watching how family members solve problems, communicate with each other, and allocate their resources, family therapists and researchers can begin to understand the underlying patterns and structures of family life. In the world of human and family systemic thinking, the idea is that you can observe the movement of the actors, how they communicate, what comes into the system, and what happens to the system (whether it be factory workers or family members). Based on those observations, one could deduce what the goals of the system are and how effective that particular system is at achieving its apparent goals.

- **Goal Seeking.** As with other theories, this theory assumes that family systems are goal directed: Families have goals they are trying to achieve. For the most part, this process is not really apparent to a typical family. They rarely sit down and discuss the overall meaning or goal of their family. In fact, it probably takes a skilled observer from the outside to watch the repeating patterns of a family before some of the underlying themes or goals surface.

These goals vary widely from family to family. In addition, there is always a good chance that one or more of the family members will not subscribe to the overall family direction, goal, aim, purpose, ambition, or aspiration. We do not know very much about this idea, as few family researchers have attempted to assess it. However, one can imagine that if the **subscription** rate were low in a family—that is, there was low consensus about what that family's mission, aim, goal, or purpose was—we would speculate that the family would be less **efficient** in solving problems, making decisions, and getting the daily business of family completed (Day, Gavazzi, & Acock, 2001). Why? Efficiencies of goal achievement (getting children educated, saving money, becoming healthy, etc.) are more likely to be achieved when all involved agree on the desired outcome. If a family member only half-heartedly subscribes to the idea of education for all, then it will take much more effort on the part of those who do value that goal to make it happen.

In sum, three take-home ideas can be gleaned from this discussion of family goal seeking. The first is that a system (including a family system) is a group of interacting parts (family members and the patterns of interaction that occur). Second, families have aims, goals, themes, and missions they are trying to attain. Further, families use strategies that are pattern-like to make those goals happen. That is, they are more likely to do the same routines over and over than they are to try some new approach to achieve goals and deal with problems that might affect goal achievement. Third, there is a subscription rate involved in the family goal attainment process. Consequently, when family members are fully subscribed and focus their energy and resources on a given theme, aim, or goal, the goal will be easier and faster to obtain.

- **Family Systems Are Dynamic.** Families and family members are characterized by constant change and adaptation on a daily, even hourly basis, because of both internal and external forces. As family entities attempt to reach goals, they must respond constantly to the changes that happen in their world—money comes in, children get sick, the local factory announces layoffs, the mother is depressed, the community faces social unrest, and so on. Family units try to reach goals by keeping life's events in balance (Figure 2.4). This may mean changing rules, adapting our traditions, and altering how we get daily chores done. In systems theory, the balancing act that families strive to perform is referred to as **equilibrium**.

that took on a life of their own. As scholars cited other scholars' views and writings related to Frazier's work, they failed to closely examine his actual empirical work. Some scholars criticized what they thought were Frazier's ideas (but weren't) and then presented ideas as their own "new" perspectives, without realizing that these new ideas were already discussed by Frazier. Additional scholars have re-examined Frazier's work (see Gaines, 2005; Platt, 1991; Teele, 2002) in an effort to reclaim his legacy.

How did this fall from grace happen? Semmes (2001) writes, "I suspect that the negative reaction to Frazier is more a reaction to how some have used Frazier to blame African American families for the effects of poverty and racism suffered by Black communities. In addition, it is probably the case that a Eurocentric bias continues to play a role in graduate education in the social sciences, such that a close and comprehensive reading of Frazier, one of America's greatest sociologists, is routinely omitted" (p. 19). E. Franklin Frazier, advocate, activist, theorist, scholar, did much to increase our understanding of African American families and was a man ahead of his time.

Questions to Discuss:

- *In your study of family or family diversity, were you ever exposed to Frazier's ideas? If not, why do you think that is?*
- *What additional lessons can be learned from the information presented?*
- *How can you avoid misrepresenting others' ideas and theories?*
- *How can you reduce your chances of trusting someone's misinterpretations? How can you strengthen your own writing when discussing another's theory?*

SUMMARY

All the theories examined in this chapter can be used to describe and understand different aspects of family life. No single theory can explain the complexities of making up a family. Some theories can be usefully combined to explain phenomena, such combining social exchange theory and symbolic interaction theory to explain family violence. Laszloffy (2004) combined systems theory with family development theory to create a process–oriented model referred to as the systemic family development model, allowing family development theory to be used with diverse families.

Whether for research, therapy, interventions, or even self-reflection, it is clear that theories can guide us on our journey. Many people are interested in childhood tantrums. Why do children have tantrums? How can we help parents and caregivers more effectively deal with them? From a social learning perspective, one might assume that the child has seen others (including parents!) throw a tantrum and is somehow reinforced for doing so. An intervention might be to avoid reinforcing the child (do not let the child have her way) and monitor one's own behavior when angry. From a symbolic interactionist perspective, one might determine that one parent sees the child's tantrum as an expression of strong will that could someday benefit the child, while the other parent might perceive the tantrum as an expression of disobedience to authority. Helping parents reinterpret the meaning of tantrums and providing parents with specific interventions within the context of that meaning could resolve the issue.

Social exchange theorists take a more rational view of the cost-benefit interactions families have. From this perspective, one will examine the behavior of each party and determine the exchange that results in a decrease or increase in tantruming. Likely, the parents and child are consciously unaware of any reward/cost exchanges surrounding a tantrum resulting in continued tantruming. If parents become aware of the exchange, they are apt to be more consistent in changing the cost-benefit ratio (i.e., be consistent in the application of consequences, as well as in preventing tantrums from occurring). Of course, tantrums are seen by conflict theorists as just the way things are. The child wants something, doesn't get it, and expresses anger and frustration.

Family developmental theorists might examine the tantrum in terms of transitions and timing. This is a typical age for children to have tantrums and perhaps there may be an increase in such behavior as families (and children) begin to transition to new stages, resulting in some stress. Patience might be the watchword of the day! Don't give into the tantrum but realize that "this is only a phase." Finally, the systems theorist might consider all aspects of the system that are in play to initiate the tantrum, respond to the tantrum, and resolve it. In this case, the problem is seen as beyond the child and may include the parent marital relationship, changes in school settings, or increased peer interactions. An intervention may be targeted or more broad, depending on the systems and subsystems involved.

From the above examples, you can see how the lens of a theory influences what we see and do. You also see that some theories are better at explaining certain aspects of family life than others. As you read the following chapters about family processes and daily life, you will begin to form a position statement about family life and likely gravitate toward a certain theory or theories. It is your task now to begin writing some of your ideas down about how families can better succeed at the difficult task of family life.

STUDY QUESTIONS

1   What is the difference between facts and theories?
2   What is a theory and why do we care about them in family science?
3   How are families different from other social groups?
4   What is reciprocal determinism? Give an example as applied to a family.
5   Why is the theory called "symbolic interactionism?"
6   Explain what is meant by equilibrium in a family system.
7   What is a family system?
8   Give an example of equifinality and explain how this idea can work in family life.
9   Look up the word *entity* and see how this term can be applied to a family.
10   What is the difference between a thesis and an antithesis?
11   Why is the idea of roles so important in the study of the family?
12   Pick your favorite theoretical orientation explained in this chapter and defend why it appeals to you.

Klein, D. M., & White, J. M. (1996). *Family theories: An introduction*. Thousand Oaks, CA: Sage.

Laszloffy, T. A. (2004). Rethinking family development theory: Teaching with the systemic family development (SFD) model. *Family Relations, 51*(3), 206–214.

Lewin, K. (1943). Psychology and the process of group living. *Journal of Social Psychology, 17*, 113–131.

London, L. (2019) Hierarchy in family systems theory. In J. Lebow, A. Chambers, D. Breunlin (Eds.), *Encyclopedia of couple and family therapy*. Cham: Springer. DOI: 10.1007/978-3-319-15877-8_280-1

Minuchin, S. (1981). *Family kaleidoscope*. Cambridge, MA: Harvard University Press.

Minuchin, S. (1996). *Mastering family therapy: Journeys of growth and transformation*. New York, NY: Wiley.

Mitchell, M., Cropanzano, R., & Quisenberry, D. (2012). Social exchange theory, exchange resources, and interpersonal relationship: A modest Resolution of theoretical differences. In K. Tornblom & A. Kazemi (Eds.), *Handbook of social Resource theory: Theoretical extensions, empirical insights, and social applications* (pp. 99–115). New York, NY: Springer Science.

Okun, B., & Rapport, L. J. (1980). *Working with families*. Belmont, CA: Wadsworth.

Overall, N. (2018). Healthy conflict makes families stronger. Retrieved from https://www.newsroom.co.nz/2018/01/16/72490/healthy-conflict-makes-families-stronger

Platt, A. M. (1991). *E. Franklin Frazier reconsidered*. New Brunswick, NJ: Rutgers University Press.

Robinson, E. A., & Jacobson, N. S. (1987). Social learning theory and family psychopathology: A Kantian model in behaviorism? In T. Jacob (Ed.), *Family interaction and psychopathology* (pp. 117–162). New York, NY: Springer.

Sabatelli, R. M., & Shehan, C. L. (1993). Exchange and resource theories. In P. Boss, W. Doherty, R. LaRossa, W. Schumm, & S. Steinmetz (Eds.), *Sourcebook of family theories and methods: A contextual approach* (pp. 385–411). New York, NY: Plenum.

Samman, S. K., & Moreno, J. (2018). Equifinality in family systems theory. In J. Lebow, A. Chambers, & D. Breunlin (Eds.), *Encyclopedia of couple and family therapy*. Cham: Springer.

Satir, V. (1972). *Peoplemaking*. Palo Alto, CA: Science and Behavior Books.

Sauber, R., L'Abate, L., Weeks, G., & Buchanan, W. (1993). *Dictionary of family psychology and therapy*. Newbury Park, CA: Sage.

Semmes, C. E. (2001). E. Franklin Frazier's theory of the Black family: Vindication and sociological insight. *Journal of Sociology and Social Welfare, 38*(2), 3–23.

Shek, D. T. L. (2001). Chinese adolescents and their parents' views on a happy family: Implications for family therapy. *Family Therapy: The Journal of the California Graduate School of Family Psychology, 28*(2), 73–103.

Sprey, J. (1969). The family as a system in conflict. *Journal of Marriage and Family, 31*(4), 6.

Teele, J. E. (Ed.). (2002). *E. Franklin Frazier and Black bourgeoisie Vol. 1*. Columbia, MO: University of Missouri Press.

Thomas, W. I., & Thomas, D. S. (1928). *The child in America: Behavior problems and programs*. New York, NY: Alfred A. Knopf.

White, J. M. (2005). *Advancing family theories*. Thousand Oaks, LA: Sage Publishing.

White, J. M., Klein, D. M., & Martin, T. F. (2015). *Family theories: An introduction* (4th ed.). Washington DC: Sage.

CHAPTER 3

How We Study Family

CHAPTER PREVIEW

In this chapter, readers will learn:

- What makes the study of family unique.
- How personal inquiry is a key way in which we understand the world, although it is one of the least reliable ways of substantiating a research hypothesis.
- The difference between nonempirical and empirical research.
- How validity and reliability are key notions in family research. A valid measure assesses what we think it is supposed to measure and a reliable measure assesses the same idea time after time with the same precision.
- The research designs we can use to measure a single point in time or across time.
- About quantitative, qualitative, and mixed methods research.
- That various research methods can be used when studying family.
- That it is important to understand correlation, causation, and spurious relationships.
- That field research seeks to understand the stories of family life by using techniques such as in-depth interviews, participant observation, and case studies.
- New trends in research, including technologies related to biological methods and big data, as well as changes in philosophy related to queering and decolonization.

INTRODUCTION

THE BLIND MEN AND THE ELEPHANT.

A Hindu Fable; Poem by John Godfrey Saxe.
I.
It was six men of Indostan
To learning much inclined,
Who went to see the Elephant
(Though all of them were blind),
That each by observation
Might satisfy his mind.
The *First* approached the Elephant,

DOI: 10.4324/9781003128717-4

And happening to fall
Against his broad and sturdy side,
At once began to bawl:
"God bless me!—but the Elephant
Is very like a wall!"
The *Second*, feeling of the tusk,
Cried: "Ho!—what have we here
So very round and smooth and sharp?
To me 't is mighty clear
This wonder of an Elephant
Is very like a spear!"
The *Third* approached the animal,
And happening to take
The squirming trunk within his hands,
Thus boldly up and spake:
"I see," quoth he, "the Elephant
Is very like a snake!"
The *Fourth* reached out his eager hand,
And felt about the knee.
"What most this wondrous beast is like
Is mighty plain," quoth he;
"'T is clear enough the Elephant
Is very like a tree!"
The *Fifth*, who chanced to touch the ear,
Said: "E'en the blindest man
Can tell what this resembles most;
Deny the fact who can,
This marvel of an Elephant
Is very like a fan!"
The *Sixth* no sooner had begun
About the beast to grope,
Than, seizing on the swinging tail
That fell within his scope,
"I see," quoth he, "the Elephant
Is very like a rope!"
And so these men of Indostan
Disputed loud and long,
Each in his own opinion
Exceeding stiff and strong,
Though each was partly in the right,
And all were in the wrong!

What does this poem have to do with research methods and researching the family? Easy enough! The men from Indostan can represent scientists studying their particular phenomena through personal observation of only *one* part of the phenomenon. That elephant can also be

FIGURE 3.1 Families, like elephants, can be explored and studied in many ways, impacting our understanding of them.

studied in other ways (Figure 3.1). One could measure it. How tall is it? How much does it weigh? What are the dimensions of its ears? One could also describe it. What is the texture and color of its skin? How does it use its trunk to wash itself, guide its young, or pick up objects? The elephant could also be observed, both within its natural habitat as well as in a zoo. And of course, one could study the inside of the elephant using various technologies to see what makes it tick and how all its internal systems interact. Now, suppose the elephant is the family and the family system. That brings us to the purpose of this chapter, especially the part about studying the inside of the family or family processes.

Like elephants, families can be observed and measured in many different ways, and how we measure matters. Whether we see a fan, a snake, or a wall can be influenced by the questions we ask, how we collect information, and how we interpret what we observe. The goals for our research, our theoretical perspective, our disciplinary training, and our methods of collecting information influence what we learn about families. Further, the very act of measuring at all can influence what we see. To illustrate this point, consider a re-telling of the *Blind Men and the Elephant* from the perspective of six blind elephants. The elephants decided to observe a man to learn more about him. The first blind elephant felt the man and declared, "men are flat." After the other blind elephants felt the man, they agreed. Werner Heisenberg (1958), a Nobel Prize winning physicist, aptly reminds us that "we have to remember that what we observe is not nature in itself, but nature exposed to our method of questioning" (p. 58).

Given the impact our research can have on the quality of information we learn, it is imperative that we understand the unique process of studying families. It is not the intent of this chapter to dig deeply into research methods, statistics, or theoretical ideas used in this discipline; however, the constructs presented here are important. They help us understand how to better evaluate and utilize the research we read—be it to support our own family or other families we aim to help.

What Is Special About Family Research?

Many aspects of the research process are similar across disciplines. Whether you are studying classroom behavior, chemical compounds, the biological origins of depression, zebrafish, or stock trends, you must be familiar with independent and dependent variables, hypotheses, theory, and how to gather and analyze evidence. However, those who embark on the journey to study family behavior and family processes soon discover the intricacies of the science of family life. Family science scholars struggle with some of the core problems of human existence. Why do some families endure and others dissolve? Why do some excel at collecting and using resources wisely and others do poorly? Why are some families plagued with chronic and destructive violence as a feature of their daily life and others are relatively violence free? Despite similarities of research across disciplines, the questions raised by family science and the characteristics of the family and family life make the process of studying families uniquely *fascinating* and *challenging* as family scientists collect data of various kinds, analyze ideas, apply theoretical notions, and try to make sense out of the world of family life. So, what are some factors that make the study of family life and family processes unique? The need for multiple disciplines, the invisibility of inner family life, and the complexity of systems.

Family Research Requires Multidisciplinarity

Understanding the family requires insights from multiple disciplines. This was evident even in the early days of family science when, in 1938, the National Council on Family Relations was started by a law professor, a sociologist, and a rabbi (NCFR, n.d.). The family is complex, and it is best explored and understood from the combined perspectives of family scientists, anthropologists, sociologists, historians, psychologists, demographers, geneticists, neuroscientists, and economists, to name a few. Each of these disciplines brings unique research methodologies and new ways of looking at the elephant that, when aggregated through a family science approach, can offer a more complete picture of the family. Family life occurs, and therefore can be studied, at many levels, including individual family members (e.g., psychology), the family group (e.g., anthropology, economics, communication), the sociocultural context (e.g., sociology, history), and finally, inside the family itself (e.g., family processes). These different focuses can lead to unique topics of exploration that help us more completely understand the family.

A multidisciplinary perspective is imperative to the study of family, yet it is also important to recognize that family science is a discipline in and of itself. The study of family science seeks to transcend the idea of self-help, goes further than even helping other families, and, instead, focuses on the collected body of knowledge that encompasses the discipline of the study of the family. As the study of family was taking root in 1946, Ernest Groves, one of the first people to teach a marriage and family class at a university, explained:

> The establishment of a definite program for the training of specialists in the field of marriage and the family means that several sciences must contribute to the instruction. The outcome will be a science of marriage and the family carried out by specialists who will draw their data from a wide range of resources. They will not be sociologists, home economists, or social workers, but persons who are committed to the gathering and the

giving of information that concerns marriage and the family, who have prepared themselves for such an undertaking, and who approach their task from a background shared
by no other science.

(1946, p. 26)

Much of Family Life Is Invisible

The study of family processes is particularly unique from, and consequently, newer than other
disciplines, such as sociology, psychology, anthropology, and economics, because of the focus
on *inner* family life. Much family life, including goal setting, communication, rules, roles, and
routines, happens inside the family and is invisible to the outside world and even to the family
itself. One reason for the relative newness of studying family processes is that most families
resist the type of scrutiny necessary to understand the events of daily life. Families are very
cautious about allowing researchers to enter their lives and do research. Further, the in-depth
family research necessary to understand processes is often expensive. These factors, among others, make the study of families challenging and require unique methodologies. For example,
some researchers reject the idea that we can research inner family life by asking simple questions like "How many times did you spank your child last week?" Instead, they argue for more
qualitative research approaches discussed later in this chapter.

Family Are Complex Systems

One of the more important questions in studying families (or any other social process) is how we
approach the complexity of social life. As discussed in Chapter 2, the family is a complex **system**
made up of interconnected individuals. As Masten (2018) explains in the context of resilience
research, "Individuals are embedded in families and other systems (e.g., peer groups, schools),
and families in turn are embedded in other systems (e.g., cultures, communities). Interactions
of individuals, families, and larger contexts affect all of the interacting systems." (p. 16).

That begs the question of how we might best go about understanding the family. Consider,
for a moment, a painting by Carmen Lomas Garza titled Camas para Sueños (Beds for Dreams).
This picture depicts two sisters atop the roof of their house looking at the night sky, discussing dreams of the future, while through the window, we see their mother making a bed. How
might we try to appreciate and understand this piece of art? Some might prefer to stand back
and take in the piece as a whole, to examine the story being told, the interactions happening
at the moment, the use of vibrant colors throughout the image contrasting with the deep blue
of the night sky, or the overall image that depicts both dreaming and daily living happening in
unison. Others, however, might lean in and record the dimensions of the image, take note of
specific brush strokes, consider the type of paper or paint that was used, or examine how the
grain of the wood was depicted in a tree. How we approach art is similar to how we might
study a family.

An ongoing debate in social science centers on the topic of **reductionism**. Reductionism
focuses on the small atomic parts of a system. Many scientists, especially those who study physics,
math, and chemistry, for example, believe that understanding comes from studying the smallest
atomic fragments of a system as a strategy to understanding how the system works. This philosophical orientation was made popular by such scientists as Galileo and Newton. A reductionist-
oriented researcher in social science might try to identify the tiny pieces of daily behavior that
make up life (Figure 3.2). The researcher would attempt to show that the parts matter and

FIGURE 3.2 This family is being reduced to small fragments—we call that a kind of research reductionism.

are connected. Additionally, a reductionist would suggest ways of intervening in a problem by targeting one or more of the parts for change.

For example, suppose we are measuring something like father involvement (Marsiglio, Amato, Day, & Lamb, 2000). Many researchers want to know if father involvement really matters in the lives of children since findings could have implications for public policy, custody issues, and what we think about children's well-being. Much of the research about father involvement has been done using a reductionistic approach, typically gathering a few pieces of data from mothers with regard to a few activities the father might do in the family. Then, researchers make some guesses about what that means for family life. Using this method, we would have to assume that one person's view of the larger activities and beliefs of a group of people is sufficient. We would assume that this person's analysis of family life (and often it is the mother's view) is accurate enough, so we use that view as a summary for what the entire family believes, thinks, and does behaviorally—and we treat that one view as reality. To many researchers, this approach has seemed less than adequate. We see that applying reductionism to social science may be a pragmatic approach but it has serious limitations, particularly in understanding complex family systems.

An alternative approach is to move away from a purely reductionistic view by gathering information from several people in the family, and then, using sophisticated statistics, researchers find shared beliefs about what has happened in a particular family. For example, if we wanted to know more about father involvement, we would ask mothers, fathers, and even children for their perceptions about what the father does and what it means to them. The idea is that by **combining the shared views of several people**, we might get closer to understanding the processes that occur in family life. Jager, Bornstein, Putnick, and Hendricks (2012) expanded beyond this idea by focusing on *differences* in perceptions of family members, exploring how those differences could help us understand positive and negative family functioning. These methods are an effort to approximate inner family life and see the family as more than a collection of individuals; but might still be considered reductionistic.

One point of view is that it might be very difficult, if not impossible, to measure the wholeness of a family by gathering information about each of its members and then somehow combining their answers to get an overall picture of the family. This suggests that more in-depth research methodologies, such as qualitative observation and deep interviews over time, must be used to allow the researcher to see family functioning and daily living as a whole rather than a sum of its parts.

Ultimately, we learn about families from many different kinds of research studies, some of which are extremely reductionistic in nature and others that are excellent examples of narrative-qualitative studies that offer deeper family insights. Our belief is that each of the approaches we use has strengths, limitations, successes, and problems. Each is another way to tell the story about family life behind closed doors. However, a clear bias found in this text is that we believe it is important to at least attempt to study families as a whole rather than only focus on the individuals within families.

Personal Experience and Empirical Research

It is wiser to find out than suppose.

Mark Twain

As you sit in the doctor's office, you spy a recent edition of *Working Woman*. You notice a short two-page article on daycare discussing its impact on children. You turn to the man next to you with a crying two-year-old and ask his opinion about day care. It turns out that the two of you have similar views. As a child, you went to daycare and your own child is currently in daycare— from what you can tell, both you and your child are doing well. Ultimately, you conclude that daycare is the way to go! On what have you based your view? Why did you come to this conclusion? How did your values, beliefs, and experiences fit into your answer? What role did research play in your conclusion? Have you actually read studies about day care and its effects (or lack of effects) on children? All of these are important questions about how we know what we know.

Personal Experience

It is important to understand that your **personal experiences** are valuable. They mean a great deal to you; they define who you are and how you experience and approach life, make decisions, and solve problems. Your personal opinion about any issue is very complex and its sources are varied and difficult to identify. Views can come from an older sister, a scene in a movie, a sermon given by a minister, or it could just be built on a "gut feeling" you have. It is not our intent to discount the sources from which we all derive opinions. However, your **personal experiential reality** (Babbie, 2006), what you know from direct, personal experience, has limitations that are important to understand, including the following:

- **Sample Bias.** One of the first problems with using personal experience or personal inquiry as the basis for making general statements about family life is what we call **sample bias**. When we conduct social research, we are trying to discover or understand a problem within a **population**, the larger group we are interested in making statements or generalizations about. Populations tend to be fairly large, so researchers will look at only a portion of the population, referred to as a **sample**. Researchers try very hard to make sure their sample is representative of the population they are studying; in this way, they are better able to generalize their findings from their sample to the population. When it comes to personal experience, our sample is limited and not representative of the population. Therefore, we very likely will get a **biased** view, meaning any efforts to generalize our observations and experiences will likely not provide us with an accurate view of the broader population. As a result, our views of family gained through personal experience usually do not represent the condensed, distilled, well-rounded opinion that we might get if we systematically interviewed, for example, 2,000 people selected carefully to represent the population of interest.

- **Overgeneralizing.** Related to sample bias is the issue of overgeneralization. To overgeneralize means to take the opinions, experiences, or observations of one person or a small, non-representative group of people and assume that what those people think or how they behave is representative of a larger group. Knowing that your friend found a particular parenting book provided advice that helped her child sleep is not grounds to conclude that the suggestions in the book are effective for others. Further, when we have limited observations, it is possible that the people and experiences we have examined are actually **outliers**, or unusual respondents, and misrepresent the broader population we hope to understand. Although researchers can learn much from those who respond in a significantly different way, we must be careful not to inadvertently think that the outlier represents the majority of the population.

- **Confirmation Bias/Fixation.** Another limitation to using personal experience as a way of knowing is confirmation bias. In many cases, this is defined as the tendency to notice and believe information that confirms your views while ignoring or being more critical of information that does not. For example, if you believe that teenagers are rude and inconsiderate, you are more likely to notice the time when a teenager pushes past you in the store and brush off the moment when a teenager says something kind to your child at the park, considering the latter to be an anomaly or exception to the rule. Klein, Phillips, Rall, and Peluso (2007) argue that the concept of fixation better explains this behavior than confirmation bias. Fixation is the process by which people create "knowledge shields" to protect themselves against information that goes against their beliefs, allowing them to stick with their initial explanations and understandings rather than having to adapt and change (Klein et al., 2007). Whether it is confirmation bias or fixation, the warning is clear—using personal experience to know about the world means we must be cautious of supporting what we believe to be true and ignoring what contradicts it.

- **Agreement Reality.** Another problem with personal experience is that, when faced with making sense of our world, we often respond to what Babbie (2006) called **agreement reality**. That is, there are things that we "just know" because everyone agrees that they are real, and we learn this through friends, family, society, and culture. We are immersed with groups of people we love and respect. They share stories and experiences that come from a limited perspective. As stories and experiences are shared with individuals and with groups, the group coalesces around ideas and promotes particular viewpoints. Sometimes, this agreement reality is not even discussed openly. For example, we "just know" that we are to agree with certain opinions or behave in certain ways in the group; we know that it is not our place to have a conversation about why we have these rules. Therefore, acting on what we "just know" as fact when it comes to learning about and understanding families is problematic and often touches on biases we are unaware of.

- **Reporting Inaccuracy.** Another problem with personal experience is that the individual's view of the world is frequently off-center. That is, humans are notorious for **reporting inaccuracy**. This does not mean that all humans are liars. Instead, it simply means that we are not very good social observers, we have remarkably poor memories, and we filter what we see and hear through years of personal experience. Now, one could easily ask, "What, then, is the point of asking 2,000 people if all of them are poor reporters?" Good question. The answer is that most social scientists would rather stand on a research finding that was the predominant response of 2,000 relatively independent (i.e., they do not know each other or are not all alike in some obvious way) observers than to just ask one or two people. At least with 2,000 participants, one might have some notion about how the event or attitudes varied across those 2,000 people (taking into consideration that some may be rich, some poor, some African American, others European American). Statistically, we could also compare their responses and find out if a belief or behavior is similar for smaller groups within a sample and more easily recognize whether some behaviors are outliers or typical for the group and subgroups in the sample.

In sum, practically everyone has vast experience in family life. As Schvaneveldt (1971) pointed out, "No other experiences are so universally experienced as childhood, family, and marriage; hence, everyone is an 'expert' or at least perceives himself as such. Many laymen seriously question the validity of family life study, believing that much of the subject matter is trivial" (p. 3). It turns out, however, that your personal experience in that one family (or even two or three families) is very limited and is, by definition, biased. That is not a critique of you, personally, but it is a caution to those who would take their personal family experience, whatever it might be, and overgeneralize that idea to the vast population of families that are not their own.

PRINCIPLE 3.1

FAMILY SCIENCE RESEARCH

Sound family science asks us to go beyond our personal experience.

Empirical Research

The process of doing family science research, therefore, is designed to go beyond personal experience and anecdotal evidence. **Non-empirical methods** emphasize these personal observations, experiences, and reflections as ways of gaining knowledge. Although non-empirical methods can be interesting, deepen insights, and lead to future research, information gained in this way is generally not **falsifiable** (i.e., it can't be proven wrong) because of its personal nature, thus impeding our ability to test knowledge and theory.

In contrast, **empirical research** aims to look at the world of family life in a scientific and more objective way. Empirical research focuses on the collection and interpretation of information through systematic means that reduce bias and increase the generalizability of the knowledge that is learned. This approach, insists that we do not accept (for the purposes of science) revelatory declarations, preferences of individuals, or proclamations by powerful public figures. Instead, the **scientific method** is an important aspect of collecting empirical data. It guides us in identifying and defining problems; asking questions and formulating hypotheses that we can test and explore; designing studies and measuring constructs in a way that allows us to test our hypotheses; interpreting and applying findings based on our observations; and refining how we view the world and the theories we hold. This is not simply a one-time process but an ongoing cycle of discovery, growth, and adaptation in how we understand what we observe and measure. Importantly, using this process, in conjunction with theoretical frameworks, allows us to build on past research, turning individual bricks (data/observations) into stable buildings.

An important consideration of empirical research is ensuring validity and reliability. **Validity** means that the measures we use are, hopefully, measuring what we think they are measuring. **Reliability**, on the other hand, speaks to the idea that each time researchers use the same measure, they get similar results. Both are important if we want to collect useful information. Suppose you walk into a clock store, and there are hundreds of clocks on the walls. You notice that they are all set to the same time. If the time on all the clocks matches the satellite broadcast of the actual atomic clock used to measure time (http://www.time.gov/), you could say that the clocks in the store have a valid measure of the correct time. Reliability, on the other hand, speaks to the long-term accuracy of the clocks. So, a clock could be very reliable—chiming 12 times every day at 11:30—but not express a valid time.

PRINCIPLE 3.2

EMPIRICAL RESEARCH IN FAMILY SCIENCE

Empirical research (empiricism) is one way to tell the story of inner family life. It attempts to do so through systematic methods to collect evidence that can be tested.

Paul Amato, former president of the National Council on Family Relations, emphasizes the importance of scientific rigor and empirical methods in the study of family, but also touches on the limitations of science in this realm of research (Amato, 2014):

> Given that the social sciences will never attain the precision and clarity of the physical sciences, does it still make sense to refer to our field as family science? I believe that it does, provided that we recognize that the term "science" is a metaphor. That is, we follow the methods of science as best we can, and we see how far that takes us. Our empirical generalizations about families have many exceptions, and they often are culturally and historically contingent. But despite the limitations imposed by our subject matter, the scientific approach still brings rigor and discipline to our work and helps to ensure that our observations are as reliable and objective as possible. Without adopting the methods of science, our "research" would not rise above the level of personal opinion. We would lose the capacity to be surprised by the results of our work, trapped in an infinite loop of reaffirming our own preconceptions.

Although the scientific approach is valuable, we also should recognize that many aspects of the human condition are not readily amenable to scientific analysis. The meanings that people attach to actions and events, in particular, are better grasped through sympathetic understanding (or empathy) rather than experimentation and quantification…Because humans have a physical body as well as consciousness and volition, the study of human behavior always will have one foot in the sciences and the other in the humanities. We need both to keep our balance. If we reject science, we lose our credibility. If we reject our humanistic foundations, we lose what is unique about our subject matter—and ourselves.

Overall, it is important to remember that science, per se, is not about finding the ultimate truth. Especially in the context of social science, science is about working with truth-like ideas—all of which, by definition—have to have the possibility of being proven false. We do the best we can at searching for ideas that are usable, make sense, and seem to stand the test of research practices. The scientific method and empirical research practices allow this iterative research process to happen, and by employing different research designs and methods, we can gain a deeper understanding of the family.

PRINCIPLE 3.3

FAMILY SCIENCE NOT ABOUT TRUTH, PER SE

Family science is uncovering our best guess about the ways things work in families. It is not about discovering absolute, immutable truths. Hence, every research project has limitations and biases.

Research Design and Methods

Research is formalized curiosity. It is poking and prying with a purpose.

Zora Neale Hurston

Chris is a woodworker who enjoys building anything from furniture to decorative wall art. Looking inside his toolbox, you will find a pencil, measuring tape, square, chisels, hand planes, various saws, glue, hammer, and sandpaper, among other items. This wide array of tools is necessary to accomplish different tasks for different projects. In fact, we would most certainly scoff at any carpenter who sets out to create a fine table or cabinet using only a hammer. What we are building and where we are at in the process of building will dictate the use of specific tools for specific purposes. Researchers, much like Chris, have a toolbox full of different designs, methodologies, and statistical techniques that allow them to accomplish different goals, including exploring, describing, explaining, predicting, intervening, or evaluating. Whether you are setting out to discover new information about family, verify theoretically based hypotheses, design interventions to make family life better, or evaluate the effectiveness of existing family-based programs—your goals and purpose matter and influence what you pull from your toolbox. Further, although some family scientists may have more expertise with particular research tools, we cannot ignore the fact that many tools are required to approach a polished product. Let's take a look at some of the considerations, planning, and tools required to build high-quality research!

Timing

In a review of family resilience research, Masten (2018) touches on the role that development plays in understanding family: "Over the life course of an individual or a family life cycle, the developmental status of each interacting system has the potential to alter the effects of challenges and recovery or transformation, as well as the nature of cascades that can be expended or averted. Individuals develop and change in multiple ways over time that can influence individual or family capacity to adapt to challenges" (p. 16). Individuals, family systems, and family contexts are constantly developing and changing. This is something we must keep in mind as we determine how we might study the family and the nature of the information we gather in family research, including whether we use a cross-sectional or longitudinal research design.

Cross-sectional research designs involve collecting data from individuals or groups at a single point in time. For example, suppose a researcher wants to know if eating meals with family is related to adolescent alcohol use. One way to do this with a cross-sectional study is to send a one-time survey to adolescents asking them to report how often they eat dinner with their family and how much alcohol they use. Cross-sectional research can be a helpful way to gather large amounts of information and learn about a population of interest at a particular time.

Cross-sectional designs can also explore change and development in a limited way. For example, if we wanted to know how frequency of family meals changes with age, a researcher might send a survey to a group of 13 year olds, a group of 16 year olds, and a group of 18 year olds. No participant would be surveyed more than once, but a researcher could consider how responses might differ across these different age groups. Alternatively, a researcher might use a repeated cross-sectional design to try to understand how frequency of meals with families are changing over time by sending a survey to 16 year olds in 2000, 16 year olds in 2010, and 16 year olds in 2020. Once again, each individual is measured only one time, but the researcher could gain insight into trends within this group.

A drawback of cross-sectional research is that a single point in time, even with a repeated cross-sectional design, fails to fully capture developmental processes and other changes in individuals, families, and sociocultural contexts. Additionally, such designs do not allow researchers to make inferences about cause and effect. Researchers (like everyone else) are interested in knowing what causes things to happen or what causes people to be the way they are. Unfortunately, simply collecting data at one point in time does not always tell us the cause of things. Sometimes, it appears that we know the cause, but often, we are making a mistake by assuming **causation**. One of the biggest errors one can make is to assume causation based on correlational data. A **correlation** is simply collecting two sets of data and seeing if they relate ("co-relate"). Just because two things appear to happen together does not mean that one is causing the other to happen. For example, consider the link between eating dinner together as a family and child and adolescent well-being. Research suggests that eating meals together more frequently relates to improved nutrition (Gillman et al., 2000), decreased substance abuse (Eisenberg, Neumark-Sztainer, Fulkerson, & Story, 2008), and improved academic performance (Eisenberg, Olson, Neumark-Sztainer, Story, & Bearinger, 2004). Further, popular media has often touted the benefits that come from frequently eating meals together. However, in a review of research relating to family mealtime, Fiese and Schwartz (2008) point out that most research on the subject is cross-sectional, thereby limiting conclusions we can make about cause and effect. For example, by measuring only one point in time, we are unable to determine whether more frequent family meals result in healthier parent/adolescent relationships OR whether healthier parent/adolescent relationships result in more frequent family meals. It would take a method that follows the same people over time in order to understand the relationship between these two factors.

In contrast to cross-sectional designs, **longitudinal** research designs involve collecting data from the *same* people over time. By measuring across time, it is possible to understand how behaviors, characteristics, and qualities may change. As Berthoud (2000) aptly explains, longitudinal research provides us with "a movie rather than a snapshot" (p. 15). Longitudinal research can take a number of forms. Quality longitudinal designs allow researchers to more fully explore how individuals, not just groups, change over time and to identify what factors cause particular outcomes. However, such research is typically more expensive, requires more time, and requires the researchers to deal with the loss of participants over time. If you are interested in more details relating to cross-sectional and longitudinal designs, see Menard (2002).

Quantitative, Qualitative, and Mixed Methods

If you think back to the elephant, you will remember that it can be studied in many ways, from measuring its height and weight to observing how it uses its trunk in its natural environment to support its young. These ways of studying the elephant reflect, in a very simplistic way, the differences between quantitative and qualitative methods.

Quantitative methods, as the name implies, refer to methods related to **quant**ifying, including measuring and counting. In quantitative research, responses or observations of individuals and families are reduced to a series of recorded quantifiable numbers. In quantitative research, we might ask: How often do you spank your child? How happy is your family on a scale from 1 to 10? How many years have you been married? Typically, quantitative research begins with a research question and a hypothesis, followed by the collection and analysis of data in an effort to find objective answers to the research question. In quantitative research, the investigator strives to control as many elements as possible (e.g., setting, participant qualities) in order to attribute outcomes to specific **variables** of focus. A variable is a measurable trait or quality (e.g., religion) that can vary across the people, families, or groups that we study. Quantitative methods come with a number of strengths, including efficiency; the ability to collect data from a large number of people, which enhances the generalizability of the findings; increased objectivity and, ideally, reduced opportunities for bias; and the relative ease of replicating such research.

Qualitative methods, on the other hand, focus on **qual**ities rather than quantities. Instead of counting and measuring, qualitative research focuses on the meanings people attribute to their experiences and the world around them. James Spradley (1979), a cultural anthropologist and author of a number of books on qualitative research and ethnography (a type of qualitative research), offers insight into a qualitative researcher's approach: "I want to understand the world from your point of view. I want to know what you know in the way you know it. I want to understand the meaning of your experience, to walk in your shoes, to feel things as you feel them, to explain things as you explain them. Will you become my teacher and help me understand?" (p. 34).

Whereas quantitative research tends to be a (theoretically) linear process of research question/hypothesis > research design > data collection > answer, qualitative research tends to be less linear by design. In qualitative research, research questions and constructs can grow out of observations and interviews, thus qualitative data collection may precede research questions and hypotheses.

Michael Agar, author of *The Professional Stranger: An Informal Introduction to Ethnography*, touches on the differences between the quantitative and qualitative process when he explains:

> It's not necessarily that ethnographers don't want to test hypotheses. It's just that if they do, the variables and operationalizations and sample specifications must grow from an understanding of the group rather than being hammered on top of it no matter how poor the fit. You can't specify the questions you're going to ask when you move into the community; you don't know how to ask questions yet. You can't define a sample, you don't know what the range of social types is and which ones are relevant to the topics you're interested in.
>
> (1980, pp. 69–70)

Strengths of qualitative research methods include an appreciation of context (e.g., cultural, historical, situational), more natural research settings, an insider's perspective and interpretation of phenomena, flexibility that allows for changes throughout the study, and the ability to see and understand systems and groups beyond the individuals that make them up. As Gabb (2008) explains, "a qualitative approach lends itself more readily to the messiness and particularities of family relationships and everyday intimate life" (p. 29).

It is not uncommon to see people debate quantitative *versus* qualitative methods; however, to see these as opposing approaches or a competition between which one is "right" is shortsighted and inaccurate. Instead, when examining the strengths and weaknesses of these two methods, you will find that they actually complement each other. While one allows us to collect large amounts of data efficiently, for example, the other adds context and depth to our understanding. For this reason, **mixed methods** have become increasingly popular and important. Plano Clark, Huddleston-Casas, Churchill, O'Neil Green, and Garrett (2008) define mixed methods research as "consisting of a set of designs and procedures in which both quantitative and qualitative data are collected, analyzed, and mixed in a single study or series of studies" (p. 1546). Mixed methods designs can come in different forms as researchers vary the timing (when each type of data is collected/used), weighting (which is emphasized more), and mixing (how data/results are brought together in the study) of qualitative and quantitative data. Plano Clark et al.'s review of mixed methods in family research suggests such research is happening, but they also point out that not all researchers use established mixed methods terminology, nor are they necessarily using complex quantitative and qualitative techniques, suggesting that there is room for growth in this area. As family researchers deepen their understanding of what qualitative and quantitative techniques have to offer and collaborate with experts in these different forms of research, it is likely that our understanding of family life can deepen and expand.

Data Collection

Ultimately, a researcher's goals, purpose, resources, theories, and questions come together to determine the method of research and data collection. All methods of gathering data have strengths and weaknesses and, together, offer us unique ways to look at the inner workings of family.

Experiments

Traditionally seen as the gold standard in research, experimental designs *randomly* assign participants to either experimental groups, where participants are exposed to some stimulus or treatment, or control groups, where participants are not exposed to any treatment. Researchers strive to control as much as possible between these two groups, manipulating only the **independent variable** for the experimental group. The independent variable refers to the variable that we believe influences the **dependent variable**, the outcome we are interested in. By allowing only the independent variable to change, the researcher can more accurately attribute differences in the dependent variable at the end of the study to the particular manipulation or treatment that participants were exposed to. Thus, the experimental design is ideal for avoiding **spurious relationships**. A spurious relationship is one in which two events seem related, but, on further examination, we find that both are related due to some third event. For example, ice cream sales and shark attacks may appear to be related, but it is not actually ice cream sales causing shark attacks but the high temperatures of summer influencing both ice cream sales and the number of people in the water.

Experiments can be conducted in either a controlled lab setting or in the field. An interesting example of a field experiment is the Moving to Opportunity Experiment (Chetty, Hendren, & Katz, 2016). In this study, families living in high-poverty neighborhoods were randomly assigned to receive housing vouchers to allow them to move to lower-poverty neighborhoods. They found that children who moved to lower-poverty neighborhoods when they were younger than 13 were more likely to attend college and, as adults, earn a higher income and live in lower-poverty neighborhoods.

Quasi-Experiments

Given the complex nature of family research, it is rarely possible to randomly assign individuals and families to particular groups, control certain aspects of a study, or ethically expose families to particular stimuli or treatments that we might be interested in. For example, consider a researcher who wants to understand how a parent's alcohol abuse influences children. It would be unethical to randomly assign parents of children to abuse or not abuse alcohol. Instead, we need to find families that already abuse or don't abuse alcohol. This is referred to as a quasi-experiment. In a quasi-experiment, researchers find and compare naturally occurring groups; they still strive to hold certain aspects of the situation/context constant and use a control group for comparison, but it is not nearly as rigorous as a true experimental design. Peters, Maas, Hovinga, Van den Bogerd, and Schuengel (2020) used a quasi-experimental design to understand how being exposed to nature influenced parental well-being and parent-child relationships when living in a family shelter in The Netherlands. Rather than randomly selecting and assigning participants to particular conditions, all participants were simply asked certain questions while they were participating in typical daily activities with their child(ren) inside the shelter (control condition) and while they experienced natural environments at or near the shelter (treatment condition). Interestingly, they found that a single exposure to nature at the shelter appeared to support the parents' well-being, potentially improving parent-child relationships and interactions.

Surveys

Surveys are a very popular method of collecting data. You are no doubt familiar with surveys as you have likely been asked to participate in more than a few over the years, whether by phone, e-mail, mail, website, or an in-person interview (see Field Research on the following text for more information on qualitative, in-depth interviews). Collecting data through surveys is typically less expensive and more convenient than other methods, making it easier to gather information from large numbers of people. A key consideration in survey research is the quality of the questions used to collect information. It is relatively easy to create a survey, but it is less easy to create a quality survey that is both valid and reliable. Questions must be unambiguous, measure information that the participant knows or is aware of, and be clear, avoiding issues like jargon, double-barreled items, and loaded questions. Additionally, different types of surveys can result in different concerns; for example, a personal interview could introduce bias from the interviewer's demeanor, and phone or internet surveys may leave some people out because they do not have access to one or both. Additionally, as you are probably aware, participants are not always eager to complete surveys in any form (when was the last time you threw away a survey printed on your receipt or hung up on someone who wanted to ask you just a few questions?), and there is a chance that some populations may be less likely to respond than others, making the sample less representative.

Despite this, surveys can allow us to gather vast amounts of information and are an important tool in our research toolbox. Consider, for example, the University of Pittsburgh's Family Strengths Survey, an online or phone survey that families can complete to help researchers understand mental health, health care, access to food, online learning, and financial needs and assistance for children and parents during COVID-19. As of March 2021, this survey has revealed that most parents and caregivers have felt unable to support their children's well-being or their own emotional and mental health, that over 50% of children lack necessary supervision related to online learning and that food assistance rates as the number one resource families needed during COVID-19 pandemic.

Diary Studies

Much of family life is made up of the day-to-day activities of the family and, as described earlier, can often be invisible or seem unimportant to members of the family. This can make it difficult for family members to accurately recall past events and family interactions. Diary methods, however, offer one way for researchers to gain access to these everyday activities, behaviors, and feelings as they happen. When using diary methods, participants are asked to provide their thoughts, feelings, and experiences in a diary. Entries can be structured (e.g., specific questions or checklists) or unstructured (more freeform); kept on paper, online, or a phone app; and entered based on different circumstances and timelines. Just as with other longitudinal designs, the timing of diary entries can vary, with participants making diary entries several times per day or once per day and being prompted to make an entry every time a certain event happens or randomly throughout the day or week (perhaps when an app on their phone signals participants to complete an entry). As explained by Laurenceau and Bolger (2005), "the primary benefit of examining marital and family processes using diary methods is that they permit examination of relationship events and experiences in their natural, spontaneous context and often reduce the likelihood of retrospection by minimizing the amount of time between the experience of an event and the account of the event" (p. 86). Bai Reynolds, Robles, and Repetti (2016) used diary methods to understand how adolescents' problems at school could influence parent-child interactions in the home. Adolescents and their parents were asked to write in an online journal every weekday at bedtime for 8 weeks. Researchers used this information to see if academic and peer problems influenced parent-child relationships on the day the problems occurred. Results suggested that academic problems influenced the teen's perception of the relationship with one or both parents (e.g., more conflict, less warmth); however, parents did not report similar feelings. Peer problems, on the other hand, did not seem to relate to the teen's perception of their relationship with their parents. By collecting information as it happens, it is possible to draw new connections between various contexts that can influence family and family relationships.

Observation

Collecting data through observation is a fascinating process that can take on a wide range of forms! Observation in the context of family is particularly useful in gaining insights into "interactional patterns and structures that are not necessarily accessible to the participants themselves, and thus could not be accurately assessed through self-report" (Margolin et al., 1998, p. 196). Observations can be overt (the participant knows they are being observed) or covert (the participant is unaware of being observed); controlled (e.g., in a lab) or naturalistic (e.g., watching families in the mall); qualitative or quantitative. Further, the researcher can take on different roles, either through direct observation, where the researcher observes behavior from the outside in an unobtrusive manner, or participant observation, where the researcher becomes a participating member of the community they are observing and employs more qualitative techniques.

For all observational methods, researchers must be skilled at what to look for and they must take quality, in-depth notes. An observation with a quantitative focus tends to employ systematic observation methods, where the researcher is focused on specific behaviors and interactions and utilizes coding systems to define what those behaviors are and what "counts" as that behavior during the observation. This requires reliable and valid instruments to assess clearly thought-out constructs tied to theoretical ideas.

A famous example of a controlled observation is Dr. John Gottman's Love Lab (https://www.gottman.com/love-lab/), where couples could stay and be observed. Their interactions and conversations are recorded and coded, offering insights into how couples communicate, interact, address conflict, and narrate their relationship. Gottman and others have used these observations to develop evidence-based interventions to support relationships.

Field Research

In field research, the goal is not to present a statistical comparative picture of family life and does not focus so much on statistics, variables, and correlations. Instead, the goal is to provide a richer description of how the family works through the eyes of those reporting the **lived experience**. Further, field research focuses on understanding people in their natural environment and context. In-depth/qualitative interviews, case studies, qualitative observation, and ethnography are examples of field research methodologies. Here, we focus on the more commonly used field research approaches: participant observation, in-depth interviews, and case studies.

- **Participant Observation.** In participant observation, the researchers immerse themselves in situations, family groups, tribes, or communities. In using this method, researchers must have a good working relationship with the people they are observing. Participant observation research does not rely on a random sample or population-based demographics and most field research requires in-depth training and, in most cases, years of experience

FIGURE 3.3 Aka fathers hold their infants for safety.

and preparation. Participant observation field research is difficult and costly but results in wonderfully rich data that provide an illuminated image of how people conduct the prosaic of everyday life.

There are several excellent examples of this kind of research. Dr. Barry Hewlett, for example, spent decades regularly visiting the Aka people of Central Africa. Hewlett, Lamb, Shannon, Leyendecker, and Scholmerich (1998) explored how parents interact with infants in different cultures by living in the villages of two small communities, known as the Aka and Ngandu. The Aka live in small huts in camps of 25 to 30 people, moving several times a year as they search for hunting locations. The Ngandu live in larger huts alongside roads in rather established communities. The Aka are much less integrated into anything that represents a commerce-based society—they have no cash, nor do they buy or sell much of anything. They make their own clothes and kill or grow their own food. On the other hand, the Ngandu are more likely to have received some schooling and might work at jobs for pay. In this study, the researchers wanted to know how the type of living style changed how parents interacted with their children (Figure 3.3).

Hewlett and colleagues simply sat nearby and coded the infant–parent interaction while the families went about their everyday lives for days at a time. What did they find? They discovered that Aka parents held their children much more than did the Ngandu, although the Ngandu were more likely to talk and verbalize with their children. Why? These researchers suggested several reasons, from keeping children safe from insects, snakes, and other hazards to nutrition. Ultimately, however, the researchers concluded that they (the European and European American researchers) were bringing their own bias to this problem. That is, all of the potential reasons for differences that they generated were ideas that came from the minds of people who were raised in the suburbs of Western civilization and not on the jungle floor of Central Africa. They then ventured some other guesses about the number of yearly relocations each group experienced and also suggested that their worldviews about family life, egalitarian lifestyle, and the value of children might be at the heart of the difference. You are encouraged to read this interesting article and see if you have other ideas.

- **In-Depth Interviews.** The second type of field research is the in-depth interview. In this type of research, researchers locate and interview a group of individuals who share a common life experience. Usually, these researchers do not attempt to sample the whole population of possible participants, but instead, they will interview a relatively small number of individuals who are willing to tell their stories. As participants tell their stories, the researcher takes careful notes, often recording the interviews for analysis at a later time. Once the interviews are completed, the researchers have a word-by-word transcript created of each interview. This can be a lengthy and expensive process. Interviews continue until the researcher reaches a **saturation** level; that is, new interviews do not seem to be yielding any new information.

An example of the use of in-depth interview was a 2004 study by Ahmed and Bould regarding Bangladesh parents' views on having girls vs. boys. These researchers interviewed 120 mothers who were employed at a garment factory in Dhaka. There was no questionnaire filled out by the women. No attempt was made to generate an unbiased sample, nor was there any attempt to show how attitudes change over time or vary by the number and gender of the children in the family. Instead, Ahmed and Bould told the story of a small number of women who were struggling with provisioning and surviving. The researchers looked for themes in the stories of these women, taking care to note the relevant cultural or community contexts. What did they find? Over the last 20 years, the women of the family have begun to find work in garment factories, and with those wages, they have increased freedom to make choices independent of the men's wishes for them. With this newfound independence, these women are creating a better life for themselves and their families, according to these authors. Further, where women once hoped for sons, now only 10% reported that the ideal family had sons, with an increasing number of women hoping for daughters who could work with them. These women's power also seemed to increase when they were able to direct some of their income to their kin and help support them.

Another form of interviewing is called **photo elicitation interviewing**, where researchers ask participants to take meaningful photos, and those photos are then used to help drive the interview. Research suggests that incorporating photography into an interview can help the participant more clearly communicate thoughts and ideas, creates a deeper bond between the interviewer and participant, and allows the participant a more active role in the research process (Sibeoni et al., 2017). Hong and Goh (2018) further argue that this technique is particularly useful in helping children share their perspectives.

- **Case Studies.** Another qualitative technique that can help us understand the family is the case study. Case studies focus on one or a few specific cases and delve deeply into that case. A case may be a family, individual, a parent-child pair, a couple, communities, and beyond. Case studies require a great deal of time, cannot be generalized to the broader population, cannot be replicated, and may more easily allow researcher bias into the process, but they offer a depth of understanding that survey research does not. It sees and recognizes the importance of the story of the individual and how that individual or family experiences the world. Seanna Leath (2017) used a case study to understand the story of Tron, an African American man, and his experience as a new father. Through Tron's stories of his relationship with his father, playing video games with his son, embarrassment at his son's birthday party because of his inability to afford a larger gift, among others, Leath highlights the themes of African American fatherhood and intergenerational change (trying to be different from the generation before; in this case, his desire to be present in his son's life), emphasizing "Tron's story illustrates a need to counter dominant narratives of African American fathers as absent and neglectful" (p. 9).

Unobtrusive Methods

Unobtrusive methods refer to researchers accessing data without directly interacting with research subjects. Examples of unobtrusive methods include:

- **Content Analysis.** In content analysis, the researcher examines existing materials for key themes, words, and concepts. These materials can be in various forms, including text, speech, images, and videos and may come from public records, private records (such as diaries, letters, or memoirs), photos, media, and social media. For example, Johnston and Swanson (2003) reviewed articles in women's magazines to understand portrayals of motherhood. Sandbye (2014), on the other hand, argues that family photo albums are ripe for analysis.
- **Secondary Data Analysis.** Rather than collecting their own data, researchers are increasingly turning to existing sources of data, often collected by large organizations with expertise survey construction and data collection. The scale of these data collection projects means resources can be devoted to creating samples fairly representative of the population. Many of these datasets are based on large-scale surveys that individual researchers would find extremely difficult and expensive to collect on their own. Using sophisticated statistical techniques, researchers can analyze data collected by others to answer a variety of questions about issues such as child and adolescent health, family life, and the transition into adulthood. Every research project, however, has limitations and these surveys can be somewhat limited in their attention to inner family life, such as family routines, rituals, and family processes. Still, researchers and graduate students from around the world have utilized these datasets to learn more about family. Such data is often public access and can be free or relatively inexpensive. Sharing of data and publishing findings are basic tenets of the scientific endeavor and the trend appears to be moving more in this direction in terms of data sharing and archiving. Secondary data analysis is also not restricted to quantitative data, with secondary qualitative datasets available, although this is a topic of debate (see Ruggiano & Perry, 2019). Below are some popular examples of quantitative secondary data relating to children and family:
    - The National Longitudinal Study of Adolescent Health (Add Health, Figure 3.4)
    - National Survey of Families and Households (NSFH)

FIGURE 3.4 The Add Health project has surveyed more than 20,000 families in their homes, asking a myriad of questions about their personal lives and about their family.

- Fragile Families and Child Wellbeing
- National Longitudinal Surveys (NLS)
- Behavioral Risk Factor Surveillance System (BRFSS), including Adverse Childhood Experience (ACE) data
- Early Childhood Longitudinal Study (ECLS)
- General Social Survey (GSS)
- Youth Risk Behavior Surveillance System (YRBSS)
- Census and data from other government agencies

Future Directions

The study of family is constantly evolving, with innovations in existing research methods and the development of new measures and sources of information provide fascinating paths into the future of family science.

One such cutting-edge technique is the use of **biological methods** in the study of the family. Li, Fiese, and Deater-Deckar (2019) highlight biological methods in this context, including EEGs, blood tests, saliva tests, MRIs, and fMRIs. These tools help us measure factors such as hormone levels and neural activity, offering insights into factors such as stress and relationships. Li and colleagues argue that "it has never been more important for all family scientists to develop solid foundations for understanding these methods and concepts" (p. 197), explaining that "the pace and extensiveness of use of these methods is only increasing, as the technologies involved become cheaper and better understood. The inclusion of relatively simple physiological, neuroendocrine, neuroimaging, and genetic measurements has become normative in human development and psychology research, and the same will happen in family science" (p. 198).

Utilizing **big data** is another approach that has become popular and is slowly making its way into family science. Big data is an unobtrusive technique that refers to utilizing massive amounts of data that are generated incredibly quickly. Consider, for example, the data generated as people shop on Amazon, search the internet, browse/post to social media sites, or use their mobile devices. When you see ads targeted to you while online, you are seeing big data at work. As an example, Bacher-Hicks, Goodman, and Mulhern (2021) utilized internet search data to understand how families sought out online learning resources for their children during the COVID 19 pandemic. They found that families from areas with higher income sought out more resources, suggesting the potential for increased achievement gaps as a result of the pandemic. Additionally, The Fragile Families and Child Wellbeing Study utilized big data techniques to find meaning within 54 million data points, helping them understand predictors of academic achievement, poverty, employment, and grit in children (Makhijani, 2017).

Scholars are also increasingly calling on family scientists to explore and challenge traditional theoretical and methodological perspectives through the applications of approaches such as **queering methods** (Fish & Russell, 2018) and **decolonizing research methods** (Bermúdez, Muruthi, & Jordan, 2016). According to Bermúdez, Muruthi, and Jordan (2016), decolonizing methodologies "challenge the status quo and the superiority of Western academic research and focus on agendas meant to honor subjugated, marginalized, indigenous people and their local knowledge," adding that "decolonizing research methods highlight and privilege the voices that have been ignored, disregarded, and/or marginalized. This stance is especially relevant in family social science" (p. 192). Addressing queering methods, Fish and Russell (2018) explain that queering methods requires a consideration for "interlocking systems of power and privilege that shape the life experiences of those whose identities and experiences do not reflect normative expectations of gender, sexuality, and family… a queer method compels not only analytic critique but also critique of the ways that science may confront family normativities" (p. 20). Both of these perspectives ultimately call into question what has traditionally been considered "normative" and "legitimate," striving to listen to voices that have previously been unheard or unappreciated, and turns the focus from research on participants to research for the benefit of participants.

PRINCIPLE 3.4

A RESEARCH TOOLBOX SHOULD HAVE MANY TOOLS

Family scientists must utilize a variety of research designs, including considerations for timing, methodology, and data collection techniques. The tools used will be influenced by research questions, goals, and resources, and the best information comes from a constellation of research methods.

Discussions in Diversity: I Found Work at MTurk!

Imagine having access to over 250,000 people (Robinson, Rosenzweig, Moss, & Litman, 2019) who are eager to answer any questions you have! Information about family structure, sibling relationships, parenting behaviors, daily routines, and rituals—for just a small fee, this data could be yours almost immediately. Thanks to the progress of technology, this is now possible with Amazon Mechanical Turk (MTurk). The Mechanical Turk was originally a purported chess-playing machine from the 1700s; however, it was later revealed to be a hoax, with a person hiding inside the machine actually playing the game against unsuspecting opponents (Figure 3.5). Now, MTurk refers to a crowdsourcing marketplace where people and organizations can post "microtasks" to be completed by "workers"—tasks that are simply better completed by real people rather than automated processes. Examples of tasks include monitoring web content, rating photos, updating documents or spreadsheets, and tagging objects in images. Workers then get paid per microtask, with some quick and simple tasks paying just a few cents. Although MTurk was launched in 2005, it continues to be an increasingly popular method of gathering information.

How does this apply to studying families? Social scientists are now creating survey completion microtasks, drawing from the large pool of workers to create their samples. Schleider and Weisz (2015), for example, used MTurk to study the relationship between family processes and children's mental health across 3 months, not only focusing on the family, but also on the MTurk process itself, ultimately concluding that "parents provided largely high-quality data" adding that "compared to prior studies using traditional longitudinal methods, the MTurk method was (a) much lower in case and resource

FIGURE 3.5 A depiction of how the Mechanical Turk machine may have been designed.

requirements, (b) successful in enrolling fathers [a group that can difficult to collect data from], (c) comparable in participant attrition, and (d) similar in attrition bias, participant race/ethnicity, and enrollment of single parents" (p. 3236). MTurk also appears to be a better option than convenience samples too often drawn from college students as MTurk participants appear to be more ethnically and socioeconomically diverse (Cassese, Huddy, Hartman, Mason, & Weber, 2013; Difallah, Filatova, & Ipeirotis, 2018; Woods, Velasco, Levitan, Wan, & Spence, 2015).

However, every method of data collection has drawbacks and MTurk raises some important methodological and ethical considerations. For example, are MTurk workers representative of the population? Although they are more diverse in some ways, are they diverse enough and in important ways? Are MTurk workers so familiar with social science research tools that their responses are no longer accurate? Are workers paid appropriately for their work? Berg, Furrer, Harmon, Rani, and Silberman (2018) report an average hourly wage of just $6.54. Is it possible that we are taking advantage of particular groups of people, including low-income participants? Authors like Chandler, Rosenzweig, Moss, Robinson, and Litman (2019), Difallah et al. (2018), Robinson et al. (2019), Woods et al. (2015), and an unpublished paper by Moss, Rosenzweig, Robinson, and Litman (2020) have tried to address these questions, suggest steps to improve data quality and MTurk samples and propose alternative data sources, but suggestions vary and answers remain elusive. Certainly, these issues should be a consideration when conducting or reviewing research based on these methods.

Even given these challenges, MTurk opens doors and opportunities for many researchers, including individuals who may not always have the time, money, or opportunity to collect data in more traditional ways. One young researcher reports that MTurk made collecting data on school-aged children significantly easier, saving her time and money while avoiding the complications of collecting data through a school system. Additionally, she was able to collect data from a more targeted sample and do so quickly (in one study, she reached the cap of 300 participants within hours!).

Ultimately, data collection platforms such as MTurk offer an interesting opportunity for researchers! Likely, as with most information gathering, MTurk will offer researchers one additional tool to be used in conjunction with more traditional research techniques. For example, Schleider and Weisz (2015) argue that MTurk can be used as the first step in research that is later supplemented and supported by more traditional methods. Overall, as is true with all research, the key is to consider how researchers can ensure that they are using this new tool both effectively and ethically.

Questions to Discuss:

- *If many research samples consist of college students, what might be the "typical" demographic of this group? Why is that not representative of the general population?*
- *How can one access diverse groups that are representative of the same groups in the general population? For example, if you are interested in same-sex parent families, how would you access these parents? Some students have suggested "gay bars," "Pride Festivals," and sending out flyers at school. What are the problems with these suggestions?*
- *Do you think MTurk is a good idea for increasing diverse samples? Why or why not?*
- *How honest do you think participants in MTurk projects are? Explain.*
- *Discuss the ethical dilemmas presented by MTurk. How should these be addressed?*

SUMMARY

Which of these approaches is best? The answer is all of them. They are all ways of telling the story of the human condition and each is very valuable. Often those who do the more quantitative or empirical work rely on the lived experience world of the field researcher. In a like manner, the field researcher pays close attention to the findings of larger empirical, longitudinal, statistical-based research findings. Those findings inform and enlighten their efforts.

In this chapter, you have read about how family science researchers go about the task of trying to discover how to better understand family life. There are many ways researchers collect information about families. Sometimes, we use large-scale data sets like those created by the government (e.g., census data), sometimes researchers rely on historical accounts, others collect information from within clinical settings, others complete in-depth interviews with families, and still others ask family members about their beliefs and attitudes about their lived experiences. All of these methods are legitimate and useful when done carefully and with precision. All of them are attempts to tell the story of family life. It is not helpful to claim that one of them is better than another; instead, each contributes to the story of family life in a different way and each helps build a wonderfully rich mosaic—a mural of family life. When we step back and look at all the stories told by all the means possible, only then can we begin to see the richness of the whole picture.

STUDY QUESTIONS

1 What are three factors that make the study of family unique from other disciplines?
2 What five limitations are present in knowledge gained through personal experience?
3 What is the difference between non-empirical and empirical research?
4 Give an example of reliability and validity of a measure.
5 Explain cross-sectional and longitudinal research designs and give an example of each.
6 Contrast qualitative and quantitative research methods. Which is "better"?
7 What is the difference between an experiment and a quasi-experiment? Why do researchers use quasi-experiments?
8 Describe three commonly used field research approaches.
9 Why do we care about the idea of causation and correlation? In your answer include and define the idea of spurious relationships.
10 Describe the study reported in the text about the Aka and Ngandu peoples. Why was this study used as an example? Why didn't the researchers use more quantitative methods in their research?
11 How might new trends in research provide additional insight into family?

KEY TERMS

Reductionism
Personal experience
Personal experiential reality
Personal inquiry
Sample bias
Sample
Population
Biased
Systematic and random distortion
Overgeneralizing
Outliers
Confirmation bias/fixation
Agreement reality

Reporting inaccuracy
Non-empirical methods
Falsifiable
Empirical research
Scientific method
Validity
Reliability
Cross-sectional
Causation
Correlation
Longitudinal
Quantitative methods
Variables
Qualitative methods
Mixed methods
Experiments
Independent variable
Dependent variable
Spurious relationships
Quasi-experiments
Survey
Diary
Observation
Field research
Lived experience
Participant observation
In-depth interviews
Saturation
Photo elicitation interviewing
Case studies
Unobtrusive methods
Content analysis
Secondary data analysis
Biological methods
Big data

SUGGESTED READINGS

Daly, K. J. (2007). *Qualitative methods for family studies and human development.* Thousand Oaks, CA: Sage.

Greenstein, T. N., & Davis, S. N. (2019). *Methods of research on human development and families.* Thousand Oaks, CA: Sage.

Keller, M. N., & Noone, R. J. (2020). *Handbook of Bowen family systems theory and research methods: A systems model of family research.* New York, NY: Taylor & Francis.

Wheelan, C. (2014). *Naked statistics: Stripping the dread from the data.* New York, NY: W. W. Norton & Company.

REFERENCES

Agar, M. H. (1980). *The professional stranger: An informal introduction to ethnography*. Orlando, FL: Academic Press Inc.

Ahmed, F. E., & Bould, S. (2004). "One able daughter is worth 10 illiterate sons": Reframing the patriarchal family. *Journal of Marriage and Family, 66*(5), 1332–1341.

Amato, P. R. (2014, September 15). *What do we mean by family science?* National Council on Family Relations. https://www.ncfr.org/ncfr-report/past-issues/fall-2014/what-do-we-mean-family-science

Babbie, E. (2006). *The practice of social research*. Belmont, CA: Wadsworth Publishing Company, Inc.

Bacher-Hicks, A., Goodman, J., & Mulhern, C. (2021). Inequality in household adaptation to schooling shocks: Covid-induced online learning engagement in real life. *Journal of Public Economics, 193*, 1–17. DOI: 10.1016/j.jpubeco.2020.104345

Bai, S., Reynolds, B. M., Robles, T. F., & Repetti, R. L. (2016). Daily links between school problems and youth perception of interactions with parents: A diary study of school-to-home spillover. *Social Development, 26*(4), 813–830.

Berg, J., Furrer, M., Harmon, E., Rani, U., & Silberman, M. S. (2018). *Digital labour platforms and the future of work: Towards decent work in the online world*. International Labour Organization (ILO). http://www.ilo.org/wcmsp5/groups/public/—dgreports/—dcomm/—publ/documents/publication/wcms_645337.pdf

Bermúdez, J. M., Muruthi, B. A., & Jordan, L. S. (2016). Decolonizing research methods for family science: Creating space at the center. *Journal of Family Theory and Review, 8*, 192–206. DOI: 10.1111/jftr.12139

Berthoud, R. (2000). Introduction: The dynamics of social change. In R. Berthoud, & J. Gershuny (Eds.), *Seven years in the lives of British families* (pp. 1–20). Bristol: Policy Press.

Cassese, E. C., Huddy, L., Hartman, T. K., Mason, L., & Weber, C. R. (2013). Socially mediated internet surveys: Recruiting participants for online experiments. *PS: Political Science and Politics, 46*(4), 775–784.

Chandler, J., Rosenzweig, C., Moss, A. J., Robinson, J., & Litman, L. (2019). Online panels in social science research: Expanding sampling methods beyond mechanical Turk. *Behavior Research Methods, 51*, 2022–2038. DOI: 10.3758/s13428-019-01273-7

Chetty, R., Hendren, N., & Katz, L. F. (2016). The effects of exposure to better neighborhoods on children: New evidence from the moving to opportunity experiment. *American Economic Review, 106*(4), 855–902. DOI: 10.1257/aer.20150572

Difallah, D., Filatova, E., & Ipeirotis, P. (2018). Demographics and dynamics of Mechanical Turk workers. Proceedings of WSDM 2018: The Eleventh ACM International Conference on Web Search and Data Mining. DOI: 10.1145/3159652.3159661 Mining Marina Del Rey CA USA February 5–9, 2018

Eisenberg, M. E., Neumark-Sztainer, D., Fulkerson, J. A., & Story, M. (2008). Family meals and substance use: Is there a long-term protective association? *Journal of Adolescent Health, 43*, 151–156.

Eisenberg, M. E., Olson, R. E., Neumark-Sztainer, D., Story, M., & Bearinger, L. H. (2004). Correlations between family meals and psychosocial well-being among adolescents. *Archives of Pediatrics and Adolescent Medicine, 158*(8), 792–796.

Fiese, B. H., & Schwartz, M. (2008). Reclaiming the family table: Mealtimes and child health and wellbeing. *Social Policy Report, 22*(4), 1–20. DOI: 10.1002/j.2379-3988.2008.tb00057.x

Fish, J. N., & Russell, S. T. (2018). Queering methodologies to understand queer families. *Family Relations, 67*, 12–25. DOI: 10.1111/fare.12297

Gabb, J. (2008). *Researching intimacy in families. Palgrave Macmillan studies in family and intimate life*. London: Palgrave Macmillan.

Gillman, M. W., Rifas-Shiman, S. L., Frazier, A. L., Rockett, H. R., Camargo, C. A., Field, A. E. … Colditz, G. A. (2000). Family dinner and diet quality among older children and adolescents. *Archives of Family Medicine, 9*(3), 235–240.

Groves, E. R. (1946). Professional training for family life educators. *Marriage and Family Living, 8*(2), 25–26.

Heisenberg, W. (1958). *Physics and philosophy: The revolution in modern science*. New York, NY: Harper.

Hewlett, B. S., Lamb, M. E., Shannon, D., Leyendecker, B., & Schölmerich, A. (1998). Culture and early infancy among central African foragers and farmers. *Developmental Psychology, 34*(4), 653–661. DOI: 10.1037/0012-1649.34.4.653

Hong, R. T.Y., & Goh, E. C. L. (2018). Using photo elicitation interviewing to access the subjective well-being of children from poor families within an affluent Asian society: Insights for service delivery. *Children and Youth Services Review, 96*, 430–438.

Jager, J., Bornstein, M. H., Putnick, D. L., & Hendricks, C. (2012). Family members' unique perspectives of the family: Examining their scope, size, and relations to individual adjustment. *Journal of Family Psychology, 26*(3), 400–410. DOI: 10.1037/a0028330

Johnston, D. D., & Swanson, D. H. (2003). Invisible mothers: A content analysis of motherhood ideologies and myths in magazines. *Sex Roles, 49*, 21–33. DOI: 10.1023/A:1023905518500

Klein, G., Phillips, J. K., Rall, E. L., & Peluso, D. A. (2007). A data-frame theory of sensemaking. In R. R. Hoffman (Ed.), *Expertise out of context: Proceedings of the sixth international conference on naturalistic decision making* (pp. 79–96). Taylor & Francis Group, NY.

Laurenceau, J., & Bolger, N. (2005). Using diary methods to study marital and family processes. *Journal of Family Psychology, 19*(1), 86–97. http://www.columbia.edu/~nb2229/docs/laurenceau-bolger-jfp-2005.pdf

Leath, S. (2017). Being better than my dad: A qualitative case study of one African American father's journal with parenthood and intergenerational change. *Sage Open.* DOI: 10.1177/2158244017697163

Li, M., Fiese, B. H., & Deater-Deckar, K. (2019). An overview of biological methods in family science. In B. H. Fiese, M. Celano, K. Deater-Deckard, E. N. Jouriles, & M. A. Whisman (Eds.), *APA handbook of contemporary family psychology: Foundations, methods, and contemporary issues across the lifespan* (Vol 1, pp. 187–204). American Psychological Association, Washington, DC.

Makhijani, P. (2017, November 13). *Fragile families challenge uses "big data" to answer big questions.* University of Princeton. https://www.princeton.edu/news/2017/11/13/fragile-families-challenge-uses-big-data-answer-big-questions

Margolin, G., Oliver, P. H., Gordis, E. B., O'Hearn, H. G., Medina, A. M., Ghosh, C. M., & Morland, L. (1998). The nuts and bolts of behavioral observation of marital and family interaction. *Clinical Child and Family Psychology Review, 1*(4), 195–213. https://link.springer.com/article/10.1023/A:1022608117322

Marsiglio, W., Amato, P., Day, R. D., & Lamb, M. E. (2000). Scholarship on fatherhood in the 1990s and beyond. *Journal of Marriage and the Family, 62*(4), 1173–1191. DOI: 10.1111/j.1741-3737.2000.01173.x

Masten (2018). Resilience theory and research on children and families: Past, present, and promise. *Journal of Family Theory and Review, 10*, 12–31. DOI: 10.1111/jftr.12255

Menard, S. (2002). *Longitudinal research* (2nd ed.). *Series: Quantitative applications in the social sciences.* Thousand Oaks, CA: Sage Publications.

Moss, A., Rosenzweig, C., Robinson, J., & Litman, L. (2020). Is it ethical to use Mechanical Turk for behavioral research? Relevant data from a representative survey of MTurk participants and wages. *PsyArXiv Preprints.* DOI: 10.31234/osf.io/jbc9d

NCFR. (n.d.). *NCFR history.* National Council on Family Relations. https://www.ncfr.org/about/history

Oswald, M. E., & Grosjean, S. (2004). Confirmation bias. In R. F. Pohl (Ed.), *Cognitive illusions: A handbook on fallacies and biases in thinking, judgement and memory* (pp. 79–96). New York, NY: Psychology Press.

Peters, E., Maas, J., Hovinga, D., Van den Bogerd, N., & Schuengel, C. (2020). Experiencing nature to satisfy basic psychological needs in parenting: A quasi-experiment in family shelters. *International Journal of Environmental Research and Public Health, 17*, 8657. DOI: 10.3390/ijerph17228657

Plano Clark, V. L., Huddleston-Casas, C., Churchill, S., O'Neil Green, D., & Garrett, A. (2008). Mixed methods approaches in family science research. *Journal of Family Issues, 29*(11), 1543–1566.

Robinson, J., Rosenzweig, C., Moss, A. J., & Litman, L. (2019). Tapped out or barely tapped? Recommendations for how to harness the vast and largely unused potential of the Mechanical Turk participant pool. *PLoS One, 14*(12), e0226394. DOI: 10.1371/journal.pone.0226394

Ruggiano, N., & Perry, T. E. (2019). Conducting secondary analysis of qualitative data: Should we, can we, and how? *Qualitative Social Work, 18*(1), 81–97.

Sandbye, M. (2014). Looking at the family photo album: A resumed theoretical discussion of why and how. *Journal of Aesthetics & Culture, 6*, 1–17.

Schleider, J. L., & Weisz, J. R. (2015). Using Mechanical Turk to study family processes and youth mental health: A test of feasibility. *Journal of Child and Family Studies, 24*, 3235–3246.

Schvaneveldt, J. D. (1971). Role problems of the college family life educator and researcher. *The Family Coordinator, 20*(1), 3–10. https://www.jstor.org/stable/582924

Sibeoni, J., Costa-Drolon, E., Poulmarc'h, L., Colin, S., Valentin, M., Pradere, J., & Revah-Levy, A. (2017). Photo-elicitation with adolescents in qualitative research: An example of its use in exploring family interactions in adolescent psychiatry. *Child and Adolescent Psychiatry and Mental Health, 11,* 49.

Spradley, J. P. (1979). *The ethnographic interview.* New York, NY: Holt, Rinehart and Winston.

University of Pittsburgh School of Medicine (n.d.). Family strengths survey. https://www.pediatrics.pitt.edu/centers-institutes/pittsburgh-study/family-strengths-survey

Woods, A. T., Velasco, C., Levitan, C. A., Wan, X., & Spence, C. (2015). Conducting perception research over the internet: A tutorial review. *PeerJ.* DOI: 10.7717/peerj.1058

CHAPTER 4

Generations

Graphing Family Processes

CHAPTER PREVIEW

In this chapter, readers will learn:

- The difference between pedigree charts and genograms.
- How genograms are used in various disciplines and for various purposes.
- How to make and interpret a genogram.
- That the generational transmission principle speaks to the idea that families tend to transmit their style of life to each new generation.
- About the generational alliance principle that helps us understand that it is important to have clear-cut generational boundaries.
- That family genograms are part of larger social structures that might be considered.
- About the benefits of creating a genogram.

INTRODUCTION

> We all carry inside us people who came before us.
>
> Liam Callanan, *The Cloud Atlas*

> A people without knowledge of their past history, origins, and culture is like a tree without roots.
>
> Marcus Garvey

The family tree has become an object of interest for people all over the world. Consider the number of popular television programs watched by millions: *Finding Your Roots with Henry Louis Gates, Jr., Genealogy Roadshow, Who Do You Think You Are?,* and *The Genetic Detective.* According to one source, genealogy is second only to gardening as a hobby and pornography for website visits (Rodriguez, 2014)! Interestingly, research has found that knowing one's family history is associated with resilience, self-esteem, and identity in children and adolescents (Fivush, Duke, & Bohanek, 2010; Reese, Fivush, Merrill, Wang, & McAnally, 2017). Grandparents, parents, and children often work together to piece together their family trees and create elaborate pedigree charts, listening to stories and understanding the influence of historical events. These cross

DOI: 10.4324/9781003128717-5

generational interactions themselves can be strengthening to families, including immigrant and refugee families and families of elders with dementia (see Park, 2015; Yoshida, Henkin, & Lehrman, 2013). Learning about your family history can result in all sorts of surprises. It has been said that some family trees have beautiful leaves, and some have just a bunch of nuts; remember, it is the nuts that make the tree worth shaking.

This chapter goes beyond the family tree, usually set up as a **pedigree chart**, and explores an important tool used by family researchers, therapists, ministers, educators, families, and even individual self-exploration—the **genogram**. Introduced by noted psychiatrist Murray Bowen and developed by scholars Monica McGoldrick and Randy Gerson (1986), the genogram provides a method of identifying and measuring intergenerational characteristics of families, using charts or graphs that diagram the biological and interpersonal relationships of people across several generations. They also identify significant events in intergenerational relationships that can have an influence on families and individuals. In other words, a genogram is like a 3D pedigree chart on steroids. The following comparison chart can help you understand the differences between pedigrees and genograms.

Pedigree Chart	Genogram
A pedigree chart is a map of our genetic and adoptive relationships, including names, dates, and places; may be supplemented separately with family narratives.	A genogram is a map of our genetic and adoptive relationships, as well as family processes and unique individual information, in one space.
Pedigree charts tend to be direct line ancestors (child, parents, grandparents, great grandparents), with children and siblings added on separate sheets.	Genograms show all family members by generation, including child, parents, grandparents, great grandparents, siblings, aunts, uncles, cousins, all in one place.
Pedigree charts can go back hundreds (maybe even thousands) of years.	Genograms typically go back only two or three generations (maybe four).
Pedigree charts tend to be static, except for the addition of children or spouses.	Genograms change much more frequently across time (because relationships and processes change). Your genogram today could be very different from your genogram a year from now.
Pedigree charts are best created using written historical documents, such as birth certificates, based on fact as we know it.	Genograms are based both on fact and perception. Two people in the same family may perceive relationships and processes differently, resulting in unique genograms for each person.

Genograms are used in several areas and for different purposes:

- **Medicine.** Medical professionals use genograms to map family health history, making it a useful tool for understanding people's individual health issues and potential for specific diseases. Related to health, Darwent, McInnes, and Swanson (2016) had mothers-to-be create a genogram of family infant feeding history, identifying sources of support. These genograms were helpful to mothers making feeding decisions related to breastfeeding.
- **Business.** Business professor and entrepreneur Randel Carlock and others (KeBler, Kleve, & Kollner, 2020; Kets deVries & Carlock, 2007) have utilized genograms for family-owned businesses, tracing not only family events and roles but changes in the family business as well. This tool allows family members to understand the influence of family life on business events (and vice versa), leading to more open dialog, healthy decision making, and improved conflict resolution.

- **Research.** Genograms help family researchers gather rich qualitative data related to family and family processes. Alexander, Callaghan, and Fellin (2018) found that using genograms in research had unintended and transformative effects on participants in research settings designed simply to collect family data.
- **Training and Education.** Genograms have been used successfully in training social workers and family therapists on issues related to culture, religion, and even politics (Crowell, 2017; Hardy & Laszloffy, 1995; Limb, Hodge, Wark, Ferrell, & Alboroto, 2018). Thus, genograms can lead to more culturally competent therapists and human service workers.
- **Therapy and Self-Growth.** As individuals create and study their family genograms, they often gain insights into patterns of behavior and possible reasons people behave the way they do. Genograms can help us better understand the desirable and the undesirable influences that earlier generations have had on us. This can help us enjoy and appreciate the desirable effects and sometimes find ways to minimize and change some of the undesirable effects. The adaptability of genograms and the insight they provide have resulted in them being used for military families (Weiss, Coll, & Gerbauer, 2010), as well as people with autism (Turns, Handley, Story, & Hertlein, 2019).

How to Make a Genogram

A genogram can be created using a pencil and paper or with a myriad of software programs available online. It can be very simple or extremely complex. It does not require as much "digging" as pedigree charts require, but it does require extensive self-reflection. The genogram consists of four parts:

1 Chart
2 Family chronology
3 Description of family relationships
4 Description of family processes

If you choose to create your own genogram, we suggest that you do so privately unless the entire family is "all in." Otherwise, you may discover some conflict or a family member holding deep-seated pain. Your sister may not see your family the way you see your family, which can be a source of conflict or anger. If you have experienced personal difficulties or trauma, you may wish to be guided by a professional.

Let's examine the four parts of the genogram.

Genogram Chart

McGoldrick and Gerson (1986) developed a set of standardized symbols and methods for constructing genogram charts, and many of their conventions are used in this chapter. As genograms have become more common and sophisticated, additional symbols have been created, so don't be surprised if you come across symbols not presented in this chapter. Figure 4.1 shows a fairly simple genogram chart for the family of a person we will call "Sandra Jones."

Each family member is represented by a box or circle. The boxes are used to indicate males, and circles show females. Transgender people are signified by a box within a circle (man to woman) or circle with a box (woman to man), and unknown gender or nonbinary is signified

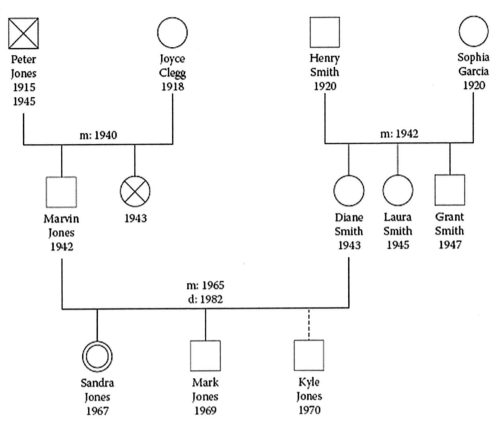

FIGURE 4.1 This is a simple three-generation genogram of the Sandra Jones family.

by a diamond. Intersex is a condition in which a person is born with reproductive or sexual anatomy that is not clearly male or female. For example, a person with androgen insensitivity syndrome (AIS) will look female but be genetically male (i.e., carry the XY chromosome). Usually, the symbols used for a person are based on their phenotype (i.e., how they look). Thus, an AIS person will usually be designated with a circle, but a notation may be made next to that circle if the person is aware of their condition.

A genogram chart is usually created to understand a particular person and is made from that person's perspective; this person is known as the **index person** and signified by double lines. Notice Sandra Jones has a double circle, indicating she is the index person for that chart. If you were doing a genogram of yourself (possibly as an assignment), you would show yourself as a double circle (or box) in the same way. It is helpful to put names and years of birth and death on a genogram, and the best method we have seen is to put them just below the box or circle. If there is just one year shown, it is the birth year, which means the person is still living at the time the genogram is made.

Children are **arranged by age**, from the oldest child on the left to the youngest child on the right. Thus, in Sandra's family, she is the oldest child. Her younger brother Mark was born in 1969, and the youngest child, Kyle, was born in 1970. The dotted line above Kyle shows that he was adopted. Sandra's parents were married in 1965 ("m. 1965"), and the marriage is shown with the horizontal line connecting them. Sandra's father, Marvin, was born in 1942 to Peter and Joyce Jones, who were married in 1940. Peter Jones died in 1945, and Joyce did not remarry, so the genogram shows that Joyce raised her son as a single parent. The other aspect of their family that is shown is that they had a stillborn child in 1943. The X inside a box or circle indicates a person died. It is helpful to include personal information for each family member, such as nicknames ("Skinny"), occupations, hobbies/interests, medical issues, addictions, roles, and other meaningful comments (e.g., "just like Aunt Tilda," explosive temper, lung cancer).

Families are seldom as simple as the information in Figure 4.2 shows. They usually have a number of complications, and the method of diagramming some of these complications is illustrated in Figure 4.2. This figure shows the same family five years later. Sandra's parents were divorced in 1982 ("d. 1982"), and the year of their divorce is placed just below the year of their marriage. Marvin, Sandra's father, remarried quickly, as he was married to Leanne Brady in 1982. Sandra's mother, Diane, was married in 1983 to Phillip Page. The dotted lines show the residential patterns of the stepfamilies. Sandra and her youngest brother Kyle live with her mother and her stepfather. Sandra's brother Mark lives with his father and stepmother.

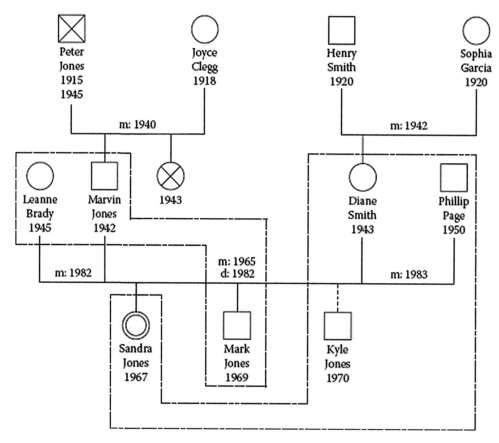

FIGURE 4.2 It is helpful to put as much information on a genogram as possible. The information can vary depending on the genogram's purpose. This chart is five years later than the first chart.

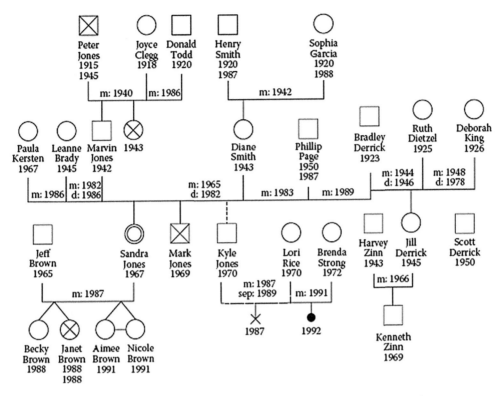

FIGURE 4.3 As life progresses, the genogram usually gets more complicated.

Figure 4.3 shows how to diagram additional complications that can occur in families. In this diagram, the stepfamily residential patterns are not shown because Sandra and her surviving brother are now married and have their own families. Sandra's brother, Mark, died in 1987, and because he died, an X is placed in the square. Sandra was married to Jeff Brown in 1987, and they have given birth to two sets of twins. The older twins are fraternal twins, and one of them, Janet, died as an infant. The younger set of twins, Aimee and Nicole, are identical twins.

Figure 4.3 also shows how to diagram relationships where two individuals are a "couple," but they are not legally married. Sandra's youngest brother, Kyle, had a relationship with Lori Rice. They met in 1987 and separated in 1989. Lori had an abortion in 1987, and it is shown with a vertical line and small "x." Later, Kyle was married to Brenda Strong in 1991, and Brenda experienced a miscarriage in 1992.

Figure 4.3 also shows that Sandra's stepfather Phillip Page died in 1987, and her mother married Bradley Derrick, a man who was 20 years older than she was in 1989. This marriage was Bradley Derrick's third marriage. He was married to his first wife, Ruth Dietzel, for a very short time, and they had a daughter named Jill in 1945. Bradley's second marriage was to Deborah King in 1948, and they had a son named Scott. Thus, Jill and Scott are stepsiblings, half-brother and sister. Jill was married to Harvey Zinn in 1966, and they had a son in 1969. Thus, when Sandra's mother, Diane, married Bradley in 1989 it created some unusual family relationships. In addition to getting a stepfather, Bradley, the remarriage also gave Sandra a stepsister named Jill, who is 20 years older than she is, and she has a nephew, Kenneth Zinn, who is 1 year older than she is. Another unique aspect of these relationships is that they did not begin until the year after Sandra was married.

On the other side of Sandra's family, Figure 4.3 shows that her father was divorced again in 1986 and married Paula Kersten, who was 19 at the time, the same age as Sandra. Thus, Sandra then had a stepmother who was the same age she was. Also, Sandra's paternal grandmother, Joyce, remarried at the age of 68. Her new husband, and Sandra's new stepgrandfather, was Donald Todd. The genogram also shows that Sandra's maternal grandparents died in 1987 and 1988. Genogram charts are sometimes helpful in giving us insights about what is happening in the lives of individuals and families, and they can help us find ways to cope and adjust to many of life's challenges. For example, we would expect that the period between 1986 and 1988 was a challenging time for Sandra and her family. During this period of time, her 18-year-old brother died, two grandparents died, and her stepfather died. Her youngest brother had a temporary relationship that included an abortion, and her father was divorced for the second time and married a woman the same age as Sandra. Shortly after this marriage, Sandra was married. With that many dramatic events happening in Sandra's family situation, it would be likely that she would have a number of emotional reactions that she and her new husband would find themselves dealing with.

Many people find a genogram chart such as this helpful in putting these events in perspective, understanding the emotional reactions, and working through the many feelings that would be occurring. If you create your own genogram, we suggest starting with yourself at the bottom of the page and then working out (siblings) and up (parents, aunts, uncles, cousins, grandparents, and so on).

Family Chronology

The second part of a genogram is a family chronology. This is a chronological listing of major events experienced in a family. Some meaningful events might include moves, changes in careers, changes in family composition such as a grandparent or other relative moving in or out, or times when a parent is gone for an extended period of time.

The family chronology will also include unfortunate events experienced by the family, such as a family member being in prison or a mental health hospital, serious illnesses such as cancer and incapacitating strokes, affairs, suicides, physical abuse, sexual abuse or incest, periods of drinking/substance abuse, runaways, financial difficulties, accidents, and homes burning. These events have an important effect on individuals and families, and they should be identified. Care should be taken in describing them to be sure that confidences are not breached, and sometimes it is best to describe some of them in general terms. For example, saying something like "Paul and Sarah not close" could mean many things to the person making the genogram, and that is what is important.

Sometimes there is a tendency to focus on the tragic and traumatic events in writing the chronology of family events, but this tendency should be avoided. Unusual positive events should also be included in the family chronology because they influence families and the individuals in them. Some examples of these are such events as a member of the family being on a championship team, times of financial affluence, periods of unusual closeness or love, getting special awards or recognitions, developing unusually meaningful friendships, having a special musical or artistic performance, special trips or vacations that are memorable, or being elected to a high office.

The following family chronology for Sandra Jones lists some of the information from her family life to show how a family chronology is written.

A Chronology of the Jones Family

1915—Peter Jones born.

1918—Joyce Clegg born.

1920—Henry Smith born. Sophia Garcia born.

1939—Henry Smith moved to Mexico.

1940—Peter Jones and Joyce Clegg married.

1942—Marvin Jones born. Henry Smith and Sophia Garcia married.

1943—Diane Smith born. Stillborn child born to Peter Jones and Joyce Clegg.

1944—Peter Jones has a severe stroke.

1945—Peter Jones died.

1952—Henry and Sophia Smith move from Mexico to South Carolina.

1965—Marvin Jones and Diane Smith married.

1967—Sandra Jones born.

1969—Mark Jones born.

1970—Kyle Jones born and adopted by Marvin and Diane Jones.

1982—Marvin Jones and Diane Smith divorced. Marvin Jones and Leanne Brady married.

1983—Diane Smith and Phillip Page married.

1986—Marvin Jones and Leanne Brady divorced. Marvin Jones and Paula Kersten married.

1987—Sandra Jones and Jeff Brown married. Mark Jones died at the age of 18. Phillip Page died. Henry Smith died. Kyle has affair with Lori Rice. Lori Rice has an abortion.

1988—Diane Jones has mental breakdown. Sophia Garcia Smith died. Twins, Becky and Janet Brown, born. Janet died.

1989—Kyle and Lori break up.

1991—Twins, Aimee and Nicole Brown, born.

1991—Kyle Jones and Brenda Strong married.

1992—Kyle and Brenda Jones have a miscarriage.

1996—Kyle graduates from local college and finds first job in construction industry.

2000—Brenda and Kyle have first child. It is a girl (Keensha); she has a serious eye defect.

2001—Keensha has a series of operations on her eyes. She will see, but the vision is limited.

2005—Keensha begins school and is placed in a special program for vision-impaired children.

2006—A second child is born to Brenda and Kyle. His name is Brandon.

2007—Brenda begins home business as a day care provider. Finds it fulfilling.

A thorough family chronology involves events from *at least three different generations* and usually has more than 50 items. The preceding list has only a few to illustrate how a family chronology is made, but it does not include many events that would be important in the family life of Sandra Jones and her extended family. A rich family chronology can be an excellent starting point for building an extensive family history.

Describing Family Relationships

The third part of a genogram is a description of the relationships among family members. These are usually fairly simple and straightforward descriptions, and some of them can be drawn on a genogram chart with the symbols shown in Figure 4.4. Usually, it is not possible to diagram all of the important information about relationships on a chart because it becomes

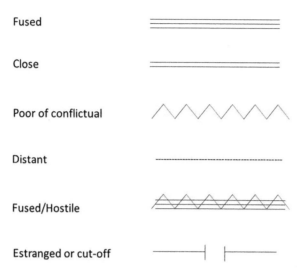

Fused

Close

Poor of conflictual

Distant

Fused/Hostile

Estranged or cut-off

FIGURE 4.4 Genogram relationship symbols.

too complicated and confusing. Therefore, most of the time, it is necessary to write the information about relationships on a few additional pages of paper.

Another way to describe relationship information is to make the basic chart and then make several photocopies of the chart. It is then possible to diagram some of the relationship information on the duplicate copies. Also, sometimes it is helpful to show the relationships at several different time periods in a family life cycle.

Figure 4.4 shows common symbols used to symbolize relationships.

The following list of questions illustrates the kind of information that is usually included in the relationships part of a genogram:

1 Who was close to whom?
2 Which individuals had conflicted relationships?
3 Which individuals were "left out"?
4 Who tended to be the family scapegoat if there was one?
5 If there was a "favorite" child of a parent or grandparent, who were they?
6 Who were the leaders? Who were the followers?
7 Who was the family peacemaker? Who was the troublemaker?
8 Who was distant from the family?
9 Were there intergenerational alliances? If so, how did those alliances influence family functioning?
10 Who was "overfunctioning" or "underfunctioning?" Overfunctioning individuals take on an excessive amount of responsibility to make sure the right things get done. Underfunctioning individuals take little responsibility and initiative as they let others get things done.

Figure 4.5 provides a simple illustration of a genogram with some relationships added. As shown in this figure (which is from Sandra Jones' perspective), Sandra felt extremely close to her mother but distant from her father. She experienced conflict with her stepmother (who married her father the same year her parents divorced). Her young brother, Mark, was seen as

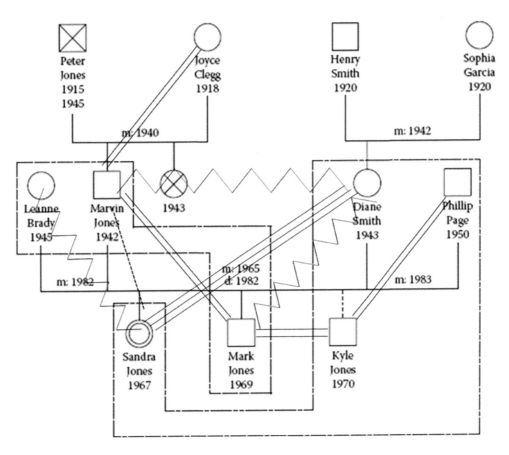

FIGURE 4.5 Genogram with relationship symbols.

close to both his father, whom he lived with and his adopted brother, who was close to his stepfather; Mark also had a conflicted relationship with his mother. Marvin and his former wife were seen as having a rocky relationship. Mapping out these relationships might be useful in determining who should sit next to whom at a wedding party!

Describing Family Processes

The fourth part of a genogram is a description of circumstances or processes that can help us understand how generational relationships influence a family and the people in it. Several examples of processes that can be helpful are things such as cliques, alliances, and coalitions in families; ways children are treated differently by the parents; favorite relatives; conflicts that are not resolved; ways of solving problems; in-law pressures; marital harmony or difficulties; feuds among family members; determining who helps out when help is needed; and difficulties coping with life's challenges. The following list of questions helps identify some of these processes:

1 How did the family react when a particular family member was born or died? Who took it the hardest? The easiest?

2 Have there been any job changes that influenced the family? How do people feel about their jobs?

3   How do people in the family get along with relatives? Are some relatives especially difficult, close, or helpful?

4   Have any members of the family had a drinking problem? What about trouble with medications or other substances?

5   Who is supportive or helpful of other family members? Who is unselfish, and who is selfish?

6   In what does the family take pride?

7   What are the leisure time and recreation patterns in the home, and how do the various members feel about them?

8   Were any individuals especially successful in school? Did any have problems?

9   What are the talents and special gifts that members of the family have?

10   Did the family have any special "program" or "plans" for a particular child?

11   Did sibling positions or relationships influence any of the children?

12   How involved was the family with churches, clubs, fraternities, or other organizations?

13   Were any life cycle transitions (births, deaths, moving away from home, marriages, etc.) especially gratifying or difficult?

14   Did any members of the family have unusual ways of gaining recognition or success?

15   What were the successes, failures, traumas, satisfactions, and themes in the home?

16   Were there any coincidences of life events?

17   Did any economic or political events such as economic depressions or wars influence the family?

18   Were there any triangles (e.g., three people who were particularly close) inside or outside the family that had an effect on people?

19   Were there any "black sheep" or "family skeletons?"

20   Were there any resources such as inheritances or unusual brilliance or beauty that influenced the family?

One can even delve deeper into such issues as trust, loyalty, and fairness (Keskin, 2017). Were children treated equally? Could parents be counted on to stand by you in times of trouble? Different colored pencils can be used to indicate the directions of these feelings, as well as the strength of these feelings.

A helpful strategy in completing a genogram is to have the index person tactfully do "research" about his or her own family history by interacting selectively with relatives. Many people find it helpful to get more "involved" with their extended family by attending reunions, weddings, funerals, and other family gatherings and by observing others and their own emotional reactions to what they experience. It is especially informing to be around extended families when important emotional feelings are occurring, such as at a birth, a marriage, a death, a special achievement, a crisis, or an illness. It usually is not very helpful to get involved with relatives to try to "straighten them out."

Interpreting a Genogram

Once the data has been collected and the genogram complete, what do we do? Several strategies are helpful for interpreting genograms. One strategy that usually helps is to try to identify some **positive things first**. This can be done by looking for events, patterns, relationships, and processes that have helped create strengths or things that are valued and desired. All individuals and all families have some strengths, good aspects, and admirable characteristics, and finding some of them builds morale and motivation. Even the most troubled and problem-ridden families have assets and strengths. In fact, sometimes, the individuals and families that have had the most challenges have an unusual number of strengths.

Another strategy that is usually helpful is to be tentative and **hypothetical** when trying to understand what a genogram means. This means it is wise to state ideas as hypotheses or guesses about the effects of various relationships or processes. Some examples of this are: "It may be that …, " "It's possible that …, " "It could be that …, " and "Maybe …. "

Look for **patterns across generations**. McGoldrick, Gerson, and Petry (2008) write, "Families repeat themselves. What happens in one generation will often repeat itself in the next—that is, the same issues tend to be played out from generation to generation, though the actual behavior may take a variety of forms" (p. 15). Researchers have developed the **generational transmission principle**. **Generational transmission** is the process of transmitting information, beliefs, traditions, and communication styles from one generation to the next. Think of how your family interacts around the dinner table. Are they loud, noisy, and animated, or quiet, demure, and thoughtful? Likely your family reflects the dinner communication patterns of your grandparents! Families with more functional, healthy generational processes tend to transmit those family styles to their children, and those children are more likely to develop a functional, healthy family life. Generational transmission seems to be more powerful for characteristics of the family realm than characteristics of the public realm. This means that there is more generational transmission with regard to ways of loving and maintaining intimate relationships than such things as political ideas, careers, leisure interests, and social class behavior (D'Onofrio et al., 2007). Quality of marriage and abuse are just two examples of behaviors and processes that are transmitted across generations. Thus, if your parents and grandparents divorced, you are much more likely to divorce (Landis, 1956).

Examine the genogram for **alliances**. The term *alliance* refers to the connections and the boundaries among subsystems in a family system. An alliance is when two or more individuals in a family become unusually close or align themselves together, so they are a clique or a semi-unique unit in the family. As they do this, they change the boundaries in the family system. One of the important and healthy alliances in families is to have a fairly clear parental alliance while the children are being raised. This means the parents form an alliance with each other in their relationships with their children. In ideal situations, this means the parents are a cohesive, integrated, and coordinated team. They are supportive of each other and unified in the way they relate to their children, and the boundaries between the parents are few and permeable. Even non-married parents living separately can have a clear parental alliance. These are **intergenerational alliances**. Not all intergenerational alliances, however, are healthy. Some intergenerational alliances, such as certain sibling alliances, can lead to emotional and interpersonal problems for all involved. **Cross generational alliances**, alliances between people of different generations, are particularly problematic alliances. A divorced parent may ally with an oldest child, trading confidences, granting privileges, and expecting additional responsibilities. The child may enjoy the extra attention but may also miss out on age appropriate experiences or become confused when the parent connects with a new partner, casting the child out of the alliance. Similarly, the idea of a mother being "best friends" with her teen daughter is not likely to work out well.

As you examine a genogram, look for people who are **transitional characters**. A transitional character is one who, in a single generation, changes the entire course of a lineage. These individuals may grow up in an abusive, emotionally destructive environment and yet somehow find ways to metabolize the poison and not pass it on to their children. They break the mold. For example, they refute the observation that abused children become abusive parents. Or, they might turn the corner and turn away from alcohol. Their contribution to humanity is to filter the destructiveness out of their own lineage so that the generations downstream will have a supportive foundation on which to build productive lives. There are many things people can do to help themselves be transitional characters, such as being deliberate in changing negative processes, developing new and distinctive family rituals, maintaining emotional distance, marrying later than average, reading good books about family life, joining family like organizations, becoming educated on positive family life, and pursuing a positive life philosophy.

Finally, when the family genogram is complete, try to envision it in **multiple contexts and larger social structures**—religion/spirituality, politics, culture, race/ethnicity, gender, sexual orientation, class (Chavis, 2004; McGoldrick et al., 2008). Surrounding the genogram itself, one could include boxes that represent various aspects of the community and the time period the family is experiencing. For example, you could include environmental boxes representing the criminal justice system, neighborhood and friendships, employment, economy, religion, healthcare, schools, pandemics, and so forth. Some of these community aspects may be more directly involved with family functioning than others, such as having a father or mother who is a police officer during societal calls to defund police, having some family members intimately involved with a religious organization, or living in an area with poor educational outcomes. These influences are likely to affect family relationships and processes. Additionally, the emerging field of **epigenetics** suggests that the environment can influence the expression of one's genes. Environmental trauma, from famine to war to family violence, has been found to affect switches that turn genes off and on, resulting in changes in health that can be passed on to future generations (Jiang, Postovit, Cattaneo, Binder, & Aitchison, 2019; Van Steenwyk, Roszkowski, Manuella, Franklin, & Mansuy, 2018). In other words, one may physically pass on reduced stress tolerance, anxiety, and propensity for obesity as a result of environmental trauma; this, in turn, influences our relationships within our families. As we study family and expand our use of genograms, we have the potential to increase understanding not only of family processes but of how external social systems influence family processes, as well.

Making Your Own Genogram

You are encouraged to make a genogram for your own family. Making one for your own family provides an "experiential" type of learning that does not occur in any other way. You learn to better understand some of the interesting, informative, and subtle aspects of your own family situation. You can also learn in a firsthand way how your generational connections have an influence on you and how you can influence your posterity. It takes several hours to make a good genogram, but many of our former students and colleagues who have made genograms for their own families have found that it is an interesting, helpful, and useful learning experience. None of us should try to use a genogram to help someone else until we have made one for our own family first.

There are a few cautions that are helpful when we try to use a genogram to help someone else. Some people have very painful experiences in their families, and the strategies they have used to cope with some of their experiences are sometimes to forget and avoid them. In some of these situations, they might be very uncomfortable when they begin to think about their earlier experiences and forcing them to think about them could do more harm than good.

Therefore, people's feelings, desires, and wishes should be respected, and they should never be forced or coerced to face or deal with aspects of their family life they are not ready to deal with. Their personal wishes and desires should determine what they do, and only when they are emotionally ready should they try to think about or understand how their earlier family experiences have influenced them.

The payoff with a genogram is that it usually gives us a lot of new information. When we are making a genogram of our own family, it usually helps us better understand why we have some of the feelings we have, why we believe some of the things we do, why we have some attitudes, and why we relate to people the way we do. This information often helps us and others become more effective in managing our lives, and it might help us cope more effectively with life's challenges and difficulties. The insights we get from genograms often help us better attain the things that most of us want in family life: closeness, understanding, love, richness, fulfillment, commitment, healthy development, support, communication, empathy, and intimacy. If we are using a genogram as an educator or therapist to try to help someone else learn and grow, it can have the same effects. The other people often gain insights about why they feel, act, relate, and think the way they do, and they can then use their new insights to better attain their goals.

Discussions in Diversity: Graphing Us

How we view ourselves and our families have changed somewhat over the last 50 years. Even the terminology we use has changed and continues to change. For example, when first introduced, genograms used symbols that were based on heteronormative and cisnormative assumptions. Heteronormative refers to the belief that heterosexuality is the normal, default, preferred interaction and relationship. Cisnormative refers to the idea that our gender identity always matches our physical, biological sex. As a result, people who self-identified or engaged in relationships outside "the norm" were not well-represented in a genogram. As Barsky (2020) writes, we (family scientists, counselors, family educators) want to respectfully and accurately depict family and relationships, so new and meaningful symbols and processes are needed (for example, see Figure 4.6).

Today, genograms are being used with and applied in many diverse contexts, weaving in historical influences (including trauma), languages spoken,

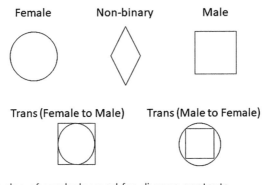

FIGURE 4.6 Examples of symbols used for diverse contexts.

sex and sexuality, spirituality, and family networks. For example, Lim and Nakamoto (2008) used genograms with Asian families, showing changes in language and life experience across generations, including cancer incidence following the bombing of Hiroshima and language changes following migrations and influencing family relationships. They also noted culturally relevant information, such as sibling position with its traditional responsibilities affecting family dynamics. Lim notes that growing up, she was never called by her name but by her sibling position (fifth sister). Thus, despite genograms being developed in the West, they can resonate culturally with people from non-Western countries, especially if therapists are trained to be culturally sensitive and responsive.

Similarly, Limb and Hodge (2010) created genograms with American Indian families, graphically representing expressions of spirituality over generations. Without research on culturally appropriate ways of conducting spiritual assessments with American Indians, it is necessary to work with individuals and tribes to begin creating better representative genograms. Limb and Hodge used color coding for spirituality and incorporated meaningful symbols (such as corn) to represent events, strengths, and other important information. They received feedback that their genograms were more fluid, more visual, appropriately included extended family, and integrated past influences on present day functioning; all said to be more consistent with American Indian cultures. Still, these scholars recommended that the language and symbols used should be client driven and not imposed by the majority culture. Pember (2016) reminds us of the tendency to group "Native Americans" into one category and apply concepts, such as "Two Spirit" (referring to gender-variant individuals in indigenous tribes), to all American Indians. With over 500 tribes recognized by the federal government and speaking several hundred languages, we are on thin ice in making such global attributions. As Pember writes, "Despite New Age and popular ideals to the contrary, there is no universal Native-American culture or spirituality."

One can find many reflection questions to aid in creating and interpreting genograms with diverse populations, but many are yet to be written. History, culture, spirituality, and sex/sexuality can add layers of depth to a genogram (Belous, Timm, Chee, & Whitehead, 2012) as we incorporate beliefs, supports, and strengths to begin to understand self, family, and the inner processes at work.

Questions to Discuss:

- *How might exploring spirituality or sexuality in a genogram "add depth" to it and its interpretation?*
- *Discuss historical events that might influence families and family processes.*
- *Many American Indians prefer to be identified by their tribal affiliation (Cherokee, Ojibwa, Sioux). If you were assisting someone in creating a genogram, would you include this affiliation? If so, how would you do it? How do you make sure your exploration is "client-led" rather than other led?*

SUMMARY

This chapter described how to make and interpret a genogram and then described strategies that can be used to conserve desirable generational ties and transmissions and liberate people from undesirable generational ties and transmissions. It described how generational processes influence families and people, including the generational alliance principle and the generational transmission principle. The generational alliance principle states that there are several boundaries between parent and child generations that are natural and desirable. When families maintain these boundaries, it contributes to the healthy development of the members of the family. Conversely, when these boundaries become blurred, it interferes with healthy development.

The generational transmission principle states that aspects of the family realm are transmitted from one generation to the next, and this includes the good, the bad, and the ugly. Three areas where there is considerable evidence that transmission occurs are marital stability and instability, abusive and nonabusive behaviors, and mental health and illness. Readers were encouraged to make a genogram for their own family because learning how to make and interpret genograms can help them deal effectively with their personal lives and learn an effective method of helping others to cope wisely with their generational processes.

STUDY QUESTIONS

1   What is the difference between a pedigree chart and a genogram?
2   What are the four parts of a genogram?
3   Draw four common symbols used in genograms.
4   What is the symbol in a genogram that tells the reader who the person of focus is?
5   Name four ways a genogram might be used in different settings.
6   Define the term *generational transmission*. Give an example.
7   What is the definition of a generational alliance?
8   Why do we care about cross-generational alliances?
9   In your own words, why is the study of generations important?
10 Why are generational alliances so problematic?

KEY TERMS

Pedigree chart
Genogram
Index person
Generational transmission
Generational alliance
Transitional character
epigenetics

SUGGESTED READINGS/WEBSITES

Beavers, W. R. (1985). *Successful marriage*. New York, NY: Norton.

Carter, B., & McGoldrick, M. (Eds.). (1989). *The changing family life cycle: A framework for family therapy* (2nd ed.). New York, NY: Allyn & Bacon.

CDC Medical Genogram (My Family Health Portrait). https://phgkb.cdc.gov/FHH/html/fhh.html?action=create

DeMaria, R., Weeks, G., & Hof, L. (1999). *Focused genograms*. Philadelphia, PA: Brunner/Mazel.

Elkind, D. (1988). *The hurried child*. Reading, MA: Perseus Books.

Fivush, R. (2019). *Family narratives and the development of an autobiographical self: Social and cultural perspectives on autobiographical memory*. New York, NY: Routledge.

McGoldrick, M. (2011). *The genogram journey*. New York, NY: W. W. Norton & Co. Inc.

McGoldrick, M. (2016). *The genogram casebook: A clinical companion to genograms: Assessment and intervention*. New York, NY: W. W. Norton & Co. Inc.

McGoldrick, M., & Gerson, R. (1986). *Genograms in family assessment*. New York, NY: W. W. Norton & Co. Inc.

REFERENCES

Alexander, J. H., Callaghan, J. E. M., & Fellin, L. C. (2018). Genograms in research: Participants' reflections on the genogram process. *Qualitative Research in Psychology*. DOI: 10.1080/14780887.2018.1545066

Barsky, A. E. (2020). Sexuality- and gender-inclusive genograms: Avoiding heteronormativity and cisnormativity. *Journal of Social Work Education*. DOI: 10.1080/10437797.2020.1852637

Belous, C. K., Timm, T. M., Chee, G., & Whitehead, M. R. (2012). Revisiting the sexual genogram. *The American Journal of Family Therapy*, 40(4), 281–296.

Chavis, A. M. (2004). Genograms and African American families: Employing family strengths of spirituality, religion, and extended family network. *Michigan Family Review*, 9(1), 30–36.

Crowell, J. H. (2017). Teaching note fostering political awareness. *Journal of Social Work Education*, 53(4), 765–770.

Darwent, K. L., McInnes, R. J., & Swanson, V. (2016). The infant feeding genogram: A tool for exploring family infant feeding history and identifying support needs. *BMC Pregnancy and Childbirth*, 16, 315.

D'Onofrio, B. M., Slutske, W., Turkheimer, E., Emery, R., Heath, A., Madden, P. A. F., … Martin, N. G. (2007). The intergenerational transmission of childhood conduct problems: A children of twins study. *Archives of General Psychiatry*, 64, 820–829.

Fivush, R., Duke, M., & Bohanek, J. G. (2010). Do you know…The power of family history in adolescent identity and well-being. *Journal of Family Life*. Retrieved from https://ncph.org/wp-content/uploads/2013/12/The-power-of-family-history-in-adolescent-identity.pdf

Hardy, K. V., & Laszloffy, T. A. (1995). The cultural genogram: Kety to training culturally competent family therapists. *Journal of Marriage and Family Therapy*, 21(3), 227–237.

Jiang, S., Postovit, L., Cattaneo, A., Binder, E. B., & Aitchison, K. J. (2019). Epigenetic modifications in stress response genes associated with childhood trauma. *Frontiers in Psychiatry*, 10, 808.

Keßler, R., Kleve, H., & Köllner, T. (2020). *Succession and family structure: Untangling legacies through genogram research*. Sage Publications: Sage Business Cases Originals. DOI: http://dx.doi.org/10.4135/9781529726909

Keskin, Y. (2017). The relational ethics genogram: An integration of genogram and relational ethics. *Journal of Family Psychotherapy*, 28(1), 92–98.

Kets de Vries, M. F. R., & Carlock, R. S. (2007). *Family business on the couch: A psychological perspective*. Hoboken, NJ: John Wiley & Sons, Ltd.

Landis, J. T. (1956). The pattern of divorce in three generations. *Social Forces*, 34(3), 213–216.

Lim, S. L., & Nakamoto, T. (2008). Genograms: Use in therapy with Asian families with diverse cultural heritages. *Contemporary Family Therapy*, 30(4), 199–219.

Limb, G. E., & Hodge, D. R. (2010). Helping child welfare workers improve cultural competence by utilizing spiritual genograms with native American families and children. *Children and Youth Services Review, 32*, 239–245.

Limb, G. E., Hodge, D. R., Ward, K., Ferrell, A., & Alboroto, R. (2018). Developing cultural competence with LDS clients: Utilizing spiritual genograms in social work practice. *Journal of Religion & Spirituality in Social Work: Social Thought, 32*(2), 166–181.

McGoldrick, M., & Gerson, R. (1986). *Genograms in family assessment.* New York, NY: W. W. Norton & Co. Inc.

McGoldrick, M., Gerson, R., & Petry, S. (2008). *Genograms: Assessment and intervention* (3rd ed.). New York, NY: W. W. Norton & Co.

Park, A. L. (2015). Do cross-generational interactions make any difference to the mental health of older adults with dementia? *International Journal of Emergency Mental Health and Human Resilience, 17*, 210–212.

Pember, M. A. (October 13, 2016). "Two Spirit" Tradition far from ubiquitous among tribes. *Rewire News Group Commentary.* https://rewirenewsgroup.com/article/2016/10/13/two-spirit-tradition-far-ubiquitous-among-tribes/

Reese, E., Fivush, R., Merrill, N., Wang, Q., & McAnally, H. (2017). Adolescents' intergenerational narratives across cultures. *Developmental Psychology, 53*(6), 1142–1153.

Rodriguez, G. (2014). Why are Americans so obsessed with genealogy?. *Zócalo Public Square.* https://www.zocalopublicsquare.org/2014/05/12/why-are-americans-so-obsessed-with-genealogy/inquiries/an-imperfect-union/

Turns, B. A., Handley, V. A., Story, M. R., & Hertlein, K. M. (2019). Identifying and enhancing meaningful relationships for individuals with ASD: The socially playful genogram. *Journal of Creativity in Mental Health, 24*(4), 447–454.

Van Steenwyk, G., Roszkowski, M., Manuella, F., Franklin, T. B., & Mansuy, I. (2018). Transgenerational inheritance of behavioral and metabolic effects of paternal exposure to traumatic stress in early postnatal life: Evidence in the 4th generation. *Environmental Epigenetics, 4*(2), 1–8.

Weiss, E. L., Coll, J. E., & Gerbauer, J. (2010). The military genogram: A solution-focused approach for resiliency building in service members and their families. *The Family Journal, 18*(4), 395–406.

Yoshida, H., Henkin, N., & Lehrman, P. (2013). *Strengthening intergenerational bonds in immigrant and refugee communities.* Philadelphia, PA: The Intergenerational Center Temple University.

Part II

Building and Establishing Families

Building and Establishing Families

Alone we can do so little;
together we can do so much.

- Helen Keller

In this section, we will examine how people come together to build a family. At the core of the family is its ideologies, beliefs, and paradigms, mostly invisible to the family and its members. Through the repetitive rituals and routines of family, we can gain a window into what it means to be a member of the family and how that motivates and guides us as individuals.

CHAPTER 5

Coming Together

CHAPTER PREVIEW

In this chapter, readers will learn:

- How and where people meet future mates.
- What makes people attractive.
- About changes in dating practices, including hanging out and hooking up.
- About different theories of love.
- About union formation, including cohabitation and marriage.
- That courtship practices around the world vary greatly. Most cultures have some form of family-involved mate selection, but others (mostly in Western cultures) have moved to love-based selection.
- That how we come together influences future family processes.

INTRODUCTION

Bethany and Nick met on a spontaneous hiking and camping trip organized by someone at their church. 21-year-old Nick was immediately smitten with 19-year-old Bethany and attempted to "connect" with her by saying, "You remind me of my first wife!" (Nick had never been married) and doing a silly dance on a rock while singing a song. Bethany rolled her eyes, but Nick persisted. Later, Nick called Bethany and asked her out. On their first date, he told her that he planned on finding a wife, getting married within 3 months of finding her, and having a baby 9 months later. He also told her he preferred women with long hair (Bethany's was very short) and at least 5'9" tall (Bethany was 5'2"), and he expected his wife to stay home and take care of the kids (Bethany was working toward an advanced degree). Bethany's reply was, "Then I'm not the girl for you. However, I have several friends that you might want to take out!" Nine months later, with a few twists and turns and some objections by Bethany's parents related to their youthfulness, the couple were married. That was over 18 years ago. They now are raising six happy, rambunctious children, have thriving careers, and a strong marriage. How does this love story reflect union formation in the United States? How might such a pairing have occurred in India or Egypt? How does how we meet and who we meet influence the family processes that develop?

Human beings around the world and across time have experienced different ways of creating and organizing families. Likely, you have never really thought much about this because "it just is" and so much of what we do and how we interact culturally is invisible to us. How we come together and create a family varies by culture, class, religion, and even family, but it is

DOI: 10.4324/9781003128717-7

this coming together that is necessary for the continuation of humanity. If you are single and hoping to one day start a family, you may or may not have a clear idea of how this will happen.

In this chapter, we will explore how one's dating and mate selection activities direct who we choose to marry and set the foundational rules about that relationship. In particular, styles of partner selection speak to issues of commitment, intimacy, passion, loyalty, devotion, romantic love, and other core ideological themes that can shape future relationships. We also will see how the way we select a partner influences family processes and patterns throughout the life cycle.

The Meet-Up

Have you ever asked your parents or grandparents how, where, and when they met? What attracted them to each other? Was love an important part of their decision to marry or not marry? Social scientists have not totally ignored such questions.

Location

Most of us meet and marry someone who is in our geographic location (**propinquity**). Our future mates are likely to be introduced to us by friends or families, be co-workers, or be part of our special interest groups (Le, 2011). Geographic location is no longer limiting for people looking for partners, however. About 30% of never married people today are choosing online meet ups and dates using phone apps or websites. Lesbian, gay, and bisexual singles are about twice as likely to use online dating apps (Vogels, 2020). This method of finding people increases the pool of available mates, which is helpful for lesbians and gays, given their small proportion of the population. Ultimately, however, it appears that meeting and dating someone online does not improve romantic outcomes (Finkel, Eastwick, Karney, Reis, & Sprecher, 2012). When comparing online with face-to-face relationships, face-to-face encounters provide us with more accurate information about the other than online interactions, which may be less than honest and keep us from seeing how people react to daily stress and strain. Interestingly, it appears that technology not only plays a role in how people get connected, but it influences how people feel about their relationship status. Most single social media users who are looking for partners report that they have seen posts about others' romantic relationships, with 2/3 saying it doesn't bother them but 1/3 saying that it makes them feel worse (Vogels & Anderson, 2020).

Attraction

What makes someone attractive? Both men and women are attracted to people with symmetrical faces (Lewandowski, 2011). Almost universally, men are attracted to women with a 0.70 waist-to-hip ratio (the waist is 70% of the width of the hips), big eyes, full lips, and small chin; and women are attracted to men with broad shoulders, "robust upper bodies," and square chins (Lewandowski, 2011; Sorokowski, Koscinski, Sorokawska, & Huanca, 2014). Likely, these attractions are a result of evolution and related to good gene pools and fertility. In terms of emotional attraction, the saying "opposites attract" does not appear to be true; rather, "birds of a feather flock together" (Le, 2011). When seeking partners online, Bruch and Newman (2018) found that heterosexual men and women tended to seek out people about 25% more desirable than themselves. Interestingly, they also found men's desirability increased up to age 50 but women's desirability decreased from 18 to 60.

Interactions

In the United States, dating (a somewhat more formalized way for a couple to get to know each other) has given way to hanging out or hooking up. **Hanging out** refers to groups of mixed gender young people getting together at someone's home, in someone's yard, at a park, or at the mall (to name a few places). These groups may also get together to play online party games, such as Jackbox. Online "meet up" groups for people with similar interests or desire to participate in new activities and adventures are also available. Whether or not these groups are more fertile ground for finding suitable mates and lead to satisfactory marriages is unknown at this time but could make an interesting study. Hanging out is mostly platonic but sometimes may lead to pairing up.

Hanging out comes with certain benefits. It allows for much less pressure related to sex, without worries about kissing/not kissing at the door or making out in a car. Also, there are no worries about being rejected because most of these gatherings are spontaneous and sometimes even ritualistic (every Friday we go to the mall together). No longer do young people need to agonize over making a phone call to ask someone out or reject such a request. Costs are born fairly equally, too. Still, hanging out is not without its detractors. These arrangements may not allow one to get to know another on a more personal level, the comfort level may result in a lack of motivation for moving a relationship, and boundaries/relationship status may be confusing. Indeed, one might end up moving into the horrifying "friend zone," with a mismatch between romantic/platonic feelings and difficulty moving out.

Hooking up (and somewhat similar relationship encounters, such as "Netflix and chill," friends with benefits, and booty calls) usually refers to casual sexual encounters with no strings attached, in other words, no commitments and no expectations. These sexual encounters can run the gamut from kissing (what is commonly referred to as making out) to intercourse (oral, anal, vaginal). They may or may not lead to a relationship later, which can be problematic if one of the participants wants more from the relationship. How frequent is hooking up among college students? Not as much as you might think. On average, a college student is likely to have less than eight hook-ups over his or her entire college career (Ford, England, & Bearak, 2015). Most college students tend to grossly overestimate how often their peers are hooking up, which could put internal pressure on them to hook-up to be more like their peers, despite not being ready or interested in such an experience (Weissbourd, Anderson, Cashin, & McIntyre, 2017).

Hooking up can have physical, social, and emotional consequences for the participants, disproportionately affecting women. Women are less likely than men to experience orgasm during the hook-up, which shouldn't come as too much of a surprise as young men in these encounters tend to be more concerned about themselves than their partners. Many hook-ups occur during parties and drinking, so people may not take precautions to reduce the possibility of a sexually transmitted disease or pregnancy, again disproportionately affecting women. Socially, unfortunately, one might acquire a negative reputation; a woman may be viewed as a "slut" against the man's status as a "player." Emotionally, Strokoff, Owen, and Fincham (2015) found that hooking up can leave people with one of four emotional reactions: happy-hopeful, content realist, used and confused, and disappointed. Almost 2/3 of their sample fell within the first two categories. The remaining groups experienced more negative reactions, including depression, loneliness, and poorer social adjustment.

Considering the above, it appears parents and educators are not doing a very good job of preparing young people for caring romantic and sexual experiences (Weissbourd et al., 2017).

In their report, *The Talk*, these researchers provide tips for parents and resources for educators to help young people develop healthy romantic relationships and reduce misogyny and sexual harassment. From our perspective, this "talk" begins at birth, through our examples related to self-respect and respect for others. How and even whether families have this talk, along with beliefs about hooking up, hanging out, and dating, are tied to our family processes, which are explored in future chapters.

What's Love Got to Do with It?

Would you marry someone you didn't love? Several studies have found that the vast majority of American men and women would not marry someone they didn't love, even if they were practically perfect in every way (Berscheid & Regan, 2017, p. 366). Love as the basis of marital relationships is a relatively recent and growing global phenomenon. Previously, the choice of a mate was pretty much related to survival and economics. Love may have grown into the relationship, but it wasn't the initial basis as it is today.

Defining "love" is not easy. In fact, "What is love?" is one of the top questions about love, according to Google Trends. Yet, to understand and study it, we must define it. In the social science literature, you are likely to see words other than "love" used: attachment, bonding, nurturance, warmth, support. Operationalizing love in this way divorces it from emotion; yet, these terms are only subsets of love. Famous experimental psychologist Harry Harlow once snapped at a visitor who attempted to move him away from using the "l-word," saying, "Perhaps all you've known in life is proximity. I thank God I've known more" (Blum, 2002, p. 2). Scientists have not completely stopped theorizing about love; following is a brief overview of philosophical and scientific conceptions of love:

- **Love Is an Art.** Psychoanalyst Erich Fromm (1900–1980) wrote a landmark book, "The Art of Loving" (1956), exploring all aspects of love, from love of God to romantic love to brotherly love. For Fromm, love consists of four key elements: care, responsibility, respect, and knowledge. He saw love as an art; it is a skill that can be taught and developed and one that begins with self: *The affirmation of one's own life, happiness, growth, freedom, is rooted in one's capacity to love*, i.e., in care, respect, responsibility, and knowledge. If an individual is able to love productively, he loves himself too; if he can love only others, he cannot love at all—(1947a: Man for Himself. An Inquiry into the Psychology of Ethics, New York (Rinehart and Co.) 1947, p. 130).
- **Love Is a Color.** Sociologist John Lee (1933–2013) introduced a color wheel of love with his book, "Colours of Love: An Exploration of the Ways of Loving" (1973). Using the color wheel as a metaphor, Lee identified the three primary types of love as eros (red; erotic type of love), ludus (blue; game playing type of love), and storge (yellow; friendship/caring type of love). Secondary types of love include mania (violet; obsessive love), pragma (green; business-like love), and agape (orange; selfless love). Again, this typology allows us to examine love beyond romantic love and in all types of family relationships. The Love Attitude Scale was developed based on Lee's six types of love and has been used to study factors associated with love styles, including gender, age, and culture (Hendrick & Hendrick, 1986). For example, gender differences have been found, with males significantly more ludic than females and females significantly more storgic, pragmatic, and manic than males.

- **Love Is a Language.** Author, theologian, talk show host, counselor Gary Chapman (b. 1938) wrote, "The Five Love Languages: How to Express Heartfelt Commitment to Your Mate" (1992). According to Chapman, each of us has a "love language" that makes us feel loved and appreciated. These five love languages are affirmation, quality time, physical touch, receiving gifts, and acts of service. From this perspective, knowing our partner's love language can strengthen our relationship. Chapman's books and ideas enjoy wide popularity. What does the research say? Bunt and Hazelwood (2017) looked at couples to see if they matched in their love language and if it made a difference in the quality of their relationships. They found that people who matched in their love languages were not happier than those who didn't. They also found that most people already knew their partner's love language; if they didn't, however, learning about it didn't improve the relationship. One interesting finding was that when there were love language mismatches, the couple did better if the woman adapted to her partner's needs and modified her behavior. In short, "love language alignment and/or knowledge of a partner's love language does not enhance relationship satisfaction, but self-regulatory behaviors do. Hence, exploration of a spouse's love language alone may not improve relationship satisfaction, but such programs and interventions have the capacity to be effective if they catalyze relevant self-regulatory change behaviors" (Bunt & Hazelwood, 2017, p. 288).
- **Love Is a Story.** Psychologist Robert J. Sternberg (b. 1949) wrote an article on "A Triangular Theory of Love" (1986) that is probably one of the most popular theories taught today. Sternberg wrote that love can be understood through three basic components at the corners of the triangle: passion, compassion, and commitment. These three components combine to create eight subsets of love: nonlove, liking, infatuated love, empty love, companionate love, fatuous love, and consummate or complete love. One day, while reflecting on his theory, Sternberg realized that the theory was a description of "what is" and did not provide any insight into "how we got here." To this end, he developed a new theory based on extensive research: "Love is a Story: A New Theory of Relationships" (1998). Sternberg and his colleagues created an instrument to measure and test aspects of the love story theory (Sternberg, Hojjat, & Barnes, 2001). According to this perspective, people develop their own "love stories," partially based on experience and partly on personality. They then seek others who fit their storyline. Perhaps they view love as a garden, something to be tended to and watched over. These people would seek similar "gardeners." A few might prefer horror stories and will tend to seek out similar "characters" to play out their story of violence and abuse. Have you wondered why people you know seem to end up with very similar mates when a relationship doesn't work out? This theory may provide an explanation. Sternberg and others have found that relationships tend to be happier when the people involved have compatible stories. They have also found some interesting gender differences in preferred love stories. No single story guaranteed successful or long-lasting relationships, but some were more likely to predict doom. What we like about the love story theory is that, though difficult, it allows one to change the plot, rewrite a story, or perhaps move to more healthy genres.
- **Love Is a Physiological Drive.** For anthropologist Helen Fisher (b. 1945), love is biologically based. Interestingly, she is the chief scientific advisor for singles site, Chemistry.Com. Over six million people have viewed her 2008 TED talk, "The Brain in Love." According to Fisher (1998), lust, attraction, and attachment are all categories of love, and each has its own set of hormones. Lust is associated with estrogens and androgens, attraction with catecholamines

(stress hormones), and attachment with oxytocin. Based on her research findings, to keep love alive, she advises people to do things to drive up these hormones, including have regular sex, cuddle, and engage in novel activities (Fisher, 2016). As an aside, it is known that taking someone on an adventurous date, such as rock climbing, going on a roller coaster, or visiting a haunted house, is linked to increased attraction, and hormones may be the cause.

- **Love Is a Process.** Psychologist Harry Harlow (1905–1981) spent his life working with monkeys. If you have ever taken a psychology class, you likely learned about his famous experiments involving baby monkeys and their response to softly padded wire monkey "mothers" and unpadded wire monkey mothers with a bottle; his findings led to the "contact comfort theory" showing the importance of touch to infants. As early as 1958, Harlow encouraged the study of love: "Love is a wondrous state, deep, tender, and rewarding. Because of its intimate and personal nature, it is regarded by some as an improper topic for experimental research. But, whatever our personal feelings may be, our assigned mission as psychologists is to analyze all facets of human and animal behavior into their component variables. So far as love or affection is concerned, psychologists have failed in this mission. The little we know about love does not transcend simple observation, and the little we write about it has been written better by poets and novelists" (1958, p. 673). Harlow saw love as a process, writing "From the developmental point of view, the general plan is quite clear: The initial love responses of the human being are those made by the infant to the mother or some mother surrogate. From this intimate attachment of the child to the mother, multiple learned and generalized affectional responses are formed" (p. 673). One of Harlow's revolutionary ideas was that fathers, as well as mothers, could be appropriate caregivers for infants.
- **Love Is a Family Process.** Family scientist Wesley Burr (b. 1936) and colleagues (1993) take the position that love is a basic and enabling family process. It is considered normative in the sense that we expect family members to love each other, even if they don't. For these researchers, the kind of love necessary for a healthy individual and family life has four characteristics. First, it is other-oriented and desires to support and foster the growth of the other, rather than the self. It allows the giver to sacrifice without feeling depleted. This type of love requires humility in the sense that the family member recognizes the interdependence of all family members. Second, healthy family love is action-oriented. This means that actions *showing* love are more important than feelings. In their words, "one learns to love by loving not by being loved and to serve by serving not by being served" (p. 477). The third characteristic of healthy family love is that it is unconditional. Being loved is not conditioned on accomplishment or behavior but simply because one is part of the family. Finally, healthy family love is enduring. One does not expect it to end in the future (Burr, Day, & Bahr, 1993).
- **Love Is an Open Door.** (See the movie, "Frozen.") ★smile★

Just Say Yes

Give your all to me
I'll give my all to you
You're my end and my beginning
Even when I lose I'm winning
'Cause I give you all of me
And you give me all of you

(John Legend, 2013)

For most people, past and present, part of the human experience is to find a mate and start a family. How, when, and where that happens is as diverse as the number of songs written about love, family, and marriage.

Cohabitation

The study of union formation (how we get together) is extremely complex, and with rapid changes in union formation across cultures and groups, research today is replete with gaps and inconsistencies (Sassler & Lichter, 2020). One such rapid change is the rate of **cohabitation**, living together as partners without being officially married. Cohabitation has been the norm in Scandinavian countries for several decades. In Sweden, 99% of couples live together prior to marriage (Liazos, 2004/2015). It has been said, "As Sweden goes, so goes the world"; in the case of cohabitation, it might be true. In the not too distant past, cohabitation was referred to as "living in sin" and was deeply frowned upon in the United States. Today, it has surpassed marriage as the most common union experience for young adults, and about 2/3 of women who expect to marry, expect to live with their husband first (Lundberg, Pollak, & Stearns, 2016; Manning, Smock, & Fettro, 2019). This living arrangement hasn't just increased among the young. Between 2007 and 2016, cohabitation rates among those over 50 increased 75% (Stepler, 2017)!

The reasons for cohabitation vary widely across cultures and subgroups, from being an alternative to marriage to being one step in the marriage process (Hiekel, Liefbroer, & Poortman, 2014). While most US marriages today are preceded by cohabitation, cohabitation typically does not lead to marriage (Sassler & Lichter, 2020). In fact, most cohabitation relationships break up within three years, and only one in ten lasts longer than five years (Bumpass & Lu, 2000; Lundberg, Pollack, & Stearns, 2016). It is often thought that living with someone is good practice to assess compatibility. Is this the case? Unfortunately, no. Research has consistently found that, except for two circumstances, cohabitation is associated with marriage instability and dissolution even across all education groups (Rosenfield & Roesler, 2019; Stanley, Rhoades, & Markman, 2006). What are the two exceptions? First, if a couple is engaged *before* they cohabit, they have similar marriage success and outcomes as those who marry without cohabitating (Rhoades, Stanley, & Markman, 2009). The second exception relates to the first year of marriage. People who cohabit and then marry are less likely to divorce during the first year of marriage compared to those couples who did not cohabit; however, they are more likely to divorce in the long run, thus experiencing "shorter term benefits and longer term costs" (Rosenfield & Roesler, 2019, p. 42).

It is unknown why cohabitators are at increased risk of divorce and marital distress. Some family scholars have suggested a **selection effect** (Stanley et al., 2006). According to this perspective, people who choose not to marry are different from people who do. Perhaps they have problems with commitment or trust or lack confidence in marriage; in other words, these people might have more risks when it comes to marriage, to begin with. This means that the living situation itself is not the cause of poorer outcomes but the people entering the situation are. However, other evidence suggests that the experience of cohabitating results in risks *beyond* the selection effect. It may be that after two people move in together, they may choose to get married simply because "that's the next step," even if they do not have the highest quality relationship. This has been described as "**sliding**" into marriage rather than "**deciding**" to marry and leads to poorer outcomes (Stanley et al., 2006).

With the increase in cohabitation and the increased instability in these relationships, it should come as no surprise that children, either born into the union or brought into it from a previous relationship, are increasingly affected (Manning, 2016). In general, outcomes for women and children are poorer in cohabiting relationships than married relationships (Carlson & VanOrman, 2017). Children in cohabiting relationships are more likely to experience child abuse, school difficulties, delinquency, and poorer health, but careful parsing of the literature leads to a much more complex understanding of these outcomes. For example, outcomes are related to the age of the child and the type of relationship of the parent/s. Children born into a cohabiting relationship appear to have enduring difficulties. Young children in stepparent cohabitation relationships also tend to have more problems; adolescents, however, do not. The water is further muddied when you consider social class, race/ethnicity, diverse genders and sexualities, multipartner fertility, and serial cohabitations (Manning, 2016).

Marriage

I didn't marry you because you were perfect. I didn't even marry you because I loved you. I married you because you gave me a promise. That promise made up for your faults. And the promise I gave you made up for mine. Two imperfect people got married and it was the promise that made the marriage. And when our children were growing up, it wasn't a house that protected them; and it wasn't our love that protected them—it was that promise.

Thornton Wilder, 1942 *The Skin of Our Teeth, Act II*

Billionaire investor and philanthropist, Warren Buffet, has made many important decisions in his lifetime, yet he says that the most important decision anyone can make is who they marry (Moss, 2017). Research provides some support for this statement. Together with her colleagues, psychologist Brooke Feeney (Feeney, Van Vleet, Jakubiak, and Tomlinson, 2017) gave married couples a choice between completing a simple puzzle or competing for a prize worth up to $200. Those participants with encouraging spouses were more likely to take on the challenge. Additionally, 6 months later, they found those individuals with supportive spouses rated higher in improved well-being as measured by personal growth, happiness, relationships, and feelings of self-efficacy. Feeney explained, "Significant others can help you thrive through embracing life opportunities or they can hinder your ability to thrive by making it less likely that you'll pursue opportunities for growth" (Monahan, 2017).

Aside from supportiveness, what characteristics do you think are important in a future spouse? Buss, Shackelford, and Kirkpatrick (2001) help us understand some of the more dramatic shifts over the last 80 years in our ideas about what's important in a spouse. They gathered data about mate preference across six decades (1939–1996). These researchers assessed 18 characteristics or ideas that were asked of men and women as they thought about people they would like to marry. Regional and gender differences were found, although most findings were strikingly similar.

The first preference listed was a dependable character. This idea about partner character does not seem to have changed much over the years. Both men and women expect a partner to be dependable, reliable, and committed to the relationship. Additionally, past and present, both sexes have reported that the physical attractiveness and financial prospects of a potential mate are important. At the other end of the spectrum, having a similar political background was *not* very important in 1939 and still was not in 1996. It's quite possible, though, that the current political climate could result in different findings. Wakefield Research (2017), an independent and nonpartisan organization, found that over one in five Millennials has broken up with someone because of political differences!

Some characteristics, however, have made significant shifts. Chastity is the most notable. In 1939, men ranked this attribute as number 10, ahead of education and even good looks. By 1996, men rated chastity 16th on their list of desirable characteristics behind such things as good health, refinement and neatness, education, and good looks. The men of our day are much more interested in a woman who is healthy, neat, educated, and good looking and care very little if she has had other sexual partners.

On the other hand, women in our day prefer to be with a man who is in love with them, emotionally stable, has a pleasing disposition, is educated, and has a good strong desire to have children and provide a home. Interestingly, most (in this survey) cared very little about his previous sexual behavior. That represents a dramatic change from the 1939 data.

Similar data has been gathered in other countries, including China and Brazil. In China, dependability was identified as important, and good financial prospects increased in importance; virginity decreased in importance (Chang, Wang, Shackelford & Buss, 2011). Gender differences were found in the importance of attractiveness and resources, with men preferring young, attractive, and healthy women; and women preferring men with resources or ability to provide. These findings were mirrored in Brazil (Souza, Conroy-Beam, & Buss, 2016). Women valued resources/resource acquisition in men; and men valued qualities related to fertility (attractiveness, youth). Apparently, some desired characteristics of potential mates are fairly universal.

How we choose a marriage partner is influenced by culture. In the past and in many parts of the world today, a mate was chosen by family members. Over the past century, however, the trend toward choosing a mate is based on love. Let's look a bit closer at arranged (family-involved mate selection [FIMA]) vs. free choice marriages (love-based mate selection [LBMS]).

Family-Involved Mate Selection

Perhaps you have seen the movie or musical *Fiddler on the Roof*. In this poignant story, Tevya, a local milkman and rural Jewish father (circa 1900) of four marriage-aged young women, tries to find partners in several different ways—each one challenging the matchmaking system of the time in rural and agricultural Jewish communities in Europe. In one scene, the daughters sing a lament about the capricious process of finding a husband through the local matchmaker. As they sing, it is clear they could find themselves married to people who really do not know or care about them. In the United States and Western culture, it is hard for us to have even a vague understanding of the idea that a young girl is betrothed to a man she might not even know.

In the relatively recent past, marriages around the world were almost exclusively arranged using matchmakers or through direct family contacts. Even today, in highly traditional societies, such as in Asia, South America, or the Middle East, as well as some religious groups, choosing a partner is a **family-involved mate selection** (FIMS) process. Selection criteria often are centered on social class and position. Typically, fathers and mothers warn children about playing with other children from another class, and, at a very early age, parents begin the search for a suitable marriage partner for their child. "Helpers" or matchmakers assist in making sure the family (and the young person) does not make a poor choice. In a FIMS system, there remains a strong push by family members, teachers, and even matchmakers to pick partners within one's own social class and economic status. To reiterate, most couples worldwide do not secure a marriage partner in the "regular" American way: See someone attractive, give him or her a call on the phone, ask for a date, and go to a movie—and then see what evolves from there. Instead, in most Asian and Muslim cultures, for example, someone expresses interest in a person, a host of gatekeeper relatives and friends consider the bid, families potentially gather and introduce the young people and they (while not looking directly at each other) "court" in the presence of on-looking relatives.

Consider Egypt. Prior to the 1950s, marriages were almost exclusively arranged using matchmakers or through direct family contacts. According to Sherif (1999), dating situations are slowly changing: Young people are now permitted to meet potential marital partners through work or other social situations. However, for many couples in Egypt today, the courting process usually involves an element of family negotiation. That is, the man requests the hand of a woman through very formal channels (Nasir, 1990; Sherif, 1999). Sometime during these negotiations (and well before the potential couple have really spoken in depth with each other), the man will approach the woman's family and the inquiries begin. Both families seek to find out as much as they can about the status of the family, position in the community, and potential for future status attainment.

At some point, when the negotiations seem to be going well, the man will consult with his mother, sisters, and friends as he considers the purchase of a *shabka*. The shabka is a gift given to the prospective bride and usually is of the highest quality and price the man can afford. In wealthier families, this is usually a fine piece of jewelry (Sherif, 1999). During the next phase of this very structured courtship or *khutba*, either party can bow out of the preliminary contract. It is during this time that the couple gets to know one another and can talk together. However, this getting-to-know-you phase is very structured. Families get together for dinners, outings might be planned, and the two families begin to intertwine. If all goes well, the families negotiate a contract for marriage. The contract is signed, often long before the actual marriage, but the contract is very formal and binding.

Before you think that FIMS is something not seen in the United States, think again. We know several people living in the United States (and born in the United States) who entered arranged marriages. One of our friends, who is Muslim, met her husband through her parents. They spent a couple of weeks under close supervision, getting to know each other, and then had the option to accept the match or not. They did. That was over 15 years and 4 children ago! Our friend has an MBA, and her husband is a surgeon. For people from other countries living in the United States, the desire to marry someone from their birth country can be strong. Advertisements on the Internet and social media contacts can provide opportunities for meeting future mates from other countries.

Love-Based Mate Selection

In most Western, modern, and industrialized countries, young people are more likely to have the first and final say about who they marry. This is a new and emerging world trend. These types of love-based unions spread rapidly in the 20th century, as the ideals of Western-style individualism spread. The type of dating and mate selection system we find in places like Europe or North America is referred to as **love-based mate selection** (LBMS). These relationships might or might not result in marriage, per se. In many Western cultures, cohabitation rates are very high, with individuals experiencing several premarriage partners before a marriage choice is made. Again, it is important to note that general cultural stigma about this type of system is faint at best. In these countries, the cultures have decided that the individual choice trumps religious, extended familial, or other community concerns or needs.

Western-style individualism has brought with it the notion that marriage and sexual activity are not as connected as they once were. Societies that move toward decreased religious orientations and increased liberal and individualistic ideologies are more likely to adopt the idea of LBMS, within which the individual should have first and final say about personal choice in such matters of the heart. This type of individual choice also brings with it—or can bring with it—the choice to choose and act on sexual desire outside of religious or family sanction. One of the keys to understanding this move toward LBMS is the advent and worldwide acceptance of birth control and the general liberalization of abortion practice. With these two widely accepted practices in hand, the cultural idea of sex for recreation has flourished. One can, in a purely LBMS system (devoid of religiously proscribed sexual activity), choose to have multiple sexual partners with impunity and with decreased worry about unintended pregnancy (more on this topic appears later).

Highly religious, traditional, and conservative cultures that still embrace the ideal of FIMS see themselves as being in a desperate fight to keep their cultures from drifting toward Western ideas of individual choice and the rejection of historic and traditional ideas about marital union. These cultures hope to keep young people free from the emergent Western-style morality. Many of these cultures view this type of individual choice and self-chosen sexual contact as the very definition of evil and offense to God.

The differences in these mating and courtship styles are stark. Reflect on what this type of courtship practice might mean for the quality, durability, and strength of the future relationship. As can be imagined, when cultures shift from FIMS dating to LBMS individual-based decision making, that shift has an impact on the general kinship family system. Consider the following:

1   In FIMS, match-making parents have much more power over who does what and how resources are spent. They have been heavily involved in the selection of the new family member and might have chosen him or her for economic reasons. It is also likely in FIMS that there is a built-in expectation that the newlywed couple will be a part of the farm, business, or family enterprise.
2   In an LBMS, there is not as much pressure to adopt the family system patterns of daily living from the previous generation. Couples feel far less pressure to do their daily life routines in the ways done by their parents and have more freedom to choose their own style of relationships and patterns of family life.
3   In FIMS, the connection and value of kinship are enhanced. Once your family has been deeply involved in the marriage choice, they are also more likely to feel a connection and investment in the outcome of that relationship, the number of children born, what the children's names are, who the godparents are, and even how far you live from the epicenter of family life.
4   On the other hand, in LBMS, the wants and wishes of the individuals are enhanced. If they choose not to have children, or name the child for a popular rock star, or even move to a faraway country, the kinship wishes and wants become secondary to the couple's wishes.
5   In LBMS, relationship dissolution is the purview of the couple—not the family.
6   Conversely, in FIMS, one would expect the larger kinship system, the church or religion, and even the government to have a say over relationship dissolution. After all, they had a say in the formation of the relationship, they have a keen investment in the family connections

created through the contractual negotiation and, therefore, will probably have a lot to say and pressures to bear when things are not going well for the couple. In more religious and traditional societies, one would expect the couple to be reminded of religious covenants, promises, and mandates that govern marriage. Government agencies would want to regulate these activities if informal unions pay different tax amounts or require different provisions for health care and social safety net benefits.

7 In FIMS, it is much more likely that having and rearing children will take on greater importance. Children represent family continuity, name transfer, and inheritance perpetuation. The government always has an interest in future workers, future soldiers, and the well-being of future taxpayers. All of those values center on the maintenance and enhancement of family prestige, power, and status.

When considering family involved mate selection and LBMS, which type of mate selection do you think leads to a happier marriage? Regan, Lakhanpal, and Anguiano (2012) compared arranged and free-choice marriages among Indian–Americans living in the United States. They expected to find that people in arranged marriages would show higher commitment levels but lower levels of satisfaction and love compared with love-based marriages. Instead, they found "regardless of the nature of their marriage (i.e., whether the spouse had been selected by family members or matchmakers, or was personally and freely chosen), the participants in this study were extremely – and equally – happy with their relationships. Love, satisfaction, and commitment appear to be common outcomes in both arranged and love-based marriages, at least among Indian adults living in the U.S." (p. 922).

Not only has culture shaped how we choose marriage partners, but our partner-choosing folkways influence culture. Cultures have historically moved from family-based mate selection (FIMS) to love-based marriages (LBMS). This change has direct impacts on the goals, themes, loyalties, and general family functioning of the forthcoming generations. This change also has a direct impact on community and larger governmental plans and programs.

Discussions in Diversity: Mail Order Brides

In 2003, at age 21, Ukrainian-born Valeriya Sorokina married 44-year-old NY record producer Steve Loeb. While the 23 years age difference between these two might have raised a few eyebrows, their manner of meeting raised even more. Valeriya ("Lera") was the modern-day version of the "mail order bride." The couple shared their story six years later in a 2009 Glamour Magazine spread, "Yes, This Woman is a Mail Order Bride" (Loeb & Pilot, 2009). In the article, Lera is described as a "smart, independent and hip blogger" wildly in love with her doting and supportive husband. The description was in stark contrast to pictures painted by critics of international marriage brokering agencies, the source of "mail order brides" and "mail order husbands." Many critics express concern about powerless women in violent relationships, as well as scams against men. In fact, in order to protect non-citizen women brought to the United States for the purpose of marriage, Congress enacted the International Marriage Broker Regulation Act of 2005.

FIGURE 5.1 Schwartz, Lewis, & Young (1918).

Source: Library of Congress

Advertising for marital partners in the United States is not a 21st century phenomenon. Economic and social forces in the 19th Century resulted in a shortage of women on the Western American frontier (with an estimated 200 men for every woman) and a shortage of men in the East following the Civil War (Enss, 2015). As a result, newspapers and magazines frequently printed advertisements for potential marriage partners. Just as today, articles of the time detailed the successes and failures of these pairings or potential pairings.

Today, American citizens can obtain a K-1 visa, allowing an engaged partner from another country to enter the United States and marry the "sponsor" within 90 days. In 2017, 35,000 K-1 visas were issued, with most to unemployed or student women in their late 20s (Rapid Visa, 2021). Their sponsors tended to be white males in their early 40s, with retirees and professional drivers overrepresented.

Where do most of today's foreign-born spouses come from? Visas issued to Filipino citizens outstripped the next five countries (Vietnam, Dominican Republic, Mexico, the United Kingdom, and China) together. Of course, the media has capitalized on the public's interest in these couples with the popular reality television series, 90 Day Fiancé. Beginning in 2014, the series has enjoyed eight seasons, with several spinoffs.

Some people might look at mail order matches and believe them to be about love and marriage. Others might look at mail order matches as being about poor female "products" of white male consumerism. Still, others might see the female participants as intelligent, independent women making a choice. Perhaps it's about all of these and more, and we must recognize the great diversity that exists in these relationships. Surely, mail order marriages may offer a poor, naïve, uneducated woman a chance to find a comparatively wealthy "sponsor" in another country and a way out of her situation. So, too, might mail order marriages provide an Indian-American man with a well-educated wife from the man's home country and culture, a woman who desires the relationship and who is more likely to share his language, history, and culture.

At this point, there is little research attesting to the success or failure of these matches. According to North (2015), almost half of all K-1 visas do not result in marriage. How these marriages fare across time and how family processes might differ are questions for the future.

Questions to Discuss:

- *How do mail order marriages differ today than in the past? Do you think these differences may result in different long-term outcomes of marriage?*
- *Do you believe mail order marriages are ethical?*
- *Why might someone turn to potential partners from other countries rather than looking for someone closer to home?*
- *What barriers and difficulties might these couples experience compared with "typical" couples?*

SUMMARY

Family scholar James M. Harper compares family relationships, interactions, and patterns to a dance (Harper, 2002). When you dance, you pay attention to your partner, manage your distance, follow certain patterns, have verbal and nonverbal exchanges, and attempt to stay in rhythm and synchrony with your partner (or group in the case of line dancing). His analogy expertly captures family processes. This chapter, then, addresses what happens even before the dance that can ultimately influence the dance: Meeting, deciding, and then asking someone to dance.

The way we meet, date, and mate around the world has changed in the last 100 years. Courting and formal dating have been replaced with hanging out together as friends, and technology has increased our pool of available mates. We have experienced a dramatic shift away from the connection between relationship commitment and sexual intimacy. Very quickly, many young people today have disconnected those two ideas. That disconnection has had a significant impact on such issues as abortion, age at marriage, the divorce rate, and the overall meaning of marriage today.

A major shift has also occurred in how we view love. This chapter presented several theories of love and its view as an art, a color, a language, a story, and a family process. It was not until the modern era that romantic love was even a part of the marriage equation and now it is considered by many as a necessity. But what is it about love—or what is it *within* loving relationships—that informs, builds, strengthens, and potentially enhances the quality of family life? Family process theory helps us understand love as a pillar of strong and effective family life.

As the mores and folkways surrounding mating change, the culture seems to be experimenting with different forms of relationships and patterns of pairing, as seen in the acceptance of cohabitation in much of the modern world. Cohabitation is crossing class and age lines, with more children being affected by these relationships. Unfortunately, cohabitation has not led to more stable relationships, but often just the opposite.

Similarly, we are experiencing changes in how we select mates. For the most part, many cultures are moving away from family-based involvement in mate selection and toward love-based selection. The latter system reflects the growing idea that young people do not want to rely, nor do they have to rely, on family and parents for support and decision making about such things as future partners. This shift has many implications for how we view marriage and marriage-like relationships (e.g., long-term cohabitation).

Recalling the principle of epigenesis in relationships, the type and style of relationship one adopts early in the relationship defines and directs the relationship as it emerges and matures over time. For example, if the relationship lacks commitment early on, it will be more difficult to generate commitment later. Further, those relationships that are passionate, intimate, and committed should produce relationships that are more efficient in solving problems and better at fending off crises, allowing the couple to make more effective decisions. Family well-being is an outcome of numerous decisions, roles, and responsibilities made by the family and reflective in family processes (Manning, 2015). Family processes are influenced by how the family was formed, and how the family was formed influences family processes.

STUDY QUESTIONS

1 Where do you think is the best place to meet a future mate? As you consider propinquity, who would you be more likely to marry?

2 Ask your friends what they find attractive in other people. How do their answers match with the findings reported in this chapter?

3 Do you consider hanging out a good way to find a partner? Why or why not?

4 What gender differences might there be in hook up experiences?

5 Which philosopher described love as an art? What did he mean by this?

6 Which "love types" (colors) can you apply to various family relationships (husband/wife, parent-child, grandparent, sibling)?

7 What are the components of love according to Sternberg's triarchic theory of love? How does this theory differ from his conception that love is a story?

8 How important do you think is the physiological basis of love?

9 What are the four components of family love as outlined by Wesley Burr (love as a family process)?

10 If your friend asked you your opinion of cohabitation and if it could improve marriage satisfaction, what would you say?

11 What do you think is the best explanation for why cohabitation does not seem to have positive outcomes in relationships or marriage?

12 Explain what is meant by family-involved mate selection and love-based mate selection.

13 Comment on your world: How do the young people you know (or even the older ones) seem to be hooking up, dating, and choosing partners? Does the analysis in this chapter support what you are seeing around you?

14 Would you ever consider (or have you ever considered) living with someone before marriage? Explain your views in this regard: Why would you (or wouldn't you) entertain that as a possibility?

15 What does how we meet our future mates relate to our examination of family processes?

KEY TERMS

Propinquity
Hanging out
Hooking up
Cohabitation
Selection effect
Sliding/deciding
Family-involved mate selection
Love-based mate selection

SUGGESTED READINGS

Berscheid, E. (2006). *Dynamics of romantic love: Attachment, caregiving, and sex.* New York, NY: Guilford.

Crouter, A., & Booth, A. (Eds.). (2006). *Romance and sex in adolescence and emerging adulthood: Risks and opportunities.* Mahwah, NJ: Lawrence Erlbaum Associates.

England, P., & Edin, K. (Eds.). (2007). *Unmarried couples with children.* New York, NY: Russell Sage.

Fahmy, H. (2020). *That can be arranged.* Kansas City, MO: Andrews McMeel Publishing.

Harlow, H. F. (1974). *Learning to love.* New York, NY: Jason Aronson, Inc.

Reczek, C. (2020). Sexual- and gender-minority families: A 2010 to 2020 decade in review. *Journal of Marriage and Family, 82,* 300–325.

Weissbourd, R., Anderson, T. R., Cashin, A., & McIntyre, J. (2017). *The talk. Making caring common project.* Cambridge, MA: Harvard Graduate School of Education.

REFERENCES

Berscheid, E. S., & Regan, P. (2017). *The psychology of interpersonal relationships.* New York, NY: Routledge.

Blum, D. (2002). *Love at Goon Park: Harry Harlow and the science of affection.* New York, NY: The Berkley Publishing Group.

Bruch, E. E., & Newman, M. E. J. (2018). Aspirational pursuit of mates in online dating markets. *Science Advances, 4*(8), eaap9815. https://advances.sciencemag.org/content/4/8/eaap9815

Bumpass, L., & Lu, H. H. (2000). Trends in cohabitation and implications for children's family contexts in the United States. *Population Studies, 54*(1), 29–41.

Bunt, S., & Hazelwood, Z. J. (2017). Walking the walk, talking the talk: Love languages, self-regulation, and relationship satisfaction. *Personal Relationships, 24*(2), 280–290.

Burr, W. R., Day, R. D., & Bahr, K. S. (1993). *Family science*. Pacific Grove, CA: Brooks/Cole.

Buss, D. M., Shackelford, T. K., & Kirkpatrick (2001). A half century of mate preferences: The cultural evolution of values. *Journal of Marriage and Family, 63*(2), 491–503.

Carlson, M. J., & VanOrman, A. G. (2017). Trajectories of relationship supportiveness after childbirth: Does marriage matter? *Social Science Research, 66*, 102–117.

Chang, L., Wang, Y., Shackelford, T. K., & Buss, D. M. (2011). Chinese mate preferences: Cultural evolution and continuity across a quarter of a century. *Personality and Individual Differences, 50*(5), 678–683.

Enss, C. (2015). Getting personal on the frontier: Mail order brides. *Wild West, 27*(5), 44–51.

Feeney, B. C., VanVleet, M., Jakubiak, B. K., & Tomlinson, J. M. (2017). Predicting the pursuit and support of challenging life opportunities. *Personality and Social Psychology Bulletin, 43*(8), 1171–1187.

Finkel, E. J., Eastwick, P. W., Karney, B. R., Reis, H. T., & Sprecher, S. (2012). Online dating: A critical analysis from the perspective of psychological science. *Psychological Science in the Public Interest, 13*(1), 3–66.

Fisher, H. E. (1998). Lust, attraction, and attachment in mammalian reproduction. *Human Nature, 9*, 23–52.

Fisher, H. E. (2016). The science behind maintaining a happy long-term relationship. *Big Think*. https://bigthink.com/videos/helen-fisher-on-how-to-sustain-a-long-term-relationship

Ford, J., England, P., & Bearak, J. M. (2015). The American college hookup scene: Findings from the online college social life survey. *PowerPoint published in TRAILS: Teaching resources and innovations library for sociology*. Washington, DC: American Sociological Association. http://trails.asanet.org

Harlow, H. (1958). The nature of love: Address of the president at the 66th annual convention of the American psychological association, Washington, DC, August 31, 1958. Reprinted in. *The American Psychologist, 13*(12), 673–685.

Harper, J. M. (2002). The family dance. *Marriage and Families, 8*, 9–15. https://scholarsarchive.byu.edu/cgi/viewcontent.cgi?article=1057&context=marriageandfamilies

Hendrick, C., & Hendrick, S. (1986). A theory and method of love. *Journal of Personality and Social Psychology, 50*(2), 392–402.

Hiekel, N., Liefbroer, A. C., & Poortman, A.-R. (2014). Understanding diversity in the meaning of cohabitation across Europe. *European Journal of Population, 30*, 391–410.

Le, G. (2011). What's the best way to meet someone? In G. W. Lewandowsk Jr., B. Le, & M. E. J. Gleason (Eds.), *The science of relationships (chapter 1)attraction & relationship initiation* (pp. 13–19). Dubuque, IA: Kendall Hunt Publishing Company.

Legend, J. (2013). *All of Me* [Lyrics]. Retrieved from https://genius.com/John-legend-all-of-me-lyrics

Lewandowski, G. W. Jr. (2011). What makes someone hot and others not? In G. W. Lewandowsk Jr., B. Le, & M. E. J. Gleason (Eds.), *The science of relationships (chapter 1) attraction & relationship initiation* (pp. 1–5). Dubuque, IA: Kendall Hunt Publishing Company.

Liazos, A. (2004/2015). *Families: Joys, conflicts, and changes*. London: Taylor & Francis.

Loeb, L., & Pilot, J. (2009). Yes, this woman is a "mail-order" bride. *Glamour*. https://www.glamour.com/story/yes-this-woman-is-a-mail-order-bride.

Lundberg, S., Pollak, R. A., & Stearns, J. (2016). Family inequality: Diverging patterns in marriage, cohabitation, and childbearing. *Journal of Economic Perspectives, 30*(2), 79–102.

Manning, W. D. (2015). Family formation processes: Assessing the need for a new nationally representative household panel survey in the United States. *Journal of Economic and Social Measurement, 40*, 197–219.

Manning, W. D. (2016). Cohabitation and child wellbeing. *The Future of Children, 25*(2), 52–56.

Manning, W. D., Smock, P. J., & Fettro, M. N. (2019). Cohabitation and marital expectations among single millennials in the U.S. *Population Research and Policy Review, 38*, 327–346.

Monahan, P. (2017). Supportive relationships linked to willingness to pursue opportunities. Dietrich College of Humanities and Social Sciences, Carnegie Mellon University. https://www.cmu.edu/dietrich/news/news-stories/2017/august/supportive-spouses-brooke-feeny.html

Moss, W. (2017). Why who you marry is the most important decision you make. https://www.wesmoss.com/news/why-who-you-marry-is-the-most-important-decision-you-make/#:~:text=Buffett%20refers%20to%20marriage%20as,advantage%20to%20have%20a%20wonderful

Nasir, J. (1990). *The Islamic law of personal status*. London: Graham & Trotman.

North, D. (2015). Large number of cold feet among those applying for the k-1 (Fiancé) visa. *Center for Immigration Studies*. https://cis.org/North/Large-Number-Cold-Feet-Among-Those-Applying-K1-Fiance-Visa

Rapid Visa (2021). K1 Fiancé Visa Statistics and Trend Report. *Rapid Visa*. https://rapidvisa.com/k1-visa-report/#1

Regan, P. C., Lakhanpal, S., & Anguiano, C. (2012). Relationship outcomes in Indian-American love-based and arranged marriages. *Psychological Reports, 110*(3), 915–924.

Rhoades, G. K., Stanley, S. M., & Markman, H. J. (2009). The pre-engagement cohabitation effect: A replication and extension of previous findings. *Journal of Family Psychology, 23*, 107–111.

Rosenfield, M. J.,, & Roesler, K. (2019). Cohabitation experience and cohabitation's association with marital dissolution. *Journal of Marriage and Family, 81*, 42–58.

Sassler, S., & Lichter, D. T. (2020). Cohabitation and marriage: Complexity and diversity in union-formation patterns. *Journal of Marriage and Family, 82*, 35–61.

Schwartz, J., Lewis, S. M., & Young, J. (1918). *Wedding bells will you ever ring for me* [Notated Music]. New York, NY: Waterson, Berlin & Snyder Co. Retrieved from the Library of Congress, https://www.loc.gov/item/ihas.100007958/

Sherif, B. (1999). The prayer of a married man Is equal to seventy prayers of a single man: The central role of marriage among upper-middle-class Muslim Egyptians. *Journal of Family Issues. 20*(5), 617–632. DOI: 10.1177/019251399020005003

Sorokowski, P., Koscinski, K., Sorokowska, A., & Huanca, T. (2014). Preference for women's body mass and waist-to-hip ratio in Tsimane' men of the Bolivian Amazon: Biological and cultural determinants. *PLoS One, 9*(8), e105468. DOI: 10.1371/journal.pone.0105468

Souza, A. L., Conroy-Beam, D., & Buss, D. M. (2016). Mate preferences in Brazil: Evolved desires and cultural evolution over three decades. *Personality and Individual Differences, 95*, 45–49.

Stanley, S. M., Rhoades, G. K., & Markman, H. J. (2006). Sliding versus deciding: Inertia and the premarital cohabitation effect. *Family Relations: An Interdisciplinary Journal of Applied Family Studies, 55*(4), 499–509. DOI: 10.1111/j.1741-3729.2006.00418.x

Stepler, R. (2017). Number of U.S adults cohabiting with a partner continues to rise, especially among those 50 and older. FactTank. Pew Research. https://www.pewresearch.org/fact-tank/2017/04/06/number-of-u-s-adults-cohabiting-with-a-partner-continues-to-rise-especially-among-those-50-and-older/

Sternberg, R. (1986). A triangular theory of love. *Psychological Review, 93*(2), 119–135.

Sternberg, R. J., Hojjat, M., & Barnes, M. L. (2001). Empirical tests of aspects of a theory of love as a story. *European Journal of Personality, 15*, 199–218.

Strokoff, J., Owen, J., & Fincham, F. D. (2015). Diverse reactions to hooking up among U.S. university students. *Archives of Sexual Behavior, 44*(4), 935–43.

Vogels, E. A. (2020). 10 facts about Americans and online dating. FactTank, Pew Research Center. https://www.pewresearch.org/fact-tank/2020/02/06/10-facts-about-americans-and-online-dating/

Vogels, E. A., & Anderson, M. (2020). Dating and relationships in the digital age. Pew Research Center. https://www.pewresearch.org/internet/2020/05/08/dating-and-relationships-in-the-digital-age/

Wakefield Research (2017). New Wakefield research study: The Trump effect on American relationships. https://www.wakefieldresearch.com/blog/2017/05/10/new-wakefield-research-study-trump-effect-american-relationships

Weissbourd, R., Anderson, T. R., Cashin, A., & McIntyre, J. (2017). The talk. *Making caring common project*. Cambridge, MA: Harvard Graduate School of Education.

Wilder, T. (1942). *The skin of our teeth*. New York, NY: Samuel French, Inc.

CHAPTER 6

Family Ideologies and Paradigms

The Core of Family Life

CHAPTER PREVIEW

In this chapter, readers will learn:

- That an *ideology* is a set of ideas or beliefs. The ideological part of family systems is different from the generational and emotional parts, and all three are important.
- How some aspects of family ideology are more abstract than other aspects. Three levels of abstraction are explained.
- That family paradigms are an important part of families and are the enduring, fundamental, shared, and general assumptions families develop about the nature and meaning of life, what is important, and how to cope with the world they live in.
- How family paradigms develop and change.
- About four general types of family paradigms: open, closed, random, and synchronous.
- About the ideology principle, which teaches us that many of the other elements of family processes are built on the themes, paradigms, and shared fundamental beliefs found in the family's ideological core.
- That the exaggeration principle helps us understand that when families encounter stress they have a natural tendency toward exaggeration of the processes created by their paradigmatic beliefs.

INTRODUCTION

The long running, popular television program, *The Simpsons*, features the free-wheeling, chaotic Simpson family, including father Homer, mother Marge, and their three children. Homer is a bumbling, somewhat dimwitted, yet usually caring and protective father. The Simpsons' next-door neighbor is honest and sincere Ned Flanders and his two children. The Flanders' household is very different from the Simpson's. It is organized, clean, and highly religious. Both families

DOI: 10.4324/9781003128717-8

are white, middle class, and attend the 1st Church of Springfield (part of the Western Branch of American Reform Presbylutheranism), yet both families are extremely different.

These are cartoon families, but what about reality? I have stayed with families that never locked a door and kept their keys in the ignition of their car parked on the street. I have also seen families that have three locks on their front door and would never dream of leaving the keys in the car! Obviously, these families (cartoon and real) see the world differently and their perceptions influence not only how they interact with each other but with the world at large.

How we see the world and interact with it is influenced by our **ideologies**. The root of the word *ideology* comes from the Greek term *ide*, which means *idea*. Therefore, ideology refers to the body or group of ideas that exist in a group, society, or social movement. When we focus on family ideology, we are focusing on *the cognitive or intellectual* aspect of family systems that is reflected in their beliefs, thoughts, myths, symbols, ideals, aspirations, values, worldviews, philosophy of life, or doctrines. This is very different from the emotional and generational aspects of family systems. The emotional part is an affective process experienced as sensations or emotions rather than thoughts. Generational processes (discussed in Chapter 4) also are not part of the "idea" part of family systems. Rather, they are connections, continuities, discontinuities, and other processes that occur between parents and children—even when families are not aware of them intellectually. In short, emotional and generational processes are fundamentally different from family ideology; however, ideas or beliefs about these emotional and generational processes can become part of the family ideology. Deeply held ideologies form what is called the family paradigm. This chapter deals with this very fundamental and important part of the family system.

What's the Big Idea? The Continuum of Abstraction

To fully grasp the idea of family paradigms, it is helpful to understand **the continuum of abstraction**. At one end of the continuum is **concrete, logical thinking**. This type of thinking relates to the observable, tangible, and measurable aspects of life (and science). At the other end of the continuum is **abstract thinking**. Abstract thinking is not confined to physical objects present in the here and now; instead, it allows us to think of intangibles and objects not present, as well as complex ideas, philosophy, and principles. It allows us to think of the possible. Such thinking is an important cognitive ability required for academic and scientific endeavors.

So how does this relate to our discussion of family? There is a difference between thinking about our own personal experiences in family life and imagining family in general. Our own version of family life is a specific and concrete example. On the other hand, when we think of family life generally, we imagine a wide-ranging way of organizing humans, which is much more abstract. Frequently, we make the mistake of jumping from one level of abstraction and of generalizing that experience to a broader, less concrete feature of the same experience. For example, if you were to assume that your personal version of family life and that the family you were raised in (concrete) is the norm, the typical, or even the ideal (abstract), you could run into a host of problems.

Family scientists recognize that all families, regardless of form, class, race, ethnicity, or culture, are complex systems that create and manage rules that govern universal tasks that families undertake (Anderson & Sabatelli, 2011; Broderick, 1993; Hess & Handel, 1959; Kantor & Lehr, 1975). Families, in their own unique ways, must contend with boundaries (who's in and who's out of the family), identity of the family and its individual members, activities of daily living (from eating meals to cleaning to managing finances), and the emotional roller coaster of family life. These tasks and more operate at different levels of abstraction (Watzlawick, Weakland, & Fisch, 1974). For our discussion here, we will divide these family tasks into two levels of abstraction in family systems, from specific and concrete to highly abstract: **first-order processes** and **second-order processes**.

First-Order Processes

First-order processes refer to specific and concrete ways of behaving and organizing family life. They center on patterns of daily living: solving daily problems, making decisions, and keeping the daily business of the family humming. These first-order processes or ways of thinking about family life are simple, fairly visible skills and contain rules that are, for the most part, more specific, observable, and concrete. Most of the rules and skills families have fall in this category. If we were observing family interaction and taking notes about first-order processes, we would want to know what family members are talking about and with whom they communicate. We would try to assess if their communication styles were effective. We might take note about how they solved a financial problem, celebrated a special holiday, and managed to get a room in the house painted. Additionally, we would take notes on family boundaries. Families have a first-order task of deciding who belongs in the family, who is not in the family, and how far from home family members should roam. Each family also has the first-order task of role allocation. That is, they have to decide who performs which roles, and they have to negotiate the sequences of daily practices (e.g., when children rise in the morning, when the lawn is mowed and who is in charge).

Another first-order task in family life is the development of life skills that help define personal competence (Beavers, 1985). Well-being in family life is, in part, a function of how competently family members can make decisions, solve problems, take leadership, and make desired goals happen. According to Gontang and Erickson (1996), family well-being can be assessed by examining the ability families have to perform skills that are crucial as families choose between individual needs and group needs. On the one hand, family members experience individual wants and needs. We all feel the pressure to take from the group what we want. Stronger families, according to these authors, can balance the needs and wishes of the individual with the needs and wants of other family members. The group agenda is considered along with the needs of the individual. For example, a family might need a new or different car to meet the group needs of transportation, such as a teenager needing a car to get to work or school. Stronger families can balance that general group need with the need of the individual family member who is pushing the group to spend extra funds on a personal want. Observing families from a first-order view is observing how skillful they are at implementing this choice. Families that are more competent and experience better outcomes are more balanced and flexible in solving first-order processes. In this case, they find ways of successfully balancing the needs of the teenager and the larger needs of the family group. They know how to both be flexible and show concern for the needs of the weakest or youngest in the group.

A typical family system has thousands of specific "ideas" about how family systems should operate. For example, most families think they should put beds in bedrooms rather than in living rooms, and they think it is okay to show physical affection to each other—as long as it is appropriate. Of course, families differ in what they think is appropriate. Some families express affection a great deal, and others express it less. Most families have ideas about where people should and should not eat and how family members should dress. They also believe that lawn mowers and garden tools should not be left in driveways, electrical appliances should be kept safe, and toys should not be left on stairs.

Some family processes are more subtle and unspoken. Sometimes (think now of the continuum of abstraction), even first-order family processes start to slip from obvious view and are hidden even from the family. These patterns of acting or task-oriented behaviors are subtle, implicit, and often unknown even to the family. For example, a family might have an implicit idea that "Dad can criticize other members of the family, but the other members cannot criticize Dad." Or, some members of a family might think that "Stephen is the mother's favorite child," but the mother might think she has no favorites. More competent families have skills that promote openness, emphasize generosity, and communicate caring. Families who struggle are more likely to be rigid, less caring, and more authoritarian about interactions.

You will notice that the rest of the chapters in this text could be organized around first-order elements of family life. Only this chapter focuses on the more complex and invisible second-order layer of family functioning. Further, most of the research about family life focuses on first-order elements. For example, there is an emerging line of research about how family rules emerge. Researchers ask questions about how families make rules, negotiate rule behavior, and handle rule violations.

Although first-order processes are not very abstract, they can be markers of something much more complicated and fundamental to a given family. It is interesting that by observing the skills and rules families adopt to solve daily problems, we can begin to get some idea about deeper, strongly held ideologies to which they subscribe. These much less visible, abstract, and vague elements of family life are rarely measurable; however, the more visible first-order processes and strategies for completion are breadcrumbs along the trail. We observe what we can and use those data to extrapolate about the secret inner life that is usually inaccessible.

Second-Order Processes

Second-order processes identify the deeper inner patterns and beliefs that are held by the collective family group. These include the themes that bind the family together, the beliefs they share, and the patterns of daily living. Second-order processes center on how the family negotiates and subscribes to (or decides not to subscribe to) key themes, ideologies, and core beliefs. It is from these core themes and ideologies that much of what is family arises.

These abstract ideas are difficult to articulate and define clearly because they are, by their very nature, general and diffused rather than specific and concrete. Nevertheless, they are an important part of family systems. People's abstract beliefs influence their major goals in life, the ways they try to attain their goals, and how they behave. In fact, first-order family processes, what families do, grow out of second-order family processes, what families believe. For example, if education is a core belief of a family (i.e., second-order family process), then family behaviors (i.e., first-order family processes), such as study time, family discussions about school, and trips to museums and libraries, will reflect this and grow out of that belief.

It is important to introduce the term *schema* at this point. *Schema* is a Greek word that means shape or plan. In the social sciences, the most prominent use of this term comes from the work of Piaget, a Swiss philosopher considered to be the father of developmental psychology. The plural form of schema is *schemata*. Schemata are the mental structures that represent one's understanding of how things are organized, shaped, and linked. Family members, especially as each one passes the age of 12 or so, build mental schemata about their personal world; part of that construction is very vague, deeply held, and core to their worldview. This core belief structure or schemata we label ideology.

These family ideological elements are very abstract, vague, and certainly influenced by other family members. However, when we are talking about this kind of deeply held, abstract, and vague schemata, we probably cannot identify a certain moment when those elements of our being were formed, who shaped them, and why we adopted them. Ideological schemata are not usually openly negotiated by family members; they are very general ideas basic to the way we think and believe.

Sometimes the deep ideological schemata found in family members represent general summaries that shadow the things a person believes about the world. For example, some family members might believe that the world is a hostile place to be feared, whereas others might believe that the world is a garden of opportunities to be experienced and embraced. Other core ideological schemata deal with values such as the nature of reality and how to cope with it. Some might believe the world is basically simple, black and white; others believe it is complex, complicated, and intricate. Some might believe they have control over their destiny and others think they have little control over what happens to them. It is also important to note that families have a difficult time changing these deep beliefs. Sometimes, in a severe crisis, they might rethink whether or not there is a God or really examine who they are, but most of us rarely even think about these deeply held ideas that direct our lives.

In summary, it is helpful to think about the different levels of abstraction in family systems. First-order processes refer to specific and concrete ways of behaving and organizing family life. Second-order processes are highly abstract schemata residing within family individuals, probably shared but rarely discussed. Some of the ideological schemata we hold come from the training and years of exposure to our families of origin. Other schemata come as the result of our own experience, and still others are formed deliberately as we make decisions about the meaning of life. Together, these are part of an even more abstract construct—the family paradigm.

THE FAMILY PARADIGM

The highest level of abstraction governing both first- and second-order processes is the **paradigm** (pronounced "para-dime"). Noted family therapist and researcher David Reiss (1981) wrote a book called *The Family's Construction of Reality*. In this well-known scholarly book, he developed a concept that helps us understand how the ideological schemata of family members can be shared; he called the sharing of values, beliefs, and viewpoints **family paradigms**. By way of definition, a family paradigm (or deeply held family ideology) is the shared, enduring, fundamental, and general assumptions or beliefs to which family members subscribe about the nature and meaning of life, what is important, and how to cope with the world they live in (Reiss, 1981). He even demonstrated that family members constructed and shared ideological schemata, despite disagreements, conflicts, and differences. Indeed, the core of an individual's membership in his or her own family is acceptance of, belief in, and creative elaboration of these abiding assumptions (Reiss, 1981, p. 1).

Family paradigms inform much that is done in family life, and we assume that the core beliefs held by family members direct behavior. For example, if parents believe that the development of a love for learning is a key aspect of family life, the daily behaviors chosen by those parents should, for the most part, reflect what they truly believe. If educational pursuits are at the core, they will find a way to allocate time, money, space, and personal energy to that end.

Family paradigms are the fountainhead from which the rest of family life seems to emanate. When we believe the world exists in a certain way, we organize the rest of our life's activities to reflect that notion. For example, if a family believes the world is a hostile place, they likely have more strict boundaries, have tighter rules about daily events, and take more care about activities outside the safety of the home.

Family paradigms are rarely explicit or conscious in families. They are like an iceberg beneath the surface, hidden from the view of outsiders and, at least most of the time, from the families themselves. We see only a small fraction of the total; the rest of the ideological core is usually hidden from observers, and even the family members have difficulty identifying their own paradigms. Constantine (1986) noticed this phenomenon and suggested that the invisibility of family paradigms is so complete that usually, families never become aware of them. He did note, however, that even though invisible, this deeply held ideological core is so pervasive and powerful that it becomes a template for the actions, decisions, and strategies families use to attain goals (Constantine, 1986, p. 16).

Occasionally, family paradigms will surface in family life and become known to family members. For example, they are much more likely to appear and be noticed during times of extreme crisis, including major transitions such as divorce or remarriage. In times of crisis, the very existence of the family can be threatened, and family members turn to their most basic shared beliefs to help them manage their way through the crisis. When these periods of crisis are resolved, the basic beliefs recede into the assumed foundation of daily life, and attention can again be given to everyday and routine challenges.

Family paradigms play a key role in managing processes. You will remember from our discussions that families have goals. Simply put, the ideology a family creates, and thus its governing paradigm, either *helps* or *detracts* from the family's ability to attain its goals. Several analogies illustrate the role of family paradigms. A family paradigm is like the north star in a family's attempts to navigate a complicated world. Another way to describe the power of a paradigm is to imagine it as the family's constitution that is used to govern itself. Reiss (1981) described this role by saying that family paradigms are the "central organizer" that does the "shaping," "fashioning," and "guiding" of what families do when they regulate, order, and transact with their environment.

Development of Family Paradigms

Only in recent years has the word *paradigm* been used widely. In his landmark book, *The Structure of Scientific Revolutions*, philosopher Thomas Kuhn (1969) wrote about the changing ways the science community approached what science is and how it is studied. He asserted that the science community could possess what he labeled a paradigm. In the 1969 edition of his top-selling book, he clarified what he meant by a paradigm: A paradigm was an entire constellation of beliefs, values, and techniques, and so on, shared by the members of a given community (Kuhn, 1969, p. 34). With the term *paradigm,* we move beyond schemata. Like any community collection, family members can and do share schemata about beliefs, values, and viewpoints. Schemata, therefore, reside within the individual. When taken together, the constellation of collected schemata about beliefs, values, and viewpoints, when shared by a community, such as the family, becomes a paradigm. Thus, paradigms are properties of communities.

We are just beginning to learn about how families construct, modify, and maintain their deeply held beliefs and paradigms. As with so much of human development, the construction of paradigms within relationships is likely related to our culture. Cultural conceptions of family, roles, living arrangements, gender, class, religion, and ethnicity influence our beliefs, values, and ideology. Our family paradigms are also influenced by our family heritage across generations. In addition, the dynamic nature of family and relationships influences paradigm development and change as the family determines what we want as we live life and even negotiate with family members as we merge different family ideologies. Just as paradigms themselves, much of these influences are invisible to family members.

Kuhn (1970) speculated a five-stage pattern in the development of scientific paradigms. These five stages can be adapted for family paradigm development (Bodman & Peterson, 1995).

Pre-Paradigm

The first stage is referred to as the **pre-paradigm stage**. When a couple come together, each individual brings into the relationship schemata that have been under construction for many years. It is shaped by our family life experience, subsequent life experiences, images we incorporate from media, and from ideas we consciously adopt. As we initiate relationships with others, our core ideological schemata bump into theirs, so to speak. When we notice ideological differences, one of two processes (or a combination of two processes) occurs: assimilation or accommodation. These terms also come from the field of human development, especially within the area of cognitive development. Assimilation means that we adopt the difference, and accommodation implies that we actually reorder our internal schema to make room for a new idea—a new addition to our existing "house of ideas."

Suppose a young man is talking with a young woman and they are mutually attracted. During their conversation, the topic of sports comes up. She, it turns out, is an avid Boston Red Sox fan and would not miss a game. He, on the other hand, is a true blue, dyed-in-the-wool New York Yankees fan. Let's pick up this process from his point of view. His personal ideological schemata (values and beliefs) dictate to him that the Yankees are the most important baseball team to have ever played the game. As he listens to her rave about the Red Sox, we would want to know if he assimilates or accommodates during this exchange. Someone who assimilates, in his case, would have a place within his existing schemata structures for "weirdoes and kooks" who do not really understand baseball. Her rantings do not move him to change his worldview—instead, he takes what she is saying and tucks it away into the worldview he already has shaped.

On the other hand, someone who accommodates during these types of exchanges might listen carefully to her stories about the Red Sox and the path to glory during the 2004 World Series as they swept past the hapless Cardinals to take their place in baseball history. He pauses; he reflects. He builds a slightly different view and begins to realize that he has not taken this earth-shattering event seriously. Accommodation is about change in schemata, whereas assimilation is about finding room for an idea to reside within a schema that already exists. An earth-shattering event like this could, in fact, create an ideological schemata shift, in which case, he would realize the sports faux pas of his whole life and toss out his ill-conceived previous worldview about the New York Yankees.

In this facetious example, one can easily see how the individual schemata are shaped and changed as we go through life. As we enter into close relationships, the process is more serious.

There is probably nothing more important in courtship and partner selection than finding out about the other's core ideological schemata and finding out if the ideological core of two individuals matches, can merge, and somehow combine into a solid family paradigm that is compatible for both individuals. A clear application of this information is that relationship formation is best achieved when one pays close attention to ideological differences but also (and maybe even more important) to how each partner deals with assimilating or accommodating to differences. If, for example, one partner is pushed to change and accommodate or even reject a deeply held belief, one would expect relationship trouble to emerge. However, one would expect greater success when there is a comfortable fit of important ideological values and worldviews. We would also expect future family systems to be more efficient when the key adults in those systems know how to negotiate ideological differences effectively.

Paradigm Emergence

One of the relationship tasks of the couple is to decide, consciously or unconsciously, what their new family will be like. In most situations, the two individuals grew up in a family that had constructed its basic ideology or paradigms. As they grew up, the beliefs their parents held were assumed to be the "normal" way of viewing the world. If the individuals who are beginning to form a close relationship ignore this vital topic and superficially adapt for a temporary fix, we would expect to see relationship problems later on. This formation stage can last for several months for most couples. During this time, they talk with each other at great length. These discussions are usually exciting and filled with discovery. Somewhere along the way, a couple bonds and joins their thoughts. The two individuals discover what they share as common. They might also redefine who they are as they attempt to create something new.

This sense of richness and depth that is almost universally experienced probably is partly because each couple goes through a process of constructing their unique set of meaningful and basic assumptions about what the world "really is" like for them. This process is a combination of consciously and unconsciously selecting some aspects from the family each person grew up in and from other families that are respected and developing some entirely new assumptions and beliefs (Steinglass, Bennett, Wolin, & Reiss, 1987, p. 308).

Paradigm Established

Family scientists believe that the first paradigms of a new family are borrowed and invented. As various aspects of the relationship are identified, talked about, tested, and revised, they come and go in consciousness. They remain conscious as long as there is uncertainty, ambiguity, and conflict, and when they are resolved, they slip into the implicit, implied, unconscious part of the gradually growing family paradigm.

Once a family's paradigm is firmly established, it becomes a part of the family's daily life and is reflected in their total lifestyle. Established paradigms provide a sense of meaning and order, and they are used as the guiding beliefs in selecting goals, making decisions, and managing resources. As long as things go smoothly, the paradigm will remain unchanged. In fact, it is difficult to change established paradigms partially due to their invisibility and its unconscious automatic components of everyday thinking. But life rarely is without problems. In times of crisis, the typical pattern is for families to begin to question old ways of thinking and doing things and to construct new ways of defining the stressful situation and new strategies for trying to cope with the stress. In other words, the paradigm begins to change.

Paradigm Shift

If one is using the definition proffered by Kuhn and his scientific community, an individual cannot experience a paradigm shift, per se. A change in ideological orientation or a reevaluation of one's personal ideological schemata should, in proper terms, be labeled an ideological schemata shift. That sounds a bit awkward, but it makes two important points. First, individuals create and maintain ideological schemata about how the world is constructed. Those collected views can (and often do) change. However, changes in one family member's worldview are not the same as a community change. The second point, therefore, is that a community of individuals can share viewpoints, beliefs, and values. Those shared beliefs can (and sometimes do) change, and when they change, we call that a **paradigm shift**.

A paradigm shift can occur for many reasons, including education, experience, or family crisis. Reiss devoted much of his research and a book to showing ways family crises influence paradigmatic beliefs. He found that the strategies that families use to recover from the crisis are found in the collective part of the family paradigm. That is, the individuals in a family share some idea about how best to solve the problems they encounter. They interact in certain ways that they believe will be effective in resolving their crisis. When the crisis is very severe, the family sometimes changes. They might even have to change the foundational, core ideologies they have to get through a crisis situation, and the original paradigm dissolves.

Paradigm Re-Emergence

Original paradigms can dissolve and be replaced by entirely new paradigms or slightly altered paradigms depending on family needs. The longer a family experiences difficulty in coping with a stressful situation, the more the parts of their ideology are called into question, eliminated, or revised, and new definitions and perceptions emerge. If the new constructs are effective in coping with the stress, the general and abstract parts of the new beliefs are assimilated into the family paradigm. The new or revised paradigm can once again offer the family meaning and order.

Unfortunately, there is also a "worst of times" aspect to these processes. Some families are rigidly attached to some of the ideas they hold, and they do not have the flexibility, creativity, or other resources to change. This inability to change can keep a family in a state of chronic difficulty until they can get outside help.

Types of Family Paradigms

The concept of family paradigms is so new that scholars have not conducted much research about them. One of the reasons is that they are very hard to measure and discover. A few scholars, however, have begun this process, and their ideas are helpful. For example, Kantor and Lehr (1975) and Constantine (1986) described four kinds of family paradigms that seem to appear repeatedly when counselors and therapists work with families. They labeled these four paradigms closed, random, open, and synchronous families.

Closed Families

A *closed family paradigm* is the most common type of family paradigm. In this paradigm, the family has a cluster of fundamental beliefs that emphasize continuity, steadiness, and conventional ways of doing things. They believe that security and belonging are very important. They

FIGURE 6.1 The closed family: Some families organize boundaries in such a way that the family seems like it is a castle—surrounded by a moat, with doors and windows that do not allow much to come or go.

prefer stability whenever possible and are concerned about deviations from what they believe are the "right" ways to do things. The motto in closed families could be described as "stability through tradition and loyalty" (Constantine, 1986, p. 20).

When families have a closed paradigm, it leads them to adopt well-defined goals with clear boundaries (Figure 6.1). For example, when a family adopts a closed ideology, the parents are more likely to be concerned about their children's friends, and there are many more locked doors, careful scrutiny of strangers in the neighborhood, parental control over the media, and supervised excursions (Kantor & Lehr, 1975, p. 121).

Families with this paradigm tend to organize their time, so it is predictable and stable. They pay attention to the past and to the future, frequently seeking to preserve or restore something that was, or attain or achieve something that has not been accomplished. They tend to have a well-understood pattern in using time, and the individuals tend to fit their schedules to the family pattern.

The method of making decisions in closed families tends to be relatively authoritarian. Tradition or aspirations are important, and what the parents think is important. These two qualities tend to create a more authoritarian power system and method of government than exists in open and random families.

Random Families

The opposite of a closed family paradigm is the random family paradigm. When families have a *random family paradigm,* their core ideology emphasizes discontinuity, and they maximize the change in a radical focus on the present. In the random paradigm, the guiding images are novelty, creativity, and individuality. The motto of a random paradigm family might be "variety through innovation and individuality" (Constantine, 1986, p. 20). Random families are flexible regarding traditions and established ways of doing things, but they tend to be fairly rigid in emphasizing individuality, little restraint, and high levels of freedom.

These abstract beliefs are used to manage family resources in ways that are quite different from closed and open families. The use of space has some predictability, but less so than with

FIGURE 6.2 The random family is organized around the idea that routines, boundaries, and expectations are ever changing and malleable.

closed or open families. For example, eating and sleeping can occur in many places. Expressions of anger, affection, and joy might occur in the street as well as behind the closed doors of the home.

The method of making decisions and governing tends to emphasize individuality. The family interests are considered, but what is important to the family is that the individuals are free to fulfill their needs and goals. Therefore, the individuals are quite free to "do their own thing," make their connections, set their goals, and arrange their schedules.

Time is irregular and can be used and viewed very differently at different times and by different individuals or groups in the family. The preference is for evolving and spontaneous patterns that emerge from and out of what happens rather than because it is part of a plan or structure (Figure 6.2).

In random families, family members might engage in meals and entertainment patterns singly or in groups. Such physical and emotional refueling is fluctuating and changing, as family members have great freedom to seek the type of fueling they want. Foods tend to be prepared more individually. Music and entertainment are more spontaneous and varied.

Open Families

Conceptually, the open family paradigm lies between the closed and random family paradigms. When families have an *open family paradigm,* they believe in a style of life that emphasizes dialogue, communication, patience, and a willingness to change. These families believe in adaptability and innovation, and they are looking for new ways to do things. They believe in negotiation and collaboration as the fundamental ways to live and cope.

Space in open families is more movable and flexible than in closed families, and the individuals have more freedom in what they can do (Figure 6.3). They are allowed to self-regulate

FIGURE 6.3 The open family organizes itself around the notion that people, ideas, and information can come and go pretty freely.

and they are freer to choose their own destinations as long as they do not interfere with the rights and space of others. Frequent guests, unlocked doors, and lower levels of monitoring typify these families. The parents are much less likely to be intrusively involved in keeping track of family members' movements.

The method of governance that is more consistent with this style of life is less authoritarian than the closed type. Therefore, there is usually more discussion, sharing of ideas, democracy, and flexibility. The approach tends to be to try to find consensus rather than to try to find what is "right" or proper.

Synchronous Families

The *synchronous family paradigm* emphasizes harmony, tranquility, and mutual identification. When families have this paradigm, they believe they will be able to move through life with little conflict, and they will be able to easily resolve the conflict that does occur. These families depend on family members thinking alike, not to control, but to avoid conflict. Many of these family decisions will be based on *consentience* (the root word here is consent and the word means a non-intellectual sense of unity) and they will try to function with consentaneity and try to act in harmonious agreement. Some have commented that families who adopt this ideology have a distinctly utopian, mystical, or magical flavor to their family climate. The motto of synchrony might be "harmony through perfection and identification" (Constantine, 1986, pp. 20–21).

Other Paradigms

The four paradigms already discussed are only the beginning of the many deeply held beliefs that families can have. For example, in the many years I have taught the course associated with this text, I have heard hundreds of hours of discussion by students about the themes, beliefs, and deeply held paradigms their families hold. Some of these include such ideas as "education is to be revered above all"; "our family will succeed in business"; "we will do everything we can to assure that our children make it to heaven"; and "our family members will prove themselves at sports at all costs."

The last one mentioned is particularly interesting. Not long ago, in a class using this text, a young woman took about 10 minutes of class time explaining how her family was a water-skiing family. At first, it was difficult to believe that what she was saying was really an explanation of how paradigms work in families. But, after a few minutes, one could see her point.

From an early age, her father had decided that she was going to be a world-class water skier. She explained the deep core ideology was about success and winning. She went on to say that attached to that winning notion was a very closed family ideal. She was not allowed to have friends unless the friends were willing to help with the water-skiing workouts. The only magazines found in the house were about fitness and water-skiing-related topics. Schoolwork was even scheduled around practices. Meals in the home were designed for fitness and energy and every part of her life was regulated around ski meets, winning certain events, and progressing to the championship.

Additionally, the family finances were organized around this one idea (ideology, ideal, and paradigm). The family lived in Seattle and they purchased a home next to a lake that included a dock so that travel time for practice would be minimized. The mother took an extra job to make payments on a very expensive state-of-the-art ski boat. The family vehicle had to be one that could pull the boat and take the family on weekly ski trips.

Although this is an extreme example of a family paradigm, it does illustrate how the principle works. Now, imagine for a minute if the girl had been diagnosed with cancer and could no longer water ski. Or—and this was part of the story—imagine if one day she said, "That's enough" and refused to ski. This brings us to the exaggeration principle.

The Exaggeration Principle

The **exaggeration principle** suggests that when faced with a crisis, instead of finding a new deep purpose or ideology, families instead turn up the volume of the old one and try to make it work. In other words, under stress, a family tends to exaggerate the family ideologies (paradigms) rather than change. When confronted by problems, families do the best they can to solve the issues at hand. Again, they maximize their resources and try the best strategy they know to survive and attain the goals they have at their core. One strategy that most families try when something goes wrong is to try harder. "Trying harder" is itself defined paradigmatically: Families try harder by doing more of the same. Instead of changing strategies or changing their ideology, they turn up the volume of the strategy they already use. Thus, by using the available resources, each family under stress has a natural tendency toward exaggeration of its own special character.

In the case of the young woman who decided she no longer wanted to water ski, this is exactly what the family did; there was a younger sister who became the next family skier. The young woman related how her family thought of her as a traitor and she was barely allowed to visit the family home. The story was obviously a painful and traumatic one for her. Until she read the material for class, she really had not realized what had happened. What would you do to comfort her?

A family paradigm represents a commitment to certain priorities that direct family action in one direction or another as they seek to overcome difficulties. A family's methods of managing its resources consist of essentially stable structures maintaining coordinated family processes.

The regime is resilient and not likely to change fundamentally in response to stress, especially as it is guided by the family's paradigm.

The stability of a paradigm can be appreciated if it is remembered that a family paradigm is the family's way of perceiving the world, including their problems, as well as their way of approaching and solving problems. Thus, the most likely response to any challenge from within or without is for a family to respond in a manner consistent with its paradigm and organization. The more difficult and intractable the situation, the more extreme are the measures that will be taken; extreme, that is, in a way consistent with the family paradigm. The longer an impasse is sustained, the greater the degree of typical exaggeration.

The closed family confronted by problems relies on tradition, authority, and loyalty to solve them. The more difficult the problem proves to be, the stronger are the attempts to control, to pull the family into line, and to maintain consistency against a threatening world. Thus, closed families tend to become more isolated from the world, more strongly and intensely connected internally, and more rigid as they become increasingly disabled. The rallying cry is essentially "Fall in! Toe the line!"

The random family relies on spontaneity and creative individuality to find solutions to problems. As members work with increasing independence to find more creative solutions, family process becomes more chaotic and less coordinated. The random family tends toward greater separateness and chaos as it becomes more disabled. In the random family, the appeal is "Be more creative. Find something new" (which, it must be noted, does not imply a change of basic tactics; finding something new is what the random family does normally).

When initial attempts fail, the open family hangs in there, trying to hammer out a consensual solution. They gather more and more information and try harder to communicate. They become inundated with information and overwhelmed by hashing things through. As they question more and more of their basic rules, less and less is clearly known. They go around in circles. If problems remain, they become more and more enmeshed in a process that generates chaos. Their rallying cry is "We've got to work this out. We'll talk it through again and consider it more thoroughly!"

The synchronous family relies on its essential agreement to enable it to solve problems in a coordinated way while acting independently. When this consentaneity breaks down, the family moves toward greater separateness. To remain coordinated and true to its paradigm, it narrows its scope and restricts its actions to those on which there is the closest agreement. Thus, it becomes more rigid and stereotyped in its behavior while also becoming less connected. As synchronous families are based on similarity and do not deal as well with difference, which would contradict their synchrony, it becomes increasingly necessary to deny differences and problems, hiding these under a veneer of agreement and competence. As it becomes disabled, the synchronous family attempts to continue "business as usual" and insists, "There is no real problem. As always, we are really in agreement about this." Less and less happens as they become increasingly "dead" as a family or increasingly disconnected from their real problems (Constantine, 1986, pp. 182–183).

According to Constantine's ideas, most of the time, when families become disabled, it is not the family paradigms that are the root of the problem. The family paradigms are the abstract beliefs, and most families have defensible, coherent, and healthy basic assumptions. It is the less abstract processes that occur at the first two levels that become disabled. In other words, it tends to be the management that becomes disabled rather than the ideology that guides the system. It is the family's strategies for clarifying goals, making effective decisions, and managing resources that become dysfunctional.

When families find themselves in deep trouble, they tend to seek help. Closed families are more cautious about whom they turn to and how they do it, but closed, open, and random families seek help in their own ways. They turn to books, friends, relatives, educators, therapists, ministers, Ann Landers, psychiatrists, social workers, and so on.

The strategy for using the exaggeration under stress principle to help families is to help them learn how to "borrow" management strategies used in other family paradigms. It is usually easier for a closed family to use open strategies than random strategies. It is usually easier for random families to use open strategies than closed strategies.

Discussions in Diversity: Cultural Competence

As stated earlier, family paradigms have been compared to icebergs. Icebergs are interesting because of their varied shapes and sizes and the fact that "the tip of the iceberg" is literally the tip of something massive underneath the surface of the sea. Icebergs have been used as metaphors for many complex concepts, including knowledge, education, emotions, violence, and culture and diversity (Loewen, 2017).

Just as cultural anthropologists use of the iceberg for understanding culture itself, we can apply the same concepts to family paradigms and the continuum of abstraction. In this case, first-order family processes would be those things above the water, and second-order family processes and schemata would be those things underneath the water. The paradigm encompasses the entire iceberg, above and below and all round. The different shaped icebergs (yes! Icebergs can be identified by shapes, such as blocky, domed, irregular, tubular, weathered) represent different family paradigms, with the recognition that they can change over time often slowly but occasionally quickly in the face of crisis. Understanding family paradigms can help us understand families and family processes, ultimately helping us understand others and ourselves, even those who we perceive as quite different.

Dr. Jerome H. Hanley, a professor with the University of South Carolina Department of Neuropsychiatry and Behavioral Science, child psychologist, and Director of the Office of Multi-Cultural Affairs for the South Carolina Department of Mental Health, also used the iceberg metaphor when he wrote (1999) "Beyond the Tip of the Iceberg," addressing cultural competence (Figure 6.4). He wrote, "Understanding the cultures of those we serve requires more than words and good intentions. The journey toward cultural competence requires the willingness to learn from one's experiences and act... One of the most valuable skills we can have is cultural competence—the ability to work across cultures in a way that acknowledges and respects the culture of the person or organization being served." For us to be culturally competent, Dr. Hanley writes, "We must look within and without for a deeper understanding of ourselves and the cultures of the people we serve. We must also act on the knowledge, turning our understanding into more effective programs and services." Cultural competence is more than cultural awareness, cultural humility, or cultural respect. It goes well beyond viewing the tip of the iceberg. For Dr. Hanley, "Striving for cultural

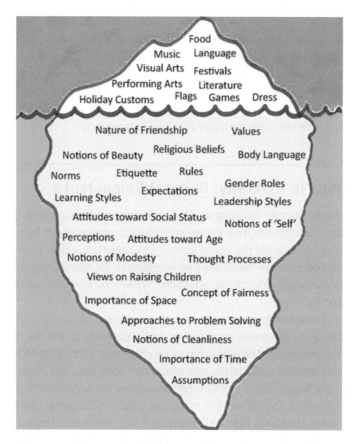

FIGURE 6.4 Created by James Penstone, licensed under Creative Commons.

competence will help you break through these stereotypes and enter the deep waters of culture…where you can effect positive, lasting change for the better."

Questions to Discuss:

- *What do you think might be the most effective way to develop cultural competence?*
- *How does cultural competence differ from cultural awareness, cultural humility, or cultural respect?*
- *Why might cultural competence be important in human service work?*
- *How might cultural competence assist us in understanding and serving families?*

SUMMARY

This chapter focused on what Reiss called family paradigms. Family ideologies or paradigms are the fundamental, general, abstract, and guiding beliefs families construct about their world. It was suggested that an individual develops a private schema about how the world is organized but that families have a collective, communal notion about how it should operate. This familial view is called a family paradigm. Further, it was suggested that families could have an open, closed, random, or synchronous family paradigm. They can also have identified themes that drive family behavior and choices. Having this concept helps us better understand how family systems work and how we can help families regardless of the stage of life cycle.

A key idea in this chapter was that some parts of family paradigms are more abstract, central, and fundamental than other parts of paradigms. This idea helps us realize there is great flexibility in the way families can organize themselves and be successful. It is not usually helpful to think that families need to conform to one particular mold or style of life if they are to be successful. There are plenty of examples of successful families who are close, open, cautious, frugal, religious, adventurous, or whatever the overall core belief is. Like snowflakes, no two families have the same way of organizing their lives, managing rules, negotiating role divisions, and establishing boundaries.

A real problem occurs if an ideology becomes too extreme in any of the many directions it could take. Problems also arise when families get stuck in ways of doing things that are too narrow and restricted because their way of behaving can interfere with their ability to cope with new developmental, cultural, or technological changes. This can happen when family members are assigned roles that fit some predetermined ideal, and there is a belief that to change how activities are done would be to damage the family.

As seen throughout this chapter, the concept of family paradigms, although a relatively recent conception, has been embraced by human service professionals. Ward (1997) suggests that utilizing paradigms could lead to more successful adoptions of older children as adoption professionals match family strengths to children's needs. The use of family paradigms has also been proposed for effective clinical decision making related to family-centered practices (Hidecker, Jones, Imig, & Villarruel, 2009). Sometimes when we try to help families, however, we wish they would change easily and quickly. We naively want our therapy, advice, or educational programs to make big differences in families. When we realize how earlier generations are involved in family paradigms, how slowly and gradually they are initially formed in courtship and early marriage, how they are intricately tied up with deeply experienced affective states, and how they are probably changed only by severe crises, it helps us realize that these basic assumptions are not fleeting and flexible ideas that can change easily. They are the most fundamental rudders in the ship of life, and once they are formed, they only change slowly and only when there are very unusual circumstances. Once we understand the nature of family paradigms and the role they play in family life, we can better understand what families are going through when they are experiencing enough stress that they are changing their paradigms. Also, we can adapt our attempts to help them so we focus on the parts of their systems that can change.

STUDY QUESTIONS

1 Define ideology and give an example.
2 What is the "continuum of abstraction?" Provide your own example that helps explain this idea.
3 Give examples of first-order and second-order family processes. Do first-order processes grow out of second-order family processes or vice versa? Explain.
4 How does the family paradigm relate to first- and second-order family processes?

5 Name all four types of family paradigms, give the definition of each, and provide an example of what each of those family styles would be like.
6 Explain why most of us never really think about family paradigms.
7 Provide four clear examples of how you could apply the principles in this chapter to make family life stronger.
8 Is an ideology different than a paradigm? Explain.
9 Why do you suppose that families exaggerate the core family ideology when they are under stress?

KEY TERMS

Ideology
Levels of abstraction
First-order family processes
Second-order family processes
Schema/schemata
Paradigms
Open/closed/random/synchronous paradigms
Exaggeration principle
Paradigm shift

SUGGESTED READINGS

Boszormenyi-Nagy, I., & Spark, G. (1973). *Invisible loyalties*. Levittown, PA: Harper & Row.
Constantine, L. L. (1986). *Family paradigms: The practice of theory in family therapy*. New York, NY: Guilford.
Constantine, L. (2007). The structure of family paradigms: An analytical model of family variation. *Journal of Marital and Family Therapy*, *19*, 39–70.
Hanley, J. H. (1999). Beyond the tip of the iceberg: Five stages toward cultural competence. *Reaching Today's Youth*, *3*(2), 9–12.
Hess, R. D., & Handel, G. (1959). *Family worlds*. Chicago, IL: University of Chicago Press.
Kantor, D., & Lehr, W. (1975). *Inside the family*. San Francisco, CA: Jossey-Bass.
Letourneau, N., & Joschko, J. (2013). *Scientific parenting: What science reveals about parental influence*. Toronto: Dundurn.
McCubbin, H. I., Thompson, E. A., Thompson, A. I., & McCubbin, M. A. (1993). Family schema, paradigms, and paradigm shifts: Components and processes of appraisal in family adaptation to crises. In A. P. Turnbull, J. M. Patterson, S. K. Behr, D. L. Murphy, J. G. Marquis, & M. J. Blue-Banning (Eds.), *Cognitive coping, families, and disability* (pp. 239–255). Baltimore, MD: Paul H. Brookes Publishing.
Reiss, D. (1981). *The family's construction of reality*. Cambridge, MA: Harvard University Press.

REFERENCES

Anderson, S. A., & Sabatelli, R. M. (2011). *Family interaction: A multigenerational developmental perspective* (5th ed.). Boston, MA: Pearson.
Beavers, W. R. (1985). *Successful marriage*. New York, NY: Norton.
Bodman, D. A., & Peterson, G. (1995). Parenting processes. In R. D. Day, K. R. Gilbert, B. H. Settles, & W. R. Burr (Eds.), *Research and theory in family science* (pp. 205–225). Pacific Grove, CA: Brooks/Cole Publishing Company.

Broderick, C. B. (1993). *Understanding family process: Basics of family systems theory.* Newbury Park, CA: Sage.

Constantine, L. I. (1986). *Family paradigms.* New York, NY: Guilford.

Gontang, R., & Erickson, M. T. (1996). The relationship between Million's personality types and family systems functioning. *American Journal of Family Therapy, 24*(3), 215–116.

Hanley, J. H. (1999). Beyond the tip of the iceberg: Five stages toward cultural competence. *Reaching Today's Youth, 3*(2), 9–12.

Hess, R. D., & Handel, G. (1959). *Family worlds.* Chicago, IL: University of Chicago Press.

Hidecker, M. J. C., Jones, R. S., Imig, D. R., & Villarruel, F. A. (2009). Using family paradigms to improve evidence-based practice. *American Journal of Speech-Language Pathology, 18,* 212–221.

Kantor, D., & Lehr, W. (1975). *Inside the family: Toward a theory of family process.* San Francisco, CA: Jossey-Bass.

Kuhn, T. 1970. *The structure of scientific revolutions* (3rd ed.). Chicago, IL: University of Chicago Press.

Loewen, D. (2017). Tip of the icebergs: Cliched metaphors in education. http://www.davidloewen.org/blog/2017/5/22/tip-of-the-icebergs-clichd-metaphors-in-education

Reiss, D. (1981). *The family's construction of reality.* Cambridge, MA: Harvard University Press.

Steinglass, F., Bennett, L. A., Wolin, S. J., & Reiss, D. (1987). *The alcoholic family.* New York, NY: Basic Books.

Ward, M. (1997). Family paradigms and older-child adoption: A proposal for matching parents' strengths to children's needs. *Family Relations, 46*(3), 257.

Watzlawick, P., Weakland, J. H., & Fisch, R. (1974). *Change: Principles of problem formation and problem resolution.* New York, NY: Norton.

CHAPTER **7**

Family Rituals and Routines
Windows of Family Identity

CHAPTER PREVIEW

In this chapter, readers will learn:

- The differences and similarities between family routines and family rituals.
- How family rituals and routines develop within a family.
- The effect of family rituals and routines on the family, as a whole, as well as on the members of the family.
- Five ways to manage family routines and rituals.
- That families can be creative in making new rituals and changing old ones.

INTRODUCTION

Last year, at the age of 91, Louella died in hospice. While in hospice, she was surrounded by her children, her grandchildren, and her great grandchildren. Visits were simultaneously joyous and painful. Louella had always said she didn't want a funeral. She saw funerals as creepy, macabre, and negative, saying she wanted to be remembered for the vibrant human being she was than the lifeless corpse she would become. After attending funerals for some close family members, she changed her mind. She said she saw that funerals seemed to help the family cope with the loss of their loved ones. Indeed, at her funeral, family and friends came from different states. They laughed, cried, hugged, sang, ate, prayed, and shared stories. When it was over, many of the participants felt a sense of relief and hope and connection, not just to each other but to life itself. After Louella died, the weekly routine of family taking her out to dinner evaporated. It was interesting how something so small now seemed so significant.

In the last chapter, we introduced the concept of family paradigms. Recall that a family paradigm is "the shared, enduring, fundamental, and general assumptions or beliefs that family members subscribe to about the nature and meaning of life, what is important, and how to cope with the world they live in" (Reiss, 1981, chapter 4). In this chapter, we explore particularly powerful family activities deeply entwined with family processes—family rituals and routines. These activities are not the same as "traditions," which often refer to something handed down from the past (sometimes distant past and sometimes within the past of the family), although some

DOI: 10.4324/9781003128717-9

rituals and routines may be traditions, and some may lead to new traditions. Family rituals transcend the mundane, prosaic, ordinary features of life and become a seminal and elegant collection of shared, enduring, fundamental activities that make powerful statements about what our shared beliefs are, what is foundational, and what are the assumptive beliefs of a family group. Daily family routines may seem ordinary, especially compared to rituals, but they are no less important to family. As clinical researchers and family scholars, we have found family routines and rituals serve as a window into a family's underlying shared identity and family paradigm, providing special access to the behavioral and emotional tenor characterizing each family (Wolin & Bennett, 1984, p. 401). If the family were an art project, rituals and routines would be the glue and color that bring it to life!

WHAT ARE RITUALS AND ROUTINES?

Although you may not realize it, most of you are already familiar with family rituals and routines. For example, many rituals occur on holidays, such as Christmas, Thanksgiving, the 4th of July, Passover, Juneteenth, Eid al-Fitr, or Dia de los Muertos. On these special days, families do several things in ways that are different from the ordinary. They trim trees, wrap and open presents, bake turkeys in a special way, color eggs, decorate sugar skulls, have religious ceremonies, go to parades, attend church, eat special foods, abstain from eating food, watch football games, wear special clothing, and so on. Some rituals related to self occur only once in a lifetime, such as (hopefully) one's marriage or (not surprisingly) funerals, although these rituals may be experienced many times for family and friends.

Routines, on the other hand, are more ordinary and tend to be repeated daily. For example, we give each other kisses and hugs in special ways and wave goodbye as we leave for work and school. We tuck small children into bed, tell bedtime stories, eat certain meals at certain times and in certain ways, complete household chores, and have special places to sit and read.

Even though we are all familiar with family rituals and routines, when we try to study this part of the family realm, we discover that the terms we use are fairly vague and elusive, and they also are complicated. In the words of Wolin and Bennett (1984), the term *ritual* is "an elusive concept, on the one hand transparent and conspicuous in its enactment, on the other, subtle and mysterious in its boundaries and effects on participants" (p. 401). Scholars in many fields study rituals and routines but they have had difficulty agreeing about just what they are (Boyce, Jensen, James, & Peacock, 1983; Fiese, 2007). For example, anthropology, sociology, psychology, and family science all have a body of literature about them. Because the scholars in each of these disciplines have differing perspectives, they study different aspects of rituals and do not agree on how to define the terms (Gillis, 1996), and some even use these terms interchangeably.

For the purposes of this text, **rituals** are defined as a set of actions for behaviors that contain symbolic meaning, sacred meaning, or both. The act of performing ritual behavior provides utility to the family group as they attempt to meet the demands of life and attain desired goals. In other words, families that have appropriate ritual systems are more efficient and effective in solving problems and attaining desired goals. **Routines** are also a set of actions engaged in regularly by the family, but they do not carry symbolic meaning. While we have separate definitions for rituals and routines, it is important to keep in mind that these activities often intertwine and may have characteristics of both (Spagnola & Fiese, 2007). We might eat dinner regularly, but occasionally, we have a special dinner with an honored guest or for a certain family celebration. Thus, the ordinary takes on special significance and meaning for the family, blending the routine with ritual. Perhaps an easy way to distinguish between rituals and routines is to compare their commonalities and differences (Figure 7.1).

Rituals and Routines—Commonalities and Differences

Family rituals and routines have several things in common:

1   Family rituals and routines both always involve more than one member of a family.
2   They both have overt or visible behavior or action. Thus, just thinking about something is not a ritual or routine.
3   Family rituals and routines show repetition in the form and in the content of what is done. The form refers to *how* something is done, and the content refers to *what* is done. Some rituals are repeated many times by the same family members, and some are just experienced once in the lifetime of a family member, but other individuals repeat them.
4   **Morphostasis** (the pull for sameness) and **morphogenesis** (the pull for a change) are seen in both rituals and routines. This means they all have some continuity over time, but they also all evolve and change over time as individuals and families develop and as the external environment of families changes.

The following list of attributes and dimensions illustrates differences and helps us distinguish ritual from routine:

1   **Communication.** Routines focus on communication styles that are *functional and instrumental*. That is, we know it is a routine if the communication about the activity communicates something like, "this task needs to be completed before we leave for the movie." On the other hand, the communication that flows from a ritual tells the family members about *identity and informs them about "who they are."* Imagine a Jewish family in the United States performing the rituals associated with Passover. One of those activities may be a spring mega-cleaning, during which every morsel of *chametz* is removed from the home. Chametz is bread, grains, or leavened products that are not used during Passover. These leavened products may be set aside, donated, or perhaps destroyed by burning. Unleavened bread (or matzo) is then purchased or prepared, as are other special items to be used during the Seder, the special meal shared by the family during the Passover holiday. The Seder includes traditional songs and scripted prayers. Part of the ritual includes traditional questions that may be asked by the youngest family member to the oldest family member, who answers with scripted responses that retell the story of the Jewish people leaving the land of Egypt. This ritualized holiday communicates to the new generation a clear identity. It also helps remind the older generations who they are and what values they hold dear.
2   **Commitment.** Rituals and routines are also different with regard to commitment. Routines require little commitment, are usually perfunctory, and take little thought. Taking a morning shower, for example, is not a ritual, per se. It is, however, a valued routine for many—but it requires no interpersonal commitment. *Rituals capture the ideal of commitment.* Remembering someone's birthday is a signal that you are committed to that relationship. Attending a religious service shows commitment to one's God and religion.

3 **Continuity.** Rituals and routines are different with regard to continuity. Routines can change without fanfare, but this is not the case with rituals. For example, if someone decides to eat at 5:30 instead of 6:30, no one is really going to care much. But, if one changes the menu at Thanksgiving and decides to have spaghetti instead of turkey, there could be a revolt. Continuity also exists at an even higher level. Fiese (2007) says that the meanings created with rituals "extend across generations" (p. 11). She also says that rituals communicate across generations about who we (as a family group) will continue to be across generations.

4 **Emotion.** Rituals and routines differ in the amount of emotion that is involved. A great deal of emotion is felt or expressed during weddings, funerals, children leaving home to go to school, the birth of a new child, a Bar Mitzvah, and celebrations of important holidays, such as Christmas and Thanksgiving. When these traditions involve *important emotionality* they become ritualized, and the best term for them is family rituals. There is relatively little emotion in more ordinary events, such as kissing each other hello when returning home each day, talking about the events of the day, vacuuming the carpet once a week, doing dishes, and helping children with their homework. Thus, such activities are referred to as family routines.

5 **Symbolism.** Rituals and routines are different in the amount of **symbolism** involved. Some traditions tend to involve many symbols. Weddings, for example, symbolize leaving the old households, being "given away," making important commitments and covenants, maturity, a **rite of passage** from being single to being married, and so on. Other events such as funerals, Christmas, Bar Mitzvah, infant "welcoming" ceremonies, and christening have several different levels of symbolic meaning, and *the symbolism in these events makes them rituals.* On the other hand, family events or activities that have little symbolism and are ordinary are family routines. For example, daily brushing of one's teeth carries little symbolism and thus is considered a routine.

Some family scholars in recent years have used the term *metaphor* (Imber-Black & Roberts, 1992) to try to describe the symbolic aspect of family rituals. A metaphor in this context refers to an abstract set of ideas or beliefs that is understood and shared but difficult to put into words. Rituals can provide a somewhat tangible representation of the more abstract idea in the metaphor and thereby have a symbolism that provides meaning, purpose, and a sense of completeness and integration that is difficult to acquire in more rational ways of behaving or conversing.

The symbolism in the Thanksgiving holiday illustrates the metaphorical aspects of a typical American ritual. The unity of the family huddled together over a table of food is a metaphor for the unity of the family wherever they are in the world. They give thanks for the bounty before them as a symbol of the end of the harvest.

Some metaphors in family rituals are less desirable and less healthy. One family, for example, celebrated most holidays with alcohol as a prominent feature. Almost always, harsh words were eventually spoken, tempers would flare, and the celebrations would turn into a living hell. Unintentionally, this reoccurring ritual was a mini-version of their entire life. The family was chaotic and had unresolved conflicts that had gone on for several generations, but they were never brought into the open and dealt with. The family retreated into distance, anger, and hostility, and the dependency on alcohol was an escape. All attempts to end the alcohol problem ended in disappointment. It was not until Bob, one of the sons, insisted on the abstinence from alcohol at holiday celebrations (even if it meant the absence of his drinking father) that the family was able to begin to have the healing effects of warm, peaceful holidays and greater harmony and peace in general.

FIGURE 7.1 During the life course, we experience a rainbow of changes and events that are connected together by rituals and passages that define those transitions.

6 **Ordinary vs. Extraordinary.** Rituals and routines differ in how ordinary versus extraordinary their behaviors are. When traditions are part of the usual ways of behaving and they are not special or "staged," the term *routine* is a good term to describe them. Routines involve more ordinary ways of doing things. For example, English families tend to use a knife and fork to eat vegetables, and American families just use a fork, and these patterns are part of the routines for family life. Getting up in the morning rather than the evening, eating three fairly sizable meals rather than ten small meals, and turning the lights out before going to bed are routines.

On the other hand, rituals tend to have *behavior that is relatively unique, unusual, or extraordinary* (Fiese, 2007). For example, when family members bow their heads, are quiet, and say a prayer together in a reverent manner before eating a meal, these are "special" behaviors. Even if these special behaviors occur fairly frequently in the family, they still have a certain "uniqueness" or lack of "routineness" in them. When families get dressed up to celebrate the New Year and they have a special meal, these are fairly unusual ways of behaving and they are, therefore, rituals. Some rituals are so unusual and out of the ordinary that they are sacred or highly dramatic, and it is easy to tell them from routines. Other rituals are just barely unusual. For example, using the special China for certain meals, cleaning the house extra carefully when the company is coming, and getting ready for a special date might be unusual enough that they become family rituals. Even events such as reading the daily newspaper or watching certain television programs can evolve from routine to ritual if they become unusual enough. For example, if family members like to get a certain combination of refreshments, lighting, seating, and emotional involvement while watching certain television programs, these become family rituals.

7 **Preparations and Follow-Up.** Rituals and routines are different in preparation for the event and the follow-up activities. "Ritual is not just the ceremony or actual performance, but the whole process of preparing for it, experiencing it, and reintegration back into everyday life" (Roberts, 2003, p. 8). Even rituals that are fairly frequent have a preparation phase and a back-to-normal phase, and these phases are important parts of the ritual. Routines do not have the same three phases because they are such a normal part of everyday life. An example of these phases is the preparation for the ritual of Thanksgiving dinner. Many American families put a great deal of time into inviting relatives and preparing the food and their home. Many schedules are temporarily changed as miles and miles are traveled in preparation for the Thanksgiving feast and get together. The meal is then eaten, perhaps at one table or many tables; perhaps "buffet style" or "family style." Following the Thanksgiving meal, the family may watch television, attend a movie, or sit and talk (reintegration). If someone does not think these processes are important, witness the lack of students at college campuses during such holidays. When students cannot go to their own home, it is painful to stay alone, and hence many homes "adopt" these students who are unable to return home into their own family rituals.

In summary, rituals, and routines both involve more than one individual, behavior rather than just thinking, repetition, morphogenesis, and morphostasis. Rituals are different from routines in that they tend to involve more emotion, symbolism, and stylized or staged behavior; and they have the three stages of preparing, experiencing, and shifting back into the ordinary. Even though many rituals tend to be quite different from many routines, it is important to also realize that there are some situations where there is overlap and the differences are not clear.

PRINCIPLE 7.1

RITUALS AND ROUTINES ARE ESSENTIAL BUT DIFFERENT

Families who are strong and efficient in goal attainment activities are also effective in creating and maintaining rituals and routines. Rituals are different from routines.

FAMILY RITUALS AND ROUTINES: HOW DO THEY DEVELOP AND HOW DO THEY INFLUENCE US?

In the Garcia household, dinner is usually served around 6 p.m., and bedtime starts at 7:30 p.m. after spot cleaning is done around the house. Five of the six children are off to school by 7:15 a.m., returning at various times of the day. Afternoons often involve family biking or playing at the park. Birthdays are marked with pinatas, cake, and family visitors. The family recently participated in a very special religious ceremony upon the adoption of two children; the ceremony symbolized the eternal nature of the family and the family's commitment to each other. Sundays involve regular church attendance and dinner with the grandparents.

In the Williams household, dinner time varies depending on the sports practices each child is involved in. Lights out bedtime is 9 p.m., often preceded by the family television viewing of America Ninja Warrior. Wake up is 7 a.m., with children off to school by 8:15 a.m. Afternoons are filled with homework before practice. The Williams have a yearly birthday celebration, celebrating the births of all of the children on one day (because their birth dates are close together) with family, friends, and neighbors. Saturdays are reserved for chores if games don't interfere, and Sundays tend to be on the lake.

Both of these families are healthy and thriving, yet both vary in their routines and rituals. How did these routines and rituals develop? What does scientific research say about the influence of family rituals and routines, not only on the family as a whole but also on the individual members?

Development of Rituals and Routines

Bossard and Boll (1950) found that rituals and routines originate in two ways in families. Some rituals and routines are part of cultural traditions, and they are handed down from one generation to the next. Many "traditional" rituals involve holiday celebrations and religious activities, such as having a Thanksgiving dinner, Chinese New Year and Spring Festival, going to the mosque for Friday prayers, and sending Christmas cards.

The second way family rituals and routines originate is for families to create or invent their own. These rituals arise out of immediate family interaction in a specific situation, such as going to bed, getting up, eating meals, doing household chores, relaxing over weekends, and vacationing in the summertime. Whereas the traditional rites are usually rich pageants, the spontaneous ones are relatively simple. They are, however, more numerous, more frequently practiced, and related to a stricter utilitarian purpose. For this reason, they are often more quickly subject to change (Bossard & Boll, 1950; Fiese, 2007). As you examine your own family, you are likely to realize that your family has developed their own routines and unique rituals. For example, in our family, we had the "birthday bunny," that would hide gifts about the house for the birthday child to find. This tradition developed when our family had little money but discovered young children often enjoyed "the thrill of the hunt" more than the gift itself! What routines and rituals are unique to *your* family?

Many family rituals and routines develop over time following a developmental sequence related to the family life cycle (Fiese, 2007). When a new family begins with the union of two or more people, they pull from their past to develop unique family rituals. Routines begin as the couple negotiate schedules, priorities (clean house or not?), daily needs, and past experience. During the formative stage of the family life cycle, there also tends to be a searching for events that can be ritualized. For example, when two people start dating, they usually create rituals around events that would otherwise be minor things. For example, they might pick out a song that is "their song," and whenever they hear it, they enact their own special ritual of hugging, smiling, and commenting on it being something special to them. Or, they might have anniversary celebrations of things such as the day they met, their first date, the day they got engaged, the day they decided to live together, and so on. Other possibilities are they might develop rituals about certain places that had unusual importance to them, such as the place where they decided to get married.

As families continue to acquire new rituals, some of the rituals they created in the formative stages of family development fade away and are no longer remembered or celebrated in the childrearing stage. Further, the way rituals and routines are emphasized changes at different stages of the family life cycle. When families have children between 2 and about 12 years old, they find themselves creating and experiencing routines and rituals for bathing, bedtime, eating, and visiting certain friends and relatives. Also, during this childrearing stage of family development, many families find they emphasize some of the traditional holidays, such as Easter and Christmas, in elaborate ways that center around the children.

As families move into the stages where they have teenage children and are launching children, their rituals and routines continue to evolve. Youth and young adults are more mobile and independent, often necessitating changes in family routines and rituals as outside pressures enter the scene. They often prefer lively rituals that involve friends, music, and action, while the parents usually find themselves preferring more sedentary and symbolic rituals. Parents may also find themselves dealing with adolescent autonomy and the young person's desire to not participate in certain family routines or rituals. This may result in family conflict. Fortunately, most families are able to weather such changes well.

The post-childrearing stages of the family cycle may bring new routines and rituals. Grandparenting ushers in routines and rituals such as taking small children to parks and zoos, walking young children around the neighborhood, reminiscing, and telling stories about how things "used to be." Often the younger generations patiently, and sometimes not so patiently, listen over and over again to stories that become part of the family folklore. The routines and rituals of aging couples become even less energetic, but they remain an important part of the emotional and symbolic fabric of the family life of the elderly.

Influence of Family Routines and Rituals

When reviewing the literature on family routines and rituals, one is struck by their importance for both family and individual well-being, affecting us physically, socioemotionally, cognitively, relationally, and culturally. Fiese et al. (2002) reviewed 50 years of the scientific literature and found family routines and rituals are associated with children's health, academic achievement, adolescent identity, stronger family relationships, and marital satisfaction. It's not difficult to imagine the long-term influence of even the most mundane routines, such as handwashing (decreasing transmission of viruses), regular sleep schedules, and family mealtimes that allow for regular family interchange. The benefits of family routines and rituals also are found in families who have a member with a chronic health condition (Crespo et al., 2013). Routines and rituals are associated with more positive outcomes for the person with the chronic condition, as well as the other members of the family. Fiese et al. (2002) write, "Although families may be challenged to meet the busy demands of juggling work and home, there is reason to believe that routines and rituals may ease the stress of daily living" (p. 388).

Family scientists have identified at least seven specific goals that family rituals and routines can help with: (1) creating **healthy emotional ties**, (2) **membership changes**, (3) **healing**, (4) **identity definition** and redefinition, (5) providing **rites of passage**, (6) creating a sense of **meaning and purpose**, while dealing with paradoxes and ambiguities, and (7) **providing a sense of order and predictability**.

1 **Creating Healthy Emotional Ties.** Rituals tend to deal with the more cheerful and optimistic aspects of life providing positive emotional bonds. Rituals also provide a reservoir

of such things as goodwill, feelings of "we can do it," "we're together," and trust. This helps families cope with the tragic and challenging aspects of life. Homeless families who were randomly assigned to participate in monthly birthday parties at their shelter showed higher levels of happiness, hope, and feelings of parental empowerment compared with those who didn't participate (Leong, Berzin, & Lee, 2019). In their study of LGBT adults, Hanke, van Egmond, Crespo, and Boer (2016) found that family rituals and routines help these adults to flourish, providing a sense of closeness, positive family environment, connection, and support resulting in increased psychological well-being.

Rituals and routines also can help provide a sense of "home" and a feeling that the world is, at least in some ways, a good and comfortable place. They provide memories that lead to the often-told stories and myths that create a mythology helpful to the sense of family. Rituals and routines include many soft, tender, and affectionate moments, helping family members learn that emotionality is appropriate and desirable.

2 **Membership Changes.** Families deal with membership changes in many ways. Some changes are major events such as births, deaths, marriages, and divorces; most cultures and families have rather elaborate rituals that help them deal with these major transitions (Gillis, 1996). For example, weddings help individuals, families, and friends make the adjustment of two families of origin coming together and a new family unit being created. Announcements, christenings, and other baby-naming rituals help new members be assimilated, and funerals and wakes help families cope with death. A Bar Mitzvah redefines membership in the family and in the Jewish community, and graduation ceremonies help families redefine the relationship of parents and children and their involvement with school systems.

Some major family events have few rituals making the symbolic and emotional adjustment of family members more difficult. For example, there are few rituals associated with divorce and adoption. There are none when couples begin living together or stop living together. Even though the number of stepfamilies has increased dramatically in recent years, there are few ways to ritualize the formation of a stepfamily. Weddings are used to create the marital part of stepfamilies, but the children have a peripheral role in the wedding, and sometimes they are even excluded. One consequence is that often the marital part of the new stepfamily is formed symbolically and emotionally, but the family system is not usually formed as gracefully and effectively.

An extreme example of this can be seen in a stepfamily that came for therapy due to stepparent–stepchild conflict that was rapidly leading to the exclusion of a child. This couple's wedding was celebrated with extended family and friends, but their five children from their prior marriages, ages 6 to 12, were barred from attending. The wedding ritual had publicly affirmed the new couple, but not the new stepfamily (Imber-Black, 1992, p. 69).

3 **Healing.** All individuals and families encounter situations in which healing is needed. Healing is needed after periods of conflict or when there is pain and grief, reconciliation, or death. When other major changes occur, such as retirement, disabilities, and midlife crises, rituals provide a vehicle that can help healing. Doty (1986) explained that rituals can be transformative, which is part of their wonderment and power. When transitions, catastrophes, and unexpected events occur in a family, rituals have a healing power that allows, encourages, and facilitates changes.

4 **Identity Definition and Redefinition.** Rituals and routines can help individuals and families create, maintain, and change identities. Weddings, for example, do more than just redefine memberships. They transform identities by some members of the family becoming a spouse and others becoming in-laws. Rituals and routines, such as birthday celebrations, daily goodbyes and greetings, and goodnight kisses, reaffirm who the individuals are, their importance to the family, and the emotional connections that maintain identity and create enduring intimacy.

Many of the religious, ethnic, and cultural rituals in which families participate have important implications for identity creation, change, and maintenance. In them, specific foods, dresses, and ceremonies might serve to symbolize the identity theme. Such celebrations define an individual's identity as part of a larger cultural group. For example, the stomp dance practiced by various Eastern and Southeastern American Indian tribes (including Cherokee, Algonquian, Seminole, and Choctaw) involves men, women, and children moving counterclockwise around a fire. The fire symbolizes the life-giving, sacred sun, and the dance brings generations together in community identity (Conlan, n.d.).

In the multiethnic society of the United States, participation in such rituals as the Chinese New Year or Greek Orthodox Easter allows even highly assimilated persons to stay connected to their ethnic and religious identity. Cultural rituals, such as Veteran's Day, Mother's Day, and Father's Day, all involve the identity theme, as these mark and celebrate particular aspects of people's identities (Imber-Black, 1992, p. 73).

Interesting use of family rituals and routines is found in families that have transracial adoptions (Nelson & Colaner, 2018). A White family may use special routines for a Black child's skin and hair care. Children adopted from China may find their adoptive parents incorporating aspects of their birth culture into their daily lives, from meals to art. Participation in ethnic festivals or recognition of holidays from the birth culture may be done in an effort to connect the children to their roots. Interestingly, this use of routines and rituals also influences the adoptive family's perspective and family identity (Nelson & Colaner, 2018).

5 **Rites of Passage.** Some rituals provide the vehicle for rites of passage that facilitate growth and change. There are few rites of passage during adolescence in American culture, but some cultural groups such as Judaism and several American Indian cultures have a number of rituals that help families and individuals mark the transitions from childhood to adulthood. In the Southwestern United States, on the Mesclarao Apache reservation, young women reaching menarche participate in a multi-day ritual called the "Isánáklésh Gotal" (Tribal Wisdom, n.d.). This ritual has been handed down for generations. Through song and sacred rituals, the girl is symbolically transformed from girl into deity and then into an Apache woman. This ritual not only solidifies a tribal identity but also an identity of the woman. Upon completion of the ritual, the young woman's status within her tribe also changes.

Rites of passage rituals also have the power to be therapeutic. For example, the ritual in funerals helps the participants move from one stage of life, through grief, and on to another stage of life.

6 **Meaning and Purpose.** Fiese (2007) suggested that rituals help families deal with the deepest levels of shared meanings and values. Not only is it shared meaning of what things

are now, but how things should be and can be. There are many abstract and ultimate concerns that are important to people that are difficult to understand, and clear answers are elusive. For example, questions about the origins of life, the purposes of even existing, the nature of reality, the role of birth and death, the role of the sacred, and the possibility of life after death are challenging concerns. They are challenging intellectually and emotionally because many of them are ultimate and profound, and it is difficult for individuals and families to come to terms with these concerns.

Rituals provide a vehicle that helps families find and maintain solutions to these complicated and ultimate concerns. The symbolism in rituals, such as christening, baptism, funerals, new year celebrations, Thanksgiving, and Easter, each help provide a sense of meaning and purpose that would be elusive and difficult to have without these or similar rituals.

Rituals and routines also help with another aspect of meaning and purpose. Life has many forms of injustice and inequity. Bocknek (2018) observes that African American children experience a world "made even harsher by racism, [and] family rituals may protect and buffer risk" (p. 704). African American families identify racial socialization as one of the most important aspects of parenting in a world where racism exists (Carter-Black, 2001); rituals and routines that involve interactions with immediate and extended family can assist children in dealing with this challenging world, building personal strengths, developing skills, and strengthening identity.

In short, we face many aspects of life in which there is little sense of control and many contradictions and paradoxes. Rituals can help families deal with these complexities. As Roberts (2003) observed:

> Ritual can hold both sides of a contradiction at the same time. We all live with the ultimate paradoxes of life/death, connection/distance, ideal/real, and good/ evil. Ritual can incorporate both sides of contradictions so that they can be managed simultaneously. For instance, a wedding ceremony has within it both loss and mourning and joy and celebration. People say, "You're not losing a daughter, you're gaining a son–in–law." Parents give their child away at the same time as they welcome a new member to their extended family.
>
> (p. 17)

7   **Order and Predictability.** Families can also use rituals and routines to help create a sense of order and predictability in life. They help create a sense of "home." For example, routines such as preparing and eating meals, leaving and returning home, dressing and undressing, preparing one's self to be dressed and groomed in an acceptable way, and having a favorite chair to relax in at the end of a day provide a sense of continuity, comfort, and peace that is an important part of life (Gillis, 1996).

It is likely that rituals and routines contribute in different ways to this goal. Rituals probably provide a sense of order and predictability about the more important issues, questions, and paradoxes of life, and routines seem to contribute in a different way. They help provide a sense of order in the daily rhythms and cycles and contribute to a sense of comfort. The daily routines probably contribute to homes being a haven or place of refuge, a place where people can let their hair down, be "offstage," and escape from the competitiveness and aggression of the marketplace or school.

Many reasons have been given for *how* rituals and routines help families accomplish these goals, including their numerous repetitions in family interactions. Meredith, Abbott, Lamanna, and Sanders (1989) summarized additional reasons:

> Family rituals, first and foremost, encourage contact between family members, usually in a relaxed, enjoyable setting. Family conflicts and problems are temporarily set aside …. Rituals may help to bridge the intergenerational gaps that separate family members by providing activity between parents and children and extended family members. A major theme of most family rituals is appreciation of one another and the enjoyment of life together; therefore, commitment to the family may be renewed by the regular observance of family rituals. Family values and beliefs may be learned and perpetuated through rituals fostering a sense of unity and oneness. In sum, rituals may be family strengthening for many reasons.
>
> (p. 77)

Wise use of rituals tends to help families create continuity, solidarity, integration, and bonds (Meredith, 1985; Meredith, Abbott, & Adams, 1986; Meredith et al., 1989; Schvaneveldt & Lee, 1983). Sacred family rituals, such as the Latter-Day Saint Family Home Evening or scripture study, can enhance structure, meaning, and family unity; and even family prayer can influence relationships, bringing family together and providing intergenerational transmission of religion (Chelladurai, Dollahite, & Marks, 2018; Marks et al., 2020). Rituals and routines also seem to provide a protective and stabilizing influence for children in homes experiencing challenges related to divorce, remarriage, poverty, disasters, migration, death, racism, or single parenting (Boles et al., 2017; Fiese et al., 2002; Masten, 2018).

PRINCIPLE 7.2

RITUALS AND ROUTINES

Family rituals and routines are valuable resources, and when they are wisely used, they can help families attain important goals, such as unity, closeness, intimacy, meaning, membership changes, and so on.

MANAGING RITUALS

Rituals and routines are not inherently healthy and facilitating. They can be unhealthy and destructive if families are not wise in the way they create them and carry them out. Further, managing routines and rituals can be difficult in certain circumstances. For example, compared with families of typically developing children, families with adolescents who have autism have fewer meals together as well as more difficult mealtimes (Touhy & Yazdani, 2018). In addition, having an adolescent with autism appears to limit family participation in community activities, effectively increasing the social isolation of the family.

Considerable variability exists in how many and the types of rituals families have (Wolin & Bennett, 1984, p. 406). It is important to note that people and families differ in the amount of ritualization that is desirable. Some families find it helpful to have a relatively large number of rituals and others find it effective to invest less of their time and energy in rituals. There is some evidence that the parental and grandparental generations like more family rituals than teenagers and young adults (Meredith et al., 1989).

So how can families be wise and effective in their use of rituals and routines? Research and clinical experience have identified four ideas that can help families in this area: (a) amount of ritualization; (b) distinctiveness of rituals; (c) balance stability and change of rituals; and (d) appropriate use of rituals.

Amount of Ritualization

Overall, research suggests a *moderate* amount of ritualization is helpful to families; it is usually disruptive to have too much (**over-ritualization**) or too little (**under-ritualization**) (Bossard & Boll, 1950; Meredith et al., 1989).

Over-Ritualization

Over-ritualization can occur when families try to incorporate too much input from people or organizations outside the family. It can be overwhelming if young couples try to incorporate all of the rituals from both parental families and also try to include the rituals that are encouraged by various cultural, civic, religious, and fraternal groups. Couples need to selectively adopt and include rituals in their new family.

Over-ritualization also can occur when families never give up rituals that have lost their usefulness. For example, many families who have young children find it meaningful to have a large number of rituals around Christmas time. Later, however, as the children mature, some of the rituals are less relevant and important, and if some of the members of the family try to continue them, it can lead to being overwhelmed by the rituals.

Under-Ritualization

Under-ritualization occurs when families have few or no rituals. Our fast-paced society emphasizes economic, occupational, and materialistic parts of life, creating a hustle-bustle attitude in which many families have little time with the whole family or even much of the family together. Further, a family emphasis on passive entertainment, such as watching television and listening to music with headphones on, can lead to reduced attention to family rituals. The result of this is a loss of family and individual identity, loss of structure and stability, and little cohesiveness.

Families may experience many important or traumatic events that currently do not have adequate ritualization. Such events could include early retirement due to health changes, divorce, rape, coping with physical abuse or incest, miscarriage, and life-course transitions. Rituals addressing such circumstances could help unite people, strengthen families, provide support, allow containment of emotions, and move participants on to acceptance and positive growth (Laird, 1988; Quinn, Newfield, & Protinsky, 1985). Consider the following two examples where events are typically under-ritualized:

The first example shows how under-ritualization was disabling in one family's experience with a stillborn child. The family had an unwritten rule that no one was to talk about the death. The body of the baby was taken from the mother soon after the birth. The mortuary flew the baby inside a casket, while the family drove in a car, from one state to a distant, desired state of burial. The casket was taken from the airport to the burial plot in the back

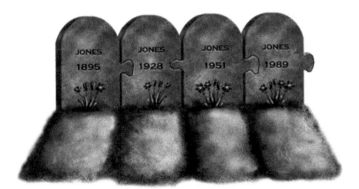

FIGURE 7.2 The death of a family member can shake the foundation of a family. It can also be a time of growth and healing.

of a station wagon, while the family rode in a separate car. The father declined to carry the casket from the car to the graveside before a very short memorial service. Few visits were made to the cemetery and talk about the child was almost nonexistent resulting in a family entrapped in their grief. What a change could have taken place if rituals had been used along the way, even onetime rituals!

Rituals could have helped this family work through their feelings of loss and facilitated conversations about their grief and crushed expectations. For example, it could have helped if someone were in charge of transporting the casket and baby and if a more elaborate funeral or graveside ceremony occurred, where people could express consolation, support, and understanding. A funeral followed by a luncheon, dinner, or time to visit where family and friends could gather could provide opportunities for the parents and children to express their deep-felt emotions and allow for acceptance and moving on. Such rituals can incorporate both sides of the contradictions involving life and death, and allow the participants to see, understand, experience, and cope with these paradoxes (Figure 7.2).

In our second example, an unexpected ritual provided the support needed as a result of a very unusual but traumatic event. One of our students managed a river tube rental company along the shores of a popular river. One day, she was notified that a patron had slipped off a tube and was feared drowned. She quickly grabbed one of her employees to help search the banks of the river for the missing man. Unfortunately, she and her employee, a Diné (Navajo), had to pull his body from the river and wait for the sheriff to arrive. Touching a corpse is a huge taboo among the Diné, and the employee looked visibly frightened. Both the manager and employee were shaken by the horror they experienced. A short while later, the employee told his manager that he had arranged for a Navajo medicine man to perform a purifying ceremony for the employee and his manager, if she agreed. Our student readily agreed. Following the ceremony, she said she indeed felt better and was able to move on without the awful experience weighing on her as it had been. Rituals in these traumatic areas can acknowledge the destructive aspects of these experiences and help create new structures for the future. They can help celebrate the survival of the participants rather than leave them as victims, and this can help open communication about the events, use more of the family and community resources, and create cohesion rather than fragmentation in the families.

Distinctiveness of Rituals

A group of researchers discovered an idea that can help families be wise in the way they manage their rituals. The idea has to do with the *distinctiveness* of family rituals. They found that when families have an undesirable characteristic, such as alcoholism, it is helpful to keep the rituals distinctive from or separated from the problem. Apparently, if family rituals and routines can be separated from the family problems, there tends to be less generational transmission of the problems. For example, if families with alcoholics are able to keep alcohol separate from their holiday celebrations, it decreases the likelihood that alcoholism will be passed on to future generations. Similarly, if families are able to have pleasant dinners together without alcohol, even though they have an alcohol problem in the family, it helps decrease the likelihood that the alcohol problem will be passed on.

This idea probably works with other kinds of family problems, too. Thus, if families have problems, such as physical abuse, fighting, closeness avoidance, aggressiveness, excessive competitiveness, or lack of intimacy, it is probably true that the more they can separate these problems from their family rituals, the greater the likelihood the problems will not be passed on to future generations. A practical implication of this is to try to agree to "not fight," "not drink," "be nice," or "be home" during family rituals—such as at Thanksgiving or birthdays.

Balance in Stability and Change

One of the paradoxes of rituals is that they are stable and change simultaneously. They need to have some stability and be repeated over and over again to be rituals, but at the same time, individuals and families are continually developing and changing, and rituals need to adapt to these changes.

Healthy flexibility is seen with the Muslim tradition of Eid Al-Fitr, a joyous three-day celebration marking the end of Ramadan and the Breaking of the Fast. The celebrations involve generous gift giving (including money), new clothes, visiting friends and family, and lots of sweets. Eid is celebrated more elaborately when there are small children in a home. As the children get older, however, the celebrations continue but are simpler. It also is illustrated when families with teenagers find themselves doing many of their rituals without the teenage children. Parents of small children and school-age children enjoy such rituals as family picnics and family reunions, but adolescents are in the middle of individuating, so forcing the teens to attend could have more undesirable effects than desirable ones. It is possible that teenagers and young adults have so many other demands, challenges, activities, and developmental tasks they are trying to manage that this is a period of life when it is effective to be less involved in family rituals. Being less involved in family rituals might actually help young adults disengage from their parental family and create their own family. Then, as they create their own new family, they might find it enabling to get selectively reinvolved in some of the rituals in their larger family and create their own for their new family.

Healthy flexibility occurs when the type of birthday parties given for children change as they grow older. Young children enjoy small family parties with games, cakes, and singing, but teens are different. They tend to want more friends over or to go out somewhere for a movie or other activity. Rituals must be flexible enough to change over time, so they are meaningful to the participants and carry the power that is potentially available in them. It is wise to "include" members of a family in rituals to promote the shared aspect of them, but this, too, should not be overdone.

Too much stability occurs when families get "stuck" in certain developmental stages and try to maintain rituals after they have outlived their usefulness. Some families maintain rituals in rigid, repressive, and degrading ways to preserve the status quo. These rigid patterns appear sometimes when families experience serious problems, such as incestuous behavior, and they try to have rigid rituals to keep their secrets from getting out.

Another form of rigidity can occur when substance abuse, such as alcoholism, dominates rituals. When all of a family's activities end up with heavy drinking, it can dominate what is done so much that new ways of doing things cannot emerge. Changing such rituals, though, can be difficult, as found by one man who had joined Alcoholics Anonymous and informed his large family that the yearly Easter celebration would be alcohol free. Some of his adult siblings refused to attend the celebration. On a positive note, however, the remaining family celebrated a calm and enjoyable Easter without the drama of fights or even police presence, and future holidays followed suit.

Family reunions also illustrate the need for balance in stability and variety. If the only activity in a family reunion ritual is to sit around and talk about ancestors not known to the young people, and the young people are forced to listen for hours, it soon becomes drudgery for them. Compare that to reunions in which food is part of the ritual, different activities are available, such as short programs, games, prizes, treats, hiking, swimming, and so on. Which would attract future attendance at a family reunion?

Avoid Inappropriate Use of Rituals

Rituals can be abused in many ways. For example, parents can use rituals to try to control children long after the children should be in control of their own lives. Also, rituals can be used to perpetuate pseudo-mutuality, skeletons, cross-generational alliances, avoiding letting children go, avoiding independence, and so on. They are enormously powerful because they tap into a set of dimensions that are hard to identify, define, articulate, and understand, as they deal with deep emotions implicitly and symbolically rather than with simple, overt, cognitive processes. Attempts to defy them can be defined as disloyalty.

Another way rituals can be abused is to adapt them to certain family members while ignoring others. This is referred to as *skewed ritualization* (Roberts, 2003). For example, one wife emphasized her traditions and demanded that the husband's traditions be eliminated. They visited her extended family, to the exclusion of the husband's, and her past family's rituals became the present family's rituals. Not only was the husband's wealth of experiences and memories lost, but also a number of new problems were created by the lack of balance.

PRINCIPLE 7.3

MANAGING RITUALS AND ROUTINES

Managing rituals in terms of amount of ritualization, distinctiveness, balance, and appropriate use can be enabling to families, allowing them to thrive while supporting the individual members.

GUIDELINES WHEN CREATING OR CHANGING RITUALS

Family scientists have discovered that deliberately trying to create new rituals can help families accomplish their developmental tasks and cope with life's difficulties. One couple, for example, was struggling with past incidents of anger, mistrust, hurt, and lack of understanding. Extramarital affairs were present, as well as verbal declarations of wanting something different than what they had. A second wedding and honeymoon and burning and burying of symbolic items from the dark past helped them create a new start. They ritualized the end of the past ways of doing things and creatively used new rituals to make things better and different. As a result, the couple was able to change. It was a powerful way of getting "permission" to start over while cutting off the old way.

In the 1970s, a group of Italian scholars began prescribing new rituals as a strategy for dealing with problems and difficulties for families seeking family therapy (Palazzoli, Boscolo, Cecchin, & Prata, 1977, 1978; Palazzoli, Cirillo, Selvini, & Sorrentino, 1989). Gradually, more and more family therapists and family life educators gained experience in helping families with rituals and developed a few guidelines that are helpful for families who are trying to create or modify rituals (van der Hart, 1983; Whiting, 1988). Although much of this work has focused on rituals in the context of family therapy or psychotherapy, other family professionals and even individual families can likely adapt this information to create and modify family rituals in a positive way.

When trying to deliberately create or modify rituals, it is important to consider the following: (a) the goals, which are the purposes or objectives; (b) the form, which refers to how the rituals are carried out; and (c) the content, which refers to what is symbolized and what the behaviors are.

Goals

When someone wants to design or modify a family ritual, it is helpful to have at least a vague idea about what it is one wants to accomplish. Imber-Black (1992) referred to this part of rituals as the "ritual theme." A large number of scholars refer to this part of rituals as the functions of the rituals (Doty, 1986). The term in ecosystems theory that describes this part of rituals is the term *goal*. Seven goals were described earlier in this chapter, but that list of goals is illustrative rather than exhaustive. There can be many other goals. Some additional examples are celebration, adventure, and preserving memories.

Often when people want to design or change rituals, they are dealing with more than one goal. Further, goals can be vague and difficult to describe, perhaps little more than vague impressions, images, metaphors, or similes. That is okay—it is not always necessary to have a clear statement of goals and how they will be quantified or measured.

Form

Counselors are not sure whether it is wise to focus on the form or the content first. They seem to both gradually evolve in a "chicken and egg" manner as ideas about what to do influence ideas about how to do it and vice versa. Eventually, however, it is helpful to think through the form of the ritual. Whiting (1988) called this part of designing rituals the "design elements."

It refers to issues such as how open or closed the rituals will be, how time and space will be used, and how much repetition will occur.

The open versus closed aspect of rituals refers to how much the ritual is rigid versus flexible. In rituals that are quite closed, there is little room for innovation or variation and there are understandings or rules that clearly define what is to be done. Of course, all rituals require some closed or structured aspects. More open rituals have fewer rules and more flexibility for innovation, creativity, and individual differences. Rituals vary widely in how closed versus open rituals they are, as they are tailored to different situations and to the family's personal preferences, values, and lifestyle.

When developing rituals, timing and placement of our family rituals are critical. Of course, this implies that attention must be paid to planning and organizing these events to achieve the goals of the ritual. (Whiting, 1988, p. 89).

Finally, repetition is an important aspect to consider when creating or modifying rituals. The frequency of family rituals will be repeated varies depending on goals and context. For example, a prayer or a period of silence before eating a meal and kissing each other hello and goodbye are two rituals that are performed daily in many families. Conversely, giving a person a name or having a funeral are rituals that occur only once. Families might want to create a ritual that will occur once to help them deal with unique situations, such as adoption, letting go of a relationship, accepting a family member back into the family after the person has been excluded, or coping with personal or financial failure.

Content

In many ways, this is the most important aspect to consider when designing or modifying rituals because it gets to the heart of what rituals are about. The content deals with at least three different parts of rituals: (a) the behaviors that are performed, (b) the symbolism in what is done, and (c) the emotional aspects of the ritual.

The Behaviors

Whiting (1988) identified several ritual techniques or symbolic actions that help us understand the kinds of behavior or action that can be used in designing rituals. One of the categories he identified is *letting go*. By letting go, we mean that during several kinds of rituals (death, marriage, graduation) there is a time when it is appropriate for the family members to express a willingness to release the individual(s) who are leaving. You will notice that in many rituals, there is a time when final hugs are given, a flower is placed on the casket, or some other signal is given that it is time to let the person leave.

A second category of behaviors Whiting identified is *giving and receiving*. The exchanging of food, gifts, verbal expressions, and cards are the hallmarks of some rituals. For example, when a teenager is ready to begin driving, the parents could give the child a set of keys to the family automobile to symbolize the new status in an important step toward adulthood. When young adults are ready to leave home to attend college, families can use giving and receiving behaviors in rituals to help them accomplish this transition. The parents could give the student a computer that could say, "You're in charge of your life, and you can do it." We heard a story about one young adult who, on leaving home, gave his parents an apron to use during family barbecues. He had an extra string sewn on that was broken. He wanted to remind his dad that family life would go on even though he was moving away. In the United Kingdom, there is frequently a major birthday party for someone turning 21 years of age, sometimes called a key party. During this time, the birthday person is symbolically given the "keys" to the house, indicating they have moved into the status of adult and no longer need to rely on someone else to let them in. Most birthday cards in the United Kingdom for this occasion will sport some type of key emblem.

A third category of behavior in Whiting's model is *documenting*. This is the process of writing something in an "official" way to document something, such as an event, a change, or a transition. Sending thank-you cards is a simple example. Getting a marriage license and writing a will are other documenting processes that have enormous symbolism and can be used as rituals.

Love letters document commitment, care, concern, and interest. Many families have a ritual of sending notes of appreciation and love. Even something as subtle and minor as knowing that family members will text to let others know they have safely arrived at a destination is a form of documentation, and when it is ritualized in a family, it can have many positive effects.

Documenting rituals can be used to help family members remember pleasant experiences. For example, putting the pictures from a family vacation into a special album or electronically posting them on a website, thus making a place for it among other precious belongings documents and cements the positive aspects of the experience. Having a picture enlarged and hung in a special place in the home documents membership, importance, unity, and special events.

The Symbolism

The second part of the content is the symbolism, and it is one of the most important parts of rituals. As Turner (1967) argued, "the symbol is the smallest unit of ritual" (p. 19). Thus, as people create or recreate rituals, consideration of symbols is key. Symbols are tangible or observable things that represent something else. Many different things can be symbols. For example, they can be tangible objects, emblems, tokens, words, phrases, images, figures, or signs. The symbol derives its meaning from the object, idea, or other part of reality that it represents.

Families and individuals differ in the kinds of symbols that are important and can be important to them. Some families find symbols of the past, both of the current generation and of previous generations, to be important. Other families studiously avoid symbols of the past. Some families find religious symbols meaningful, and others find them empty and uncomfortable.

One way to try to understand the symbolism in a family is to try to identify the family paradigms that guide the family's thinking, images, and beliefs about what is important. Because family paradigms are highly abstract ideas, it is sometimes helpful to look at more specific parts of families to get clues about their paradigmatic beliefs. An examination of a family's main goals can provide helpful clues about these abstract ideals and beliefs. Also, clues can be acquired by observing the tangible objects families put on their walls, the way they dress, the way they decorate their home, and the way they relate to their community.

A helpful clue about what is symbolized in a family is to identify the events or things that evoke strong emotion. It is our experience that when the parts of life that bring out strong emotions can be identified, an understanding of the family's symbols and things that are symbolized is close.

The Emotion

There are few ideas that all family scientists can agree on, but an idea where there is widespread agreement is that the emotional aspects of the family realm are extremely important.

As a result, family theorists, family researchers, family therapists, and family life educators all pay great attention to emotional processes as they try to understand and help families. This makes it doubly ironic that the literature in the field about rituals almost ignores the emotional aspects of rituals. All the scholars who have studied rituals highlight the cognitive aspects: the symbolism, the meanings, the metaphors, and perceptions. They also pay a great deal of attention to the repetition, the staging, the functions, and the therapeutic and developmental value of rituals. Unfortunately, however, the role of the emotional aspects of rituals is almost ignored in the literature about family rituals.

Therapists and educators who use rituals to help families include the emotional aspects, but when they write books and papers to describe what they are doing and what rituals are, the emotional aspects are hardly ever mentioned. This is an unfortunate omission. We are convinced that it is the combination of the symbolism and emotionality that makes rituals such a rich and helpful part of the family realm. Therefore, it is helpful to think about the emotional aspects of rituals whenever we try to help families develop or change rituals. Also, when families want to change or invent rituals, they would be well-advised to pay as much attention to the emotional aspects as any of the other aspects of rituals.

Emotional aspects deal with how people feel as they are involved with rituals. Are they attracted or repulsed? Do they experience feelings such as warmth, closeness, integrity, peace, or fulfillment? Or are the feelings generally negative? For example, is a graduation experience an inconvenience or a fulfillment? Is a wedding and reception or open house viewed as a charade and superficially irrelevant experience? Are family celebrations of holidays an ordeal that is annoying or a fulfilling emotional experience?

Most family rituals involve some degree of emotional involvement, and some of them are extremely intense. One of the issues that is either overtly or covertly dealt with when designing and changing rituals is what type of emotion is expected and tolerated. How much intensity is desirable or considered appropriate culturally? At funerals, for example, some individuals in the immediate family may exhibit crying, wailing, and other forms of emotional distress; whereas in other families, emotions are meant to be inhibited. At weddings, there are almost always tears.

The analog messages and the relationship messages that are sent with rituals help define what is appropriate emotionally, and occasionally it might be wise to turn these nonverbal communication processes into verbal communication. For example, when a family is designing a healing ritual to cope with a loss or serious problem, it might be helpful to observe that this is a time when it could be acceptable, even desirable, to experience some deeply felt emotions.

The neglect of the emotional aspect of rituals by family scholars means that thus far, we have few ideas about how or when to deal with the emotional aspects of family rituals. Often, this may be due to the invisible influence of culture, which may result in misunderstandings. We hope this deficiency will be corrected in the coming years.

Discussions in Diversity: Family Strengths and Resilience

Sanchez, Letiecq, and Ginsberg (2019) suggest a new theoretical framework of family strengths and resilience. They point out that most family theories do not integrate an indigenous lens and contrast Bronfenbrenner's bioecological theory, of layered nested circles from the individual to the overarching macrosystem (culture), with a spiral indigenous cosmological "wheel of life" that represents the dynamic, expanding, connectedness aspects of life (Figure 7.3).

From this unique perspective, they examine five domains related to family strength and resilience, including family rituals. As discussed previously, family rituals have been found to increase family cohesion and assist in identity

FIGURE 7.3 Conceptions of family include Bronfenbrenner's nested circles and the indigenous "Wheel of Life." Adapted from Sanchez et al, 2019.

development, not only as an individual but as a family. Further, family rituals transmit cultural information, values, and beliefs.

Sanchez et al. (2019) demonstrate how the rituals of indigenous cultures "reflect their alignment with life's transcendental goals: staying connected to the creator (i.e., source of life), nature, and staying centered and aligned with their most deeply held values and principles…[sustaining] harmony in life on the individual, family, and community levels" (p. 570). They go on to describe an Inkan ritual of Yuyaymanay (meditation):

> This particular family ritual takes place after dinner, with the eyes closed, under the guidance of the elder of the household. The meditation starts with the youngest family member, who recalls each event of the day aloud, from the moment she or he wakes up in the morning to the present, as if by a narrator in a movie in which the narrator doubles as the main actor. After the youngest family member has finished, the next youngest member does the same, and so on, until every person has a turn. Throughout this process, the self-correcting nature in each person provides feedback in the form of short realizations of right and wrong or correct and incorrect deeds and aha moments.
>
> (p. 570)

Questions to Discuss:

- *How does the wheel of life differ from the nested circles described by Bronfenbrenner?*
- *What routines and rituals does your family engage in that you believe helped your family in times of difficulty and crisis? Conversely, if your family did not engage in regular routines or many rituals, how could they have assisted in such times?*
- *What family routines and rituals have you observed (or participated in) in families that were "different" from yours? What feelings did these rituals seem to evoke in participants?*
- *How can diverse families use routines and rituals to maintain cultural and generational connections?*

SUMMARY

Family rituals and routines are valuable resources, and when they are wisely used, they can help families attain important goals such as unity, closeness, intimacy, meaning, membership changes, and so on. Seven family goals with which rituals and routines can help are creating healthy emotional ties; making changes in family membership; healing, forming, and redefining the identities of individuals and families; providing rites of passage that help families and individuals make developmental transitions; helping families create a sense of meaning and purpose; and creating an adequate sense of order and predictability.

Rituals and routines can be enabling or disabling in families. Therefore, families should be wise in how they create and enact them. Four ideas that can help families be wise are to have moderate ritualization, to have distinctiveness when there are problems a family does not want to pass on to future generations, to have a balance of stability and change, and to avoid using rituals in inappropriate ways.

Family scientists and practitioners have developed a set of guidelines to assist family in developing healthy rituals, focusing on goals, form, and content of rituals. Anyone interested in changing the roles of rituals and routines in their family may find their guidelines helpful.

STUDY QUESTIONS

1 What is a ritual?
2 Define the term *routine*.
3 Name three ways rituals and routines are different.
4 What is meant by overritualization?
5 How does staging make rituals important?
6 Why do rituals play an important role in building family strength?

KEY TERMS

Ritual
Rules
Routines
Morphostasis
Morphogenesis
Healthy emotional ties
Rite of passage
Metaphor
Overritualization
Underritualization
Distinctive rituals
Symbolism
Form and content

SUGGESTED READINGS

Doherty, W. J. (1999). *The intentional family: Simple rituals to strengthen family ties.* New York, NY: HarperCollins.
Fiese, B. (2007). *Family routines and rituals.* New Haven, CT: Yale University Press.
Fiese, B. H., Hooker, K. A., Kotary, L., & Schwagler, J. (1993). Family rituals in the early stages of parenthood. *Journal of Marriage and Family, 55*(3), 633–642.
Imber-Black, E., Roberts, J., & Whiting, R. A. (2003). *Rituals in families and family therapy* (2nd ed.). New York, NY: W. W. Norton & Company.
Smith, C. (2007). *Soul searching: The religious lives of American teenagers.* Oxford, UK: Oxford University Press.

REFERENCES

Bocknek, E. L. (2018). Family rituals in low-income African American families at risk for trauma exposure and associations with toddlers' regulation of distress. *Journal of Marital Family Therapy, 44*(4), 702–715.

Boles, R. E., Halbower, A. C., Daniels, S., Gunnarsdottir, T., Whitesell, N., Johnson, S. L., & Johnson (2017). Family chaos and child functioning in relation to sleep problems among children at risk for obesity. *Behavioral Sleep Medicine, 15*(2), 114–128. DOI: 10.1080/15402002.2015.1104687

Bossard, J. S., & Boll, E. S. (1950). *Ritual in family living.* Philadelphia: University of Pennsylvania Press.

Boyce, W. R., Jensen, E. W., James, S. A., & Peacock, J. L. (1983). The family routines inventory: Theoretical origins. *Social Science Medicine, 17*, 193–200.

Carter-Black, J. (2001). The myth of "The tangle of pathology:" Resilience strategies employed by middle-class African American families. *Journal of Family Social Work, 6*(4), 75–100.

Chelladurai, J. M., Dollahite, D. C., & Marks, L. D. (2018). "The family that prays together …": Relational processes associated with regular family prayer. *Journal of Family Psychology, 32*(7), 849–859. DOI: 10.1037/fam0000432

Conlan, P. (n.d.). "Dance, American Indian," *The Encyclopedia of Oklahoma History and Culture,* https://www.okhistory.org/publications/enc/entry.php?entry=DA008

Crespo, C., Santos, S., Canavarro, M. C., Kielpikowski, M., Pryor, J., & Feres-Carneiro, T. (2013). Family routines and rituals in the context of chronic conditions: A review. *International Journal of Psychology, 48*(5), 729–746.

Doty, W. G. (1986). *Mythography: The story of myths and rituals.* Tuscaloosa, AL: University of Alabama Press.

Fiese, B. H. (2007). *Family routines and rituals.* New Haven, CT: Yale University Press.

Fiese, B. H., Tomcho, T. J., Douglas, M., Josephs, K., Poltrock, S., & Baker, T. (2002). A review of 50 years of research on naturally occurring family routines and rituals: Cause for celebration? *Journal of Family Psychology, 16*(4), 381–390.

Gillis, J. (1996). *A world of their own making: Myth, ritual, and the quest for family values.* New York, NY: Basic Books.

Hanke, K., van Egmond, M. C., Crespo, C., & Boer, D. (2016). Blessing or burden? The role of appraisal for family rituals and flourishing among LGBT adults. *Journal of Family Psychology, 30*(5), 562–568. DOI: 10.1037/fam0000214

Imber-Black, & Roberts, 1992. *Rituals for our time.* New York, NY: Harper Perennial.

Laird, J. (1988). Women and ritual in family therapy. In E. Imber-Black, & J. Roberts (Eds.), *Rituals in families and family therapy* (pp. 69–102). New York, NY: Vintage Books.

Leong, A. D., Berzin, S. C., & Lee, H. (2019). Birthday celebrations as a family homelessness intervention: A mixed-methods analysis. *Journal of Children and Poverty, 25*(1), 21–36. DOI: 10.1080/10796126.2018.1555520

Marks, L. D., Dollahite, D. C., Hatch, T. G., Goodman, M. A., Phillips, T. M., & Kelley, H. H. (2020). The real book of Mormon musical: Latter-day Saint family home evening as a weekly ritual. *Marriage & Family Review, 56*(5), 425–448. DOI: 10.1080/01494929.2020.1726852

Masten, A. S. (2018). Resilience theory and research on children and families: Past, present, and promise. *Journal of Family Theory & Review, 10*, 12–31. DOI: 10.1111/jftr.12255

Meredith, W. H. (1985). The importance of family traditions. *Wellness Perspective, 2*, 17–19.

Meredith, W., Abbott, D., & Adams, S. (1986). Family violence: Its relation to marital and parental satisfaction and family strengths. *Journal of Family Violence, 4*, 75–88.

Meredith, W., Abbott, D., Lamanna, M. A., & Sanders, G. (1989). Rituals and family strengths: A three-generational study. *Family Perspectives, 23*, 75–84.

Nelson, L. R., & Colaner, C. W. (2018). Becoming a transracial family: Communicatively negotiating divergent identities in families formed through transracial adoption. *Journal of Family Communication, 18*(1), 51–67. DOI: 10.1080/15267431.2017.1396987

Palazzoli, M. S., Boscolo, J., Cecchin, G., & Prata, G. (1977). Family rituals: A powerful tool in family therapy. *Family Process, 16*(4), 445–453.

Palazzoli, M. S., Boscolo, L., Cecchin, G., & Prata, G. (1978). *Paradox and counter-paradox.* New York, NY: Jason Aronson.

Palazzoli, M. S., Cirillo, S., Selvini, M., & Sorrentino, A. M. (1989). *Family games: General models of psychotic processes in the family*. New York, NY: W. W. Norton & Company.

Quinn, W. H., Newfield, N. A., & Protinsky, H. O. (1985). Rites of passage in families with adolescents. *Journal of Family Processes, 24*, 101–111.

Reiss, D. (1981). *The family's construction of reality*. Cambridge, MA: Harvard University Press.

Roberts, J. (2003). Setting the frame: Definition, functions, and typology of rituals. In E. Imber-Black, J. Roberts, & R. A. Whiting (Eds.), *Rituals in families and family therapy* (pp. 3–48). New York, NY: W. W. Norton & Company.

Sanchez, R. O., Letiecq, B. L., & Ginsberg, M. R. (2019). An integrated model of family strengths and resilience: Theorizing at the intersection of Indigenous and Western paradigms. *Journal of Family Theory & Review, 11*, 561–575.

Schvaneveldt, J. D., & Lee, T. R. (1983). The emergence and practice of ritual in the American family. *Family Perspectives, 17*, 137–143.

Spagnola, M., & Fiese, B. H. (2007). Family routines and rituals: A context for development in the lives of young children. *Infants & Young Children, 20*(4), 284–299.

Touhy, R., & Yazdani, F. (2018). Family routines of adolescents with an Autism Spectrum Disorder: A literature review. *Degenerative Intellectual & Developmental Disabilities, 1*(4). DIDD.000519. 2018.

Tribal Wisdom (n.d.). Mescalero Apache Rite of Passage. https://www.tribal-wisdom.org/page/427/t-mescalero-apache-rite-of-passage. Downloaded November 2020.

Turner, V. (1967). *The forest of symbols: Aspects of Ndembu ritual*. Ithaca, NY: Cornell University Press.

van der Hart, O. (1983). *Rituals in psychotherapy: Transitions and continuity*. New York, NY: Irvington.

Whiting, R. A. (1988). Guidelines to designing therapeutic rituals. In E. Imber-Black, J. R. Roberts, & R. A. Whiting (Eds.), *Rituals in families and family therapy* (pp. 96–139). New York, NY: Norton.

Wolin, S., & Bennett, L. A. (1984). Family rituals. *Family Process, 23*, 401–420.

Part III

Maintaining Families—Ties That Bind

Maintaining Families: Ties that Bind

You can cut the ties that bind but not without losing a part of yourself. You can walk away and hide from the people who made you, but you'll always hear them calling your name.
- Lisa Unger

In this section of the text, we will explore family processes, from rules and rule sequences to communication and distance regulation. We finish the section with a focus on positive or facilitating family processes, those processes that build and strengthen families, including forgiveness, kindness, hope, and gratitude.

CHAPTER 8

Rules and Rule Sequences

CHAPTER PREVIEW

In this chapter, readers will learn:

- What family rules are.
- The difference between mores and folkways.
- That social norms and family rules are similar terms but have slightly different meanings.
- How rules emerge and take shape in family life.
- That rules and rule systems are a part of the paradigmatic orientation found in families.
- The types of rules that exist in families.
- The difference between explicit and implicit rules in families.
- The power of rule sequences and how those sequences can create family growth or family dysfunction.
- That rules have distinct purposes including helping with family member accountability, boundary maintenance, distance regulation, and resource allocation.
- How to manage rules and rule sequences effectively.

INTRODUCTION

Humans are rule loving creatures. We are surrounded by rules, from street signs to posters in cafes, airports, workplaces, classrooms, and yes, even our homes (Figure 8.1)! In the last chapter, we explored routines and rituals, which should not be confused with rules. While routines and rituals are events, rules are beliefs or understandings that govern how these events are carried out in the family. In other words, routines and rituals have rules. So do family processes!

Rules deal with the "should" in our lives. They define how we should do millions of daily things, such as how to use the utensils at the meal, closing doors when it is cold, knocking on a door rather than walking directly into someone's house, and not asking a parent for a favor when they are in a bad mood.

You may not realize it, but your family has thousands of rules, both formal and informal, that regulate and direct family life (Hoopes & Harper, 1987). For example, think of the mail each family receives every day. Who goes to the mailbox and retrieves the mail? Where is it placed? Is it sorted and delivered to each person's room? Can anyone in your family open the "junk" mail? Can parents open the children's mail? Are there certain types of letters that do

DOI: 10.4324/9781003128717-11

FIGURE 8.1 Many families post "family rules" as reminders for how to treat each other.

not have to be shared at all? Most of the rules that govern "mail collection" and other family interactions emerge without any fanfare or even much negotiation, but they have the power to direct and dictate much of what we do. Rules might direct where one sits at dinner, what is watched on television, and when homework is done (if at all). The family rule system can also specify which towels to use in the bathroom, where to store holiday decorations, who should replace the empty toilet paper roll (and if it's over or under), and even what should be discussed when and by whom.

Families even have rules about rules! Most rules are "invisible" to you, though, until the rule is broken. Rules are often automatic and often exist in sequence. They are not discussed, questioned, or labeled; they just "are." Think about how your family behaves when others (non-family) are present and then how they behave when they are alone. Our family interactions are governed by rules that provide the structure for the family, and "the maintenance of balance or survival of the structure is one purpose or goal of the family rules" (Hoopes & Harper, 1987, p. 5). Because rules regulate and direct your family life, they are very powerful.

In the following discussion, we more deeply define rules and explore where rules come from, the type of rules that influence family life, the purposes of rules and how they influence family life, and finally, how we manage rules and rule sequences.

WHAT ARE RULES AND WHERE DO THEY COME FROM?

Jackson (1965a) noted that "the family is a rule-governed system" (p. 6). He described rules as "relationship agreements" that limit our behaviors and keep our interactions organized and stable. They provide connections between family processes and individual behavior (Ford, 1983). Rules govern intimacy, communication, emotional expression, boundaries, autonomy, and even daily activities (when to do the washing and how to clean the bathroom). As with family processes themselves, family rules tend to be invisible to the family member. In fact, one usually must infer rules from patterns of behavior. Rules can find their way into family systems through many ways, from social norms to repetitions of family interactions.

Rules from Social Norms

Some rules are quite simply anchored in **social norms** and culture. Social norms are beliefs that exist in a culture that prescribe certain behaviors and proscribe others. Thus, they deal with "shoulds" and "shouldn'ts" that get communicated to us by the groups of people we are around each day. Social norms can apply to minor acts, like what utensil one uses at the dinner table, or to more major occurrences, like who should be chosen as a sexual partner.

Sociologists have developed several concepts that help us tell the difference between norms that deal with less serious behaviors and those that deal with more serious matters. They refer to norms dealing with behaviors that are preferred but more or less optional as **folkways**. Folkways are more specific behavioral expectations that might, for example, pressure us to dress our children in certain ways and speak to our spouses in a particular way.

Norms considered especially important are called **mores** (pronounced "morays"). Mores are a bit stronger than folkways. They are customs or conventions that are essential to the maintenance of community life. For example, mores dictate an ideal about parent–child behavior within a culture. From mores and folkways, we learn who we are and how we fit into society, and they have a powerful influence with regard to how we manage family business. Beyond mores and folkways, we have laws, which are society's rules that become formalized over time.

Children learn many social norms in their family that deal with the family realm. The families of origin of a newly married couple have an enormous impact on what the couple adopts as the normative elements of their family life. Additionally, family behavior can be greatly influenced by where the parents work, their religious orientation, and even the neighborhood in which they live. Every affiliation, and to some degree every past affiliation of a family member has an influence on the norms that a family consciously and explicitly accepts, as well as the tacit or "hidden" understandings, the "taken-for-granted" definitions that often are brought to light only when violated.

Because social norms are an important part of family processes, it is important to consider how families teach, adopt, and change the norms they use. Additionally, understanding the nature of social norms helps us understand some of the sources of stress in families. For example, teenagers might learn something new from their peers and try to introduce that idea into their own families.

One distinct property clearly identifies the nature of a social norm or rule: simplicity. In other words, normative social rules are not complex. They do not describe behavior sequences, nor do they necessarily rely on other rules as a requirement for their existence.

PRINCIPLE 8.1

FOLKWAYS AND MORES

Folkways and mores are different. Mores focus on more serious matters than folkways. Further, mores focus on the ideal, whereas folkways focus on the behaviors that emanate from mores.

Rules from Family Interactions

Family rules can be created in ways that do not represent standard social norms. Instead, they are created as family life emerges or in response to specific events in everyday life as we raise children and become involved in other complicated family activities. Further, some are copied from the family of origin and are brought into the new relationship by the couple.

From the time of birth, we assimilate and learn the rules we need to follow to live successfully within our families. In Chapter 6, we discussed the idea of inner schemata that form together to define and circumscribe one's world. In addition to the values, beliefs, and ideals that were discussed, one also collects and builds schemata about managing and surviving daily family life (and nonfamily life as well). As we gain experience in family life, we slowly acquire, moderate, build, tweak, and shape a family rule schemata for our own point of view (Figure 8.2).

Sometimes old, well-used family rules follow us into our new relationships. These old schemata reside within us, planted there by years of watching the adults in our life as we grew up. This collection of rules first resides in the mind of the couple when forming a relationship. They bring with them ideas and history about who should do the dishes, make beds, discipline children, clean the windows, and paint and repair the broken door. It is inevitable that when a partnership is forming and two people are merging their worlds, there will be some disconnect about how the two competing rule schemata (one from each partner) should come together and a clash can occur. One of the purposes of courtship is to begin the process of rule discovery, negotiation, and creation. It is during this time that partners begin to adopt

FIGURE 8.2 Newly formed families construct family life and it emerges as a new creation day by day. The rules, routines, and rituals they build create the "frame" of the home they construct.

some rules from one person's family of origin and some from another, discovering they have some rules in common.

This process of **assimilation** and **accommodation** is critical. Power imbalance is a key to understanding strength and efficiency in family life. If, during the formation of the relationship, one partner dominates and only assimilates—expecting the other partner to accommodate, change, and adapt—trouble will probably not be far behind. Each of us, by definition, comes with elaborate family rule schemata in place about how "things" should be done. When we enter a new relationship and assume our rule collection is the "right and true" way of doing things, we will tend only to expect minor assimilation for ourselves; but we probably expect the other person to see the light and to change, accommodate, get on board, and adopt the better way of doing things from our point of view.

We can also adopt by choice or simply accommodate beliefs and rules from external influences. For example, movies and television are sources of influence from which we might adopt bits and pieces of how to act in family life. This is a risky strategy because, typically, family life in such venues can be represented in ways that are unrealistic, oversimplified, and even inaccurately portrayed. Think about it. In 22 minutes (actual running time without commercials), the Pritchetts in *Modern Family* are able to successfully solve a host of problems! Given the makeup of the family (a May-December marriage with a stepchild, a gay couple with an adopted Vietnamese daughter, and a dual earner professional family with three children), the family is not at a loss for dealing with complex problems. People may watch such programs and think of their own lives as deficient because they are not living up to a fantasy portrayal of what someone thinks family life "should" be like. Of course, problems arise when a young couple believes that the fantasy Pritchett family in *Modern Family* is how their life should be emerging in the harsh flurry of daily reality.

Family members can also adopt rules of daily life by negotiation. This process can include discussion about such mundane issues as who sleeps on which side of the bed, who sits where at the table, who puts their clothes in what closet, and whether to squeeze the toothpaste in the middle or at the end of the tube. Negotiation also is used for rules about deeper issues, such as who controls the money, the distribution of other resources, and the division of labor.

Many family rules can appear through a series of multiple interactions (Galvin & Brommel, 1991; Haley, 1963). Through the processes of trial, struggle, error, conflict, and resolution, family members adopt what seems to work for them. By "work for them," we mean the processes that families find helpful in keeping the system in balance, free from chaos, and working in harmony. Eventually, they learn, adapt, assimilate, and accommodate. Not everything chosen is best for all members, although those within the system believe what they are doing is necessary to keep the system in working order. The process begins with the couple meeting for the first time and continues on as a developmental process. They cannot avoid the process as it occurs with or without their approval or knowledge. Every transaction results in the creation, modification, or support of rules. Thus, rules are created through repetitions of behaviors across time.

Consider the following. When the first grandbaby entered our family, it was decided that this child should be part of his great grandmother's life. "Granny" had played a limited role in her grandchildren's lives due to her living far away; however, in her later years, she returned to live near her children and grandchildren, thus providing this opportunity. Granny was asked if we could bring the great grandbaby and dinner over one Sunday, and she readily agreed. During the dinner, it was suggested we return again next Sunday. After a month of Sundays, this visit had become a rule. It could only be broken under extreme circumstances (illness or out-of-town vacations), and all family members knew when and where Sunday dinner would be held. Nobody wrote this rule down or informed family members, "Beginning now, all Sunday dinners will be at Granny's!" just as nobody upon getting engaged asks, "And once we are married, how shall we collect the mail?!" Yet, the rules are created, subtlety and unintended, through multiple repetitions and interactions.

Rules and Paradigms

In Chapter 6, it was noted that the term *paradigm* invokes the idea of a collected worldview held by a community or specified group of individuals. This, as you will remember, implies a subscription rate. That is, a paradigm only exists when the group members buy into or share certain ideals, beliefs, and views. A part of the family paradigm extends beyond the shared view about values and beliefs (as discussed in Chapter 6). It also includes the negotiated, collected, and shared view family members have about rules. Of course, a mother could have in her head that it is terrible for other family members to be unkind to one another. But that personal ideological schema does not transcend into a family paradigm unless it is a rule that is adopted and shared by the group.

Unfortunately, this is one of those areas of research in family life about which we have little knowledge. The research agenda for this topic would need to include a careful cataloging of shared and nonshared family rules. One would expect that some families experience high levels of consensus about rules, rule implementation, and what to do when rules are violated. We would expect that a key to creating an effective family would be the ability to adapt rule structures as group membership matures and changes; the creation and careful maintenance of clear and equitable rules; and the ability to discard rules that are simply historical and have little real utility.

PRINCIPLE 8.2

RULES CAN COME FROM MANY SOURCES

We learn rules and rule patterns from our culture, family, friends, and media. Sometimes the rules we learn in one place conflict with expectations or rules we learn in another place.

TYPES OF RULES

Family rules are multidimensional and can be classified in several ways, allowing for research and intervention. A common classification is based on how aware family members are of the rules resulting in explicit and implicit rules (Satir, 1972). On the other hand, Blevins (1993) categorized rules along four poles: overt-covert, appropriate-inappropriate, flexible-rigid, healthy-toxic. Additionally, scholars have identified other types of rules that have been found to be related to family functioning, including facilitating and constraining rules, disabling rules, and metarules. Recognizing the various ways rules are categorized can help in our understanding of family processes.

Explicit Rules

Some rules are very visible and **explicit**. Explicit rules are the beliefs that are recognized, acknowledged, and known by a family, and often they can be overtly talked about (Larson, Parks, Harper, & Heath, 2001). Such rules are easily identified and may even be written out. For example, explicit family rules may involve chores, curfew, allowance, and bedtimes. Many families today have explicit rules related to media use, such as "no cell phones during dinner" or restrictions related to Instagram. Explicit rules are a little different than daily requests that require a specific and perhaps a one-time response. They take on the form of regulating behavior over time, as a generalized guideline, meant to be in force "forever" or "until altered."

Another example of an explicit rule is, "Your grandmother and I have decided that all children should get some type of allowance, on a weekly basis." This type of rule has the necessary components. First, it implies that two or more people have discussed the need openly. Second, it has a long-term element to it, prescribing an action over time. Third, it is meant to regulate the flow of resources within the system or perform some other function. Also, it helps to maintain order and prevent debilitating chaos.

Implicit Rules

Most family rules, however, are created quietly over time, almost subconsciously, such as your mail rules or rules related to roles within the family. These types of rules are **implicit**. Implicit rules are hidden from view. They are not discussed and have not been thought of or labeled by family members, making them very powerful. Implicit rules take on the status of something never questioned or even considered as changeable. They quite simply (and ultimately complexly) are the "way things are."

For example, implicit rules govern how we greet one another. After a long absence, do family members hug, shake hands, or just smile? In this example, the norm reflects what the family has decided is appropriate about distance regulation: how close and affectionate family members should be. They also govern how/if we express emotions. Many families have implicit rules against sharing special feelings. They might go to great lengths to "help" family members learn ways to express or suppress how they feel. Suppose a family has an implicit rule that only good topics and feelings should be discussed. The belief might be that to talk about the negative parts of life is a destructive process. The negative feelings and experiences could go unexpressed. These negative feelings may remain unspoken but probably not unfelt. It could be very dangerous for a family to create a system in which significant and important feelings cannot be discussed. Still, healthier families tend to have more implicit rules, such as "have fun and play together" or "make decisions together as a family" than explicit. The more explicit rules a family has, the less healthy a family tends to be. Thus, implicit rules tend to be more desirable.

Facilitating and Constraining Rules

Several scholars (e.g., Crane, Harper, Bean, & Holmes, 2020; Feinauer, Larson, & Harper, 2010; Satire, 1988) have identified facilitating and constraining family rules and linked these rules to various family outcomes. Facilitating rules are those rules that provide guidelines and support the family to allow for healthy growth. They are flexible, promote openness, and encourage positive feelings of acceptance, intrinsic worth, and care. They encourage intimacy, cooperation, problem-solving, and improved communication. Crane et al. (2020) found that facilitative family process rules were directly and positively related to prosocial communication in adolescents.

Conversely, constraining rules work in the opposite manner. Constrain means to compel, force, and restrict. These rules impose structure and limitations on family interactions resulting in poorer communication and fragmented family relationships. Some rules limit expression and keep family members from disagreeing openly, without reprisal (Satir, 1972). As a result, this can limit personal growth, as well as family growth, keeping family members trapped in their roles and unable to branch out. Such rules can limit freedom, exclude individuals, and make family members feel like outsiders in their own family system. In Crane et al.'s (2020) study, they found that constraining family rules related to more antisocial communication in adolescents.

Disabling Rules

In some family systems, some rules are disabling. Disabling rules can cause family members to interact in unhealthy and damaging ways, and this interferes with families accomplishing their goals. Also, when rules are disabling, energy and a sense of direction dissipate.

Examples of ineffective or disabling rules are those that result in abuse to system members. A family could have a rule legitimizing the hitting of family members by those who are bigger and stronger when someone violates a boundary. Another type of ineffective rule is one that labels individuals as having little value to the system. The rules might eliminate a person from important decisions, important conversations, and problem-solving processes. Unfortunately, other family members often might not realize that they have established simple rules at the expense of one of the system members. Unintended results can abound.

Another type of family rule that is destructive is to have rules that communicate mistrust (Lidz, 1963). In these situations, a child might be taught to mistrust everything and everyone. Rules also might exist that prohibit family members from testing ideas in the outside world. The "facts" of the world are distorted to meet the needs of family members. Consequently, the children might not learn to test reality but are trained to accept the particular brand of irrationality constructed by the family as reality.

Some ineffective family rules might suggest two rather powerful yet contradictory behaviors. For example, a family might have consciously selected a democratic parenting style, encouraging individual expression and growth, but at the same time censuring family members for seeking a life outside the family. They construct two competing rules: (a) we are an open and accepting family and (b) we accept only certain types of choices about really important life decisions. In an extreme case, the family might be filled with a milieu of inconsistencies and contradictions. The result can be people acting in inconsistent and unpredictable ways.

Metarules

Another type of rule is the **metarule**. The word *meta* means about. Therefore, **metarules** are rules about rules. The metarules that family scientists focus most of their attention on are metarules about how to create new rules, eliminate old rules, or change rules. Referring to metarules, Laing (1972) observed that sometimes "there are rules against seeing the rules, and hence against seeing all the issues that arise from complying with or breaking them" (p. 106).

There are many examples of metarules. When families have young children, it is common to have a metarule that it is parents and not children who make and change the family rules. A metarule that qualifies this could be that if the children want a rule changed, they can ask the parents and even express their desires, but the parents decide. As the children in families mature, the metarules usually change. For example, a typical metarule when the children are teenagers could be that the ones who are the most upset by old rules and make the biggest scene determine the rules.

Hopefully, families have a metarule structure that assists them when rules no longer work. This issue is closely tied to the ideas of adaptability. As rules become obsolete, an adaptable family will have a viable metarule structure that allows them to replace, alter, and negotiate new rules that might be more appropriate for the situation. Some families do not have an adequate set of metarules about how to change their rules. When this occurs, families tend to become "stuck" in ways of doing things that were appropriate for earlier stages of development, and they have difficulty making the transitions into new stages of development.

One of the important ways family therapists help families is to help them develop metarules that help them change and grow. As Greenberg (1977) observed in his analysis of one of the main schools of thought in family therapy, "It was postulated that a central function of the therapist entailed the facilitation and the development of rules for change" (p. 396).

When families try to take a step back and think about their metarules, they can gain great insight. For example, assume a young man is studying family science, and after he studies these ideas, he realizes that he has been locked into a struggle with his parents about rules. He realizes the struggle is a standoff and he is not getting anywhere. He wants to have the freedom to decide what to study at the university, where to work, who to associate with, and so on. His parents, however, want to have a considerable say in his life. He now wants to talk about the metarules to see if they can find a better way to change the family rules. He could initiate this type of conversation by saying things like this: "Mom and Dad, I'd like to see us change some of the ways we do things in our family, but I don't know how to do it. What should one of us do if we want to make some changes? What would we say to get the others' attention, and how do we change things? What do you two do when one of you wants to make some changes, and how do you decide to make a change?"

RULE SEQUENCES IN FAMILY LIFE

In the 1950s, a group of family scientists led by Jackson and Bateson discovered that family systems have rules that are different from the rules families get from society or invent themselves (Jackson, 1957, 1965b). These rules are patterns of behavior in family systems that are repeated so regularly that they are a governing or regulating part of the structure of the family systems. They are much more abstract than the daily rule structures about the ordinary events of life. Instead, **rule sequences** are about the patterns of interactive behavior that seem much like a play: She says "X"; then Dad says "Y"; then Billy says "Y-not"; then she says "X"—and the pattern begins again.

The family scientists who discovered these rules found that usually, the rules "tend to be implicit and they are rarely, if ever, explicit or written down" (Ford, 1983, p. 135). Therefore, the only way to identify the family rules is to infer them from the repeated or redundant patterns in the behavior in a family (Larson et al., 2001). Clinicians have long recognized the value of understanding the deeply held rule patterns within families (Constantine, 1986; Ford, 1983; Satir, 1972). They would make the claim that one, especially a clinician, cannot begin to intervene or even really understand a family until one understands the rule patterns that lie beneath the surface. According to this line of research, the rule patterns regulate and govern family interaction (Larson et al., 2001). Further, they would claim that these rule systems either promote growth and strength in family life or they perpetuate dysfunction and instability. These rule sequences can empower families to attain goals and create patterns of efficiency. On the dark side, rule patterns can create communication problems, cause low self-esteem, internalize shame and guilt, and even disrupt intimacy in young adults (Ford, 1983).

An example of an implicit rule sequence is found in the writing of Jackson (1965b). They presented a real family case within which the family had a pattern that the only time the parents were able to act together was when they teamed up against a rebellious child. The parents rarely went out together, and they maintained a pattern of discord most of the time. The father was not generally in charge of the family, but he gained control with occasional violent outbursts. These researchers claimed that in this family system, we could infer that "it seems as if" the family has some rules that discord must be maintained at all costs, the parents shall not cooperate unless it is to gang up on the child, and the father shall gain power only by violent outbursts (Jackson, 1965b).

Another interesting example of a family rule sequence is found in a book by Caine (1974), *The Personal Crisis of a Widow in America*. A woman's husband is dying of cancer, and as the story unfolds, he is dealing with the devastating feelings of knowing his life is about to end. Caine describes how this crisis debilitated their relationship. A source of major stress in the woman's situation was a hidden rule sequence that the subject of the husband's death could not be overtly talked about. The sequence developed slowly and informally. In this story, you do not see anyone declaring a rule prohibiting talking about death. Instead, the power of this story is about how skillful the family members become at learning and reinforcing the rule sequence designed to avoid the topic of death. If the topic of dying starts to arise, someone steps in and offers a diversion or finds a way to take the conversation somewhere else. In a very poignant and depressing part of this story, the author shares her deep and troubled feelings following the death of her husband. She reports how much she wished she would have changed the rule sequence (our term here) and talked to him about the end of his life and the hundreds of issues that needed to be resolved. However, the rule sequence had prevailed at the cost of never discussing what was uppermost on their minds. Rule sequences like these regulate what can and cannot be talked about. The point of this story is that sometimes the rule sequence can prevent us from being as effective in family life as we would wish.

Haley (1976) was another researcher and therapist who helped develop the idea of rule sequences. He indicated that a rule sequence occurs when there is a connected series of rules that govern a complex pattern in the behavior of several individuals in a family system. He further suggested that these sequences tend to have a cyclic pattern to them. Most families have many healthy rule-bound sequences covering such activities as time management, allocation of scarce family resources (i.e., space, money, affection), interaction with those outside of the kin system, and every aspect of general family functioning. An example of a positive rule sequence is a family that has a pattern of the parents getting up a few minutes earlier than they would need to so they can visit for a minute with their child and express affection before beginning the daily routines. When the parents conform to this rule, it tends to begin a cycle of other rule-bound behaviors in the family, such as the children and adults being more pleasant, listening to each other, doing favors for each other, and so on. When the parents do not follow this pattern (family rule), a different cycle can usually be precipitated in the family, such as the children and adults being less patient, more irritable, more short-tempered, or more critical as they begin the day.

Some rule sequences are disabling and destructive (Figure 8.3). When they deal with negative or disabling patterns, we often refer to them as *vicious cycles* (Haley, 1976). For example:

1   When one parent has a bad day at the office, he or she comes home and is critical of the other parent.
2   The second parent takes the anger out on a child.
3   The child picks a fight with another sibling or kicks the dog.

The following example illustrates an oversimplified situation where there is a father, mother, and child, and each of them is either competent or incompetent. Because these sequences tend to be cyclic, there is a series of steps that lead to the next and they eventually lead back to the beginning again. We could start the description at any point in the cycle.

Step 1. *Father—ineffective.* The father behaves in an upset or depressed way, not functioning to his capacity.

Step 2. *Child—misbehaving.* The child begins to get out of control or express symptoms.

Step 3. *Mother—ineffective.* The mother ineffectually tries to deal with the child and cannot, and the father becomes involved.

Step 4. *Father—competent.* The father deals with the child effectively and recovers from his state of incompetency.

Step 5. *Child-behaving.* The child regains his composure and behaves properly or is defined as normal.

Step 6. *Mother—competent.* The mother becomes more capable and deals with the child and father in a more competent way, expecting more from them.

Step 7. *Father—ineffective.* The father behaves in an upset or depressed way, not functioning to his capacity, and the cycle begins again (Haley, 1987, p. 113).

Several elements of this sequence illustrate how rule sequences usually operate. First, the steps seem to occur in a cyclic pattern, and the pattern repeats itself over and over. Second, it is quite arbitrary where the cycle begins because it can begin with several of the steps. Punctuation is an attempt to identify where complex patterns begin and end, but it usually distorts the cyclic reality of these patterns.

Third, the strategy the mother uses to "change" the husband and child by increasing her expectations actually has the opposite effect. The more she tries to get them to improve, the more they go in the opposite direction. This points out how these repetitious rules can be painfully obscured from the vision of those who participate in them. A major element of family interaction patterns is that most of them are hidden from immediate view. Often, only an outside observer or a person trained to focus on systemic processes can piece them together.

Fourth, the details of the behavior might change in different situations, but when the pattern in the cycle is rule-governed, it will reappear over and over again in different forms. It is critical to remember, however, that most of the time, the family members are unaware they are choosing behaviors that are rule-governed or pattern-like. Most people are surprised when such rules are brought to light in counseling sessions or by a skillful observer.

FIGURE 8.3 Sometimes, the rule sequences in families are not helpful and can lead to a fracture in the fundamental relationship strength.

These patterns help us understand more about a family's paradigm and what they really believe is important. The individuals are tied together and try to solve problems using rules of interaction that have somehow emerged over time, which might have worked in the past, and are now reemployed to respond to life's changes and challenges. By solving problems and allocating resources, we begin to understand what kinds of beliefs, values, and viewpoints are the most important to the group. Therefore, one way to see into a family's paradigmatic world is to take careful note of the rule sequences that emerge over time.

These rule sequences also help us understand the way different perspectives influence how we try to help families. A common approach to assisting families with problems is to focus on the individuals rather than the family system. In the preceding situation, a therapist with an individualistic orientation might encourage the mother to be more assertive or let the child "solve her own problems." The therapist might tell the parents to let the individual consequences of individual behavior take over. A therapist with a family process approach in mind might, instead, try to identify problematic rule sequences and then help the group interrupt those sequences that were destructive.

PRINCIPLE 8.3

RULE SEQUENCES ARE POWERFUL

The rule sequences families create and maintain can create great efficiencies but can also generate dysfunction. Harmful rule patterns are very powerful, potentially destructive, and extremely difficult to change in families.

Generational Rule Sequences

Sometimes, rule sequences involve three generations. The following example is a case study presented by Haley (1987, p. 117) in which a single parent has returned to live with her mother after a divorce. Think of the principles found in Chapter 4 as you read the following. In particular, note how the following is an example of the cross-generational alliance.

Step 1. Grandmother takes care of grandchild while protesting that mother is irresponsible and does not take care of the child properly. In this way, the grandmother is siding with the child against the mother in a coalition across generation lines.

Step 2. Mother withdraws, letting grandmother care for the child.

Step 3. The child misbehaves or expresses symptomatic behavior.

Step 4. Grandmother protests that she should not have to take care of the child and discipline him. She has raised her children, and the mother should take care of her own child.

Step 5. Mother begins to take care of her own child.

Step 6. Grandmother protests that the mother does not know how to take care of the child properly and is being irresponsible. She takes over the care of the grandchild to save the child from the mother.

Step 7. Mother withdraws, letting the grandmother care for the child.

Step 8. The child misbehaves or expresses symptomatic behavior.

Again, it is impossible to identify the beginning or the "causes" of the problems in these situations because they are ongoing cycles that have no beginning and no end. A systems theory perspective, however, suggests it is helpful to view these situations as rule-governed cycles. When we think of them this way, it reduces defensiveness, helps us better understand the system characteristics that help maintain problems, and opens up several possibilities for improving the family system.

WHAT PURPOSES DO RULES SERVE?

In the big scheme of things, rules provide structure, stability, and organization to the family system. They also serve several specific purposes.

- **Accountability.** Rules hold system members accountable for actions within and outside of the system (Cronen, Pearce, & Harris, 1979). In Chapter 6, we learned that families have expectations and usually create a family paradigm that speaks to group values, desired outcomes, preferred activities, and common goals. From a family paradigm, simple family rules become a mechanism and useful tool for performing in ways that meet those generalized expectations.

- **Boundaries.** Family rules also help family members know the boundaries that exist between a family and its environment. Each family exists in a complex network of other family systems and external systems, and it must maintain a certain amount of uniqueness and distance from the others or its own existence fades. Therefore, norms are developed to define the boundaries that represent the interface between each family and its environmental systems. Boundary rules dictate how permeable the family and subsystem boundaries can be and specify limitations of individual family member freedom to roam beyond the immediate limits of the system.

For instance, if the adults in a family are having a serious conversation and the bedroom door is closed, rules about boundaries specify to other family members about when (if at all) they can interrupt that conversation. When the group is in a public setting, boundary rules can also specify the limits of conversation and disclosure. For example, the rules might specify that it is inappropriate to speak of a forthcoming pregnancy. Boundary rules also can spill over into rules about visitors. Our family rule schemata usually dictate the limits of knowing when (or if) it is appropriate to bring outsiders home.

These types of rules maintain system boundaries. Families are more effective when the group members know the rules and are willing to abide by them. Without implicit knowledge of boundary rules, it is very difficult for the family system to be a system at all. It is important, however, to note that when family rules begin to be questioned and challenged, often it is the rules about boundaries that are being questioned.

A healthy family system has effectively created functional and healthy rule systems that tell family members where the system begins and ends, where they can and cannot go, and what they can and cannot do. This is assuming, of course, that the system has created a flexible and nondestructive rule system.

- **Distance Regulation.** One specific purpose of simple rules is that they regulate distance or the amount of closeness (see Chapter 10 for a discussion of this idea). Maintaining appropriate **distance regulation** means that the group has learned how to manage a pattern of separateness and connectedness (Day, Gavazzi, & Acock, 2001; Gavazzi, Anderson, & Sabatelli, 1993; Hess & Handel, 1959; Kantor & Lehr, 1975; Minuchin, 1996; Olson & McCubbin, 1982). Family rules tell us how and when we should be close and when we should be separate. Rules also help us to know how to disengage when there is too much closeness.
- **Resource Allocation.** Another purpose of rules is to regulate how families allocate and exchange resources. These rules govern how scarce resources should be divided up within the system. This includes how family money should be spent, rules about living space, and rules about intangibles like time and affection. For example, if there is extra cash, a father might have the first choice about whether he will spend it on a new tractor part or a mother might have the first choice about whether she will invest it.
- **Rules of Responsibility.** Rules of designated authority are rules about the division of responsibility. Mother might be in charge of anyone who feels blue. An older grandparent living with the family might be in charge of relieving tension when the pressure of an argument gets too intense. A father might be charged with the responsibility of the first reaction in times of emergency. At times of divorce or death, rule and role reallocation might occur to fill the void created by the absent family member.
- **Implementation.** Many of the rules we have in private life have to do with implementation. Rules of implementation exist for the purpose of implementing other rules and expectations. A family might have a series of rules about a topic (how much schoolwork), but they also have a series of rules that designate how they go about getting the work done. For example, suppose one's family paradigm centers on achieving educational excellence. The rules that become part of that family paradigm would probably include rules

about grade performance, studying, and allocating group resources to make that happen. That particular family would, no doubt, develop a series of implicit and explicit rules that direct the system to assist children in fulfilling the established goal.

- **Exceptions.** Families can also have rules for exceptions. Exceptions allow the system to deal with the unexpected and regulate necessary behavior even when an important family rule cannot be followed. In the schoolwork example, an exception might go like this: "Jill is very athletic, and we believe personal talents should be enhanced. But we also believe everyone needs to get better grades." In Jill's case, both of these things are not going to happen, so the rule exception in these types of cases emerges as: "We will let her choose where she will put the emphasis of her time."

- **Violation.** Another purpose of family rules is related to rule violations. What happens in a family when a member gets bad grades and has violated the rule about good grades and achievement? What happens when someone does talk about death or negative ideas when the family has proscribed that kind of interaction? These actions will trigger rules that specify what is to be done following such violations.

HOW DO WE MANAGE RULES AND RULE SEQUENCES?

A number of important strategies can help family members manage the rule parts of their family systems. Among them are developing a clear understanding of how and when to be adaptable, understanding developmentally appropriate rules, avoiding rule rigidity, and learning to avoid disabling rules.

Be Adaptable

The idea of change is an important idea. When family rules are too rigid, the family could break instead of bend when the winds of stress come their way (Haley, 1976). If families are willing to be flexible or adaptable in their rules, it is very helpful. An example of little adaptability is seen in what occurred after a mother died. Before her death, the rules of family functioning were clear. Everyone knew the goals and how to accomplish what needed to get done. When this mother died suddenly, the system went into almost complete shutdown because there was no provision for flexibility. Therefore, when she died, there were great gaps left in the system's ability to function.

Before her death, she had taken care of the bills, managed money matters, run the household, maintained connections with other relatives, and made many of the decisions about the growing children. It was months before this family could reorganize, change the rules, reallocate responsibilities, and begin functioning again. The vitality of systems lies in a balance between the chaos of undefined competing rules and the rigidity of inflexible and less adaptable rules. As Haley (1987) suggested, "it is the rigid, repetitive sequence of a narrow range that defines pathology" (p. 112).

The rule part of families can develop several different kinds of problems that need adaptability. Some of these problems are that rules can become developmentally inappropriate, rigid, or disabling. When problems such as these occur, flexibility and adaptability are important, especially as developmental changes occur.

When families have rules that are disabling, it is helpful to have enough adaptability and creativity that the old rules can be adjusted or new ones invented. In these situations, honesty, openness, and willingness to compromise and try new ways of doing things can make the difference between a family being enabling and helpful in achieving personal and family goals or disabling and destructive. When there is adaptability, the rule part of families can serve as a generative mechanism that is capable of creating regularity out of chaos.

Keep Rules Developmentally Appropriate

Families sometimes create rules and rule sequences that are effective for one developmental stage, but they find it difficult to change as growth occurs. An example of this is a family that creates a group of rules that the children must obey their parents. The rules could be appropriate when the children are young and immature, but as the children mature, they increase in their ability to think for themselves, and it is developmentally appropriate to gradually let the children have increasing amounts of autonomy and control over their lives. As they mature in these ways, the rules that they must obey become less and less useful and more and more inappropriate.

There are several situations in which it can be difficult for parents to change rules about obedience. One situation is when the rules about obedience are tied in with emotional fusion or chronic emotional tensions in the family system. In these situations, the emotionality in the family system might be so powerful that it interferes with the ability of the parents to understand that the rules are becoming inappropriate, and they might put extreme pressure on mature children to continue to be obedient.

Another situation in which it can be difficult for parents to change rules about obedience is when the rules are closely tied to family ideologies. When the parents in a family place a high value on obedience and conformity, they might be unwilling to let the system change so the children can become autonomous and independent.

A third situation in which it can be difficult to change rules about obedience is when parents have high standards for their children, and they have a child that is not meeting their standards. For example, if a child is rebellious or independent, or if a child gets into trouble often, the parents might be inclined to try to help the child by trying to enforce rules about obedience long after they are developmentally appropriate.

Developmental changes are continually occurring, necessitating the need to change rules. For example, a young family may have a rule that children should go to bed at 8:30 p.m. The rule might emerge for several reasons when the children were young: Children need a lot of sleep when they are in grade school, parents need free time in the evening, and having a set time allows for easy planning and makes the day orderly. However, if the parents were still trying to make the children go to bed at 8:30 p.m. when they are in high school, it would be unreasonable and developmentally inappropriate. Thus, it is wise to expect that rules in family systems will always be in a state of flux. Much of the time, the rules evolve and change gradually without anyone paying attention to them, but in some situations, it is helpful to consciously make adjustments and modifications.

Avoid Rule Rigidity

Rule rigidity occurs when families do not have enough flexibility in rules, or they are resistant to change (Figure 8.4). Sometimes rule rigidity occurs when rules are appropriate in some situations but not in others. The following story is an example of this type of rule rigidity.

FIGURE 8.4 Sometimes rules are like an unsolvable puzzle; they are too rigid, and family members might not know how to change the rule or cope with the effects of the rules that are in place.

A young newlywed is preparing Sunday dinner. He was preparing the roast when, to the surprise of his wife, he cut the end off of the roast, wrapped it up, and put it in the refrigerator. His astounded wife asked him why. "I don't know," he replied, "that's the way my mom does it. I guess it's good to have a little left over."

When the puzzled wife was visiting the mother-in-law, she asked her the same question, and got the same answer. Later, during a holiday, they all were at the grandmother's house, having a roast, and to the wife's amazement, the grandmother cut off the end of the roast, wrapped it, and continued on with preparations. "Could you tell me why you just did that?" asked the wife. "Well," the grandmother said, "I bought this roasting pan many years ago, and as you can see it is quite small. There is hardly a roast I buy that fits."

Of course, the point of this apocryphal story is that sometimes rules and rules sequences persist long after we know why they were initiated. The rule rigidity element of this story is that even though the principal actors did not seem to have a clue why they were cutting the roast, they continued doing so. Any suggestions to change that would probably be met with some (if not strong) resistance.

The rule emerged, and it was necessary at a period of time. Later, it became obsolete, but it remained as an unexamined, submerged family rule. So are many of the rules families sustain. They have lost their purpose, but they continue on as if breaking or changing them would be harmful. Sometimes families act as if changing a rule means destruction. In actual fact, to not change and adapt creates a better chance for destruction than holding on to outdated and useless rules.

Keep in Mind That Implicitness Is Desirable

Reiss (1981) developed an idea about what happens in families when they find attention is focused on the rules that are usually implicit. He reasoned that:

> The first sign of a disorganizing family is the falling away of implicit regulation and coordination. In a smoothly running family, shared objectives, understandings, role allocations, and norms do not often have to be stated. Even when they are, limit-setting messages can

be very brief and can often be conveyed as gestures. When a family finds it is engaged in laying out verbally explicit rules of itself, it is already in the midst of a stressful situation—although it may still be far from a full-blown crisis.

(Reiss, 1981, pp. 179–180)

Apparently, when a family encounters a situation that is so unusual or stressful that its normal rules do not adequately deal with the situation, the family's attention is diverted to the rules it uses to manage. As a typical consequence, old rules are modified, new ones are invented, or both. Many times, these situations are handled without disrupting the normal operation of the family system, and the new version of family rules recedes into the implicit. However, when families are not able to devise a system of rules that cope with the new situation, a disorganizing cycle tends to occur.

The disorganizing cycle is that when greater attention is given to rules, more of them are made explicit, and the family becomes more disorganized. The disorganization apparently occurs for several reasons. As a family's attention is diverted to its rules, members' concentration on coping with other aspects of life decreases. This results in chores not getting done, missing work, meals being disrupted, and so on. Also, the family realm has such complicated and yet intimate systems that they bog down when attempts are made to explicate very many rules. In the public spheres, where relationships are more limited, rational, and efficiency oriented, it is helpful to bureaucratize and formalize laws, rules, and policies. In the family realm, however, this strategy is the "kiss of death." Families can only operate when the majority of the beliefs they use to govern themselves are shared, implicit, and affectively comfortable.

Thus, Reiss's idea is that when families find it necessary to divert a substantial amount of their attention to explicating rules, it tends to disable them from doing other things, and these processes frequently become parts of a vicious cycle.

PRINCIPLE 8.4

IMPLICITNESS IN SOME FAMILY RULES IS DESIRABLE

When families frequently divert energy and attention to rule making, maintaining, and explicating, they tend to be less efficient and more likely to fail at essential goal attainment.

This idea is helpful in understanding many disabling cycles in families. For example, many families have a difficult time adapting their implicit rule structure in a comfortable way during the teenage years. Parents and teens try to solve this problem by developing long lists of elaborate rules about what teens can do and cannot do, and the rules become part of the problem. Also, when one member of a family begins to deviate from the behaviors that have traditionally been acceptable in a family, a typical response is to "lay down" rules about what is appropriate and acceptable, but the rules seldom help. It does not matter whether the "deviant" behavior is alcoholism, using prohibited drugs, or a religious conversion; explicating rules tends to set up disabling cycles.

Several stages of the family life cycle might be exceptions to the generalization that families are functioning the best when rules are implicit. One exception is during the formative stage of a family. When couples are engaged or newly married, they find it enjoyable and helpful to focus a great deal of their attention on defining their rules and beliefs. At this stage of family life, it is enabling to focus on their values and rules as it helps them lay the foundations of their family system. Gradually, as they construct rules they can live with comfortably, they move beyond this stage, and the rule part of their system becomes implicit.

The same process can also occur somewhat when families encounter major transitions in the family life cycle. For example, when a new child is born, children reach adolescence, children start leaving home, retirement is near, or a death occurs, families seem to find it helpful to spend some time defining and redefining their rules. Usually, however, this occurs without the cycle escalating excessively, and the family is gradually able to let their new "understandings" recede into the realm of the implicit.

Think Sequences

Even though most sequences and common family rules are submerged, families can become aware of some of them, and they can learn skills that help manage at least some of them. In fact, even families that are not well-educated and not very resourceful find it relatively easy to modify vicious cycles when they become aware of them. Several skills can help families become aware of rule sequences.

One skill is to occasionally try to "think sequences" or "think cycles" rather than just "think individuals" when problems occur in a family. Another strategy that sometimes helps is to explore the possibility that the "problem" is a reasonable response to a vicious cycle the family has not noticed. As Haley has observed, it is difficult for people in families to recognize cycles that are more complicated than three steps, but it is possible. Also, only identifying two or three steps in a cycle frequently is enough to be helpful. Often when families recognize two or three steps, these insights lead to the discovery of other steps that are not readily apparent.

Another skill that can help families recognize rule sequences is to ask people who are not in the middle of the situation if they see any vicious cycles operating. When we learn to think this way, members of the family who are not caught up in the vicious cycles can sometimes recognize what is happening and make suggestions that can help those who are involved recognize what is going on. The following situation illustrates how an undesirable rule sequence was repeated in a family many times before a family member that was not involved recognized it.

Step 1. The father's emotional distress would occasionally increase. Many incidents could be the ones to reactivate the cycle after a dormant period. For example, pressures at work, health frustrations, in-law troubles, personal disappointment, and so on could activate his stress.

Step 2. The father would behave in less patient and more critical or obnoxious ways. The first and second steps were a minicycle that would increase both conditions with the father getting more emotionally distressed, less patient, and more critical around the home. Eventually, he would become angry or obnoxious enough that Step 3 would occur.

Step 3. The teenage daughter's room was usually messy and when the father was not upset, he would usually ignore it. However, when he was upset and noticed the daughter's room was messy, he would get after the daughter to clean her room.

Step 4. The daughter would clean her room according to her father's standards rather than her own.

Step 5. The father's pressure on the daughter would increase her emotional distress. Often this was because she would feel angry and resentful.

Step 6. The daughter's behavior in some areas of her life would be less desirable. This could take many forms. It could be she was more irritable or critical, did not do well at school, or misbehaved.

Step 7. The father's emotional distress would increase, and he would be less patient, and so on.

The cycle would repeat again and again until something occurred to disrupt it. The cycle also had several variations. For example, sometimes the mother would get involved instead of the father, and sometimes both parents would get upset before pressuring the daughter. During one of the family "scenes," an older brother happened to notice the connection between Steps 3 and 5. What he saw was 3 then 5 then 3 then 5 then 3 then 5 then 3 then 5, and so on. He described what he thought he saw, and it was enough for the family to eventually recognize they had a rule-bound vicious cycle. Once the cycle was in the consciousness of the family, they were able to see the other steps and devise several ways to disrupt it.

One strategy they devised was to work harder to find a compromise on the standards of cleanliness for the daughter's room. They realized that the ongoing negative tension could be contributing to the cycle, and if the father and daughter were more comfortable about the standards for the room, it might help disrupt the feedback loop.

A second strategy emerged from the belief that high levels of negative emotion were a key factor or at least a good barometer. A few strategies were then consciously devised to help each other find ways to reduce negative emotion when it was recognized. After that, the members of the family were a little more alert to their own moments of distress and the emotional distress in others, and they looked for ways to help each other calm down when upset.

This situation illustrates several important ideas. It illustrates that families can learn to manage at least some rule sequences that involve vicious cycles. It also illustrates several strategies that can be helpful in managing these sequences.

Discussions in Diversity: Grieving Rules

When Dominic (not his real name) was 12 years old, he saw his "crazy" neighbor walking up the street with a rifle. Dominic quickly ran home to tell his mother, who stepped outside to see what was happening. At that moment, a shot rang out, and Dominic's mother fell back to the ground, mortally wounded with a gunshot to her heart.

Recalling this event as an adult, tears filled his eyes. He recounted that his father quickly married, and all pictures of Dominic's mother were removed from the house. Dominic followed the unspoken household rule and was not allowed to talk about his mother or her death, resulting in disenfranchised grief or grief that is minimized or unrecognized by others (see Doka, 2018/1989; Kastenbaum, 2004). Dominic's pain ran deep throughout his life. He grew up to be very successful in his chosen profession (police officer), but he rarely talked about this trauma, not recognizing the invisible rule that brought so much pain.

FIGURE 8.5 The loss of a loved one often involves great grief, although grieving rules may dictate how that grief is expressed.

Source: Alessio Damato / CC BY-SA 3.0 Creative Commons – free to use

Grieving rules are often culturally determined (Figure 8.5). In some cultures, loud wailing and beating of the chest symbolizing one's grief are expected; in others, a quiet, reserved response is the order of the day. Within families, grieving rules are experienced, as well. Peskin (2019) discusses hierarchies or rankings of grief according to family status (parents vs. child, for example, with children being in the lower rank) influencing one's mourning and adaptation to the loss. With the loss of a child through miscarriage, the father might be expected to be stoic and supportive of the mother, while the mother might be expected to openly express her grief. Both parents may deeply feel the loss of the child, yet implicit grieving rules may only allow one parent to show it.

Rules develop around expectations and may help or hinder one's grief experience, especially if the rules aren't shared by other family members. In our family, an older member born in Mexico followed traditional grieving rules related to the loss of a family member. One of those rules was that women (mother/wife) should wear only black for 365 days following the death of a family member. In this situation, the grandchildren of this woman did not approve of the "all black" rule and even purchased colorful clothing for her to wear, hoping that doing so would shorten her grief over losing her son. However, she refused to wear anything but black until the year was finished. Perhaps this rule shortened her grief in the long run, as each day, she laid out her clothing, thought of her dead son, said a prayer, and lit a candle. We cannot assume that how one grieves and the rules one follows are related to the bereaved person's feelings. It is a mistake to assume grief is the same for others.

Although we don't think of it this way, grieving is not an individual endeavor. We are all part of a system with rules, and it is our relational dynamics that influence this experience (Rosenblatt, 2017). We may have grieving rules, but as stated by Peskin (2019), the right to mourn is a fundamental human right.

Questions to Discuss:

- *What grieving rules are you aware of in your family?*
- *How might gender, class, race, ethnicity, religion, and relationships influence grieving rules in a family?*
- *In what ways might grieving rules help someone who has experienced a loss (any type of loss, including non-death losses)?*
- *In what ways might they hinder a person's adaptation to a loss?*

SUMMARY

In this chapter, we learned that rules are "relationship agreements" that limit, guide, and connect us in our family dance (Jackson, 1965b). Simple rules arise from social norms, but more complex family rules arise from many sources, including our family of origin and through daily interactions and negotiation. Family rules are multidimensional and can be classified in many ways. Some of these rules are implicit and unknown to the family (even though they follow the rule). Other family rules are very explicit, negotiated, and monitored by the group.

We also learned that rules can be facilitating and supportive of family growth, as well as constraining and limiting to family growth. Disabling rules result in family members interacting in unhealthy and damaging ways. Families also have rules about rules. These rules are referred to as metarules.

Rules often occur in rule sequences, which are patterned ways of behaving that involve sequences of behavior of several individuals. Rule sequences usually have a cyclic aspect to them, and most families are not aware of them. These sequences can be healthy and enabling, or they can be disabling and help keep a family "stuck" in earlier developmental stages. The rules and rule sequences in family life become part of the package of beliefs, goals, aims, and worldview we label the family paradigm.

This chapter revealed that rules have many purposes. They regulate the way resources are managed, regulate emotional distance, clarify boundaries, control the implementation of decisions, clarify how to deal with exceptions and violation of rules, and so on.

Problems sometimes occur in the rule part of family systems, and when this occurs, families need to consciously manage this part of their systems. Family scientists have discovered several strategies that can be helpful in managing this part of family life. When rules become developmentally inappropriate, too rigid, or disabling, learning to be adaptable is a helpful strategy. Usually, the more implicit rules are, the better. Therefore, when families find it necessary to deal explicitly with their rules, it is desirable to deal with them as little as possible and then let them slide out of awareness.

STUDY QUESTIONS

1 Define what a rule is.
2 How are rules and social norms different?
3 Compare and contrast mores, folkways, and laws.
4 How do rules develop in families?
5 Compare and contrast: explicit rules and implicit rules; facilitating rules and constraining rules.
6 Give three examples of disabling rules.
7 How do metarules differ from other types of rules?
8 What is a rule sequence? Give an example of one.
9 What is a generational rule sequence?
10 Describe eight purposes of family rules.
11 What are some ways to manage rule sequences in families?

KEY TERMS

Rules
Social norms
Folkways
Mores
Laws
Assimilation/accommodation
Implicit rules
Explicit rules
Facilitating rules
Constraining rules
Disabling rules
Metarules
Rule sequences
Generational rule sequences
Distance regulation
Grieving rules

SUGGESTED READINGS

Cigoli, V., & Scabini, E. *Family identity: Ties, symbols, and transitions.* Mahwah, NJ: Lawrence Erlbaum Associates.

Coleman, J. (2021). *Rules of estrangement: Why adult children cut ties and how to heal the conflict.* New York, NY: Harmony.

Pleck, E. (2000). *Celebrating the family: Ethnicity, consumer culture, and family rituals.* Cambridge, MA: Harvard University Press.

REFERENCES

Blevins, W. (1993). *Your family your self.* Oakland, CA: New Harbinger Publications, Inc.

Caine, L. (1974). *The personal crisis of a widow living in America.* New York, NY: Morrow.

Constantine, L. L. (1986). *Family paradigms.* New York, NY: Guilford.

Crane, J., Harper, J. M., Bean, R. A., & Holmes, E. (2020). Family implicit rules, shame, and adolescent prosocial and antisocial communication behaviors. *The Family Journal: Counseling and Therapy for Couples and Family, 28*(2), 72–82.

Cronen, V., Pearce, W., & Harris, L. (1979). The logic of the coordinated management of meaning: A rule-based approach to the first course in inter-personal communication. *Communication Education, 23*, 22–38.

Day, R. D., Gavazzi, S., & Acock, A. (2001). Compelling family processes. In A. Thornton (Ed.), *The well-being of children and families: Research and data needs.* Ann Arbor, MI: University of Michigan Press.

Doka, K. J. (2018). Is there a right to grieve? Enfranchising the disenfranchised. *Psychology Today.* https://www.psychologytoday.com/us/blog/good-mourning/201811/is-there-right-grieve

Feinauer, I. A., Larson, J. H., & Harper, J. M. (2010). Implicit family process rules and adolescent psychological symptoms. *The American Journal of Family Therapy, 38*(1), 63–72.

Ford, F. R. (1983). Rules: The invisible family. *Family Process, 22*(2), 135–145.

Galvin, K., & Brommel, B. (1991). *Family communication: Cohesion and change* (3rd ed.). Glenview, IL: Scott & Foresman.

Gavazzi, S. M., Anderson, S. A., & Sabatelli, R. M. (1993). Family differentiation, peer differentiation and adolescent adjustment in a clinical sample. *Journal of Adolescent Research, 8*, 205–225.

Greenberg, G. S. (1977). The family interactional perspective: A study and examination of the work of Don D. Jackson. *Family Process, 16*, 385–412.

Haley, J. (1963). *Strategies of psychotherapy.* New York, NY: Grune & Stratton.

Haley, J. (1976). *Problem solving therapy.* San Francisco, CA: Jossey-Bass.

Haley, J. (1987). *Reflections on therapy and other essays.* Washington, DC: The Family Therapy Institute.

Hess, R. D., & Handel, G. (1959). *Family worlds.* Chicago, IL: University of Chicago Press.

Hoopes, M. H., & Harper, J. M. (1987). *Birth order roles and sibling patterns in individual and family therapy.* Salem, MA: Aspen Publishers, Inc.

Jackson, D. D. (1957). The question of family homeostasis. *Psychiatric Quarterly Supplement, 31*, 79–90.

Jackson, D. D. (1965a). The study of the family. *Family Process, 4*(1), 1–20.

Jackson, D. D. (1965b). Family rules: Marital quid pro quo. *Archives of General Psychiatry, 12*, 589–594.

Kantor, D., & Lehr, W. (1975). *Inside the family.* San Francisco, CA: Jossey-Bass.

Kastenbaum, R. J. (2004). *Death, society, and human experience* (8th ed.). Boston, MA: Pearson.

Laing, R. D. (1972). *The politics of the family.* New York, NY: Vintage Books.

Larson, J., Parks, A., Harper, J., & Heath, V. (2001). A psychometric evaluation of the family rules from the past questionnaire. *Contemporary Family Therapy, 23*, 83–104.

Lidz, T. (1963). *The family and human adaptation.* New York, NY: International Universities Press.

Minuchin, S. (1996). *Mastering family therapy: Journeys of growth and transformation.* New York, NY: Wiley.

Olson, D. H., & McCubbin, H. I. (1982). The circumplex model of marital and family systems VI: Applications to family stress and crisis intervention. In H. I. McCubbin, A. C. Cauble, & J. M. Patterson (Eds.), *Family stress, coping and social support* (pp. 132–150). Springfield, IL: Thomas.

Peskin, H. (2019). Who has the right to mourn? Relational deference and the ranking of grief. *Psychoanalytic Dialogues, 29*, 477–492.

Reiss, D. (1981). *The family's construction of reality*. Cambridge, MA: Harvard University Press.

Rosenblatt, P. C. (2017). Researching grief: Cultural, relational, and individual possibilities. *Journal of Loss and Trauma, 22*(8), 617–630.

Satir, V. (1972). *Conjoint family therapy: A guide to theory and technique*. Palo Alto, CA: Science and Behavior Books.

Satire, V. (1988). Family reconstruction: The family within—A group experience. *Journal for Specialists in Group Work, 13*(4), 200–208.

CHAPTER 9

Communicating in Families

CHAPTER PREVIEW

In this chapter, readers will learn:

- We can't *not* communicate with those around us, especially family members.
- Several important aspects of communication that we must attend to as we understand how families interact, including the intent and content parts of a message.
- The difference between language and communication and how understanding both helps relationships.
- Types or kinds of messages, such as small talk, control talk, non-sequitur, correcting and lecturing, superlatives, sarcasm and cutting humor, distancing, martyring, and meta-communication.
- Several types of positive communication styles, including straight talk, seeking clarification, reinforcing, seeking congruence, and appropriate self-disclosure.
- How gender differences play a large role in understanding family communication.
- The types of family secrets and how they affect current and future generations.
- Gottman's findings pertaining to communication in marriage relationships.
- Specific strategies one can use to improve family communication.

INTRODUCTION

> The goal in marriage is not to think alike, but to think together.
>
> Robert C. Dodds

Communication is at the heart of expressive family processes. Remember that family processes are strategies that families use to achieve goals, maintain ideological focus, and cope with life's changes and turbulence. Although some of those strategies are hidden from view, many goal-attaining strategies are more visible and expressive. How family members communicate, what they communicate about, and how they resolve differences are examples of these expressive family processes.

Berger, Kellner, and Hansfried (1973) observed, "We converse our way through life." The most frequent activity you do with friends and family members is, most probably, talk. Communicating is a fundamental activity of life. We communicate about who we are, our dreams, our goals, and what we think is good or bad. We critique those around us, negotiate conflict, start fights, and try to find forgiveness. When we communicate, we reveal our weaknesses and strengths and explore our expectations, hopes, and disappointments (Duck, 1997).

DOI: 10.4324/9781003128717-12

Obviously, communication is more than just talking. Communication is the process by which meaning is created and managed (Krauss & Fussell, 1996). As an early founder of the study of family communication once wrote, "We do not originate communication, we participate in it" (Watzlawick, Weakland, & Fisch, 1974). Watzlawick and his colleagues also described another important mantra of family communication: You cannot *not* communicate. In other words, it is impossible to avoid communicating with those in your world. Even if you decide you will never speak to someone again, that is still a type of communication. The point is that communication is a fundamental aspect of relationships; it is the way in which we discover each other, define relationships, and define who we are. We cannot avoid this important family process.

PRINCIPLE 9.1

COMMUNICATION IS A FUNDAMENTAL ACTIVITY OF LIFE

We cannot avoid communicating. Communication is an essential and inescapable element of all relationships.

Communication begins when people meet and begin to establish a relationship. With each person in our world, we create a private and somewhat individualized message system (Tannen, 1986). As we become more involved and committed to a particular relationship, the rules and patterns of interaction take on a richer texture and fuller meaning. In some ways, these emerging relational patterns are mysterious. That is, we do not sit and consciously plan them out; each conversational choice builds on the previous exchange.

We develop these special communication relationships from an early age. First, we watch and communicate with our parents and close family members. Then we branch out and watch the interaction of people on television and movies; we observe how our siblings solve problems and communicate with their friends; we continue to learn by watching our parents and other significant adults.

Each time a new friendship or relationship is formed, our ways of communicating and interacting change and adapt. The changes are not apparent, and most of the time, we do not talk about how we communicate to each other; the patterns just seem to unfold. Some have suggested that this unfolding is like peeling back the layers of an onion (and sometimes we even cry).

In this chapter, we explore the power of family communication. In addition, we discuss several communication principles, along with suggestions for making family communication stronger. The goal is for you to consider the power of communication in primary relationships. We do not spend much time on how one communicates and builds ties with friends or the intricacies of communicating in the workplace. Instead, we focus on communication in families and other close relationships. Specifically, we explore the importance of communication in primary relationships, types of communication, communication styles that build stronger personal bonds, and the role of disclosure in important relationships. The problems inherent in relationship communication are covered only superficially. A later chapter is devoted to those issues. Additionally, we address gender differences in communication: It has become apparent to researchers that men and women communicate differently in close relationships. It is important that we learn about these differences as we make decisions about how to build stronger bonds with family members. This chapter also provides some insights into family secrets. Finally, the latter part of this chapter focuses on several strategies for making partner and family communication more effective.

THE ESSENCE OF COMMUNICATION

Quite simply, communication is an exchange of information. All animals communicate through sounds, smells, body language, touch, and even electrically or chemically! The process is the same (Figure 9.1).

Communication involves a sender that *encodes* (sends) a message to a receiver that *decodes* (receives and hopefully understands) the message. The message may be sent through various means (*medium*), including verbal, written, and other sensory forms. During the communication process, *noise* may interfere with the message. Noise can be actual environmental noise, but it can also be bias, poor attention, or not understanding the meaning of the message. Last, the communication process includes *feedback* from the receiver. Feedback provides the sender with information that the message was received and understood. The communication process is extremely complex and dynamic, with overlapping layers of meaning and experience.

Two fundamental elements of communication are **overt (content)** and **covert (intent) messages** (Watzlawick et al., 1974). The word *overt* means obvious, explicit, observable, and visible. The overt or content element of a message is the "report" part of the message. It is the explicit and obvious raw data of the message, often sent in words. The word *covert* means hidden, disguised, or concealed. The covert or intent element of a message is the message beyond the words, often sent non-verbally.

Intent or covert messages are the most powerful kinds of messages we send. **Intent messages** are usually more concealed, not obvious, but implicit and hidden from view. The covert

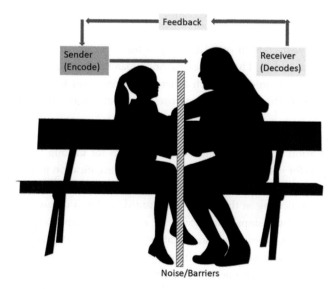

FIGURE 9.1 The process of communication.

intent messages we send are much more subtle and harder to define than overt messages. However, these powerful intentional messages have the potential to override the actual words being used. The intent messages are carried in our tone of voice and things like the small sighs that slip out and the way our eyebrows curl down and tell the receiver we disapprove, for example.

Noller (1984) showed that the intent (non-verbal) element of communication can convey three important messages. First, intent messages can reveal our interpersonal attitudes toward the sender, toward the topic, or toward the situation. The intent messages provide small clues about the assessment of the receiver. The receiver naturally extrapolates from those clues and has to guess what we think of them. The receiver does not have much to go on but will make a guess about our judgment of them based on those limited observations. Most adults are fairly skilled at picking up tones and facial clues that reveal our attitude toward them.

Second, intent messages tell the receiver how we feel about ourselves. Some of us have bad "poker faces." Whether we are having a miserable or great day seems to be written on our foreheads. Some people have the enviable skill of emotional constancy; even if they are having a rotten day, it is hard to tell. For most of us, though, our daily moods are frequently communicated in the message packages we send to those around us. Even if we don't intend on doing so, we tell people with our intent messages if we are depressed, confused, elated, excited, or bored. For most of us, those important intent messages about feelings seem to leak out and people collect the evidence and wonder if we are ill, what we are happy about, or why we are depressed. Especially in close relationships, partners and children read the mood messages that seem to be chained to the content messages. As the saying goes, "if mom ain't happy, ain't nobody happy!" and mom's happiness is often communicated covertly.

The third aspect of intent messages focuses on our interactions with others. We monitor the gaze and posture of others, looking for clues of when to end the conversation, when to let them have a turn, when to laugh, and when to not respond. As Noller (1984) wrote, "One would expect that married couples who communicate well with one another would get to know each other's conversational patterns, and as well, get to know each other's nonverbal cues" (p. 6).

Some messages are sent and the receiver does not decode or interpret them in the same way we were hoping they would. At other times, neither the sender nor the receiver is able to send or receive what they intended. Being clear in one's messages and accurately **decoding** messages from others takes a fair amount of practice and skill for most of us. Few things in life are more puzzling and even aggravating to people than when the messages they send are lost, misunderstood, or misjudged.

We can judge the quality of a relationship by listening to the style of communication revealed in close relationships. To an astute observer, how we think and feel about the other person (and ourselves) is exposed by the way we communicate and talk with them. If we are condescending and hurtful, we have one type of intention; if we are kind and gentle, we have another type of intention.

Language and communication are not the same. **Language** is a uniquely human tool that aids in their communication (Rabiah, 2012). A newborn infant can communicate with its parent through a series of cries, grunts, and vocalizations; however, language does not fully develop until later as shared symbols become known. At that point, communication is much clearer and simpler. Language involves symbols (spoken and written words are symbols for ideas, objects, feelings) that provide shared meaning for the participants and can be broken down into receptive language (understanding, listening. reading) and expressive language (speech, gestures, writing). Further, it can be verbal and non-verbal, direct and indirect. A partner might indirectly let a partner know about a desire to see a movie by leaving a movie review open on a website or hinting around at going to a movie; directly, the partner might say, "Let's go see a movie tonight!" Language is constantly growing and changing across time and across culture (hence the "lift" refers to the "elevator" depending on whether or not you are in London or New York), with different meanings attaching to similar words, even within a family. In our family, grandchildren are frequently referred to as "baby" even though they are beyond the baby stage; this term of endearment is accepted by the grandchildren but someone outside of the grandparents will quickly be told, "I'm NOT a baby!" Telling a spouse that she looks "cute" could result in a smile or a snarl, depending on how the spouse understands the word "cute." Right from birth, humans are drawn to learning language (Thompson, 2016), and by default, the family culture and the culture at large.

TYPES AND KINDS OF FAMILY COMMUNICATION

The study of communication in families is like looking at a ray of light shining through a prism and projecting a rainbow pattern on the wall. The rainbow of information we see tells us about the hidden goals, deeply held beliefs, power differences, and expectations of daily life within families and close relationships. Communication is the process of making and interpreting meaning: As we interact, the rainbow of feelings, dreams, and wants are exposed.

Most family scientists agree that effective communication is at the heart of understanding family strength. Conversely, when couples are experiencing relationship difficulty, it is often the communication style, content, and intent that one turns to for some understanding. Virginia Satir, an author and family therapist, wrote several books and articles about family communication. She showed us how communication is at the center of understanding family life: "Once a human being has arrived on this earth, communication is the largest single factor determining what kinds of relationships he makes with others and what happens to him in the world" (Satir, 1972, p. 30).

Researchers continue to explore the various facets of the communication process in order to begin to understand the various colors in the prism of family communication. Miller, Nunnally, and Wackman (1988) illuminated the kinds of messages we send to our partners. These family scientists suggested that communication in close relationships could be organized into four types. We have reworded and updated their categories and call them (1) small talk, (2) competitive and control talk, (3) meta-communication, and (4) cooperative or straight talk.

Small Talk

When we encounter a friend, stranger, or family member, we often just want to chat. Small talk topics usually focus on news items, the recent rainstorm, daily routines, something silly a child said, or what's for dinner. The purpose of this type of conversation is to build trust and establish bonds of connection. People who are not skilled at making small talk are sometimes seen as intrusive when they skip it and move immediately to requests, lectures, or inquiries. Conversely, if one only knows how to engage in small talk, then it is difficult to build lasting relationships with others.

One type of small talk is **shop talk** (Miller et al., 1988). Shop talk is really small talk that happens at or about the workplace. Often when we meet with friends or colleagues who work with us, we talk about office politics, work-related issues, and events related to employment. This type of small talk can become divisive or boring. Many people do not want to carry work into their home life or recreational settings.

Competitive and Control Talk

Frequently, we try to influence others. Control talk is about influence and change. When we praise, lecture, direct, request, or suggest things to family members, we are using control talk. Parents often supervise their children, monitor their activities by asking where they have been, and teach them while the children are doing homework. All of these activities are control related.

As can be easily imagined, too much control talk can lead to trouble. Sometimes when we push too hard, expect too much, and demand multiple requirements of family members, they understandably fight back.

Fight talk is usually in response to someone pushing us to do or believe something when we do not want to. Both Gottman (1994, 1999) and Miller et al. (1988) found that when one partner provokes or pushes too hard to get something done or changed, about 80% of the time, the other partner fights back. Most family scientists agree that using force to affect change in someone is ineffective. This idea is captured in the communication and change principle.

PRINCIPLE 9.2

COMMUNICATION AND CHANGE

The strategies we use to change someone or something a person is doing often make the situation worse and decrease the chance that the desired change will occur.

Any time we resort to compulsion, attempt to control someone, or try to dominate the situation with what we want to do, the generous spirit of cooperation leaves us. The following is a list of some kinds of destructive, competitive fight talk strategies that people often use. These strategies usually do not work and instead have the effect of making family life destructive.

- **Interrupting.** Often when we are impatient and controlling, we interrupt the other person and try to redirect the conversation to go in the direction we want (Figure 9.2). Sometimes we become so unaware that we interrupt one another that it seems like the natural thing to do in conversation. These interruptions are meant to change the subject, disagree, and disconfirm what is being discussed and are not supportive to the relationship.

  However, Kennedy and Camden (1983) showed that not all interruptions are bad or a sign of dominating and controlling communication, only some kinds are. According to these researchers, most of the interruptions that occurred in their study were *confirmation interruptions*, which are positive and occur when one seeks clarification, agrees with what

FIGURE 9.2 Sometimes, cutting someone off in conversations tells them that you really do not care much about what they are saying.

is being said, or supports what is being discussed. Couples who have communication styles that build relationships make fewer combative, competitive, and dominating interruptions.

- **Non-Sequitur.** The non-sequitur is another competitive fighting tool used effectively by partners who are trying to dominate others. The term *non-sequitur* is a logical term indicating that one idea does not follow from the next. One partner might be talking about work or dinner; the other (maybe even in midsentence) interrupts the flow of the conversation and interjects a thought seemingly unconnected to the conversation. For example, one partner might say, "I had a horrible day at work today!," with the other partner replying, "You should see what I planted in the garden!" Again, such controlling and dominating communication strategies destroy relationship integrity.

- **Correcting and Lecturing.** "If I've told you once, I've told you a million times," people often say. Most of us have been at the receiving end of controlling fight language that begins with sentences like that. Giving unsolicited advice, over-rehearsing a topic, and attempting to change someone through sermonizing usually creates no positive advantage. Like most competitive communication, lecturing creates resistance and resentment. This is particularly true in parent–child relationships when accompanied by harsh discipline (Swinford, Demaris, Cernkovich, & Giordano, 2000). Using harsh forms of correction can have serious unintended effects. Children who grow up where there is frequent competitive, controlling, and dominating correction are much more likely to use violent behavior with their own intimate partners when they become adults. The unintended results of using harsh correction and lecturing can be increased resentment, hostility, and revenge by the recipient.

- **Superlatives.** Another type of competitive fight talk is the use of superlatives. Superlatives are usually adverbs we throw into the conversation to exaggerate the point. These exaggerations and word-enhancing helpers are used to magnify our comments. Some examples are using *never, always,* "Ever since I've known you, you constantly …," and "You are a total idiot." Here are some more examples of superlatives: *completely, continually, incessantly, utterly, absolutely, entirely, perfectly, thoroughly,* and *extremely.* In actuality, there are few instances in which the words *never, completely*, or *continually* are accurate; *always* is a long time and has not occurred yet. We use superlatives in our language to assert control, exaggerate a point, and dominate the conversation. The usual effect is that we push people to fight back. As with other competitive fight talk strategies, the use of superlatives is ineffective in changing someone's behavior or communicating a need or want. For the next few days, count how many times you use or hear someone use superlatives; you might be surprised at the number of times they slip into your conversations. As you count how many times people use them when communicating to you, you might also be surprised.

- **Sarcasm and Cutting Humor.** Another common strategy for gaining control and dominating a relationship is using sarcasm and cutting humor to put others down. In current usage, the term *dissing* is popular. *Dis* is used as a short form of *disrespect* and means to make someone look foolish or unworthy. It also means to use wisecracks or make fun of what someone says or does. Current Western and American culture seem to thrive on the comedic repartee of dissing: This type of demeaning humor is frequently seen on situation comedies and talk shows. Again, when we use sarcasm and cutting humor in an attempt to better ourselves and make others look foolish, we are chasing away the spirit of harmony and unity in close relationships. It destroys trust and creates resentments that might be difficult to reconcile.
- **Distancing.** When we give up on the other person, decide we have had enough, and disengage, we are distancing. Rather than battling with words, we choose to retreat and build barriers.
- **Martyring.** Closely tied to distancing is martyring. The martyr seeks control through a particular type of distancing strategy. He or she will say, "Okay, I see you don't care what I think at all; I'll just go into the kitchen where I belong and make dinner. I guess I'll leave the big decisions to you." The intent is clearly manipulative and controlling. It is designed to get the other partner to say, "Oh, honey, come on. That's not what I meant. No, please stay. Come on, what do you think?"

Interrupting, use of non-sequiturs, correcting and lecturing, sarcasm and cutting humor, distancing, playing the martyr, and overuse or inaccurate use of superlatives are communication strategies that are likely to backfire. Any time we use overt or intent messages to manipulate and elicit responses from those around us, we are slipping into some form of competitive communication style.

PRINCIPLE 9.3

COMPETITIVE COMMUNICATION CAN BE DEADLY

Several forms of competitive communication, when employed, have the tendency to destroy relationships.

Meta-Communication or Search Talk

Miller et al. (1988) also listed search talk as an important type of relationship communication. When we talk about how we talk about things, we call this search talk or **meta-communication**. Meta-communication is important because it allows us to put the normal flow of decision making, problem-solving, and conflict resolution on hold. Then we step aside and ask deeper questions, such as, "Why do we argue that way?" We might express appreciation for the kind tone in a partner's voice or find ways of adjusting how we interact. A good metaphor for meta-communication is the racetrack. Most of the time, the race car is zooming around the track. In terms of communication, we would be solving problems, scheduling our lives, making decisions, and attempting to understand the needs and wants of those around us. Occasionally, however, we must pull into the pit stop area and examine the process itself. We look under the hood, so to speak, change a tire, and refuel. We do not need to do that often, but it does need to happen.

If done effectively, meta-communication can be useful in building stronger relationships. However, if done too often or not frequently enough, it can be less than helpful. As new relationships are formed, one would expect the individuals to spend more time exploring how they do things in their relationships. As relationships mature, only infrequent "pit stops" are needed, and couples spend the bulk of their time doing their relationship tasks instead of talking about how they do them. Spending too much time talking about how we talk irritates most people. In addition, if meta-communication is rare, opportunities are lost to build stronger, more effective communication bonds.

Cooperative or Straight Talk

Learning to take the "barbed wire and buckshot" out of our intimate communications with others is a lifelong effort for most people. Most of us are a bit competitive and controlling and seek to dominate others too frequently. The following communication patterns come straight from the heart, are non-competitive in their intent message, and tend to build relationship strength (Figure 9.3).

- **Seeking Meaning.** One way to send non-defensive, non-combative, non-competitive intent and content messages to those close to us is to seek meaning. When we seek meaning,

FIGURE 9.3 Cooperative communication can build strength in relationships.

we listen carefully, non-judgmentally, and without thinking about what we want to say next. Listening with the intent of seeking meaning means we are studying and learning from the sender. We ask the other person to expand their thoughts, explore ideas, and express opinions. There is no hidden agenda; there is no impatience as we wait for a place to break into the other person's story so we can give our lecture, tell a better story, or make a joke of what is being said.

Instead, we look into the sender's eyes with affection, concern, and caring; we only want to hear what they have to tell us. For many people, this is surprisingly difficult. You might be surprised, however, that when you practice this skill, your appreciation for the other person is greatly enhanced. Additionally, we learn far more in these situations than when we are impatiently waiting for a spot to jump in and tell our stories. Satir (1972) suggested that the way we frame (or interpret) what others are saying tells a lot about us. For example, if we are jumping in, being competitive, or listening for only negative elements in someone's story or comments, it might mean that we have a lower sense of self-worth. Confident and mature listeners have little need to best someone's story, make fun, be sarcastic, or interrupt.

- **Seeking Clarification.** When we seek clarification, we go beyond seeking the meaning of the interaction. In this situation, we are listening closely and find some aspects of the message unclear. Good counselors are experts at knowing how to seek clarification. They gently encourage the sender to expand an idea or give examples of what they mean, or they will connect what is being said to some other part of the sender's message. When we do this, we encourage the sender and build trust. The sender cannot help but see that we really care and want to know what he or she feels or needs.

- **Reinforcing.** As the sender is explaining an important message to us, it is important that we tell them (using both intent and content messages) that we appreciate the story or concern. We reinforce or reward the disclosure by saying simple things like "Uh-huh," "Sure," "I see," or "Really?" Remember that it is the intent part of the message that carries the relationship communication. When we encourage or reinforce people for telling us their story or expressing a need or want, we tell them that we want to be trusted, that what they want is important to us, and that we will take their story, request, or need seriously. Trust and connection are lost when we are uncaring or even lazy in developing these skills. Each new encounter during a day starts the relationship over (even if we have been married for 20 years). We define how we care for our partners each time we greet them, listen to their stories, respond to a request, or simply take note of the difficult day they are having. If we become lazy in these daily encounters, our close family and friends will begin to think we take that relationship for granted.

- **Seeking Congruence.** According to Jacob (1987), congruency of messages leads to greater relationship satisfaction. Congruency occurs when we take the time to make sure that the intent and content aspects of messages are similar or congruent. If one partner says, "I love you" with the content message, but the intent message is one of distance and coolness, then the messages are not congruent and the chances for building relationship strength decrease. On the other hand, if one's non-verbal (intent) language confirms that the partner does, indeed, love the other, the message package (both content and intent) builds the relationship. When congruence is missing, relationship confusion and anxiety are created.

When messages are congruent, family members are more likely to receive and send messages with greater clarity. Conversely, when there is less congruence (Satir, 1972;

Sieburg, 1985; Wynne, 1984), family members might have problems with relationship ambiguity. The message confusion creates relationship ambiguity and can affect how we feel about ourselves. Children can experience doubt about what parents really think about them if parents' messages are not authentic. When messages are congruent, authentic, and not confused, children (and spouses) are not left to wonder about how those important to them really feel about them.

Further, message congruence seems to have a significant effect on those within a relationship dyad (Sieburg, 1985; Wynne, 1984). These researchers suggest that when congruence is low, it is more likely that family members will have poorer self-perceptions. It seems that message confusion creates relationship ambiguity and personal weakness. Additionally, when we are more confident of our own inner self, we are more likely to communicate with greater congruence. Apparently, this is one reason why clear, direct, involved, and open communication is associated with more functional marriages (Jacob, 1987).

- **Appropriate Self-Disclosure.** One of the more powerful types of cooperative communication is the use of appropriate self-disclosure. This occurs when an individual reveals to one or more people some personal information they would not otherwise learn. We acquire information through daily interactions. As we become more confident in the reliability of those close to us, we reveal more and more about who we are, what our needs are, and what we need from others.

Waring and Chelune (1983) found that self-disclosure accounts for more than half of the variation in intimacy among couples. That is, although there are many factors that contribute to a feeling of intimacy with another, those feelings of closeness are tied to our ability to share special and private information about our inner lives. Therefore, when researchers ask couples about how much they share with one another, the result is that the more a spouse engages in appropriate self-disclosure, the more likely both partners are to be satisfied with the relationship (Bograd & Spilka, 1996; Hansen & Schuldt, 1982; Rosenfeld & Bowen, 1991).

There is an important message in the self-disclosure research for men. Bell, Daly, and Gonzalez (1987) found that wives whose husbands self-disclose more (e.g., sensitivity, spirituality, physical affection, self-inclusion, and honesty) also reported much higher levels of marital satisfaction. They also found that what was disclosed to spouses was important. They wanted to know if secrecy was something that damaged marriages. They found that men disclosing more about the relationship (with the partner) was more important than whether or not they kept some secrets about their personal life. They suggested that sometimes it is better to leave some things unsaid. A popular phrase captures this idea: Which hill are you willing to die on? One must know the difference between being honest and open about relationship issues that really matter and keeping silent about those topics that will only make things worse. Sometimes it is better to just let a topic drift away, unexplored and undiscussed.

For most of us, it takes concentration and practice to know when to comment and when to let go of a topic or issue. Baxter and Wilmont (1985) found that relationships could be strengthened when those in close relationships held back and did not "tell all." Sometimes partners' overdisclosures create a relationship threat and have the opposite of the intended effect. The intended message of the disclosure might have been to confide, build closeness, and connect. Instead, the message received is one of threat and confrontation.

On the other side of this coin, one should not keep secrets from partners as a way to deceive and manipulate. Vangelisti (1994) and Vangelisti and Caughlin (1997) found that the relationship between family secrets and family satisfaction depended on the reasons why the secrets were kept. If partners were keeping secrets to avoid evaluation or to keep from getting in trouble, these messages were perceived as divisive. However, when family members kept secrets to protect people, this strategy was seen as a sign of relationship strength.

As Sieburg (1985) found, learning the art of appropriate disclosure and secrecy are key elements of a good relationship. Timing is everything in building strong relationships. Over time, we learn when to disclose, when to hold back, and when to let the topic drop permanently. Learning when and how to employ these communication strategies takes higher levels of emotional maturity and years to perfect.

PRINCIPLE 9.4

COOPERATIVE COMMUNICATION BUILDS RELATIONSHIP STRENGTH

When employed correctly, several forms of cooperative communication have the power to enhance and enrich relationships.

Finally, to fully understand the various colors in the prism of communication, we need to explore other facets of the communication process. We have examined encoding and decoding processes, as well as the explicit report element and implicit intent element of communication. Further, we have discussed the types and kinds of family communication. An additional feature of the communication rainbow is related to who family members talk with and the topics discussed.

Dickson-Markman and Markman (1988) asked couples about the "who" and "what" of their interchanges. Not surprisingly, most couples spent far more time talking with their spouses than they did others (even friends or other family members). On average, couples had about 1.24 interactions per day that lasted long enough to be considered a conversational exchange. Those exchanges lasted an average of about 2 hours. The most frequent topics of discussion were work, home maintenance, children and other family members, conversations they had during the day with other people, and food. Notice what is missing from this list. These researchers found that couples rarely spend time talking about their own relationships. When they did talk about their relationship, it usually occurred after a sexual encounter or during an escalating conflict.

Another view of couples' interaction came from Noller and Feeney (1998), who found that couples reported an average of 22 conversations per week (about three per day), with each being about 20–30 minutes long. Of course, the length of time spent conversing with our partners is influenced by work schedules, the number of children in the home, and the age and stage of family members. Further, Roberts (2000) learned that couples who reported higher levels of marital satisfaction spent more time together at home and more time talking about personal topics. Of course, this raises the question: Does good communication add to feelings of couple satisfaction or do couples who like each other already stay home and talk more? No one has tackled that research yet.

GENDER IN COMMUNICATION

In the words of Paiczewski, DeFrancisco, and McGeough (2019), "Gender matters," and it is important to understand how gender operates in communication. Linguists, psychologists, communication, and gender studies people are just a few of the scholars studying and theorizing about gendered communication. Many findings have been consistent across discipline, but it's important to remember that gender itself is an evolving concept that intersects with class, race, ethnicity, age, sexual orientation, and ability in complex ways (Paiczewski et al., 2019). The research on men's and women's communication styles is still emerging, and it is frequently changing in findings and emphasis.

Much has been said about how men and women communicate differently in close relationships. Certainly, gender differences with respect to communication are an important topic for study. Men, generally, are socialized to communicate differently than women. They see the world of relationships with a slightly different hue. To learn how to strengthen relationship ties between men and women, one must attend to those differences. For example, Beck (1988) re-substantiated the idea that men do not talk about personal things as much as women do. He found that women think their marriages are stronger and working better when there is plenty of dialogue and exchange about the relationship. On the other hand, the men in this study generally felt the opposite. When communication turned to topics of relationships and marital evaluation, they felt the relationship was much more likely to be in trouble.

Similarly, Mackey and O'Brien (1995) found that a frequent source of tension between marital partners was the husbands' discomfort with talking about their inner thoughts and feelings. These husbands were not only uncomfortable talking about feelings but they also judged feeling-connected relationship messages as negative and harmful. Other researchers found that husbands actively try to control the amount of communication about feelings and personal topics. These researchers found that husbands are uncomfortable participating in what we labeled earlier as search talk. Correspondingly, their wives were unhappy with the lack of these relationship messages between them and their partners (Ball, Cowan, & Cowan, 1995).

Deborah Tannen, a linguistics professor from Georgetown University, developed "gender-lect theory" and wrote a popular book about this topic. Tannen (1990) emphasized that men approach life as a contest in which each party is striving to "preserve independence and avoid failure" (p. 25). Women, on the other hand, approach life as a community affair in which the goal is to connect, maintain intimacy, and avoid isolation. Men try to get out of relationships; women try to stay connected.

Similarly, several researchers have commented on the notion that men view relationships as a backdrop for attaining, maintaining, and evaluating status. When men interact, they are more likely to compare themselves to the other person, rating the position and social rank of the other and protecting information about themselves that would diminish their status ranking with the other. Conversely, women, in general, are more likely to engage in relationships for connection and association.

In the same vein, when problems arise, women usually respond with more understanding; men tend to give advice and try to solve the problems (Tannen, 1990). This can result in relationship problems. In times of distress, what might be needed are supportive, encouraging, and nurturing responses. Men may be slower to realize those needs and, instead, be quicker to give a lecture, provide solutions, and sermonize. Some have suggested that this is because men see the world as more hierarchical; women see the world as cooperative and focus on connectivity (Olson & DeFrain, 1994).

As Tannen (1990) suggested, men spend more time thinking in terms of hierarchy; they are attuned to the process of evaluating. Men frequently evaluate to determine whether they are a notch up or a notch down vis-à-vis the other. Men like to keep score and tally how many bouts they lost and how many they won. A male colleague recently described a bad day by saying, "Some days you eat the bear; some days the bear eats you."

According to Tannen, a primary goal for women in relationships is to design their communication style so that it helps them avoid isolation. Therefore, women are the networkers of the world. They are fonder of association with others than they are of keeping score. They are also more likely to seek out friends and community members who will provide that expanded associative role.

Empirical research has found the following four areas of communication differences between men and women that can affect relationships:

Topical Differences

Bischoping (1993) found that men and women communicate about different topics in casual conversation. The primary small-talk topics that both men and women seem to discuss are money and work. However, men more frequently speak about leisure. This includes sports, personal fitness, movies, and so on. On the other hand, although women do talk some about leisure, they also talk about men more than men talk about women. In fact, in this study, the women were four times more likely to talk about men than men were to talk about women. Recently, Aggarwal, Rabinovich, and Stevenson (2020) analyzed male/female postings related to COVID 19 on the Reddit discussion platform and corroborated previous findings even in this online context, with men focusing on economic and political aspects of the pandemic and women focusing on social topics.

Message Clarity

Another feature of gendered communication is that wives send clearer messages to husbands (Noller & Fitzpatrick, 1993; Thompson & Walker, 1989). These researchers also noted that husbands tend to give more neutral messages. A neutral message has an unclear or absent emotional or affective tone attached. Wives send more messages with some affective or emotional tone. Additionally, wives set the emotional tone of arguments. They are more likely to escalate conflicts and use emotional appeals and threats.

Interruptions

Interrupting was once considered a sign of dominance in relationships. Therefore, it was assumed that men would interrupt women more often because they are typically in a more dominant position relative to women. This idea has been discounted (Aries, 1996). In fact, research indicates that men and women interrupt at about the same rates and most of those disruptions are supportive and connective rather than aggressive and competitive. However, when the couples are observed participating in personal casual conversation, women interrupt men more than men interrupt women. As our understanding of this important family process has become more sophisticated, it has become clear that not all interruptions are the same. Most researchers agree (cf. Aries, 1996) that there is actually far less interrupting than family scientists once thought. Therefore, it is difficult to determine an accurate sense of what interruptions really mean to relationships when the research is based on short conversations between non-family members.

Directness

One gender difference in communication style is how direct men and women are in conversation. Women usually approach conflict indirectly. This means they will try to solve the situation and possibly take some type of conflict-reducing measures that their partners do not recognize. When men are faced with confrontation, conflict, and disagreements, they use direct approaches, such as bargaining and negotiation. Note that the root word in *bargain* is *gain*. Men spend more time positioning themselves to secure gain. They will Men ask, demand, seek closure, and stipulate. On the other hand, women drop hints, suggest, mention, propose, and defer (Noller & Fitzpatrick, 1990).

In like manner, men expect compliance, especially when talking to a woman. Women begin message exchanges expecting non-compliance (Falbo & Peplau, 1980). Another way that we see differences in directness is that women approach difficult situations in ways that involve and engage participants. Men approach similar situations expecting to promote, suggest, and even demand resolutions that feature autonomy and authority (Tannen, 1990). To that end, women are more accommodating, supportive, and socially responsive. Men, instead, provide suggestions and solutions to problems, as well as opinions and information (Aries, 1982).

An interesting window into the preceding differences can be found in the language structure women use to communicate. Women are more tentative in their language and use tag phrases such as "isn't it?" Men state things in ways that do not invite contradiction.

In sum, the approach men and women use in conversation and relationship connection is gendered. This means that men and women use different relationship strategies and, of course, implies that men and women might have different goals in relationships. Men typically see relationships as a feature of life necessary to attain other goals, such as being a notch up at work, getting a better job, winning an argument, or closing a deal. Women are more likely to see the relationship as an end in itself. There is no secondary goal. Why these differences in communication exist is a matter for debate. Males and females may be socialized differently. Perhaps such differences are the result of evolution or perhaps the brains of men and women are structured and wired differently (which may also result from being socialized differently!). An important point to keep in mind, though, is that there is much variation within each sex.

FAMILY SECRETS

Touch a family deeply and you will find a secret kept from a spouse, a child, a lover, a parent, an in-law, a friend, a boss, a teacher, or even from the secret-bearer. Secrets fashioned in one generation may be handed down like booby-trapped heirlooms, waiting to explode into symptomatic expression, even a generation or two later.

(Imber-Black, 2007, p. 15)

We all have secrets. Some secrets are innocuous and positive, such as a gift hidden in the closet. Other secrets, such as abuse or parentage, may affect how we see ourselves and deeply influence our relationships for generations.

Scholar, psychologist, and therapist Mark Karpel (1980) delineated family secrets by boundaries in the relationship system. He writes, "secrets involve information that is withheld or differentially shared between or among people…The phrase *between or among people* signals that we are squarely in the realm of interpersonal relationships and *withheld or differentially shared* immediately suggests the notion of boundaries and alliances, that is the structuring of relational systems" (p. 295). Secrets are not about feelings but about facts, real occurrences, or events. Based on boundaries, Karpel identified three types of family secrets:

1 **Individual Family Secrets.** These secrets are held by one member of the family and kept from others. For example, a partner might keep an affair secret or hide debts accrued through gambling; an adolescent might hide a love interest. In these instances, the boundary surrounds the individual and separates the secret holder from other/s. Even though the secret is held by only one member of the family, it can still color the family relationships and interactions.

2 **Internal Family Secrets.** These secrets are kept by at least two members of the family, locking other members out of the secret. Such secrets can create unhealthy alliances and result in distancing from other family members. Intergenerational alliances (such as between a father and a son who are both aware of the father's infidelity against a spouse) can be particularly problematic. Once outed, feelings of betrayal can occur. As you consider internal family secrets, recognize that the secret between two people also involves triangulation between the secret holders and others who are kept outside. These are still unknowingly part of the secret, as subgroupings occur in the family. A secret adopted child, conception through in vitro or surrogate mother, or an unexpressed genetic disorder are examples of internal family secrets. Another example is a family whose grandfather was convicted of a white-collar crime resulting in him serving three years in prison. The conviction and imprisonment were hidden from the adolescent grandchildren, who were told that grandpa was away working during the years of incarceration. Upon learning that they had been lied to, the grandchildren experienced a bewildering lack of trust and guilt. They said they wished they had known so that they could have supported him during those lonely years. They also could have learned earlier that people make mistakes and can atone for those mistakes. Of course, not all internal family secrets are problematic. Planning a 50th anniversary party for parents can be strengthening and joyous for families.

3 **Shared Family Secrets.** These family secrets are kept by all members of the family and are unknown to outsiders. Such secrets carried by all family members tend to strengthen family boundaries separating the family from the outside world. Child abuse, drug and alcohol abuse, incest, and incarceration are examples of shared family secrets that can have a lifelong impact on family members as they struggle to protect the family or even limit their interactions with others. A young family member might choose not to move away to college or independent living in an (usually unsuccessful) attempt to protect a parent or sibling from abuse, thus limiting the person's opportunity for growth. Again, however, some shared family secrets are joyful, involving traditions, celebrations, and family triumphs.

Family secrets have consequences that can cast long shadows on the lives of family members (Handler, 2019; Karpel, 1980; Vrij, Nunkoosina, Paterson, Oosterwegel, & Soukara, 2002)

FIGURE 9.4 Family secrets can cast long shadows on the lives of family members.

Source: https://www.istockphoto.com/photo/shadows-of-family-on-the-beach-gm1302352679-394120144

(Figure 9.4). These consequences can be informational, emotional, physical, relational, and even practical. Informationally, family secrets "result in deception, distortion, and mystification" (Karpel, 1980, p. 298) and create a false sense of reality (Handler, 2019).

Emotionally, family secrets can influence the entire family system knowingly or unknowingly living a lie. Feelings of anxiety, shame, and guilt can run through a family, often without family members understanding why. It is reasonable to expect that secrets can result in physical manifestations related to stress, from tension headaches to substance use and abuse (Handler, 2019).

As seen by Karpel's work, family secrets influence relationships, fueling distrust, suspicion, and resentment. The family system may be unbalanced in the face of unhealthy alliances. Together, these can have harmful practical consequences on the family members, as family bonds are broken. Additionally, Imber-Black (1998) writes that family secrets can freeze the development of individual family members, as well as the family as a whole, as they prevent relationships (and people) from adapting, changing, and evolving. Other practical consequences simply relate to the difficulty of keeping secrets secret.

We cannot provide a "how-to" manual for when and where to reveal family secrets because of the complexity of the problem. Who should be told (if at all)? When should they be told (if at all)? What is the reason for sharing a secret? How will the sharing of the secret influence the secret holder/s, the others, and even the community? It is safe to say that sharing family secrets should not happen during family rituals or transitions (such as weddings or family reunions). Some families may turn to a family therapist, who will need to carefully tread the situation and consider the effects on the entire family system (Deslypere & Rober, 2018).

Still, the revelation of many family secrets can lead to personal freedom and hope. Through a college assignment, one young man discovered that his grandfather had murdered other family members and committed suicide. This event was never discussed and kept secret from the young man. After accidentally finding out about the tragedy, he remarked that it made his whole life "make sense." He had always felt there was something being held back and affecting all the family interactions. Once he found out why, he believed he was able to move forward in a healthy way, and he now looked forward to his future with a renewed sense of optimism.

COMMUNICATION AND MARRIAGE—THE GOTTMAN WAY

For over 20 years, psychologist, researcher, and clinician, John Gottman studied couples in his "Seattle Love Lab." Couples would spend a weekend in the "love lab" apartment, where they were videotaped interacting. These recordings were then analyzed, resulting in many important and fascinating findings. Gottman's research revolutionized marriage counseling. In the past, therapists worked hard at helping couples improve their communication through active listening and sending "I messages" (Gottman, 1999). However, Gottman found that communicating through difficulty was not as important as *how couples negotiated interactions between fights*! To strengthen marriage and prevent divorce, Gottman works to "strengthen the friendship that is at the heart of any marriage" (p. 46). This method of couple therapy has been found to be effective and enduring (Davoodvandi, Nejad, & Farzad, 2018). Gottman has written several popular books related to making marriage work, including *Why Marriages Succeed or Fail* (Gottman, 1994) and *The Seven Principles for Making Marriage Work* (Gottman, 1999). These books provide readers with excellent information, as well as exercises to follow for strengthening relationships. Following is a summary of Gottman's principles as related to ideas discussed in this chapter.

The 5 to 1 Ratio

Gottman found that the ratio of competitive and control talk to cooperative or straight talk (to use the language of this chapter) was much more important in predicting marital breakup than was the overall style of communication. In fact, he found that marriages that survived for many years contained partners who could maintain at least a five-to-one ratio of positives to negatives (Gottman, 1999, p. 29). Thus, the negative, competitive, and control expressions presented earlier, including inappropriate interrupting, lecturing, scolding, using the non-sequitur, being a martyr, and the use of sarcasm should be heavily outweighed by positive straight-talk communication forms, including seeking meaning and clarification, communication congruence, and appropriate disclosure.

Harsh Startup

Gottman found that one of the most severe problems in communication styles is when we use competitive control communication to begin our exchanges with our partners. Let's label this idea the **harsh startup** principle.

PRINCIPLE 9.5

HARSH STARTUP

The tone and intent of the way we begin conversations is a sign of relationship strength. When we lead out with harsh, negative, and biting comments, it is a sign our relationship is weaker. Conversely, if we lead out with a calm, generous, gentle, and civil intent, it is a sign we care more about our partner and that the relationship is stronger.

Look back at the list of controlling and competitive forms of communication. This principle tells us that not only are these strategies destructive but their destructiveness is amplified when one of them is the first thing out of our mouths. Imagine a scene in which the wife walks in the door from work. The husband barely says hello, but then launches into a lecture: "I thought you said you were going to be home at 5:30. Did you remember that we are supposed to be at the Frogman's by 7:00? What were you thinking?" Gottman's (1999) research shows us that about 96% of the time, when a conversation begins with a harsh startup from the control and competitive communication styles listed earlier, it will end with a negative tone. It does not seem to matter if you try to make it up, either. "Oh … okay, I am sorry, that was too blunt. Let me start over." Actually, you cannot start over. The damage for that encounter cannot be recalled (Figure 9.5).

Remember, each contact with our partners is a new encounter (Ehrlich, 2000). We sometimes believe that our encounters with our close family members are continuous. Actually, they are not. Each time we meet and greet is a new scene in the relationship play. That does not mean it is a new play, but it is a new scene. Our partners read our intent tones, gather information about how we feel toward them, reflect on what information they want to disclose, and prepare messages to send to us. If we ignore this important rule and assume that the context of the new encounter is not important, we are missing an important principle of life. As Ehrlich (2000) states, "Many of the defining moments of our lives can be traced to the impact of first encounters….There is magic in the power in the first encounter … [and] all human communication encounters are first encounters" (p. 5).

Our job in close relationships is to realize that each new day, each new encounter is manageable. We can and must manage those repeated first impressions. However, most of us get lazy and act as if the repeated first encounters do not matter much, so we simply blast away with what is on our mind. If what is on our minds gets encoded into a nasty, controlling demand or lecture, it is almost certain that that segment of the relationship exchange will end on a negative tone and maybe even in a full-fledged fight. Most people, when challenged or pushed with a message that is confrontational, threatening, or demanding, do not repeatedly return the confrontation with generosity and openness. Instead, we eventually (or quickly) become resistant, combative, and even hostile.

Therefore, one place to start in building stronger relationship patterns with those you love is to plan more carefully how you express concerns, wants, wishes, requests, desires, and needs. Open the encounters with small talk that is at least neutral and, if possible, positive. Timing is crucial. Waiting for the right moment to express a need or want can make all the difference in the outcome.

FIGURE 9.5 This couple is slamming each other at the dinner table. Harsh startup (like slamming a tennis ball across the court at your partner) is usually met with the same kind of response: They slam it right back at you.

The Four Horsemen

Gottman expands our list of competitive communication styles and includes four specific types of negative communication patterns he calls the "Four Horseman of the Apocalypse," a reference to the Biblical vision in which four horsemen usher in the final demise of the world. His assertion is that when we participate in these four deadly kinds of competitive interactions, our own world of marriage and family might come tumbling down on us. These four strategies of marital doom are **criticism**, **contempt**, **defensiveness**, and **withdrawal**. As you will note, they are similar to the types of control language listed earlier. Learning about these deadly communication styles and how to avoid the use of them is an important way of building strong communication patterns, not only for marriage but all family relationships.

• **Criticism.** Criticism has many elements of destructive communication. This type of communication sends messages of disapproval, condemnation, denigration, and denunciation. It is sometimes like a heated ping-pong match, hitting comments right back at the partner with as much force as possible. We cannot go through life living with our partners without, at some time, being annoyed at something they do. It is a fact of life. The trick is deciding what type of message to send, how to encode it, and how to make sure it does not damage the relationship. Having a complaint is normal, natural, and predictable. Using criticism in response to an irritation does not help the situation; it makes things worse. It is one thing to say, "The way you talked to my mother last night concerns me. You seem to be annoyed with her lately." It is another thing to take the annoyance or concern to another level of attack and make our words more global and general. "You are a socially clumsy oaf. Every time you get around my mother, you blow her off and make her feel like a moron." Once we become less specific and more general, we begin using more superlatives, personal attacks, lectures, and sarcasm. We are much less likely to use message clarity, seek meaning, and find congruence in our communication exchanges. Gottman (1999) indicated that harsh startups are often disguises for impending criticism. We slam someone quickly with a complaint (but it is not couched in the language of seeking meaning and congruence) and then move rapidly to the general, non-specific criticism. The following is a true example of how this works.

- On a rainy Saturday night, a family decided that all of them (Mom, Dad, and 18-year-old Jacob) would go to a movie. Jacob had been up all the previous night watching movies with friends, waiting to go early in the morning to a ticket office to stand in line for tickets to a concert. After the ticket adventure, he and his friends played basketball for much of the day. Consequently, he was tired and fell asleep during the afternoon. He still wanted to go to the movie, however. Mom and Dad had some shopping to do before the movie. Jacob did not want to go shopping but instead would meet Mom and Dad at the show at 7:30 p.m.

- The pre-purchased ticket was left on the kitchen counter with a note to meet the parents at the movie. Mom and Dad saved a seat for Jacob; the movie began, but no Jacob. After the movie, Mom and Dad returned home to find Jacob with a sour face in the kitchen. Dad said, "So, what happened? You didn't wake up in time for the movie?" (It was a bit of a harsh startup, a little sarcastic, and a bit critical.) Jacob took the bait and responded with a harsh startup of his own: "Well, if you guys would ever tell me what is going on, maybe I could figure out what to do." That took Dad by surprise. He thought the evening plans were quite clear. His startup with a critical intent inevitably led to a confrontation. Dad assumed Jacob simply did not get up in time and had wasted the $7.50 for the ticket. Jacob was annoyed because Dad had made a mistake and Jacob did not know what to do.

- You see, Dad had purchased the tickets in the afternoon. Apparently, the ticket seller did not hear him correctly and had sold Dad three tickets for the afternoon matinee. Printed on the ticket was a 4:30 time for the movie. Jacob assumed that Mom and Dad had told him the wrong time, the movie was over when he awoke from his nap, and the theater would not let him in with an afternoon ticket. He was mad at Dad because of his mistake. Dad was mad at Jacob because he was being irresponsible.

- All of the relationship trouble could have been avoided. If both Jacob and Dad had not blasted a harsh startup in the new encounter after the movie, several minutes of negative, relationship-destroying conversation could have been avoided. All Dad would have had to say was, "Gee, we missed you. What happened?"

- **Contempt.** Often, the conversation boils over even more. Sometimes couples do not stop at criticism; they take it a notch higher and resort to words and intent messages that convey contempt (Gottman, 1999). Contempt can be defined as content and intent messages that convey disdain, scorn, and censure. When we see couples elevating a conflict to this level, there is a sneering and sniping tone to their voices. It often involves name-calling, eye-rolling, mockery, and sneering (Gottman, 1999). It conveys more than just a competition, going one step further and sending a message of disgust. This type of demeaning conversation destroys trust, alienates us from our partners, and sends a message that we have no respect for the person. As Gottman indicates, a common response to contemptuous comments is belligerence and increased aggressive anger toward our partners.

- **Defensiveness.** Both criticism and contempt result in sharp increases in defensive responses. Unfortunately, defensiveness does not work well. Resistance and self-protection often bring more attack rather than resolution. Attacking spouses are more likely to press on for resolution than they are to back down. Think for a minute: When was the last time someone criticized you and you respond with a defense ("I was not; I was only 20 minutes late"), and the attacking person said, "Oh, gee, that's right, I was wrong, sorry for bringing it up"? If you are like most people, that rarely happens. Defensiveness spawns more competitive exchanges and escalates conflicts. These three horsemen of the apocalypse work together, pushing us to attack, denounce, and defend.
- **Stonewalling.** Rather than continue the confrontation, sometimes a partner will tune out: "Okay, that's it for me. Do whatever you want. I could not care less." Think back to our list of competitive and controlling communication patterns. Among them, you will find distancing and martyring. Both of these are captured in Gottman's (1999) fourth deadly horseman. Stonewalling, distancing, and using the martyr strategy usually come later in relationships. Years of head-butting and competitive exchanges have conveyed the message that no change occurs in most of the relationship struggles; so one might conclude, what is the point of struggling? Gottman (1999) tells us that 85% of the time, it is the husband who retreats and resorts to stonewalling. He decides that the aggravation is not worth the effort.

IMPROVING FAMILY COMMUNICATION

Let's explore what we can do to improve communication in our close relationships and avoid the deadly effects of competitive and controlling communication. The following are a few suggestions. First, **kindness** seems to be more important than being an "effective" communicator. Couples who are more clumsy, more forgetful, and ineffective in communicating what they want in a relationship are able to meet family goals better (in spite of these communication problems) when they are kinder and more generous. Couples who are good communicators (i.e., clear messages, precise directions, and accurate expectations) are probably not as successful with their family's goals if kindness is absent. When family members think in terms of kindness rather than competition and control, we can begin to remove the criticism, contempt, defensiveness, and stonewalling from our response menus during the daily family contact.

We also are reminded that the more we try to change people, the more likely we will end up damaging close relationships. The only person you can try to change is yourself. In other words, changing communication is an individual effort. Teaching yourself another way of communicating can dramatically change your life. It pays to carefully note how many messages of kindness and generosity you are sending compared to negative, competitive, and controlling messages. It is also important for you to take note of what prompts you to retreat when attacked, when you are impatient with another, or when you want something changed in another person.

This is difficult if a partner is a died-in-the-wool competitive communicator. You might suggest to your partner that you wish to try strengthening your relationship based on some material you have been reading, and then suggest that your partner read it also. Come together and talk about how you talk about things (meta-communication). If that is unsuccessful, you might try finding a counselor who can guide you through ways of strengthening your communication strategies. Change is possible, but only if both partners are sincerely committed to change.

Gottman recommends that each new encounter with a partner begins with sincere kindness, care, and a loving connection. Also, if we seek change to change communication style with a partner, pay attention to timing, a key element in communicating effectively. We should use carefully chosen words to express a complaint and avoid slipping into the minefield of superlatives, attacks, overgeneralizations, and sarcasm. Also, more effective couples avoid mimicking and other forms of clever repartee you see on television and in movies. Although possibly humorous to watch in a movie, the sarcastic, demeaning humor portrayed in the media will not build strong relationships.

Discussions in Diversity: Family History—Connecting Our Past, Present, and Future

In 1993, communications professor, Dr. Leanne O. Wolff, presented a paper on the family narrative and how these narratives shape our lives. She suggested that "the use of family stories promotes family awareness, intergenerational sharing, an understanding of family and self, and appreciation for the uniqueness of the family. The family narrative is a part of personal heritage, uniting a family's past and its present and providing a link to future generations." Bits and pieces of family history and lore are shared among family members in a complex manner across time, sometimes at the dinner table, sometimes during family gatherings, and sometimes during crises (Bohanek, Marin, Fivush, & Duke, 2004). The sharing of family history has been found to strengthen family cohesion, assist in adolescent identity development, enhance youth well-being, and even foster resilience related to historical trauma (Bakir-Demir, Reese, & Sahin-Acar, 2020; Denham, 2008; Fivush, Duke, & Bohanek, 2010).

Not all family stories are true. Perhaps stories get embellished and passed down incorrectly or are created based on incorrect interpretations of the past; on the other hand, perhaps stories are created to hide or sanitize aspects of the past. Some family secrets disappear as narratives based on non-truths cross generations as truth. With the advent of online genealogy tools and documents, many families have uncovered secrets of abuse, desertion, and second families. We discovered that one of our ancestors was a descendent of slaves, only to pass for white beginning in the late 1920s. Such revelations can sometimes result in a renewed understanding of history, as well as self and family.

Vicki Mokuria utilizes critical family history projects in her college classroom (Mokuria, Williams, & Page, 2020). Through researching personal family histories in the context of history, economics, religion, culture, and politics, students delve into the complexities of the human experience (Figure 9.6). One of her students, "Alicia," researched her African American roots through historical documents and family

FIGURE 9.6 We can learn much about ourselves when we learn about our ancestors.

Source: New York Public Library; Public domain

stories. Her experience was transformative for herself and those she shared her story with, as she learned of her ancestors being enslaved, used as concubines, and lynched. She also learned one of her ancestors had African roots but became a slave owner himself, passing as white, while another ancestor could have passed for white but refused. "Through engaging in the research process that included uncovering and giving form to hidden narratives almost lost to Alicia and those of us who read about them, we see how dynamic, collaborative, and relational narrative inquiry can be. As a collaborator and co-researcher, Alicia birthed a 'new story' from her ancestors' lives and as these stories are further re-storied through our interactions with them, we reconstruct and re-story our understanding of the lives and experiences of enslaved Africans we possibly never considered" (Mokuria et al., 2020). Thus, through family communication, we build narratives that can influence us and the generations following.

Questions to Discuss:

- *Are you interested in exploring your family history? Why or why not?*
- *What might be some pitfalls in exploring family histories?*
- *Why do you think young people show benefits from knowing their family history?*
- *What are ways that families can learn their family history?*
- *Do you believe that recording current family history (i.e., diary or journal keeping, family photo projects) is beneficial to families? Why or why not?*

SUMMARY

The communication process is at the heart of all family relationships, and as with many family processes, much is hidden but still highly influential. The Chinese proverb "Married couples who love each other tell each other a thousand things without talking" is quite accurate. We have come to learn that families engage in several types of communication strategies, some healthy and some unhealthy, but all subject to change. Not only does our family communication affect us individually and the family as a whole, but it also has the potential to influence generations to come through the skills we learn (or don't learn) and pass on and the secrets we keep.

This chapter contained suggestions for improving family communication, as well as insights related to marriage relationships from John Gottman's research. This information is useful for individuals, families, and even practitioners. Still, all the information in this chapter (and book) is relatively useless unless you, the reader, want to change. Reading, *and not acting on*, this information will do little to assist you in developing stronger, more effective relationships with those you care about. One must be highly motivated to change something as long-lasting as a relationship pattern, plus one must put principles into action and make a serious effort. Sometimes, the help of a professional counselor may be necessary. While it is difficult to change yourself if family members are unwilling to participate and change as well, it is possible and may result in changing the entire system.

STUDY QUESTIONS

1   What is the difference between communication and language?
2   Give some examples of verbal vs. non-verbal communication. How can these influence relationships?
3   What is meant when we use the term *intent messages*?
4   Why do family scientists make the claim that "you cannot not communicate"?
5   Outline the communication process.
6   Briefly describe the different types of competitive or control talk.
7   What is meta-communication?
8   Name four ideas that reinforce the notion that it is critical to understand gender in the study of family communication.
9   What are three types of family secrets and how are they delineated?
10   How do secrets influence family processes? What are some negative outcomes of family secrets?
11   Briefly explain Gottman's findings related to marital success. What are the four horsemen of the apocalypse, as related to marriage?

KEY TERMS

Communication
Language
Encoding
Decoding

Indirect messages

Direct messages

Covert messages

Overt messages

Meta-communication

Intent messages

Content messages

Types of communication (e.g., dissing, straight talk, control talk, etc.)

Harsh startup

Types of secrets

The Four Horsemen

SUGGESTED READINGS

Booth, A., Crouter, A., Clements, M., & Boone-Holladay, T. (2015). *Couples in conflict.* New York, NY: Routledge.

Edwards, K. (2006). *The memory keeper's daughter: A novel.* New York, NY: Penguin Books.

Gottman, J. M. (1994). *What predicts divorce? The relationship between marital processes and marital outcomes.* Hillsdale, NJ: Lawrence Erlbaum Associates.

Gottman, J. M. (2001). *The relationship cure.* New York, NY: Crown.

Gottman, J. M. (2015). *The seven principles for making marriage work (Rev. ed.).* New York, NY: Harmony Books.

Gottman, J., Gottman, J., Abrams, D., & Abrams, R. C. (2019). *Eight dates: Essential conversations for a lifetime of love.* New York, NY: Workman Publishing.

Hathaway, M. (2017). *My grandma: In her own words.* Seattle, WA: Compendium Incorporated.

Imber-Black, E. (1999). *The secret life of families.* New York, NY: Bantam Books.

Noller, P., & Fitzpatrick, M. A. (1993). *Communication in family relationships.* Englewood Cliffs, NJ: Prentice-Hall.

Sleeter, C. (2020). *White bread: Anniversary edition.* Boston, MA: Brill Sense.

REFERENCES

Aries, E. (1982). Verbal and nonverbal behavior in single-sex and mixed-sex groups: Are traditional sex roles changing? *Psychological Reports, 51,* 127.

Aggarwal, J., Rabinovich, E., & Stevenson, S. (2020). *Exploration of gender differences in COVID-19 discourse on Reddit.* https://arxiv.org/pdf/2008.05713.pdf

Aries, E. (1996). *Men and women in interaction: Reconsidering the differences.* New York, NY: Oxford University Press.

Bakir-Demir, T., Reese, E., & Sahin-Acar, B. (2020). How three generations narrate their vicarious family stories: Intrafamilial similarities, gender and cross-generational differences. *Memory, 28*(4), 553–566.

Ball, F. L., Cowan, J. P., & Cowan, C. P. (1995). Who's got the power? Gender differences in partners' perceptions of influence during marital problem-solving discussions. *Family Process, 34,* 303–321.

Baxter, L. A., & Wilmont, W. (1985). Taboo topics in close relationships. *Journal of Social and Personal Relationships, 2,* 253–269.

Beck, A. (1988). Anxiety and depression: An information processing perspective. *Anxiety Research, 1,* 23–36.

Bell, R. A., Daly, J. A., & Gonzalez, M. C. (1987). Affinity-maintenance in marriage and its relationship to women's marital satisfaction. *Journal of Marriage and the Family, 49,* 445–454.

Berger, P., Kellner, & Hansfried (1973). Marriage and the construction of reality. In N. Glazer-Malbin, & H. Y. Waehrer (Eds.), *Woman in a man-made world: A socioeconomic handbook* (pp. 22–58). New York, NY: Rand McNally.

Bischoping, K. (1993). Gender differences in conversation topics. *Sex Roles, 28(1)*, 1–S18.

Bograd, R., & Spilka, B. (1996). Self-disclosure and marital satisfaction in mid-life and late-life remarriages. *International Journal of Aging & Human Development, 42*, 161–172.

Bohanek, J. G., Marin, K. A., Fivush, R., & Duke, M. P. (2004). *Family Narrative Interaction and Children's Self-Understanding.* The Emory Center for Myth and Ritual in American Life, Working Paper No. 34. Atlanta, Georgia.

Davoodvandi, M., Nejad, S. N., & Farzad, V. (2018). Examining the effectiveness of Gottman couple therapy on improving marital adjustment and couples' intimacy. *Iranian Journal of Psychiatry, 13*(2), 135–141.

Denham, A. R. (2008). Rethinking historical trauma: Narratives of resilience. *Transcultural Psychiatry, 45*(3), 391–414.

Deslypere, E., & Rober, P. (2018). Family secrecy in family therapy practice: An explorative focus group study. *Family Process, 59*(1), 52–65.

Dickson-Markman, F., & Markman, H. J. (1988). The effects of others on marriage: Do they help or hurt? In P. Noller, & M. A. Fitzpatrick (Eds.), *Perspectives on marital interaction* (pp. 33–63). Philadelphia, PA: Multilingual Matters.

Duck, S. (1997). *Handbook of personal relationships: Theory, research, and interventions.* Chichester, UK: Wiley.

Ehrlich, F. (2000). Dialogue, couple therapy, and the unconscious. *Contemporary Psychoanalysis, 36*, 483–503.

Falbo, T., & Peplau, L. A. (1980). Power strategies in intimate relationships. *Journal of Personality and Social Psychology, 38*, 618–628.

Fivush, M. R., Duke, M. P., & Bohanek, J. G. (2010). "Do You Know?": The power of family history in adolescent identity and well-being. *Journal of Family Life.* Retrieved from https://ncph.org/wp-content/uploads/2013/12/The-power-of-family-history-in-adolescent-identity.pdf

Gottman, J. M. (1994). *What predicts divorce? The relationship between marital processes and marital outcomes.* Hillsdale, NJ: Lawrence Erlbaum Associates.

Gottman, J. M. (1999). *The seven principles for making marriage work.* New York, NY: Crown.

Handler, S. (2019). 5 Reasons Why Keeping Family Secrets Could Be Harmful. PsychCentral World of Psychology Blog, https://www.suzannehandler.com/noteworthy/

Hansen, J. E., & Schuldt, W. J. (1982). Physical distance, sex, and intimacy in self disclosure. *Psychological Reports, 51*, 3–6.

Imber-Black, E. (1998). *The secret life of families.* New York, NY: Bantam Books.

Imber-Black, E. (2007). *Instructor's manual: Family secrets—Implications for theory and therapy.* By Wyatt, R. C. & Seid, E. L. San Francisco, CA: psychotherapy.net

Jacob, T. (1987). Family interaction and psychopathology: Historical overview. In T. Jacob (Ed.), *Family interaction and psychopathology: Theories, methods, and findings* (pp. 242–283). New York, NY: Plenum.

Karpel, M. (1980). Secrets: I. Conceptual and ethical issues in relational contexts II. Ethical and practical considerations in therapeutic management. *Family Process, 19*(3), 295–306.

Kennedy, C., & Camden, C. (1983). Interruptions and nonverbal gender differences. *Journal of Nonverbal Behavior, 8*, 44–52.

Krauss, R., & Fussell, S. (1996). Social psychological models of interpersonal communication. In E. Higgins, & A. Kruglanski (Eds.), *Social psychology: Handbook of basic principles* (pp. 44–82). New York, NY: Guilford.

Mackey, R. A., & O'Brien, B. (1995). *A lasting marriage: Men and women growing together.* Westport, CT: Praeger.

Miller, S., Nunnally, D., & Wackman, S. (1988). *Alive and aware: Improving communication in relationships.* Minneapolis, MN: Interpersonal Communication Programs.

Mokuria, V., Williams, A., & Page, W. (2020). The has been no remorse over it: A narrative inquiry exploring enslaved ancestral roots through a critical history project. *Genealogy, 4*(2), 26.

Noller, P. (1984). Clergy marriages: A study of a uniting church sample. *Australian Journal of Sex, Marriage and Family, 5*, 187–197.

Noller, P., & Feeney, J. A. (1998). Communication in early marriage: Responses to conflict, nonverbal accuracy, and conversational patterns. In T. N. Bradbury (Ed.), *The developmental course of marital dysfunction* (pp. 11–43). Cambridge University Press. DOI: 10.1017/CBO9780511527814.003

Noller, P., & Fitzpatrick, M. (1990). Marital communication in the eighties. *Journal of Marriage and the Family, 52*, 832–843.

Olson, D. H., & DeFrain, J. (1994). *Marriage and the family: Diversity and strengths.* Mountain View, CA: Mayfield.

Paiczewski, C. H., DeFrancisco, V. P., & McGeough, D. D. (2019). *Gender in communication: A critical introduction* (3rd ed.). Thousand Oaks, CA: Sage.

Rabiah, S. (2012). Language as a tool for communication and cultural reality discloser. Presented in 1st International Conference on Media, Communication and Culture "Rethinking Multiculturalism: Media in Multicultural Society" organized by Universitas Muhummadiya Yogyakart and Universiti Sains Malaysia on November 7–8, 2012 in Universitas Muhammadiyah Yogyakart, Indonesia.

Roberts, L. J. (2000). Fire and ice in marital communication: Hostile and distancing behaviors as predictors of marital distress. *Journal of Marriage and Family, 62(3),* 693–707.

Rosenfeld, L., & Bowen, G. (1991). Marital disclosure and marital satisfaction: Direct-effect versus interaction-effect models. *Western Journal of Speech Communication, 55,* 112–133.

Satir, V. (1972). *Conjoint family therapy: A guide to theory and technique.* Palo Alto, CA: Science and Behavior Books.

Sieburg, E. (1985). *Family communication: An integrated systems approach.* New York, NY: Gardner Press.

Swinford, S. P., Demaris, A., Cernkovich, S. A., & Giordano, P. C. (2000). Harsh physical discipline in childhood and violence in later romantic involvements: The mediating role of problem behaviors. *Journal of Marriage and the Family, 62,* 508–519.

Tannen, D. (1986). *That's not what I meant! How conversational style makes or breaks your relations with others.* New York, NY: Morrow.

Tannen, D. (1990). *You just don't understand: Women and men in conversation.* New York, NY: Morrow.

Thompson, R. A. (2016). What more has been learned? The science of early childhood development 15 years after *neurons to neighborhoods. Zero to Three, 36(3),* 18–24.

Thompson, L., & Walker, A. J. (1989). Gender in families: Women and men in marriage, work, and parenthood. *Journal of Marriage and the Family, 51,* 845–871.

Vangelisti, A. (1994). Family secrets: Forms, functions and correlates. *Journal of Social & Personal Relationships, 11,* 113–135.

Vangelisti, A., & Caughlin, J. (1997). Revealing family secrets: The influence of topic, function, and relationships. *Journal of Social & Personal Relationships, 14,* 222–243.

Vrij, A., Nunkoosina, K., Paterson, B., Oosterwegel, A., & Soukara, S. (2002). Characteristics of secrets and the frequency, reasons and effects of secrets keeping and disclosure. *Journal of Community & Applied Social Psychology, 12,* 56–70.

Waring, E., & Chelune, G. J. (1983). Marital intimacy and self-disclosure. *Journal of Clinical Psychology, 39,* 183.

Watzlawick, P., Weakland, J. H., & Fisch, R. (1974). *Change: Principles of problem formation and problem resolution.* New York, NY: Norton.

Wolff, L. O. (1993). Family narrative: How our stories shape us. Paper presented at the Annual Meeting of the Speech Communication Association 7th, Miami Beach, FL, November 18–21, 1993.

Wynne, L. C. (1984). The epigenesis of relational systems: A model for understanding family development. *Family Process, 23,* 297–318.

CHAPTER 10

Regulating Distance

CHAPTER PREVIEW

In this chapter, readers will learn:

- The meaning of distance regulation.
- How sometimes a family's emotional climate can create a situation in which family members become overly connected to the family system.
- What differentiation is and how it influences the family system, including child outcomes.
- What family fusion is and how it influences the family system, including child outcomes.
- Overconnection to family might result in difficulty time separating emotions from our thinking selves.
- The difference between helicopter and lawnmower parenting.
- How culture and ethnicity may influence perception of fusion, as well as outcomes.
- The difference between acute and chronic anxiety and the latter's relationship to differentiation.
- About emotional triangles and why they are considered the basic building block of relationships and how they operate in families.
- There are four ways one can use to cope with emotional distress: using a genogram, understanding invisible loyalties, the benign assumption, and avoiding emotional cutoff.
- That the ideas about family emotional systems have several implications for families and those who try to help them.
- How family systems theory and distance regulation can provide insight into LGBTQIA issues.

INTRODUCTION

Your family did not suddenly appear one day. Instead, who we are as families evolved from an ongoing, developmental, and historical process. For example, from my family of origin, I brought certain emotional and value-oriented ties. My wife also brought with her an orientation about how one should (or could) feel about another person or group of people within a family. One of the more important aspects of how our family system functions or fails to thrive is how each of us (my wife and I) manages the emotional relationships between us and

DOI: 10.4324/9781003128717-13

between each of our five children. Families who are better able to meet goals, maintain longer and more fulfilling relationships, and meet crisis are those families who have a capacity for tolerating intimacy and individuality (Farley, 1979; Gavazzi, Anderson, & Sabatelli, 1993; Sabatelli & Anderson, 1991). An important aspect of understanding family processes is an awareness of how to balance these two ideas.

In general, when we speak of balancing intimacy and individuality, we are referring to the family task of **regulating distance**. Regulating distance implies that families can be too close or too disconnected. The ability to maintain appropriate emotional distance from other family members is a key skill in successful family life.

In this chapter, we focus primarily on the idea of learning to balance closeness in family life, drawing on Bowen Family Systems theory. This theory was developed by Murray Bowen (1913–1990), a psychiatrist, researcher, theorist, clinician, author, and pioneer in family therapy (The Bowen Center, n.d.). In a nutshell:

> Bowen family systems theory is a theory of human behavior that views the family as an emotional unit and uses systems thinking to describe the complex interactions in the unit. It is the nature of a family that its members are intensely connected emotionally. Often people feel distant or disconnected from their families, but this is more feeling than fact. Families so profoundly affect their members' thoughts, feelings, and actions that it often seems as if people are living under the same "emotional skin." People solicit each other's attention, approval, and support and react to each other's needs, expectations, and upsets. The connectedness and reactivity make the functioning of family members interdependent. A change in one person's functioning is predictably followed by reciprocal changes in the functioning of others. Families differ somewhat in the degree of interdependence, but it is always present to some degree.
>
> (Kerr, 2000)

The detail and functionality of Bowen's theory have allowed it to be applied in a myriad of settings and contexts, including business organizations, divorce, soldiers, mental health, religion, gender, addiction, slavery, medicine, society, anxiety, identity, and parenting. Following, we will examine several of Bowen's interlocking concepts and how they relate to our family dance.

CONNECTION AND INDIVIDUATION

During the course of this text, we have emphasized the idea that families can become a consensual community, working together, sharing a paradigm, and using their group strength to overcome problems. In this chapter, we take a slightly different angle on that theme and suggest that family strength is also achieved *by building independence within the individuals* who comprise the family. To some, that might sound paradoxical; however, as you will see, you can build group strength by building or creating strength in individuals.

Our experience with family **connectedness** begins early in our lives (Bowen, 1976; Gavazzi, 1993; Gavazzi & Sabatelli, 1990). One of the jobs of children is to resolve the inevitably strong connections between themselves and their parents. We all are strongly connected to what happens in our families in early life, but the climate or tone of the family environment predicts whether or not we can build our own identity separate and apart from that of our parents and early family members. As we pass into early adulthood, one of the most important psychological tasks we approach is the search for independence, autonomy, identity, or individuation. All of these terms mean essentially the same thing and refer to a person's need to separate from one's family of origin and become a unique individual while maintaining a connection to family relationships.

Differentiation

Differentiation is a complex family process that involves the interplay of connectedness and individuality (Buehler, 2020). This important but elusive concept is difficult to define in a way that captures its totality and subtle nuances resulting in misunderstanding (Foose & Cicio, 2018). Foose and Cicio write, "Bowen himself, persistently mystified by the consistent misinterpretation of differentiation, noted late in his life in one of his more cantankerous moments that he wished he'd never 'discovered' it in the first place." Consider the following definitions related to differentiation:

- The ability to distinguish between thoughts and feelings in an emotional relationship system (Bohlander, 1995, p. 165).
- The capacity to be aware of one's own unique pattern of feeling, valuing, and thinking, and to decide and act in ways that remain faithful to that *awareness*" (Cowan, as quoted by Foose & Cicio, 2018).
- Families and other social groups tremendously affect how people think, feel, and act, but individuals vary in their susceptibility to "groupthink," and groups vary in the amount of pressure they exert for conformity. These differences between individuals and between groups reflect differences in people's levels of differentiation of self (Kerr, 2000).
- Differentiation can be understood as both a process and as a personality characteristic. The process of differentiating from one's family of origin entails the emergence of oneself from a multigenerational family system characterized by various levels of emotional attachments and projections of anxiety (Jenkins, Buboltz, Schwartz, & Johnson, 2005, p. 252).
- The ability to balance emotional intimacy with one's partner with one's own sense of autonomy (Stapley & Murdock, 2020, p. 76).
- The lower a person's hypersensitivity to others, the higher their level of emotional maturity or differentiation of self (MacKay, 2017, p. 641).
- The ability to think as an individual while staying meaningfully connected to others (FSI, n.d.).
- The capacity of a system and its members to manage emotional reactivity, act thoughtfully under stress, and allow for both intimacy and autonomy in relationships (Skowron, 2005, p. 337).
- The degree to which one is able to balance (a) emotional and intellectual functioning and (b) intimacy and autonomy in relationships (Skowron & Friedlander, 1998, p. 235).

It appears that differentiation (also referred to as *differentiation of self* or DoS) recognizes our human desire to be autonomous while simultaneously feeling connected in our relationships. When members of a family are differentiated, they have a clear sense of self, making them less reactive to the emotions of others and able to think more clearly in times of stress

(Bowen, 1978; Skowron, 2005). They are able to self-regulate, separate intellect and emotions, and engage more healthily in relationships. Bowen believed that differentiation exists on a continuum, from being fully differentiated (able to separate feelings from thoughts) to being undifferentiated (unable to separate thoughts and feelings).

One young woman and her husband had regular dinners with the woman's father. Often, the dinner would end up with the young woman offended or upset by something her father said and crying on the way home. One day, her husband asked, "Why do you let your father upset you?" "Because he says things that hurt me, even though you may not realize it. I know what he is really saying!" The husband thought for a moment and said, "You know who you are. You are a successful businesswoman with a successful career. You have friends and are engaged in the community. You don't have to agree with your father, and you can still love him." Suddenly, the young woman realized that she and her father had been caught in an emotional tug-of-war, and all she needed to do was let go of the rope. The next time they had dinner together when the father said something she deemed hurtful, she nicely told him that it was time to go and kissed him goodbye. Within a few weeks, the father no longer said hurtful things (or at least the young woman no longer perceived hurtful things), and their relationship grew warm and strong.

Family researchers and therapists have long taught that it is a sign of family strength when families create a climate of increasing independence in their children. Consequently, an important task of parenting is the process of encouraging and fostering personal individuality. Families who know how to build differentiation allow individuals to express individuality and are still intimately connected (Gavazzi, 1993). As the child ages, the families are less intrusive and more supportive. Researchers suggest that differentiation levels have been linked to the family's ability to prepare and successfully launch its offspring (Carter, & McGoldrick, 1989; Farley, 1979; Gavazzi, 1994; Kerr & Bowen, 1988). Being differentiated does not mean that one disconnects from parents, nor does it imply rejecting the family's rituals, values, and beliefs. It does, however, mean that the family allows children to become separated in a healthy and supported way as they grow into adulthood.

Differentiation of self is associated with positive child outcomes in families, including academic achievement (Skowron, 2005). Adolescents who evidence differentiation of self are better able to manage chronic anxiety, engage in more effective problem solving, and are less likely to engage in problematic behaviors, such as early sexuality (Knauth, Skowron, & Escobar, 2006). Appropriate levels of differentiation in a family are more likely to produce teenagers who can build stronger relationships with other people (Sabatelli & Cecil-Pigo, 1985), have fewer problems with alcohol abuse (Bartle & Sabatelli, 1989), have higher levels of psychological maturity (Gavazzi et al., 1993) and were much less likely to have general problems at school, difficulty with peers, participation in illegal activities, and fewer problems with their families of origin (Gavazzi, 1993).

As a result, teaching families how to effectively allow their children to develop an individualized self that can thrive independently, be independent thinkers, and have the freedom to make choices, while still being healthily connected to a loving, caring, and interested family is an important goal. Empirical research is limited but emerging in this area. Schwartz, Thigpen, and Montgomery (2006) found a link between parenting style and differentiation of self, with gender difference. Parents who are comfortable dealing with emotions and engage in emotion coaching are more likely to have children who are show healthy differentiation of self.

PRINCIPLE 10.1

DIFFERENTIATION IS A POWER TOOL IN FAMILY LIFE

Differentiation refers to appropriate separateness from one's family. The goal is to develop a differentiated self while remaining close (but not smothered) by one's family.

Family Fusion

Occasionally, we hear of families whose primary theme is to ask family members to surrender all they are individually and become subsumed into the collective of the family (Figure 10.1). These highly "enmeshed" families have constructed a family paradigm of beliefs, rules, rule sequences, and values that has as a core theme the idea that the family collective is more important than the strength and well-being of the individual. This lack of differentiation (the other end of the continuum described above) is referred to as **fusion**. In Bowen's (1978/2004) words, "A major concept in this systems theory is developed around the notion of fusion between the emotions and the intellect. The degree of fusion in people is variable and discernable. The amount of fusion in a person can be used as a predictor of the pattern of life in that person" (pp. 304–335).

In the 1990s, there was a popular television program called *Star Trek: The Next Generation*. In one episode, the crew of the starship encountered an alien culture that traveled through space, completely consuming and absorbing any other culture, person, or thing that got in its way. This massive absorbing collective was called the Borg. The Borg captured all in its path. Once captured, victims became attached (literally) to the massive blob-like culture, tethered, undifferentiated, and unable to act for one's self. The voice of the Borg would announce, "Resistance is futile, you will be assimilated." In this way, the collective of space cyborgs assimilated and absorbed entire cultures and anyone who got in the way. This literary metaphor serves our discussion well. There are times when some families become like the Borg. This chapter is a distillation of about 50 years of research surrounding this topic and one of the more destructive family processes known. This catastrophic process, fusion, centers on what happens when families go past the boundary of loving and caring and journey into Borg-like behavior within which the group becomes a controlling, unstoppable collective that insists that the individual surrender any semblance of personal identity.

In families where fusion exists, families have little or no tolerance for individuality and instead demand conformity and compliance at any cost. The conflict that arises from intrusive attempts to maintain control and domination might completely squelch any kindness, generosity, or feelings of love. Usually, to achieve this domination in children, overconnected parents create a climate of chronic anxiety, animosity, distrust, and conflict. This type of family climate has the potential to create deep emotional problems for children. Bowen (1976) authored several important research papers that describe how destructive, unhealthy overconnection is in family life. At its most negative point, he suggested that occasionally family members become so connected to the family emotional system that this connection interferes with their ability to manage the other aspects of their lives.

When the goal of a family is to create a mass of undifferentiated members who have forgotten or who never knew a special purpose that resides outside of their families of origin (think of the Borg), children do not thrive. When we are young, no one really expects us to differentiate and become unique. However, as we age into adolescence, becoming differentiated is essential for the health of both the individual and the family so that each family member feels a sense of uniqueness, specialness, and individuality.

Some individuals never really move beyond being emotionally connected to their parents. It is as if they have a very long emotional umbilical cord still attached to their mother, father, or both. In recent years, this has become more apparent with the invention and mass distribution of cell phones. Imagine parents using cell phone technology to monitor every movement of their child who is now an older teen—even at college. The mother (or father) is showing her love by calling several times per day, asking how a class went, inquiring about personal conversations, reminding the college student to eat a good lunch and not eat unhealthy snacks, encouraging her to do her homework, and so on. The intrusion into daily life by technology very well could be fueling a movement toward unhealthy parent–child interactions.

Of course, many parents who are overinvolved with their children are loving and caring. Their desire to protect their young and help them be successful in life results in **helicopter parenting** (Dumont, 2021; Schiffrin, Liss, Miles-McLean, Geary, & Erchull, 2013). In helicopter parenting, parents hover around their children, swooping in to rescue them when they feel they need to. By not allowing their children to problem-solve, make their own decisions, and find their own way, young people may be stunted in their personal growth and experience depression, anxiety, and lower levels of psychological well-being. Similarly, children may

FIGURE 10.1 This drawing captures the idea that sometimes families are so fused and undifferentiated that it is hard to tell where one family member begins and is different from the others.

experience **lawnmower parenting**, with parents "mowing down" any obstacle the child might experience, again preventing the child from learning how to deal with problems on their own (Locke, Campbell, & Kavanagh, 2012).

Interestingly, as we learned in the Chapter 6 discussion of family paradigms, families who are more closed and have rigid boundaries with regard to the outside world are much more likely to be chronically anxious about making sure family members do not break any rules. Inside the family walls of fused families, however, the boundaries are usually very blurred. That is, because undifferentiated families are so intrusive, they might insist on opening everyone's mail, not letting children play behind closed doors, and forcing family members to participate in all family activities.

In family fusion, patterns, rules, rule sequences, and family paradigms conspire together to negate family members' individuality. When someone in the family tries to break free of the "Borg," so to speak, their efforts at independence are seen as disloyal and the person's actions are seen as attempts to destroy the very integrity of the family. As a part of this process, highly fused families experience life as a Borgian group: Every experience resulting in anxiety, loss, joy, pain, or other emotional experience is felt and relived by the group. The daily stories of emotional highs and certainly all the lows are broadcast to the collective, experienced as a group, and processed by the whole. The person is not allowed to experience any feature of life in private but must share all with the group.

Results of Family Fusion on Children

When family fusion exists, it is usually maintained by tension, anxiety, and even hostility. It takes high levels of energy (often negative energy such as control attempts, intimidation, coercion, and even bullying) to keep family members connected and fused. This climate of tension and anxiety can have negative results for the inner well-being of the child. Thus, not only can fusion be created at the larger social-group level, but fusion can spill over from the group process into the psyche of the individual, creating **internal fusion**. As a result of the chronic anxiety and tension in family life, internally fused children have a difficult time learning how to separate their thinking world from their emotional world. Because much of their experience in family life is highly emotionally charged, they might not have been taught to pay attention to the thinking, rational aspect of their inner self. When home life is charged with resentment, animosity, and bitterness, children seem to lose the ability to separate their emotions from their intellect. Children who are raised in a climate of family fusion have more difficulty separating their thinking world from their feeling world.

Further, when children grow up in a fused family, where anxiety and hostility are used to promote conformity and fusion, children seem to lose their ability to think for themselves, solve problems effectively, make good decisions, and regulate their emotions (Nichols & Schwartz, 2007, p. 371; Papero, 1983). They are more likely to have explosive tempers and bouts of depression and less likely to form high levels of prosocial behaviors (such as reaching out to help others). Bowen (1976) explains, "At the fusion end of the spectrum, the intellect is so flooded by emotionality that the total life course is determined by the emotional process and by what 'feels right' rather than by beliefs or opinions. The intellect exists as an appendage of the feeling system" (p. 66).

The overall result of the fusion is a young person who is very unsure of one's place in the world. The prevailing message is one of doubt, unresolved emotions, and a perpetual search for validation. Conversely, research has found that in families where the climate was more positive and where there were fewer control attempts aimed at family conformity, children were much more likely to be able to separate their thinking selves from their emotional selves and they were generally less likely to experience problems with emotional reactivity. When people are more highly differentiated, they seem to be able to maintain more objectivity and to think carefully for longer periods of time despite emotional arousal (Papero, 1983, p. 140).

Another family researcher, Kerr (1981), conducted several studies in which he found that calm people think more fairly, clearly, and objectively. However, when highly connected or fused individuals were placed in emotionally charged situations, they responded less calmly and, instead, more irrationally, and sought approval from others, placed blame on others, and tried to dominate others in the situation (Kerr, 1981, p. 237). Therefore, one application of this principle is that when family climates have less conflict, family members develop a greater sense of differentiation or personal individuality and, consequently, they do much better at solving life's difficult problems. When a highly stressful event occurs, they are much more likely to be able to think clearly about their options and generate effective solutions. As Kerr and Bowen (1988) indicated, "An anxious family elevates a facet of a problem to the cause of the problem" (p. 61).

PRINCIPLE 10.2

FUSION IN FAMILIES MAY CREATE DEEP PROBLEMS

Often, fused family members feel trapped in the family ego-mass. This feeling of being trapped creates anxiety, dysfunction, and even mental illness.

Cultural/Ethnic Considerations

Bowen (1978) considered his concept of differentiation to be universal. However, it was developed and grew within a Eurocentric worldview. As a result, this concept may not be appropriate for other cultures or diverse groups. Researchers have studied differentiation in Korean, Arabic, European, Jewish, Muslim, Japanese, Thai, and Persian cultures, with mixed results. Kim et al. (2014) found that increased levels of differentiation were associated with healthier family functioning, better family communication, and greater family satisfaction for all three of their study groups, South Koreans, South Korean immigrants to the United States, and white Americans. They did suggest, however, that "for cultures in which tight-knit families are revered, perhaps the Western mislabel of fusion may be need to be replaced by something more akin to concepts that denote collaborative health, such as solidarity" (p. 263).

Similar to Kim et al.'s findings, among persons of color, Skowron (2004) found higher levels of differentiation were associated with better psychological adjustment, social problem-solving skills, and greater ethnic group belonging. On the other hand, in their reappraisal of Bowen's theory, using a cultural lens approach, Erdem and Safi (2018) found several studies of Italian, Japanese, Thai, Korean, and Taiwanese families that were contrary to the expected findings related to fusion and individual or family adjustment. Many researchers have also noted that differences in outcomes and self-differentiation were found within groups. In other words, some families in the same cultural group with high differentiation were healthy, while others were not. Finally, Kağıtçıbaşı (1996) suggests that differentiation is not a single pole; rather, separate poles can co-exist: autonomy-heteronomy and separateness-relatedness. Thus, it is entirely possible to become more autonomous or individuated while maintaining strong connections. In short, the jury is still out with regard to the universality of Bowen's differentiation concept. Further research is likely to result in increased understanding of these concepts and healthy family functioning in diverse contexts.

OF ANXIETY AND TRIANGLES...

Anxiety is defined as "The response of an organism to a threat, real or imagined. It is assumed to be a process that, in some form, is present in all living things" (Kerr & Bowen, 1988, p. 112). As a negative emotion, it includes distress or uneasiness of mind caused by apprehension of danger or misfortune. **Acute anxiety** is different from chronic anxiety. Acute anxiety is usually a short-term response to a stressful situation, and most of the time, it is a rational response to a real (rather than imagined) problem. For example, when a couple is told by a doctor their child has a serious disease, the natural emotional response is to have acute anxiety or feelings of "distress or uneasiness of mind caused by apprehension of danger or misfortune." Acute anxiety tends to leave after a person learns to cope with the stressful situation or the danger leaves. For example, the anxiety leaves a couple when they learn how to cope with the illness or if the diagnosis is not accurate.

All individuals and families encounter situations that create acute anxiety. It occurs whenever there are serious problems to be dealt with and whenever negative emotions such as despair, futility, inadequacy, inferiority, lack of fulfillment, discouragement, emotional hurt, or serious disappointments occur. One of the challenges all families face is to find ways to deal with these problems and their negative emotions so that they do not lead to chronic anxiety.

Chronic anxiety occurs when uneasiness, distress, or apprehension endures for long periods of time. As discussed previously, family fusion and lack of differentiation in the family can lead to chronic anxiety. Usually, the sources of chronic anxiety are difficult to identify, as are the original causes, and it is an underlying condition that persists and colors many different situations. As written by Kerr and Bowen (1988):

> Anxiety "rubs off" on people; it is transmitted and absorbed without thinking. This absorption seems to be based on the physiological programming or conditioning of one person by another that occurs through prolonged association, and on the imparting and incorporation of attitudes and beliefs that foster anxiety in oneself or others. Incorporating an attitude such as "I am inferior" can create anxiety for oneself; incorporating an attitude such as "I am the greatest" can create problems for others.
>
> (p. 116)

Some types of chronic anxiety are not important in family systems. For example, people can have psychic fears or apprehensions that are related to their work, their education, or their friendships, and these forms or types of chronic anxiety often have little impact of family life. Also, people can have chronic anxiety about many other things that have little to do with family systems. They can have chronic anxiety about being in an elevator or being in dark places, and many of these chronic anxieties only occur outside the home and have little impact on family systems.

Bowen studied one type of chronic anxiety that is especially important in family systems, long-term tension or resentment. This occurs when family members feel others in their family have been unjust to them in important ways. Emotional undercurrents can occur when family members love deeply, with close bonds, and then feel betrayed, abandoned, deceived, or ignored.

The solution is for families to find ways to deal with negative emotions, such as resentment and disappointment, so they do not lead to chronic ills in their system. The healing balm of such things as forgiveness, patience, and the willingness to let ourselves and others be frail and inadequate (see Chapter 11) are strategies that can help families keep chronic anxiety low enough that it does not invisibly erode the basic structures of the family system.

Chronic family anxiety is a significant problem because it can lead to destructive emotional climates, such as general feelings of animosity, malice, rancor, enmity, and hatred. Emotions such as these create seriously disabling processes in most families because they interfere with the most positive emotions that people seek (e.g., love, compassion, care, and nurturance).

Another reason this type of chronic anxiety is usually disabling is that it keeps family members "on edge," and even minor problems can be enough to create intense emotional reactions of anger, aggression, violence, and abuse. It is similar to having a pot of water simmering, where a slight increase in temperature is enough to make it boil.

When families do not have chronic anxiety in their emotional system, they do not over-respond to minor problems, and they can marshal their resources to cope with the problems effectively. When they have ongoing tension, however, they have less ability to cope with even minor problems. The principle that Bowen developed can be called the **chronic anxiety principle**.

PRINCIPLE 10.3

CHRONIC ANXIETY PRINCIPLE

The higher the level of chronic anxiety in a family (or other relationship), the less likely they will be able to attain their goals or be adaptive.

Emotional Triangles

Family fusion, lack of differentiation, and anxiety can also result in **emotional triangles**. According to Bowen (1978/2004), the building block of all relationships is the triangle. You might think that the building block would be a dyad (two-person relationship); however, Bowen found that dyads are too unstable, and when problems occur between two people, a third person is almost always drawn into the relationship (Figure 10.2). The triangle is a naturally occurring process and "describes the dynamic equilibrium of a three-person system. The major influence on the activity of a triangle is anxiety" (Kerr & Bowen, 1988, p. 135). What does this mean and how does this work?

Suppose you have a fairly close relationship with a sister. As long as things are calm, your relationship (system) is stable. Unfortunately, you and your sister have a disagreement. Likely, you will talk to your mother, friend, or co-worker about the issue, drawing a third person into the relationship. A triangle has now been formed. Doing so actually helps distribute the anxiety caused by the disruption in your relationship with your sister and helps restore a sense of balance.

Bowen refers to triangles as "simply a fact of nature" (Kerr & Bowen, 1988, p. 134). Accordingly, Laura Brooks of the Bowen Center for the Study of the Family reminds us, "A family system is a natural system where most of what happens is automatic; the use of triangles to distribute anxiety in the system is a natural process. It's not a pathology" (Dore, 2018). Triangles are not always active; they become active as anxiety is experienced.

Bowen (1978/2004) cites two important variables in triangles: differentiation of self and emotional tension in the system. The lower the differentiation of self, the more intense the triangle; similarly, the more anxiety or tension felt in the system, the more intense the triangle (Bowen, 1978/2004). There are many targets for a triangling situation. Sometimes triangles are formed to control another family member. Other times, an attribute of a person is the target.

Emotional triangles have a number of rules that govern how they operate. Friedman (1985) said, "What Peter says about Paul tells you more about Peter than it does about Paul." In the concept of an emotional triangle, "What Peter says to you about his relationship with Paul has to do with his relationship with you" (p. 36). Friedman developed several "laws" about emotional triangles that help us understand what they are and how they operate in families (pp. 36–39). His ideas have been edited and changed here to adapt them to family life:

1   Triangles are often used to create balance, but it rarely works. One family member might try to keep the relationship of two other family members in balance by intruding in the relationship of the two others. In this case, a family member will feel it is her or his responsibility to make sure that a child (for example) has a good relationship with his father or sibling. Or a child might feel a need to get two parents closer or stop high levels of conflict. In a family paradigm that uses fusion-creating strategies, one or more family members will try to force, dominate, control, or bully another to conform by trying to change the relationship between two family members.

2   The results are usually temporary. When Mary (the mother in our example) tries to change the relationship between Justin (the son) and Michael (the father), she might see some change, but rarely for more than a few days. It is almost always the case that a relationship that is changed in this way (by the mother trying to make the son and father closer) will revert to the way it was before.

3   Triangulation makes things worse. When Mary tries to make Justin and Michael get along better, Mary's attempts almost always result in a worse relationship between Justin and Michael. The harder she tries to change their relationship (even though this is a good and wonderful goal), the more she gets an opposite result.

4   The person who initiates a triangulation attempt feels worse. As Mary tries to get Justin and Michael to have a better relationship, not only is it less likely to get better, but Mary is more likely to feel worse about their relationship and take on the stress of them not being close to one another.

5   Stop using triangulation, and things might get better. Mary has a greater chance at building stronger family relationships when she builds strong connections with Justin and Michael individually, rather than thinking she can force them to get along. She must realize that the connection between Justin and Michael is not her responsibility but is best developed by the two of them. It usually turns out that intrusive attempts to make a relationship stronger by a third person make things worse (Friedman, 1985, pp. 36–39).

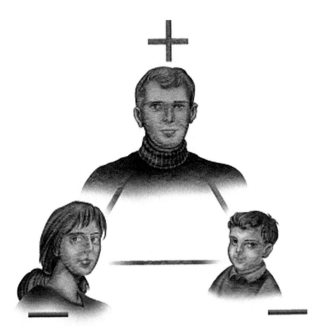

FIGURE 10.2 A triangle exists when one person does not like another person (or the actions of another)—the first person likes a third person—but the third person also likes the second person. The idea of triangles applies to likes and dislikes, difference of ideas, and even personality differences.

The roots of triangulation are ongoing, long-term anxiety (negative emotion) issues that are not resolved. The best alternative is to find ways to resolve the roots of the problem by finding ways to resolve the negative affect. The next best alternative is to find ways to manage the negative emotions so they do not disrupt healthy individual development, healthy family development, and attaining goals (Friedman, 1985).

There are several practical implications of these ideas. One of the most obvious implications is that families can avoid emotional triangles or eliminate them if they can find ways to avoid long-term negative emotions, such as resentment, tension, animosity, anger, fear, apprehension, and anxiety. Second, the use of triangulation in families is often a sign of attempts to create family fusion. Families who are anxious, worried, and distressed about lack of conformity to family paradigms often resort to these types of problematic strategies. Using triangulation to solve family problems usually makes things worse. A third implication is to try to be aware of how we might be part of family triangles. Often when someone solicits advice or help for a relationship problem, it is an attempt to triangle us into the problem situation. Being aware of the triangulation processes can provide useful ideas about how to help and how to avoid making the problem worse.

COPING WITH EMOTIONAL DISTRESS

Family scientists suggest four ways of coping with emotional distress in families: It is useful to (1) learn how to use and analyze a genogram and deal with insights it provides, (2) resolve invisible loyalties, (3) incorporate a **benign assumption** in family life, and (4) avoid **emotional cutoff**, a strategy many people try that is usually unsuccessful.

1 **Use a Genogram.** We learned about genograms in Chapter 4. Genograms can provide insights about the amount of differentiation occurring in families. One reason they are helpful is that patterns of fusion and differentiation are often carried from one generation to another. Usually, in each generation, there are some children who tend to have a little more differentiation, and there are some children who tend to have a little less; but many children repeat the patterns of the earlier generations. A trademark of Bowen's theory is his focus on at least three generations, allowing one to observe patterns and take on an active role in changing these (Brown, 2013).

Using a genogram chart, first examine and evaluate the differentiation–fusion patterns that have existed over several generations in a family. This usually provides insights about how some people have been more fused than others, and it can provide clues about a particular individual's fusion. It also helps people think about their differentiation as part of a larger pattern.

Examining your own differentiation in the context of a genogram can make you become more aware of strategies you can use to become more differentiated. For example, it might help you realize you are an autonomous individual who needs to stand on your own two feet.

Being a transitional character can change the direction of a family. Learning about these important principles means that you have the groundwork for the first step of any change process: You have the knowledge. However, having the knowledge does not mean that the knowing will, by itself, change you. There are millions of people who know that smoking cigarettes will kill them, and yet the knowledge without a daily resolve to change means that they continue living their lives as they always have, using a product that probably will kill them. The same is true for those of us who eat too much. Change is difficult and only those who practice fighting the momentum of the past can really become a transitional character.

It also might help to realize that some feelings were appropriate when you were a child, but not when you are an adult. It also might help you realize how some of the family patterns that keep you "fused" to your family system were petty sibling rivalries you have now outgrown. It might help you be able to relate to your parents as individuals who also struggle with their limitations and circumstances.

2 **Deal with Invisible Loyalties.** Boszormenyi-Nagy and Spark (1973) developed another strategy for resolving undesirable emotional connections in family systems. In their book, *Invisible Loyalties*, they described how families accumulate multigenerational patterns of obligations and rights. Some examples of positive things received are existence, love, nurturance, identity, heritage, values, bonds, and understanding.

Part of these patterns is obligations that are deeply felt emotional ties. These include such things as indebtedness, basic duties, and a sense of ethical responsibility. Boszormenyi-Nagy and Spark called these deeply felt connections invisible loyalties, and they involve such processes as giving and taking, helping and hindering, injustices and healing, teaching and receiving, and various combinations of hurting and acts of caring.

Boszormenyi-Nagy and Spark suggested that it is helpful to use the concept of a family ledger to think about these family processes. The ledger is a balance sheet of obligations and rights, debts and credits that accumulate over time. In more effective families, family members tend to balance the ledger with justice in the exchange of debts and obligations.

Sometimes, however, the justice comes too slowly, or it is insufficient, and there is too great an accumulation of injustices.

In other situations, some individuals perceive the pattern has been unjust, and this is deeply troubling. When these inequities occur, it creates chronic anxiety, resentments, and animosities that are disruptive to family members individually and collectively. One of Boszormenyi-Nagy and Spark's examples of this process is a mother who is angry at being rejected by her mother. She tries to correct this injustice by offering total devotion to her own daughter. However, in the language of balance of payments, the mother assumes the daughter should reestablish family justice by being appreciative and giving to her mother the acceptance and understanding her own mother did not give her. In this type of situation, the mother often is excessively devoted to her daughter, creating resentment rather than appreciation. This can lead to the daughter having unexplained negative feelings toward the "loving" mother. Confusion and emotional disruption prevail between the mother and daughter. Improvement results when either the mother or daughter realizes how the mother is trying to "balance the payments" or make up for her own deprivation. This can help the mother and the daughter understand what is going on and free them from the invisible emotional processes.

Family fusion can be created because the emotionally based resentments are captivating and consuming. Often, according to Boszormenyi-Nagy and Spark, the main difficulty is the invisibility of these patterns of unfinished business. Therefore, when the patterns are discovered, it is many times relatively easy to talk them through and resolve the emotional obligations.

3 **Incorporate the Benign Assumption.** Another way that family theorists and therapists have suggested to combat the potential effects of negativity and chronic anxiety in families is to develop an emotional climate that has a benign tone (Beavers, 1982). Beavers and his associates suggested that one of the more important aspects of stronger families is that they build a climate that is void of malignant attitude. An example would probably best help to define how this works.

In families where there is a malignant or highly contentious tone, each daily event that annoys or even has the potential to annoy someone is responded to with a far more negative response than the event should warrant. Suppose someone spills milk at the table. In a malignant climate, the parent might say something like, "See, that is another example of how you always try to make my life miserable. You are a brat and deserve to be punished." Families in which there is a benign assumption would probably respond with something that is far less dramatic, histrionic, animated, and nasty. Instead, the parent does not assume that each time something happens (like the milk spilling or the lost shoe) that it is a "federal case" (as my mom would say). Instead, they might even give a little laugh and say, "Oops, run and get a rag before it gets all over."

When there is no benign assumption, each day is filled with events that are interpreted as threatening and as attacks. It is as if the glass of life is always full of stress and accusation to overflowing and each creates a spill, so to speak. The application is, of course, to somehow break through the habitual over-reactivity that too many families develop. They seem to be awash in a malignant assumptive world, filled with threat, anxiety, and unresolved anger. Although you might not be able to do much about your family of origin, you certainly can begin to work on your family of procreation. Literally, nothing good comes from high levels of contention and a climate of the malignant assumption in family life. These two doses of strife only increase the distance between family members and decrease levels of intimacy.

4   **Emotional Cutoff: An Undesirable Method.** The fourth way one can cope with highly charged emotions in families is to face the problems in families head-on and not use emotional cutoff as a method of trying to deal with fusion that is generally ineffective. Emotional cutoff refers to attempts to deny fusion rather than resolve it. The result is that people might stop interacting with their family, or they might move away from their family, but they are still emotionally fused. In these situations, the fusion still has the same effects, even though the parental family might be thousands of miles away.

According to Bowen (1976), the emotional cutoff is determined by the way people handle their unresolved emotional attachments to their parents. He claimed that all people have some degree of unresolved emotional attachment to their parents, and furthermore, the more family fusion one experienced in childhood, the more likely one will experience the unresolved attachment and feelings of wanting to use emotional cutoff. Bowen indicated that the way an individual approaches the idea of cutoff greatly influences the way "people separate themselves from the past in order to start their lives in the present generation" (p. 83). He further stated:

> The degree of unresolved emotional attachment to the parents is equivalent to the degree of fusion that must somehow be handled in the person's own life and in future generations. The unresolved attachment is handled by the intrapsychic process of denial and isolation of self while living close to the parents; or by physically running away; or by a combination of emotional isolation and physical distance.
>
> (Bowen, 1976, p. 84)

Bowen is also convinced that the more intense cutoff is, the more likely one's own children are to do a more forceful cutoff with the parent in the next generation. There are many variations in the intensity of this basic process and in the way the cutoff is handled. The person who runs away from his family of origin is in serious need of emotional closeness, but at the same time, they are allergic to it. Thus, the emotional cutoff is always a less desirable solution than working through or resolving the emotional problems in a way that will promote healthy differentiation.

In some situations, however, it might not be possible to differentiate; then, emotional cutoff becomes one of the options to be considered. For example, if there is an abuse of any kind (i.e., sexual, physical, or emotional), leaving and not looking back might be the best thing and usually a prime option to be explored.

Discussions in Diversity: Mom, I'm Trans

Born and raised a boy at the age of 18, he told his parents he was gay. He told them as a pre-emptive strike after fearing he was about to be outed by an acquaintance for wearing women's clothing. Over the years, he avoided talking about his gender struggles while he wrestled with his identity: Transvestite? Cross dresser? Transgender? After settling on "transsexual," he wrote a three-page letter to his parents to "come out" once again, this time as "Juliet Jacques."

FIGURE 10.3 Gender transition can influence family perceptions of connectedness and distance.

Source: https://www.shutterstock.com/image-photo/person-holding-sign-reading-protect-trans-1449773771

In response to the letter, Juliet received an email from her father, who said they were struggling with this information, but with "time and understanding" they could continue being part of each other's lives. Difficult conversations followed. Juliet writes, "My 'becoming a woman' has not realized (my parents') worst fears… 'time and understanding' from both sides have indeed allowed us to remain part of each other's lives, thanks to our willingness to respect and share each other's concerns" (Jacques, 2010).

Research on issues related to transgender is sparse. It is safe to say that this is an extremely complex and even dynamic phenomenon (Figure 10.3). Such transitions are not single events in the lives of families but occur over time, often over years. Young children, as well as elders, are transitioning within one's self gender, and social media is filled with stories related to transgender lives. In some cases, individuals may "detransition" (or retransition) to their assigned/biological gender, further complicating identity and family relationships.

As with any major transition that involves our deepest held hopes, expectations, and beliefs, families are likely to experience a myriad of emotions that could influence one's feelings of connectedness and independence. Catalpa and McGuire (2018) studied transgender youth and found increased distance with family who don't accept their child's gender ambiguity. It appears both parents and child wrestle with uncertainty about being in or out of the family, experiencing stress and ambiguous loss. Some families experience abuse related to the situation and reconciliation may not be possible.

A similar change in identity and family process is likely experienced by families who have a parent transition (i.e., transgender parent). Many clinicians guide those in transition from their assigned/biological gender to their expressed gender (Smidova, 2019). Smidova, however, uses a family systems perspective, recognizing transition as a self-differentiation process and as a "process of balancing differentiation in the expressed gender on an interpersonal level. I believe one's experience in assigned gender is not supposed to be rejected and forgotten, but rather used for the benefit of the expressed gender and for regaining stability in the family system" (p. 34). In one family, the children were informed of their father's transition and were allowed to choose the name of the transitioning parent (Tannehill, 2016). They chose "Maddy," a combination of Mom and Daddy. Their 8th-grade daughter shared that "Maddy" became much nicer after transitioning and had seemed sad or upset prior to the transition.

Understanding family systems theory and distance regulation may provide insight into how to assist families and individuals and minimize disruptions brought about when addressing LGBTQIA issues in the family compared to utilizing individual and gender binary focus perspectives.

Questions to Discuss:

- *How do the concepts of differentiation of self and family fusion apply in this situation?*
- *How can parents help their children negotiate gender identity and sexual orientation?*
- *What would be your response if your child/brother/niece/cousin/parent said they were trans and planning to transition? Would your response differ according to your role?*

SUMMARY

In this chapter, we explored distance regulation and the delicate balance between connection and autonomy. Anchoring our discussion in Bowen's Family Systems Theory, we examined the processes of differentiation and family fusion. We suggested that the concept of fusion can be represented on a scale. On one end of the scale is differentiation. Children who are raised in a non-intrusive, non-fused family are encouraged to become independent and self-directed. It is possible, however, that family members may be so emotionally separate that bonding, support, and connection are faint and removed.

At the other end of the family fusion scale is high fusion. In highly fused families, children are expected to become part of the collective, surrender personal identity, think and act like parents and other siblings or even grandparents, conform, and become absorbed into the family collective. Families who adopt a family paradigm that focuses on fusion usually use tactics such as intimidation, high control attempts, physical force, higher levels of negativity, hostility, and animosity to achieve their goal of high conformity. It is important to note that often built into the constitution of this type of family paradigm is the idea that fusion and conforming is the ultimate family type. Family conformity and fusion are often presented as the highest ideal or even a sacred family form.

One of the outcomes of high family fusion is that children might lose the ability to think more rationally and, instead, will be consumed with an emotional, feeling world within which rational thought might be an infrequent visitor. When family fusion occurs, family members are excessively tied to the emotional system in their parental family. The result is that family members become victims of the emotionality in their lives, and when family fusion occurs, it interferes with the ability people have to use their intellect. Chronic anxiety and triangling can result from family fusion and poor differentiation and are potentially disabling processes that may prevent families from reaching their goals. Four ways of coping with emotional distress in families were provided: Use a genogram to explore generational patterns of differentiation, deal with invisible loyalties, incorporate the benign assumption, and avoid emotional cutoffs.

STUDY QUESTIONS

1   Define what is meant by the term *differentiation* in family life and how it strengthens families.
2   Give several examples of poor differentiation in families.
3   How do you balance connection and autonomy in families? Why is fusion dangerous for family members?
4   "What Peter says about Paul tells you more about Peter than it does Paul." Explain what this means within the context in which it was presented.
5   Define the emotional triangle and give an example of how one might work in a family.
6   Is fusion different than differentiation? How, if it is?
7   Tell what is meant by the term *chronic anxiety* and give examples of how it works in family life. How does it differ from acute anxiety?
8   Explain why emotional cutoff is a poor strategy for coping with family emotions.

KEY TERMS

Regulating distance
Differentiation
Connectedness
Family fusion
Helicopter parenting
Lawnmower parenting
Internal fusion
Emotional triangles
Acute anxiety
Chronic anxiety
Invisible loyalties
Emotional cutoff
Benign assumption

SUGGESTED READINGS

Cox, M., & Brooks-Gunn, J. (1999). *Conflict and cohesion in families: Causes and consequences.* Mahwah, NJ: Lawrence Erlbaum Associates.

Holodynski, M., & Friedlmeier, W. (2006). *Development of emotions and emotional regulation.* New York, NY: Springer.

Kerr, M. E. (2019). *Bowen theory's secrets: Revealing the hidden life of families.* New York, NY: W. W. Norton Company.

Kerr, M. E., & Bowen, M. (1988). *Family evaluation.* New York, NY: Norton.

Minuchin, S. (1996). *Mastering family therapy: Journeys of growth and transformation.* New York, NY: Wiley.

Titelman, P. (2015). *Differentiation of self: Bowen family systems theory perspectives.* New York, NY: Routledge.

REFERENCES

Bartle, S. E., & Sabatelli, R. M. (1989). Family system dynamics, identity development, and adolescent alcohol use: Implications for family treatment. *Family Relations, 38,* 258–265.

Beavers, W. R. (1982). Healthy, midrange and severely dysfunctional families. In F. Walsh (Ed.), *Normal family processes* (pp. 45–66). New York, NY: Guilford.

Bohlander, J. R. (1995). Differentiation of self: An examination of the concept. *Issues in Mental Health Nursing, 16*(2), 165–184.

Boszormenyi-Nagy, I., & Spark, G. M. (1973). *Invisible loyalties: Reciprocity in intergenerational therapy.* New York, NY: Gardner.

Bowen, M. (1976). Theory in the practice of psychotherapy. In P. Guerin (Ed.), *Family therapy* (pp. 42–61). New York, NY: Gardner.

Bowen, M. (1978/2004). *Family theory in clinical practice.* Lanham, MD: A Jason Aronson Book.

The Bowen Center (n.d.). *About Murray Bowen.* Washington, DC: Georgetown University Family Center. http://thebowencenter.org/theory/murray-bowen/

Brown, J. (2013). Bowen family systems theory and practice: Illustration and critique. *Australian and New Zealand Journal of Family Therapy, 20*(2), 94–103.

Buehler, C. (2020). Family processes and children's and adolescents' well-being. *Journal of Marriage and Family, 82*(1), 145–174.

Carter, B., & McGoldrick, M. (Eds.). (1989). *The changing family life cycle: A framework for family therapy* (2nd ed.). New York, NY: Allyn & Bacon.

Catalpa, J. M., & McGuire, J. K. (2018). Family boundary ambiguity among transgender youth. *Family Relations, 6,* 88–103.

Dore, J. (2018). The triangulation theory may explain why some childhoods are so stressful. *Vice, July 30.* https://www.vice.com/en/article/ev8bjm/the-triangulation-theory-may-explain-why-some-childhoods-are-so-stressful

Dumont, D. E. (2021). Facing adulthood: Helicopter parenting as a function of the family projection process. *Journal of College Student Psychotherapy, 35*(1), 1–14. DOI: 10.1080/87568225.2019.1601049

Erdem, G., & Safi, O. A. (2018). The cultural lens approach to Bowen family systems theory: Contributions of family change theory. *Journal of Family Theory & Review, 10*(2), 469–483. DOI: 10.1111/jftr.12258

The Family Systems Institute (FSI) (nd). *What is Bowen Theory? Who is Dr. Murray Bowen?* http://www.thefsi.com.au/us/bowen-theory/

Farley, J. (1979). Family separation-individuation tolerance: A developmental conceptualization of the nuclear family. *Journal of Marital and Family Therapy, 5,* 61–67.

Foose, K., & Cicio, M. (2018). Differentiation of self through the lens of mindfulness. *Counseling Today,* https://ct.counseling.org/2018/02/differentiation-of-self-through-the-lens-of-mindfulness/

Friedman, E. H. (1985). *Generation to generation.* New York, NY: Guilford.

Gavazzi, S. M. (1993). The relation between family differentiation levels in families with adolescents and the severity of presenting problems. *Family Relations, 42,* 463–468.

Gavazzi, S. M. (1994). Advances in assessing the relationship between family differentiation and problematic functioning in adolescents. *Family Therapy, 21*, 249–259.

Gavazzi, S. M., Anderson, S. A., & Sabatelli, R. M. (1993). Family differentiation, peer differentiation and adolescent adjustment in a clinical sample. *Journal of Adolescent Research, 8*, 205–225.

Gavazzi, S. M., & Sabatelli, R. M. (1990). Family system dynamics, the individuation process and psychosocial and adolescent adjustment in a clinical sample. *Journal of Adolescent Research, 5*, 500–519.

Jacques, J. (2010). How do you tell your family you are transgender? *The Guardian.* https://www.theguardian.com/lifeandstyle/2010/jul/14/tell-family-transgender

Jenkins, S. M., Buboltz, W. C., Schwartz, J. P., & Johnson, P. (2005). Differentiation of self and psychosocial development. *Contemporary Family Therapy, 27*(2), 251–261.

Kağıtçıbaşı, Ç (1996). The autonomous-relational self. *European Psychologist, 1*(3), 180–186. DOI: 10.1027/1016-9040.1.3.180

Kerr, M. (1981). Family systems theory and therapy. In A. S. Gurman, & D. P. Kriskern (Eds.), *Handbook of family therapy* (pp. 212–244). New York, NY: Brunner/Mazel.

Kerr, M. E. (2000). *One family's story: A primer on Bowen Theory.* The Bowen Center for the Study of the Family. http://www.thebowencenter.org

Kerr, M. E., & Bowen, M. (1988). *Family evaluation: An approach based on Bowen theory.* New York, NY: W. W. Norton & Co.

Kim, H., Prouty, A. M., Smith, D. B., Ko, M. J., Wetchler, J. L., & Oh, J. E. (2014). Differentiation of self and its relationship with family functioning in South Koreans. *The American Journal of Family Therapy, 42*, 257–265. DOI: 10.1080/01926187.2013.838928

Knauth, D. G., Skowron, E. A., & Escobar, M. (2006). Effect of differentiation of self on adolescent risk behavior: Test of the theoretical model. *Nursing Research, 55*(5), 336–345.

Locke, J. Y., Campbell, M., & Kavanagh, D. (2012). Can a parent do too much for their child? An examination by parenting professionals of the concept of overparenting. *Journal of Psychologists and Counsellors in Schools, 22*(2), 249–265.

MacKay, L. M. (2017). Differentiation of self: Enhancing therapist resilience when working with relational trauma. *Australian and New Zealand Journal of Family Therapy, 38*(4), 637–656.

Nichols, M. P., & Schwartz, R. C. (2007). *Family therapy: Concepts and methods* (8th ed.). Needham Heights, MA: Allyn & Bacon.

Papero, D. V. (1983). Family systems theory and therapy. In B. B. Wolman, & G. Stricker (Eds.), *Handbook of family and marital therapy* (pp. 144–190). New York, NY: Plenum.

Sabatelli, R. M., & Anderson, S. A. (1991). Family systems dynamics, peer relationships and adolescents' psychological adjustments. *Family Relations, 40*, 363–369.

Sabatelli, R. M., & Cecil-Pigo, E. F. (1985). Relational interdependence and commitment in marriage. *Journal of Marriage and the Family, 47*, 931–938.

Schiffrin, H. H., Liss, M., Miles-McLean, H., Geary, K. A., & Erchull, M. J. (2013). Helping or hovering? The effects of helicopter parenting on college students' well-being. *Psychological Science, 7*.

Schwartz, J. P., Thigpen, S. E., & Montgomery, J. K. (2006). Examination of parenting styles of processing emotions and differentiation of self. *The Family Journal, 14*(1), 41–48. DOI: 10.1177/1066480705282050

Skowron, E. A. (2004). Differentiation of self, personal adjustment, problem solving, and ethnic group belonging among persons of color. *Journal of Counseling and Development, 82*, 447–456.

Skowron, E. A. (2005). Parent differentiation of self and child competency in low-income and urban families. *Journal of Counseling Psychology, 52*(3), 337–346.

Skowron, E. A., & Friedlander, M. L. (1998). The differentiation of self inventory: Development and initial validation. *Journal of Counseling Psychology, 45*(3), 235–246.

Smidova, E. (2019). Transgender parent differentiation: A heuristic phenomenological study. Dissertation, Department of Family Therapy Dissertations and Applied Projects, Nova Southeastern University, Florida. https://nsuworks.nova.edu/cgi/viewcontent.cgi?article=1048&context=shss_dft_etd

Stapley, L. A., & Murdock, N. L. (2020). Leisure in romantic relationships: An avenue for differentiation of self. *Personal Relationships, 27*(1), 76–101.

Tannehill, B. (2016). Here's what it's REALLY like having a transgender parent. https://www.huffpost.com/entry/what-it-is-really-like-having-a-transgender-parent_b_5846c5d3e4b0707e4c817242

CHAPTER **11**

Forgiveness, Kindness, Hope, and Gratitude

CHAPTER PREVIEW

In this chapter, readers will learn:

- About some positive family processes and associated prosocial and facilitative behaviors.
- What forgiveness is and how it is different from condoning or forgetting past offenses.
- The categories and types of forgiveness.
- The costs and benefits of forgiveness personally and for the family.
- About forgiveness interventions.
- The components of kindness.
- The influence of kindness on physical and psychological health.
- The role of kindness within family.
- How hope influences individuals and family.
- About the difference between hope and reasonable hope.
- How positive illusions relate to hope.
- The four components of gratitude.
- About the similarities and variations of gratitude, even across culture.
- How families socialize gratitude.
- The effects of gratitude on family relationships.
- The effectiveness of gratitude interventions.

INTRODUCTION

Many years ago, a local grocery store handed out stamps each time we made a purchase. These stamps could be collected and pasted onto cards that we'd turn in for discounts on specific food items. Our family collected these stamps, and every November, the children would spend hours pasting the stamps on the cards to be used to purchase Thanksgiving turkeys. One year, the children made enough cards to obtain 11 turkeys at no cost (that year we had a lot of stamp licking)! We then provided turkeys to our local foodbank and families we knew who could use them.

Many families work together to provide service to their communities. They may deliver meals to neighbors, help neighbors move or mow their lawns, drive a friend to the doctor,

DOI: 10.4324/9781003128717-14

clean closets and deliver items to local charities, serve food at foodbanks, sell cookies or candy for organizations, or babysit for free under certain circumstances. Families have myriad opportunities to work together to show kindness and compassion toward people outside the family realm, and for many families, service is built into their family paradigms. However, kindness, compassion, and service within the family appear to be somewhat more difficult to master. Just as Richardson (2014) found that aggression can be expressed in many ways and varies according to relationship, forgiveness, kindness, and gratitude are also likely to be expressed differently across relationships. It is a truism that sometimes those we know well are often treated worse than those who are strangers.

In this chapter, we explore some positive family processes and associated **prosocial** and facilitative behaviors. Prosocial behaviors refer to those actions we take that benefit others and society, including sharing, cooperating, and helping (Figure 11.1). As seen throughout this text, families are complex, and peeling away the skin of the elephant to view their internal workings related to positive family processes (often invisible to the family and its members) is no easy task. For our examination of these processes, not only do we need to understand the internal processes of the family but we also need to accept and understand the "bed rock, foundational force" of individual family members, with their gender, genetics, personalities, quirks, preferences, beliefs and choices (Day, Gavazzi, Miller, & Van Langeveld, 2009, p. 121). Each of us brings our own plate to the table of family and the family itself needs to develop processes around these individual differences, with the individual and family whole mutually influencing each other in unseen ways.

FIGURE 11.1 Caring and kindness are often seen in family interactions.

Source: iStock

FORGIVENESS

> "Lydia" stood by the deathbed of her stepfather. She had not seen him in almost 25 years but had gone at his request and her half-sister's urging. She stood there remembering being kicked out of the house at 15 and learning how to take care of herself at such a tender age. She recalled the beatings, including with a hammer, that left a lifetime of physical pain and emotional scars. She remembered that he didn't like her but that she prevailed despite the pain. Now, she stood by the bed of this ailing 76-year-old man, who grabbed her hand and said, "Lydia … I always loved you. Forgive me." Lydia was awash in mixed emotions. The moment was poignant. She had forgiven him years earlier, although they had never spoken or been reconciled. It was a moment she never forgot.

We often think of forgiveness in the context of religion or as a moral virtue. Few people realize that forgiveness has been the subject of scientific inquiry, especially in the 21st Century (Fincham, 2017). Using a variety of research methods, we have come to learn what forgiveness is and how it is manifested, the benefits of forgiveness, barriers to it, and even insight into how to forgive when faced with challenging situations.

What It Is and What It Ain't

When most people hear the term "forgiveness," they think of absolving others of their wrongdoings and perhaps letting go of resentments. As with most scientific endeavors involving complex phenomena (and forgiveness is, indeed, a complex phenomenon), deciding on definitions was fraught with controversy until relatively recently (Fincham, 2017). Fincham provides a current and generally accepted definition of forgiveness utilized by scholars: "*A freely chosen motivational change in which the desire to seek revenge or to avoid contact with the transgressor is overcome* … distinct from related constructs such as pardoning …, the spontaneous dissipation of resentment and ill will over time …, forgetting …, and condoning" (p. 586, italics added). We have found that forgiveness is different across relationship types (e.g., friends, work colleagues, acquaintances, or family) (Maio, Thomas, Fincham, & Carnelley, 2008). In fact, it can even vary across family relationships.

For our purposes, we view forgiveness as a family process that is central to family functioning (Fincham, 2017). However, Carr and Wang (2012) remind us that forgiveness is not a simple process but a "vast undertaking." Indeed, we can say, "I forgive you," but much of the hard work lies after these words are spoken as we renegotiate boundaries, feelings of trust, and intimacy (Hargrave & Zasowsky, 2017). As a multidimensional construct, forgiveness involves strategies and behaviors such as these that can help families achieve their goals. It is an unusual family relationship where we do not get hurt or hurt another through words, actions, or even inactions. Such blunders interfere with family goals, and thus forgiveness is a necessity for repairing, maintaining and strengthening connectedness. In the words of Welch (2012), "Forgiveness is one of the most underutilized family processes that people can use to maintain healthy intimate and family relationships and friendships. Outside of love, forgiveness is perhaps the most important tool available for the longevity of relationships" (p. 98).

We knew a man, Glenn Kempton, whose deputy sheriff father (Martin Kempton) was killed in a 1918 shootout with Tom Powers and his family. Powers was sentenced and spent over 40 years in prison. Glenn Kempton was a young boy at the time of his father's death, and his mother was left alone to raise Glenn and his six brothers and sisters in Southeastern Arizona under very meager circumstances. Glenn recalled that he grew up hating Tom Powers and carried bitter, heavy feelings into young adulthood. At some point in his early adulthood, Glenn decided he had to forgive Tom Powers, whether or not Tom felt sorry for what he had done. The process took decades to realize. One day, on a trip home from Phoenix, Glenn and his wife decided to stop at Florence Prison, where he asked to visit with Tom Powers. Glenn recalled, "We were introduced and led into the parole room where we had a long talk. We went back to that cold, gray February morning 30 years before, re-enacting that whole terrible tragedy. We talked for perhaps an hour and a half. Finally, I said, 'Tom, you made a mistake for which you owe a debt to society for which I feel you must continue to pay, just the same as I must continue to pay the price for having been reared without a father.' Then I stood and extended my hand. He stood and took it. I continued, 'With all my heart, I forgive you for this awful thing that has come into our lives.' He bowed his head and I left him there. I don't know how he felt then, and I don't know how he feels now, but my witness to you is that it is a glorious thing when bitterness and hatred go out of your heart and forgiveness comes in. I thanked the warden for his kindness, and as I walked out the door and down that long flight of steps, I knew that forgiveness was better than revenge, for I had experienced it. As we drove toward home in the gathering twilight, a sweet and peaceful calm came over me. Out of pure gratitude, I placed my arm around my wife, who understood, for I know that *we had now found a broader, richer and more abundant life*" (Kimball, 1969, pp. 291–293, italics mine). Glenn Kempton had not only felt a release for himself through forgiveness but for his family, as well.

Forgiveness has been categorized in several ways, and Glenn Kempton's story will serve to illustrate those categories:

- **Intrapersonal (Individual) and Interpersonal (Relationship) Forgiveness.** From Glenn Kempton's story, we see the two dimensions of forgiveness elucidated by Baumeister, Exline, and Sommer (1998). The first dimension is the "intrapsychic dimension involving the victim's emotional state (and the cognitive and behavioral accompaniments)" (p. 80). This is commonly referred to as the intrapersonal level of forgiveness. Intrapersonal forgiveness is a process whereby the individual drops the weight of the offense, reducing the negative emotions (anger, bitterness, resentment) related to it. Thus, forgiveness is within the individual.

  The second dimension is interpersonal forgiveness (Figure 11.2). This is forgiveness that occurs at the relationship level (i.e., "inter," which means "between" people). This is the level of forgiveness that most people think of when discussing this topic. Interpersonal forgiveness may attempt to restore and heal relationships and result in reconciliation.

  In the example above, we see intrapersonal forgiveness occurring as Glenn Kempton decided to "let go" of his hard feelings toward Tom Powers. Meeting Tom Powers was an attempt at interpersonal forgiveness. It should be noted that these two dimensions can occur independently of each other (Cha, Hyun, Ra, & Yoon, 2010). A relationship may appear repaired while the victim still feels anger; just as a victim may no longer feel anger but the relationship is broken.

- **Decisional Forgiveness and Emotional Forgiveness.** Worthington (2003) delineated between two types of forgiveness, decisional and emotional forgiveness. Decisional

FIGURE 11.2 Interpersonal forgiveness occurs at the relationship level.

Source: https://www.istockphoto.com/photo/two-sad-teens-embracing-at-bedroom-gm820376276-132554715

forgiveness refers to one making a deliberate decision to forgive and agree to control our negative behavior toward the other. As stated by Lichtenfeld, Buechner, Maier, and Fernandez-Capo (2015), one may grant decisional forgiveness yet still hold a grudge.

On the other hand, emotional forgiveness involves changes of the heart and replacing negative emotions toward the transgressor with positive ones. Lichtenfeld and colleagues found empirical support for these two processes related to the idea of "forgive and forget," with emotional forgiveness leading to higher incidences of forgetting the offense than decisional forgiveness. When Glenn Kempton decided to let go of his negative feelings and express his forgiveness to Tom Powers, he was showing both decisional and emotional forgiveness.

- **Direct, Indirect, and Conditional Forgiveness.** According to Kelley (1998), forgiveness granting can be direct, indirect, or conditional. In direct forgiveness, the forgiver directly addresses the transgressor by discussing the issue, just as Glenn Kempton did when he confronted one of the men responsible for his father's murder. With indirect forgiveness, there typically is no discussion surrounding the offense. Instead, the forgiver might behave in a way to indicate forgiveness, such as hugging the person or acting as if nothing had happened; in other words, forgiveness is simply understood. Conditional forgiveness grants forgiveness but with strings. Kelley provides an example of a father asking a child's forgiveness as part of his recovery from alcohol addiction. The child's response? "I told him I would accept his apology; however, we both knew that there was the stipulation that he stay off of the booze" (p. 206). Such stipulations indicate that the offending behavior will no longer be tolerated (Merolla, 2008). Interestingly, both Kelley and Merolla found that forgiveness can vary by relationship type. For example, Merolla found that friends were more likely to report indirect forgiveness than dating partners, and dating partners were more likely to report conditional forgiveness.

Carr and Wang (2012) studied forgiveness within non-voluntary relationships of the family realm. Within the family, members have differing expectations and obligations and likely worry less about relationships dissolving following an offense, which may influence how (and if) we forgive. As found by previous researchers, forgiveness in family is not an event but an ongoing negotiation between and among family members across time. In Carr and Wang's study, not a single family member participant reported directly saying, "I forgive you" to another family member. Rather, family members were indirect in their forgiveness by minimizing the offense or using non-verbal displays of affection. It is believed that the permanent nature of family relationships results in this implicit approach. Still, it appears that even within non-voluntary relationships, we see differences in forgiveness. For example, Waldron, Braithwaite, Oliver, Kloeber, and Marsh (2018) found that explicit forms of forgiveness play a greater role in step-parent/step-child relationships than in first marriage/biological relationships. Clearly, family forgiveness is an area of needed research, including forgiveness between adult children and parents, children and adolescents and their parents, and siblings.

Forgiveness Has Costs and Benefits

Raj and Wiltermuth (2016) have listed several reasons why one might avoid forgiving another. For example, one might believe that forgiving another might create inequity and result in injustice. Another barrier is the belief that forgiving someone for a transgression condones the behavior and may result in future hurt; it might also make the forgiver appear weak. Indeed, research has found that spouses who forgive may have partners who might take advantage of that tendency, compared with spouses who forgive but let their partner know the behavior was hurtful and requires change (Russell, Baker, McNulty, & Overall, 2018). Sometimes, a person may fail to forgive because they have a strong sense of personal entitlement, believing that forgiveness is unfair or fearing loss of pride, as well as feeling a sense of self-righteousness (Exline, Baumeister, Bushman, Campbell, & Finkel, 2004; Raj & Wiltermuth, 2016).

Whatever the reason for failing to forgive, research has found that forgiveness (both seeking and granting forgiveness) results in numerous physical, emotional, and social benefits. These benefits are both interpersonal and intrapersonal, including:

- Increased relationship satisfaction, increased positive behaviors and thoughts about the other, and reciprocal positivity (Russell et al., 2018).
- Increased resilience as individuals and in relationships (Kelley, 2017).
- Better mental health. Toussaint et al. (2020) found that people who had experienced a lifetime of stress had worse mental health outcomes unless they scored high on measures of forgiveness; for this latter group, lifetime stress did not predict poor mental health! Toussaint said, "We thought forgiveness would knock something off the relationship (between stress and psychological distress), but we didn't expect it to zero it out!"
- Improved physical health; reduced nicotine dependence and substance abuse (Cheadle & Toussaint, 2015; Weir, 2017).
- Positively associated with psychological well-being and negatively associated with depression and anxiety, for all forgiveness types (by God, Self, and others) (Chen, Harris, Worthington, & VanderWeele, 2019; Weir, 2017).

FIGURE 11.3 Forgiveness can be learned through numerous daily interactions.

Source: https://www.istockphoto.com/photo/black-mother-and-daughter-embracing-sitting-on-couch-gm1051381418-281118775

- Positive consequences of forgiveness on individuals, family relationships, and general family environment, transforming vengeance into positive outcomes, including higher conscientiousness (fathers and children), emotional stability (fathers and children), agreeableness (mothers and children), and extraversion (fathers and mothers) (Maio et al., 2008).
- Avoids the negative outcomes of not forgiving, including destructive conflict and disruption in family relationships, cardiac and other health risks (Fincham, 2015).
- Improves the overall quality of our lives through maintaining healthy relationships (Carr & Wang, 2012).
- Promotes self-esteem in children (Shah & Sharma, 2018).
- Promotes generalized prosocial orientation and greater feelings of relatedness toward others; increases the probability of donating to charity and volunteering (Karremans, Van Lange, & Holland, 2005).

Kelley's (2017) insight that forgiveness is really about building resilience in self and relationships is an important point to remember. While some people may believe that forgiveness is for the transgressor, the findings above support the idea that forgiveness benefits the forgiver personally, the forgiver's relationship with the family, and even the forgiver's relationship with the community at large. Glenn Kempton's forgiveness of his father's purported murderer was not so much a benefit to Tom Powers but to Glenn Kempton himself.

Learning to Forgive

Everett Worthington is a scholar who has contributed much to our understanding of forgiveness through his research and writings. Despite his expertise in the area, he was called upon to put forgiveness in action when his 76-year-old mother was brutally murdered and sexually abused during a New Year's Eve burglary of her home (McNeill, 2017; Tuppance, 2009). Her body was found by Everett's brother and the trauma of it led to the brother's suicide nine years later. Everett admits that he was filled with rage and his first instinct was a desire to beat the perpetrator with a baseball bat. And then, he says, "It dawned on me that I had come through that whole day never allowing myself to think the word 'forgive.' I had just written this book on forgiveness, and I wasn't going to think about forgiveness. Who did I write the book for? Everybody else?" Indeed, within a month of the murder, Everett and his siblings all forgave the person who had done this. He doesn't describe himself as superhuman in this ability, recalling that it took him ten years to forgive a professor who had given him a "B." Instead, he says, "Mama taught us to forgive. It would dishonor her if we didn't forgive."

Likely Everett Worthington's decades of research and study in forgiveness, as well as the childhood foundation of forgiveness provided by his mother, allowed him to forgive more freely and quickly than someone else in a similar situation. However, his admission that he had difficulty forgiving a former teacher for a less than perfect grade (which seems relatively minor) provides us with an increased understanding that forgiveness is not a simple "do this, not that" approach. The dynamic and interactive characteristics of family systems mean that our relationships are both stable and in flux. We are bound to step on toes (tiny slights, such as forgetting to take out the trash when asked), as well as totally trample the other's soul (large errors, such as infidelity or financial indiscretions). Our responses to major and minor transgressions can vary depending on our relationship with the other, the context of the transgression (deliberate, unintended), and even the other's response to our response. Each experience, though, provides a lesson for the individual and the family (Figure 11.3). Physician and surgeon David Hanscom (2020) observes, "Forgiveness is both a learned skill and an ongoing daily process without a beginning or end." We are wise to remember that forgiveness, especially for major problems, can be a long process that crosses years, and we should avoid giving up too soon (Waldron & Kelley, 2008).

Our parents and caregivers are important models of behavior for interpersonal relationships, directly and indirectly sharing their values and skills with us early in life (Zimet & Jacob, 2001). This includes modeling forgiveness. Like sponges, we unknowingly absorb strategies and beliefs as we observe and interact with family members negotiating and renegotiating relationships after encountering an offense. Do we see family members withdraw from situations, engage in emotional cutoffs, or employ repair attempts that may or may not be rebuffed? As Kelley, Waldron, and Kloeber (2019) explain, some strategies may reduce hurt in the short run, but they are not sustainable in maintaining long-term positive relationships.

If we do not come from a family that valued forgiveness and find forgiveness difficult, what can we do to enhance this skill and build a healthy family foundation? Research has found that we can grow in our ability to forgive through self-directed efforts, as well as through more formal strategies developed by forgiveness researchers (Enright, 2001; Toussaint, Worthington, & Williams, 2015; Wade, Hoyt, Kidwell, & Worthington, 2014). Perhaps a first step is awareness of one's attitude toward forgiveness. We need to set aside the idea that there must be justice for us. Like we were taught as children, life's not always fair. We may not like this situation, but as one of our colleagues used to say, "What is *is*."

Kelley et al. (2019) assert that if we want strong, healthy relationships, we may need to make behavioral changes that create positive, benevolent, and more just interactions. Such changes may involve improving our communication skills and learning to listen. Further, they suggest being honest with ourselves and others, acknowledging our wrongdoings, and being gracious when others acknowledge theirs. They observe that some could benefit from "putting emotions to words, offering positive recognition, curbing the tendency to give advice, remaining constructive during conflict, or being more welcoming to new ideas" (p. 35). Other researchers have suggested developing empathy and compassion (Enright, 2001; Toussaint et al., 2015; Wade et al., 2018).

Formal intervention programs available through family life educators and counselors include Enright's (2001) forgiveness therapy process model that involves a 20-step process designed to move individuals through four phases: (1) uncovering phase, uncovering the deep-seated feelings and pain related to the offense; (2) decision phase, deciding to forgive; (3) work phase, working on forgiving; and (4) outcome/deepening phase, deepened understanding in terms of meaning and purpose in life. Enright developed the field of forgiveness education, and his program has been found to be helpful. Another intervention program is Worthington's REACH Forgiveness of Others (Harper et al., 2014). REACH stands for [R]ecall the hurt; [E]mpathize with your partner; [A]ltruistic gift, giving forgiveness unselfishly; [C]ommit to your decision to forgive; and [H]old onto forgiveness. This program has also been found to be effective, even across culture and religion (Toussaint et al., 2020). Apparently, even "grudge holders" and "revenge seekers" can become more forgiving.

Renegotiating relationships as part of the forgiveness process is never easy; however, it does allow family members to "reimagine the future" of their relationship (Kelley et al., 2019). In the words of author Paul Boese (1967), "forgiveness does not change the past, but it does enlarge the future" (p. 146).

PRINCIPLE 11.1

FORGIVENESS IN FAMILIES IS AN UNDERUTILIZED FAMILY PROCESS

Family members provide many reasons for why they resist forgiving others; however, research has found surprising benefits to those people forgiving others, including strengthening of family relationships.

KINDNESS

Elly is a rambunctious 5-year-old, with a quick smile and a story to tell anyone who will listen. She has strong feelings, and it is not unusual to see her hit or push her 2-year-old brother or stomp her foot at her mother when she is angry. Yet, you will also see her demonstrate kindness as she helps her brother get something that is out of his reach or spontaneously sits next to him and reads him a book. When Elly's father had foot surgery, Elly was first to make sure he had all he needed. She brought him cold packs for his foot, blankets to keep warm, water to drink, and even her favorite toys to keep him company. Families (and family members) are complicated.

In the past three decades, research on prosocial behavior, which includes associations with kindness, compassion, cooperation, altruism, caring, concern, and empathy, has proliferated (Gilbert,

Basran, MacArthur, & Kirby, 2019). Unfortunately, many of these (and other) terms have been used interchangeably, resulting in some confusion and misapplications. Indeed, these concepts may overlap, but they still differ in meaningful ways. For example, compassion and kindness are "different processes, with different foci, competencies, and emotional textures" (Gilbert et al., 2019). Likely this mashup of concepts is a result of the varied perspectives of who is doing the studying, including philosophers, theologians, psychologists, developmentalists, sociologists, and family scientists, each studying these constructs with a slightly different lens. Like forgiveness, kindness is considered a virtue by some, but it also refers to actions that are intended to benefit others (Curry et al., 2018).

According to Malti (2021), kindness "reflects emotions, cognitions, and inner states that convey a particular gentleness and benevolence. These orientations can be directed towards others, such as expressing concern for a needy other, or directed towards the self, such as being gentle with oneself" (p. 1). Thus, Malti identifies three components of kindness: (1) cognitive, which includes perspective-taking and self-reflection; (2) emotional, which includes sympathy, empathy, compassion, and respect; and (3) behavioral, which includes even simple prosocial acts, such as sharing, cooperating, and helping. Further, she writes that kindness creates meaning and purpose and "reflects an appreciation of the dignity of every human being" (p. 3).

Research has found that performing acts of kindness, observing acts of kindness by others, and even thinking kindly about others has psychological benefits for the person doing these things (Figure 11.4). For example, in their meta-analysis, Curry et al. (2019) found small to medium effects of helping on the helper. Performing acts of kindness for 10 days increases one's life satisfaction (Buchanan & Bardi, 2009). Even happy people become happier when they do something as simple as count their own acts of kindness for 1 week (Otake, Shimai, Tanaka-Matsumi, Otsui, & Fredrickson, 2006).

FIGURE 11.4 Research has found that kindness benefits both the doer and the receiver.

Source: https://www.istockphoto.com/photo/elementary-school-kids-doing-homework-at-home-gm1176827124-328286578

Does kindness impact health? Apparently so! Brown, Nesse, Vinokur, and Smith (2003) followed people for five years; those who provided support for others (including helping with errands, driving, housework, childcare) had a lower mortality rate than those who didn't. Because of the association of positive emotions with such behaviors, they hypothesized that helping may promote health through its association with factors that reduce the deleterious effects of negative emotion.

Nelson-Coffey, Fritz, and Lyubomirsky (2017) wanted to determine if the relationship between kindness and health might be biologically based, as well as social-emotionally based. To do this, they randomly assigned individuals to perform acts of kindness for the world, themselves, or others in their daily routines for 5 weeks and then took blood samples. They found that performing kindness for others (*not* the world or self) was causally related to changes in gene expression possibly associated with health and well-being.

But one need not *do* an act of kindness to feel better, one needs only *recall* acts of kindness to have similar effects on well-being (Ko, Margolis, Revord, & Lyubomirsky, 2021). Similarly, practicing "loving-kindness meditation," as suggested by Buddhist practitioner and teacher Sharon Salzberg, for even a few minutes, results in increased feelings of social connection and positivity toward strangers (Hutcherson, Seppala, & Gross, 2008). In loving-kindness meditation, one focuses on compassionate thoughts and well-wishes toward others, real or imagined.

Rowland and Curry (2019) were aware of these positive findings related to acts of kindness and wondered if it made a difference whether the recipients of those acts were friends (i.e., people with strong ties to each other) or strangers (people with weak ties toward each other). They randomly assigned almost 700 people to one of four groups: strong ties, weak ties/strangers, self, and observers. The participants were instructed to carry out (or observe) at least one act of kindness every day for 7 days. What did they find? Carrying out or observing kindness activities every day for a week *equally* increased happiness, no matter who the recipient was! The more kind acts provided, the greater the change in happiness.

But what of kindness in families? Do findings with friends and strangers apply to non-voluntary relationships of the family? Intuitively, it would seem that kind acts within a family would influence the entire family system through strengthening connections, improving the emotional climate, increasing member happiness, and increasing reciprocal acts by others. Dew and Wilcox (2013) found that small acts of kindness, displays of respect and affection, and a willingness to forgive one's spouse for their failings were positively associated with marital satisfaction and negatively associated with conflict. Whether high-quality marriages are *caused* by such acts or *lead* to such acts is a question of debate and future research. Likely, the relationship is interactive.

On the other hand, author Tina Viju (2019) reflected, "Why am I kinder to strangers than to my own family?" Likely, many of us have asked this same question or perhaps wondered why our partners, parents, children seem nicer to others than to us. Unless acts of kindness are pointed out, we might not even notice them in our family. The freshly hung clothes, making a favorite meal for a partner after a hard day, filling up a gas tank without being asked; such acts may be invisible connectors of family members, although some may be silent expectations. I remember my husband emptying the dishwasher and proudly exclaiming, "I emptied the dishwasher!" "Oh," I replied. "Aren't you going to thank me?" he asked. "When was the last time you thanked me for emptying the dishwasher?" I responded. The look on his face was one of amused recognition. We both worked, but for some reason, the dishes were "mine." He saw his act as an act of kindness, but my same act was viewed as an expectation. Few studies have been conducted on kindness within families, but they will certainly yield interesting results, especially as we examine the relationships and roles of family. How might kindness manifest itself between parent and child, partners, extended family, and siblings?

Speaking of siblings, much of the research on kindness in sibling relationships focuses on families of children with chronic illnesses or disabilities, such as autism. This does not mean that research has ignored siblings outside this context. Instead, many studies have explored sibling relationships within the context of prosocial behaviors, including comforting, sharing, and helping (e.g., Hughes, McHarg, & White, 2018). Likely, kindness is tangled within this context.

The non-profit organization, Doing Good Together focuses on increasing service, volunteerism, and kindness in families. They write, "We need to make kindness an unavoidable part of family life. As indispensable as brushing teeth" (DGT [Doing Good Together], 2015). In other words, we need to *do* family kindness. Through regular practice of kindness, families are more likely to experience increased positivity, connectedness, and quality of relationships. Children are likely to learn kindness through observing the kind behaviors of their parent/s and caregiver/s. Having kindness as part of the family belief system likely will spill over to relationships outside the family, including engagement with the community. Cutting a neighbor's lawn, collecting food for local food banks, visiting the elderly can not only support the community but strengthen the family as they work together in positive ways.

PRINCIPLE 11.2

DOING AND OBSERVING ACTS OF KINDNESS INCREASES HAPPINESS

Families can benefit from acts of kindness within and outside of the family, with improved connectedness, positivity, and quality of relationships.

HOPE

> Just as despair can be given to me only by another human being, hope too can be given to me only by another human being.
>
> Elie Wiesel, 1986, Nobel Peace Prize Winner/Holocaust Survivor

If you were to draw a picture of "hope," what would you draw? A butterfly? A flower growing through a crack in the asphalt? Perhaps a rainbow against scattered storm clouds (Figure 11.5). What quotes come to mind? Hope springs eternal? Or maybe Emily Dickinson's poem, "Hope is the thing with feathers/that perches in the soul/and sings the tune without the words/and never stops at all."

Family life is filled with change and challenges occurring within, and sometimes because of, developmental changes of family members, the family lifecycle, and the sociocultural context. Many families faced with challenges exhibit remarkable resilience, bouncing back stronger than before from even the most difficult circumstances (Walsh, 2003). Internal family processes allow families to adapt and successfully weather crises and difficulties, from job loss, imprisonment, or

FIGURE 11.5 For some, hope might be symbolized by this flower growing in an unexpected place. How would you symbolize "hope?"

Source: https://www.istockphoto.com/photo/petunia-growing-through-crack-in-the-concrete-gm89151966-6046299

school failure to illness and death. As Walsh writes, "resilience involves key processes over time that foster the ability to 'struggle well', surmount obstacles, and go on to live and love fully" (p. 1). Resilience is not simply within the individual but within the family as a whole. Perhaps at the center of resilience is hope. "Hope is to the spirit what oxygen is to the lungs: It fuels energy and efforts to rise above adversity. Hope is a future-oriented belief; no matter how bleak the present, a better future can be envisioned … [it allows one] to see possibilities, tap into potential resources, and strive to surmount obstacles toward aspirations" (Walsh, 2003, p. 19).

When we say "hope," what do we mean? As a noun, hope is defined as a feeling, emotion, state of mind, or perception that a goal can be reached. As such, hope is an "it" that resides within a person (Weingarten, 2010). As a verb, however, hope is anticipating, wanting, desiring; one *practices* hope rather than *feels* hope. Flaskas (2007) describes hope as a lived experience that exceeds simple feelings or emotions and exists simultaneously with hopelessness. This means that hope and hopelessness are not opposites but exist in a dialectic relationship. Hope and hopelessness struggle in their apparent contradictions yet coexist. As a result, according to Flaskas, one can "feel hopeless yet still 'do' hope" (p. 190).

Weingarten (2010) added depth to our understanding of hope by recognizing its variability and identifying **reasonable hope**. Rather than seeing one as either having hope or not, reasonable hope is an active hope that is practiced, often involving others in the process. Reasonable hope allows one to seek to attain realistic goals that might ultimately lead to ultimate goals. It can adapt and change as needed and helps us avoid false hope. In other words, if one hopes to eat an entire five course meal, reasonable hope works with one course at a time, adjusting the tempo and actions as needed while engaging with others at the table.

Hope threads throughout the entire dynamic family system, from its parts to its whole to its surrounding environment. Hope or hopelessness exists within families' lived experiences; some families have "experienced extraordinary levels of social injustice, sometimes across generations and even centuries," while others have "experienced extraordinary levels of what seems to be 'just' bad luck or even a combination of the two" (Flaskas, 2007, p. 193). Unexpected events, such as the COVID-19 pandemic, also can have a profound effect on families and individuals, derailing the most well-functioning families (Walsh, 2003, 2020). From a systems perspective, think of the difficulties many families faced during the pandemic: social isolation, job loss, deaths of family members, educational upheaval, limited food supplies. All these experiences had the potential to influence family bonds and connectedness, as well as family functioning. Bethany Van Vleet (one of the authors of this textbook) balanced full-time work at home, with two newly adopted children and four other preschool and elementary-aged children needing to be confined to the home. "School" took place behind a computer screen or with "Mom" reading and teaching the children, while "Dad" moved back and forth from home office to work office. Watching an interview of parents and children protesting teachers not wanting to return to work, we could well identify with the 10-year-old child who begged to have school open because "I need a break from my Mom!" Although such experiences can dampen even the brightest hope, many families continue to thrive and embrace a hopeful future. How does hope in family work?

We learned in Chapter 6 that family belief systems and paradigms grow organically, laying the groundwork for hope through various processes, including structure, routine, and order (Maholmes, 2014). Right from birth, parents provide a setting where children have the potential to develop positive skills, attributes, and personal characteristics, such as self-esteem, self-efficacy, self-regulation, optimism, problem-solving, and persistence, that contribute to hope (Maholmes, 2014; Seligman, 2006). As families encounter and attempt to manage unexpected and expected challenges across time, and through their invisible patterns of interaction and communication, hope (or hopelessness) can be fostered becoming part of the family's overall outlook. According to Flaskas (2007),

> In the pattern that evolves, some family members may also be better at doing hope than feeling or thinking hope, while others may find it easier to sustain beliefs around hope and a feeling of hope, and yet not be good at 'doing' hope in a concrete and pragmatic way. Patterns around hope and hopelessness can come to be gendered within and across generations and there can be stuck and invisible patterns as well as more flexible and open movements between family members around hope and hopelessness.
>
> (p. 192)

It is important to develop and maintain family processes involving beliefs, rituals, routines, organization, communication, and problem-solving that can help the family learn to balance hope and hopelessness while successfully adapting to change and challenges (Walsh, 2020). The family's *sense* of hope uniquely interweaves with *doing* hope according to the experience, family roles, and even individually inherited personal characteristics.

Sometimes, families create **positive illusions** that are powerful in fostering hope and provide the fuel to move ahead toward a family goal (Makridakis & Moeskis, 2015; Taylor & Brown, 1994). At the same time, Makridakis and Moeskis remind us that such illusions can have negative consequences and put people at risk through unreachable goals, overconfidence, or an illusion of control when control is not possible. Again, then, the family must balance reality and illusion. For example, "Carlos" had just graduated with his master's degree, applied for a position with a government agency, and received a notice of hiring from that agency. The hiring letter said that he shouldn't quit his current position (he was a full-time student and not yet working full time) until all background investigations were complete; Carlos believed he had nothing of note to worry about. His family was ecstatic as they saw him moving into a secure well-paying position in an area of interest. The entire family hoped that the background investigation would go smoothly, and Carlos was even informed that the agency had spent extra money to complete it expeditiously. The background investigator said that she rarely found such a clean background. The hope of quickly starting this new position colored the family's perspective of whether Carlos should obtain a career-oriented position while awaiting the government position. They hoped that Carlos would soon be able to start the academy training and wanted to avoid putting an employer in a difficult position of losing an employee soon after hiring. As a result, Carlos entered a series of temporary positions. With each position, he became more demoralized as he waited to start a career. He and his family continued hoping, and Carlos sporadically heard back from the agency, with encouraging information, further supporting the positive illusion of starting the permanent position any day. Three and a half years later, Carlos was still waiting, and the series of temporary positions marred rather than strengthened his resume. Discussions and disappointments led to Carlos adapting to the idea of other career opportunities while still holding out hope that his dream job would work out.

Hope in families is essential in times of difficulty and despair and useful in times of stability. Hope can vary within the family like the wind. Sometimes, one family member might lose hope, while another family member embraces it. As Walsh (2020) writes, "Family members' mutual encouragement bolsters active efforts to take initiative and to persevere. Affirming individual and family strengths in the midst of difficulties can counter a sense of helplessness, failure, and despair as it reinforces shared pride, confidence, and a 'can do' spirit." Hope springs from, as well as fuels, self-confidence, mutual encouragement, and a shared sustained belief that we shall overcome and we are here for each other. We may not be able to control everything, but we can control some things. Whether rich or poor, suffering or comfortable, happy or sad, as Maholmes (2014) so succinctly writes, "It is never too late for hope."

PRINCIPLE 11.3

HOPE AND HOPELESSNESS COEXIST

Hope is at the center of family resilience. As families balance hope and hopelessness and engage in reasonable hope, they grow and support each other. This sustains them through life's difficulties, with adaptation and change.

GRATITUDE

The deepest principle in human nature is the craving to be appreciated.

William James (1896/1920)

As we express our gratitude, we must never forget that the highest appreciation is not to utter words but to live by them.

John F. Kennedy (1963)

A simple "thank you" can mean so much, whether from a stranger, acquaintance, co-worker, friend, or family member (Figure 11.6). Even an apparent tail wag or "kiss" from a dog can bring a smile. "Thank you!" It feels good to hear it, and it feels good to say it. Research on gratitude has exploded in the last 20 years, with gratitude capturing the imagination of the public through celebrities such as Oprah Winfrey, who has posted numerous articles, videos, and book recommendations on her website. Where does gratitude fit in the family and its daily interactions?

The honor of the first formal study of gratitude probably goes to Swiss psychologist Franziska Baumgarten-Tramer (1883–1970). Baumgarten-Tramer (1938) recognized the complexity, depth, and importance of gratitude, writing, "Thanks create a relationship between people and develop their feeling of community. In other words, gratitude acts as a social cohesive … It thus appears that the feeling of gratitude is a complex one and based mainly on social and ethical elements" (p. 56).

To study gratitude, Baumarten-Tramer enlisted 2,000 school children (aged 7 to 15) in Bern, Switzerland. From this data, she identified four types of gratefulness:

1   Verbal gratefulness (e.g., saying, "Thank you.")
2   Concrete gratefulness (e.g., a desire to give an object in return, such as "I should give him a kiss.")
3   Connected gratitude (e.g., creating a "spiritual" relationship, such as "I would help him in time of need.")
4   Finalistic gratefulness (e.g., repaying a favor by doing something related to that favor, such as "I will always be on time" upon being hired for a job).

FIGURE 11.6 A simple "thank you" can help bring family members together in complex ways.

Source: Panos Sakalakis from Pexels

Since that time, gratitude has been conceptualized as a positive emotion (Tsang, 2006), a virtue (Tudge, Freitas, O'Brien, & Mokrova, 2018), a psychological state/felt sense of wonder/ emotional response to life, and source of human strength (Emmons & Shelton, 2002), an action or practice, an attitude toward life (Emmons & Crumpler, 2000), a personality trait, and part of one's character (Tudge et al., 2018; Wood, Maltby, Stewart, Linley, & Joseph, 2008). In the words of Emmons and Crumpler (2000), gratitude is "an emotion, a virtue, a moral sentiment, a motive, a coping response, a skill, and an attitude. *It is all of these and more.* Minimally, gratitude is an emotional response to a gift. It is the appreciation felt after one has been the beneficiary of an altruistic act" (p. 56; italics added). The general public has even broader conceptions of gratitude than researchers (Lambert, Graham, & Fincham, 2009).

Empirical studies have documented some fascinating findings surrounding gratitude. At once personal and public, gratitude influences all aspects of our lives and benefits self, family, relationships, and community (Emmons & Shelton, 2002; Gordon, Musher-Eizenman, Holub, & Dalrymple, 2004). A consistent finding is that gratitude is strongly associated with an overall sense of well-being (Sansone & Sansone, 2010). In their literature review on gratitude and human development, Bono and Sender (2018) reported on the increasing evidence of gratitude's relationship to decreased antisocial behavior, protection from stress, physical and mental health, improved social function and interpersonal relationships, and increased resilience across the lifespan (p. 224). Gratitude appears to act as a buffer for teenagers and is associated with decreased drug/alcohol use and depression and improved academic achievement and life satisfaction. We are happier when we are grateful; even recognizing our gratitude lifts our mood and encourages us to reach beyond ourselves. When we reach beyond ourselves, we develop a greater sense of community, building social capital and strengthening those around us.

A surprising finding relates to gender differences and gratitude. Women tend to feel and express gratitude more than men (Allen, 2018a; Kashdan, Mishra, Breen, & Froh, 2009). Where differences exist, some men find gratitude challenging and burdensome, while women find it important for relationship building and maintenance. Importantly, however, these gender differences are small and vary by culture (Sommers & Kosmitski, 1988). It appears that our emotional life, including gratitude, is influenced by sociocultural themes related to connectedness and underlying beliefs leading to different gender expectations and behaviors.

The influence of culture on the expression of gratitude is undeniable. Floyd et al. (2018) provided a fascinating look at expressions of gratitude related to everyday household and community interactions in eight countries (the Chachi of Ecuador, England, Italy, Poland, Russia, Ghana, Laos, and a group of Australian Aborigines). Across these eight countries, explicit expressions of gratitude, such as saying "Thank you," were relatively rare; however, they found significantly higher expressions of gratitude in English and the lowest expressions of gratitude among the Chachi of Ecuador. For speakers in Laos or Ghana, "thank you" is so rare that it may be perceived as "bizarre" and certainly is not seen as rude when left unsaid. Yet, the relationships among these people continue, signaling that verbal expressions of gratitude are not necessary for maintaining social interactions in some cultures.

Gratitude appears to be intrinsic to human existence, despite differences in outward displays. It may be that gratitude has a biological basis, so behavioral geneticists and neuroscientists have examined potential biological roots of gratitude and other prosocial behaviors, even observing behaviors of other species (Allen, 2018b; Steger, Hicks, Kashdan, Krueger, & Bouchard, 2007). Steger and his fellow scholars found support for previous findings of genetic influences on spirituality, leadership, hope, creativity, altruism, kindness, and gratitude. How the interplay of genes and environment work together to influence such behaviors is a subject for future research.

Similarly, neuroscientists have focused on neurological activity and gratitude (Fox, Kaplan, Damasio, & Damasio, 2015; Kini, Wong, McInnis, Gabana, & Brown, 2016; Kong, Zhao, You, & Xiang, 2020). Using brain imaging techniques (usually fMRI), gratitude has been found to be associated with regions of the brain related to socializing and pleasure (medial prefrontal cortex), as well as deep parts of the brain associated with emotions, stress relief, and pain reduction (Henning, Fox, Kaplan, Damasio, & Damasio, 2017). Other areas of the brain associated with gratitude include the parietal and lateral prefrontal cortex and the pregenual anterior cingulate cortex (Kini et al., 2016; Yu, Gao, Zhou, & Zhou, 2018).

Our discussion so far has examined gratitude in general and at the personal level, but what of gratitude in family and its relationship with family processes. Science has found a strong link between religiosity/spirituality and gratitude (Allen, 2018b). Let's consider a Muslim family and the role of gratitude in their lives and interactions. According to Ali, Ahmed, Bhatti, and Farooq (2020), gratitude is considered one of the highest virtues and is mentioned throughout the religious writings of Islam. In fact, the first two verses of the Quran, the most sacred Islamic book, provide praise to God, using the term "Alhamdulilah," expressing gratitude in everyday life (Pervez, 2018). Two of the pillars (core beliefs and practices) of Islam involve gratitude. One is praying five times per day, not asking for anything but praising God; the second is fasting, which is designed to lead toward gratitude during the holy season of Ramadhan. In Islam, there are three levels of thankfulness: (1) Realize and appreciate blessings within the heart; (2) give thanks with the tongue; and (3) express gratitude by the body (i.e., do good deeds). It is believed that gratitude will lead to more abundance. Against this backdrop, it is clear how family interactions, communications, and behaviors (including rituals) will be influenced by this belief system.

Gratitude at an emotional, cognitive, or behavioral level runs through all family systems, as families navigate caregiving duties, obligations, division of labor, distribution of resources, communication, beliefs about self and shared beliefs of family, and rules related to gratitude. Whether seen as an emotion or behavior, gratitude is fostered within the family setting through direct and indirect teaching and modeling (Hussong et al., 2019). In turn, our families are influenced by their social context, culture, and even personal family paradigms. Thus, whether and how families feel and express gratitude can vary.

It is easy to see how families explicitly teach children gratitude and gratitude rules (Naito & Washizu, 2019). We often hear, "What do you say?" when a child is given something (from a gift to a glass of water). Halloween may seem like a time for dress up and candy, but it is also a time for teaching children social niceties ("Don't forget to say, 'thank you' when you are given candy!"). Parents and caregivers may require their children to write thank you notes (or draw a "thank you" picture) in reciprocity for a gift. Some parents may emotionally coach their children ("How did you feel when your friend helped you?"). Through these very direct means, parents are providing children with insight into relationship building and maintenance, roles, meaning, and beliefs regarding who they are and where they fit. This is further reinforced indirectly through unspoken modeling of behavior. Rothenberg et al. (2017) found that parents high in gratitude are more likely to provide experiences and activities for children that can help children develop gratitude, which resulted in increased expressions of gratitude in children.

Feelings and expressions of gratitude are positively related to couple satisfaction (Barton, Futris, & Nielsen, 2015; Gordon, Arnette, & Smith, 2011; Park, Impett, MacDonald, & Lemay,

2019). Interestingly, however, expressed gratitude may not always result in marital satisfaction. It is important that one perceives an expression of gratitude as sincere; if not, marital satisfaction declines (Leong et al., 2020). Webb (2020) writes, "Gratitude is a mechanism that can remind couples of their love for one another and bind them closer together, functioning as a communal process that can result in positive outcomes for the well-being of the marital relationship" (p. 1).

We believe that a picture is often worth a thousand words, and this may be the case here as family members interact with each other, explicitly and implicitly expressing gratitude. The dynamic nature of relationships within the family (and outside the family) may reinforce expressions of gratitude and felt gratitude, as family members experience reciprocity and are further motivated to engage in other prosocial behaviors. Gratitude supports bonds within relationships, helping to create and maintain positive communication and responsiveness to others' needs (Webb, 2020). Thus, sincere gratitude is not only a source of human strength but a source of family strength. Emmons and Shelton (2002) write, "Gratitude provides life meaning, by encapsulating life itself as a gift. Within such a framework, it can come to dominate one's entire life outlook, seemingly even when sources of gratitude are absent … A grateful focus can also enable an individual to confront and overcome obstacles by means of thanksgiving for the newly acknowledged strengths that result from such challenging confrontations" (pp. 468–469).

Given that gratitude has a documented beneficial effect on individuals and family, it would be helpful to find ways to foster and even increase our feelings and expressions of gratitude (Figure 11.7). Indeed, a quick search of the Internet reveals 93 million web pages addressing this subject, with the first few websites alone offering 7, 8, 10, 15, and 40 ways for improving gratitude! The subject has captured the public's imagination and fits in nicely with the mindfulness movement. Nevertheless, popular ideas (however well-intended) are not always informed or supported by evidence. Is there evidence supporting the use of gratitude interventions?

FIGURE 11.7 Gratitude can be expressed in numerous ways and benefits individuals and family.

Source: Panos Sakalakis from Pexels

Hussong, Coffman, and Thomas (2020) developed an online 45-minute "Gratitude Conversations" program for parents. The program informs parents of the importance of gratitude, provides strategies in communicating about gratitude, allows for reflections on conversations, and has parents select specific goals for change. The program was fairly effective in helping parents talk about gratitude and increasing children's gratitude. Most gratitude interventions, though, are not as formal or in-depth (see Baumsteiger, Mangan, Bronk, & Bono, 2019; O'Connell, O'Shea, & Gallagher, 2018; Franks, 2020). For example, consider these common suggestions for increasing happiness through fostering gratitude:

1 Keep a "gratitude journal." Write three to five things that you are grateful for.
2 Make a "gratitude jar." Keep slips of paper next to it, and on each slip of paper, write something you are grateful for. Try to write three to five slips a day.
3 Reflect and meditate on gratitude for 5 minutes.
4 Write a letter to someone you are grateful for.
5 Give someone a small gift or do them a favor.
6 If in a couple relationship, express sincere appreciation for your partner.

Research on the effectiveness and durability of these interventions is limited. In a randomized study, O'Connell et al. (2018) found that keeping a "traditional" gratitude journal, where one writes lists of everyday things they are grateful for, resulted in short- and long-term improvements in friendship and life satisfaction, with the potential of sustained improvements in subjective well-being. Improvements were not seen in the groups that participated in general journal writing or even writing about gratitude for interpersonal relationships and other people.

Dickens (2017) undertook a series of meta-analyses investigating the effectiveness of gratitude interventions. Gratitude interventions could have "positive benefits for people in terms of their well-being, happiness, life satisfaction, grateful mood, grateful disposition, and positive affect and they can result in decreases in depressive symptoms" (p. 204). Other researchers have found self-help gratitude interventions had only modest effects on anxiety and depression (Chegg & Cheavens, 2021). As Dickens suggests, one should not expect life-changing outcomes from devoting 5 minutes a day to grateful meditation; however, while most gratitude interventions may have only small to modest effects, there are a few downsides to practicing them in terms of financial cost, time investment, or difficulty. In fact, they may lead to more generalized outcomes as such activities transform one's inner self and become part of one's daily interactions. Further, individuals and families facing challenges that can be addressed through gratitude intervention may find additional support through family life educators or counseling. Again, we find fertile ground for research that could provide positive changes to self, family, and community.

PRINCIPLE 11.4

GRATITUDE IS INTRINSIC TO HUMAN EXISTENCE

With possible roots in genetics and biology, gratitude is a source of human and family strength and a facilitator of relationships with self and others. Gratitude is influenced by culture and can be socialized and learned.

Putting It Altogether

For decades, family scientists at the University of Nebraska have studied families from all over the world to seek an answer to the question, "What makes strong families?" (DeFrain, Swanson, Friesen, & Brand, 2008). The answers, it seems, are remarkably similar from the high rises of New York City to the pop-up settlements in Mogadishu, Somalia, on the Horn of Africa. Those answers reflect much of what is written in this chapter and have been summarized as six strengths:

1 Appreciation and affection. Our focus on gratitude and kindness support these strengths, as families show care and respect for each other.
2 Commitment. A hallmark of strong families is commitment the family members have to each other and to their underlying paradigm. The sense of trust, honesty, and faithfulness gird up their commitment to each other and to the family. Surely forgiveness, kindness, gratitude, and hope are part of this.
3 Positive communication. Forgiveness and gratitude make up part of positive communication and help strengthen families.
4 Enjoyable time together. This strength is marked by spending quality time together in shared activities.
5 Spiritual well-being. Part of spiritual well-being is hope, compassion, and a perspective of being one with humanity. So, in addition to hope, this strength ties into forgiveness, kindness, and gratitude.
6 Successful management of stress and crises. Resilience is at the core of this strength, and we have seen that forgiveness, hope, and gratitude have all been identified with family resilience.

Effective family processes protect families from crises and help individuals and families flourish (Day, Gavazzi, Miller, & Van Langeveld, 2009). Positive family processes work at insuring members' self-worth and dignity, fostering cooperation, positive communication, cohesion, support, and prosocial behavior (Yeung, Chen, Lo, & Choi, 2017). Further, these positive family processes underlie and make up forgiveness, kindness, hope, and gratitude, and tend to lead to positive outcomes. As families internalize these values and strengthen their connections, they develop empathy that serves as a driver for kindness, compassion, and forgiveness (Decety, Bartal, Uzefovsky, & Knafo-Noam, 2016). Focusing on positive family processes offers much hope for strengthening the family.

Discussions in Diversity: Self-Forgiveness

Each reader of this textbook likely has done something they regretted and may still be carrying the hurt of that choice. It has been said that the hardest person to forgive is yourself, as we cope with "one of the most fundamental aspects of being human" (Woodyatt, Worthington, Wenzel, & Griffin, 2017, p. xiii). Long after one has committed an offense and even been "punished" for it, one may feel self-incrimination, shame, guilt, remorse, and regret, perhaps affecting our feelings of self-worth (Figure 11.8).

Self-forgiveness was once referred to as the "stepchild" of forgiveness research because it was largely ignored in the burgeoning forgiveness literature

FIGURE 11.8 Sometimes it seems that forgiving one's self is more difficult than forgiving others.

Source: https://www.istockphoto.com/photo/tears-gm92268523-1146227

(Hall & Fincham, 2005). Today, the field is thriving as scholars responded to the call to attend to self-forgiveness, exploring how it relates to situations such as substance abuse, smoking, gambling, parenting, and eating disorders (Griffin, Worthington, Davis, Hook, & Maguen, 2018; Woodyatt et al., 2017).

Everett Worthington and colleagues (2013) developed the REACH Forgiveness project and created a free workbook to promote self-forgiveness—Moving Forward: Six Steps to Forgiving Yourself and Breaking Free from the Past. Their work is based on the Dual Process Model of Self-Forgiveness, which has its roots in Social Cognitive Theory of moral development (Griffin et al., 2018). Self-forgiveness is conceptualized as a moral repair strategy that involves two processes: (1) accepting responsibility for one's behavior and aligning it with one's values in the future and (2) replacing negative emotions of guilt, self-recrimination, and condemnation with positive emotions to restore esteem. Worthington outlines six steps to self-forgiveness:

Step 1—Divine forgiveness. Seek and receive forgiveness available in God, nature, or humanity in general.

Step 2—Repair relationships. In the process of self-forgiveness, recognize the critical importance of people outside ourselves and make amends with those we have wronged.

Step 3—Rethink rumination. For self-forgiveness, we need to rethink our tendency to dwell on negative thoughts, focusing on the worst parts of our lives. Rethinking this will allow us to begin the process of psychological self-healing.

Step 4—Explicit decision plus REACH emotional self-forgiveness. Understand that self-forgiveness doesn't occur overnight. This step involves making a sincere decision to forgive self and then use the REACH forgiveness method.

Step 5—Rebuild self-acceptance. Acknowledge that we are human and make mistakes, but we are still valuable and have the ability to do and be better.

Step 6—Resolve to live virtuously.

The workbook takes approximately 6 hours to complete, and follow-up research suggests that this self-directed program assists one in forgiving one's self (Griffin et al., 2015).

Questions to Discuss:

- *Why do you think self-forgiveness is so difficult?*
- *How might self-forgiveness be interpreted by others as a "free pass" for the perpetrator?*
- *What are the advantages of a workbook for self-forgiveness? What are the advantages of counseling for self-forgiveness?*

SUMMARY

In this chapter, we explored forgiveness, kindness, hope, and gratitude. All of these strengths are related to "emotional intelligence," also referred to as EQ. High EQs appear to be more important to life success than IQ (Ackley, 2016). It is in our families that we begin to develop our attitudes, beliefs, values, and relational skills that influence EQ and carry us through life.

Forgiveness is more than a virtue. As a multidimensional construct, it involves strategies and behaviors that help families achieve their goals. Although we may sometimes be resistant to forgiving others, research suggests that doing so brings great benefits to the individual and family.

Kindness takes many shapes and forms, which we would expect when we recognize its cognitive, emotional, and behavioral components. Performing acts of kindness and even observing acts of kindness benefit us psychologically and physically. Small acts of kindness within our family can strengthen connections, increase positive feelings, and improve the quality of family relationships.

Hope is a seed that has the potential to grow strong and healthy families even in the face of diversity. To avoid becoming overconfident or losing hope when confronted with difficulties, it is recommended we apply the idea of reasonable hope. Reasonable hope allows us to achieve reasonable goals that can ultimately help us achieve our final goals. Family processes involving our family beliefs, rituals, routines, communication, and problem-solving help families balance hope and hopelessness as we face challenges that are bound to confront in our daily lives. Hope benefits all families and its members.

Gratitude has been studied for almost 100 years. From its four types (verbal, concrete, connected, and finalistic) to its layered characteristics as virtue/emotion/attitude/trait/skill, we have learned that gratitude crosses the globe and benefits us as individuals, family, and community. It is intrinsic to human existence and may have a biological base. The family teaches and reinforces the expression of gratitude and felt gratitude, according to the sociocultural context of the family, benefiting the individual and the family. Gratitude interventions have been found to have generally positive effects on individuals and families.

Taken together, these positive family processes overlap, interface, and interact, strengthening families and providing a healthier context for individual development. Like most family processes, families may be unaware of all aspects surrounding these processes and the powerful influence they have the family.

STUDY QUESTIONS

1 What is the difference between forgiving and condoning?
2 What is the difference between interpersonal and intrapersonal forgiveness? Give a specific example.
3 Give examples of direct, indirect, and conditional forgiveness.
4 List and compare benefits of forgiveness, kindness, hope, and gratitude.
5 Why might some people choose not to forgive?
6 What are the three components of kindness identified by Malti?
7 Discuss the biological bases of kindness and gratitude.
8 What are some physical outcomes related to forgiveness, kindness, and gratitude?
9 Do you think you are kinder to strangers than to your family? Why?
10 How is reasonable hope different from "hope?"
11 What are the benefits and drawbacks of positive illusions?
12 Discuss the effectiveness of gratitude interventions.
13 What are four types of gratefulness, identified by Baumarten–Tramer?
14 How can parents help children to express and feel more gratitude?

KEY TERMS

Prosocial behavior
Interpersonal forgiveness
Intrapersonal forgiveness
Direct forgiveness
Indirect forgiveness
Conditional forgiveness
Decisional forgiveness
Emotional forgiveness
Reasonable hope
Positive Illusions

SUGGESTED READINGS

Hargrave, T. D., & Zasowski, N. E. (2017). *Families and forgiveness: Healing wounds in the intergenerational family* (2nd ed.). New York, NY: Routledge.

Kelley, D. L., Waldron, V. R., & Kloeber, D. N. (2019). *A communicative approach to conflict, forgiveness, and reconciliation: Reimagining our relationships.* New York, NY: Routledge.

The International Forgiveness Institute. https://internationalforgiveness.com/

Worthington, E. Commonwealth Professor Emeritus. Forgiveness Researcher; No Cost Resources. http://www.evworthington-forgiveness.com/

Worthingon, E. L. Jr., & Wade, N. G. (Eds.). (2019). *Handbook of forgiveness* (2nd ed.). New York, NY: Routledge.

REFERENCES

Ackley, D. (2016). Emotional intelligence: A practical review of models, measures, and applications. *Consulting Psychology Journal: Practice and Research, 68*(4), 269–286.

Ali, S. A., Ahmed, M., Bhatti, O. K., & Farooq, W. (2020). Gratitude and its conceptualization: An Islamic perspective. *Journal of Religion and Health, 59*, 1740–1753.

Allen, S. (2018a). Do men have a gratitude problem? *Greater Good Magazine.* https://greatergood.berkeley.edu/article/item/do_men_have_a_gratitude_problem

Allen, S. (2018b). The science of gratitude. White paper for the John Templeton Foundation, Greater Good Science Center. https://ggsc.berkeley.edu/images/uploads/GGSC-JTF_White_Paper-Gratitude-FINAL.pdf

Barton, A. W., Futris, T. G., & Nielsen, R. B. (2015). Linking financial distress to marital quality: The intermediary roles of demand/withdraw and spousal gratitude expressions. *Personal Relationship, 22*, 536–549.

Baumeister, R. F., Exline, J. J., & Sommer, K. L. (1998). The victim role, grudge theory, and two dimensions of forgiveness. In E. L. Worthington (Ed.), *Dimensions of forgiveness: A research approach* (pp. 79–106). Radnor, PA: Templeton Foundation Press.

Baumgarten-Tramer, F. (1938). "Gratefulness" in children and young people. *Journal of Genetic Psychology, 53*, 53–66.

Baumsteiger, R., Mangan, S., Bronk, K. C., & Bono, G. (2019). An integrative intervention for cultivating gratitude among adolescents and young adults. *The Journal of Positive Psychology, 14*(6), 807–819.

Boese, P. (1967). Forgiveness. *Quote, 53*(8), 146.

Bono, G., & Sender, J. T. (2018). How gratitude connects humans to the best in themselves and in others. *Research in Human Development, 15*(3–4), 224–237.

Brown, S. L., Nesse, R. M., Vinokur, A. D., & Smith, D. M. (2003). Providing social support may be more beneficial than receiving it: Results from a prospective study of mortality. *Psychological Science, 14*(4), 320–327.

Buchanan, K. E., & Bardi, A. (2009). Acts of kindness and acts of novelty affect life satisfaction. *The Journal of Social Psychology, 150*(3), 235–237.

Carr, K., & Wang, T. R. (2012). "Forgiveness isn't a simple process: It's a vast undertaking": Negotiation and communicating forgiveness in nonvoluntary family relationships. *Journal of Family Communication, 12*(1), 40–56.

Cha, S. Y., Hyun, M. H., Ra, Y. S., & Yoon, S. Y. (2010). The effects of intrapersonal-interpersonal forgiveness on negative affect, perceived control, and intention to terminate the relationship in victims of dating violence. *Asian Women, 26*(4), 61–83.

Cheadle, A. C. D., & Toussaint, L. L. (2015). Forgiveness and physical health in healthy populations. In Toussaint L., Worthington E., Williams D. (Eds.), *Forgiveness and health* (pp. 91–106). Dordrecht: Springer. DOI: 10.1007/978-94-017-9993-5_7

Chegg, D. R., & Cheavens, J. S. (2021). Gratitude interventions: Effective self-help? A meta-analysis of the impact on symptoms of depression and anxiety. *Journal of Happiness Studies, 22*(1), 413–445.

Chen, Y., Harris, S. K., Worthington, E. L. Jr, & VanderWeele, T. J. (2019). Religiously or spiritually motivated forgiveness and subsequent health and well-being among young adults: An outcome-wide analysis. *The Journal of Positive Psychology, 14*(5), 649–658.

Curry, O. S., Rowland, L. A., Van Lissa, C. J., Zlotowitz, S., McAlaney, J., & Whitehouse, H. (2018). Happy to help? A systematic review and meta-analysis of the effects of performing acts of kindness on the well-being of the actor. *Journal of Experimental Social Psychology, 76*, 320–329.

Day, R. D., Gavazzi, S. M., Miller, R., & Van Langeveld, A. (2009). Compelling family processes. *Marriage & Family Review, 45*, 116–128.

Decety, J., Bartal, I. B., Uzefovsky, F., & Knafo-Noam, A. (2016). Empathy as a driver of prosocial behaviour: Highly conserved neurobehavioural mechanisms across species. *Philosophical Transactions of the Royal Society B: Biological Sciences, 371*, 1686.

DeFrain, J., Swanson, D., Friesen, J., & Brand, G. (2008). Creating a strong family: What is a strong family? NebGuide, #1885. University of Nebraska—Lincoln Extension, Institute of Agriculture and Natural Resources. https://extensionpublications.unl.edu/assets/pdf/g1885.pdf

Dew, J., & Wilcox, W. B. (2013). Generosity and the maintenance of marital quality. *Journal of Marriage and Family, 75*, 1218–1228.

DGT (Doing Good Together) (2015). The true power of family kindness: Kindness practice, why we matter. https://www.doinggoodtogether.org/bhf/blog/power-of-a-kindness-practice

Dickens, L. R. (2017). Using gratitude to promote positive change: A series of meta-analyses investigating the effectiveness of gratitude interventions. *Basic and Applied Social Psychology, 39*(4), 193–208.

Emmons, R. A., & Crumpler, C. A. (2000). Gratitude as a human strength: Appraising the evidence. *Journal of Social and Clinical Psychology, 19*(1), 56–69.

Emmons, R. A., & Shelton, C. M. (2002). Gratitude and the science of positive psychology. *Handbook of Positive Psychology, 18*, 459–471.

Enright, R. (2001). *Forgiveness is a choice.* Washington, DC: APA Books.

Exline, J. J., Baumeister, R. F., Bushman, B. J., Campbell, W. K., & Finkel, E. J. (2004). Too proud to let go: Narcissistic entitlement as a barrier to forgiveness. *Journal of Personality and Social Psychology, 87*(6), 894–912.

Fincham, F. D. (2015). Forgiveness, family relationships and health. In L. L. Toussaint, E. L. Worthington, Jr., & D. R. Williams (Eds.), *Forgiveness and health* (pp. 255–270). Dordrecht: Springer. DOI: 10.1007/978-94-017-9993-5_17

Fincham, F. D. (2017). Translational family science and forgiveness: A healthy symbiotic relationship? *Family Relations, 66*, 584–600.

Flaskas, C. (2007). Holding hope and hopelessness: Therapeutic engagements with the balance of hope. *Journal of Family Therapy, 29*(3), 186–202.

Floyd, S., Rossi, G., Baranova, J., Blythe, J., Dingemanse, M., Kendrick, K. H. … Enfield, N. J.(2018). Universals and cultural diversity in the expression of gratitude. *Royal Society Open Science 5*(5). DOI: 10.1098/rsos.180391

Fox, G. R., Kaplan, J., Damasio, H., & Damasio, A. (2015). Neural correlates of gratitude. *Frontiers in psychology, 6*, 1491.

Franks, H. M. (2020). Activities to practice and cultivate gratitude in the physical education setting. *Journal of Physical Education, Recreation & Dance, 92*(1), 36–41.

Gilbert, P., Basran, J., MacArthur, M., & Kirby, J. N. (2019). Differences in the semantics of prosocial words: An exploration of compassion And kindness. *Mindfulness, 10*, 2259–2271.

Gordon, C. L., Arnette, R. A., & Smith, R. E. (2011). Have you thanked your spouse today? Felt and expressed gratitude among married couples. *Personality and Individual Differences, 50*(3), 339–343.

Gordon, A. K., Musher-Eizenman, D. R., Holub, S. C., & Dalrymple, J. (2004). What are children thankful for? An archival analysis of gratitude before and after the attack of September 11. *Journal of Applied Developmental Psychology, 25*(5), 541–553.

Griffin, B. J., Worthington, E. L. Jr., Davis, D. E., Hook, J. N., & Maguen, S. (2018). Development of the self-forgiveness dual-process scale. *Journal of Counseling Psychology, 65*(6), 715–726.

Griffin, B. J., Worthington, E. L. Jr, Lavelock, C. R., Greer, C. L., Lin, Y., Davis, D. E., & Hook, J. N. (2015). Efficacy of a self-forgiveness workbook: A randomized controlled trial with interpersonal offenders. *Journal of Counseling Psychology, 62*(2), 124.

Hall, J. H., & Fincham, F. D. (2005). Self-forgiveness: The stepchild of forgiveness research. *Journal of Social and Clinical Psychology, 24*(5), 621–637.

Hanscom, D. (2020). Forgiveness is a learned skill. *Psychology Today* (blog post). https://www.psychologytoday.com/us/blog/anxiety-another-name-pain/202002/forgiveness-is-learned-skill#:~:text=Forgiveness%20is%20both%20a%20learned,take%20that%20away%20from%20you.&text=Circumstance%20or%20person%20who%20has,Blame

Hargrave, T. D., & Zasowski, N. E. (2017). *Families and forgiveness: Healing wounds in the intergenerational family* (2nd ed.). New York, NY: Routledge.

Harper, Q., Worthington, E. L. Jr, Griffin, B. J., Lavelock, C. R., Hook, J. N., Vrana, S. R., & Greer, C. L. (2014). Efficacy of a workbook to promote forgiveness: A randomized controlled trial with university students. *Journal of Clinical Psychology, 70*(12), 1158–1169.

Henning, M., Fox, G. R., Kaplan, J., Damasio, H., & Damasio, A. (2017). A potential role for mu-opioids in mediating the positive effects of gratitude. *Frontiers in psychology, 8*, 868.

Hughes, C., McHarg, G., & White, N. (2018). Sibling influence on prosocial behavior. *Current Opinion in Psychology, 20*, 96–101.

Hussong, A. M., Coffman, J. L., & Thomas, T. E. (2020). Gratitude conversations: An experimental trial of an online parenting tool. *The Journal of Positive Psychology, 15*(2), 267–277.

Hussong, A. M., Langley, H. A., Rothenberg, W. A., Coffman, J. L., Halberstadt, A. G., Costanzo, P. R., & Mokrova, I. (2019). Raising grateful children one day at a time. *Applied Developmental Science, 23*(4), 371–384.

Hutcherson, C. A., Seppala, E. M., & Gross, J. J. (2008). Loving-kindness meditation increases social connectedness. *Emotion, 8*(5), 720–724.

James, W. (1896/1920). Letter to his class at Radcliffe college, 6 April 1896. *Letters, 2*, 33.

Karremans, J. C., Van Lange, P. A. M., & Holland, R. W. (2005). Forgiveness and its associations with prosocial thinking, feeling, and doing beyond the relationship with the offender. *Personality and Social Psychology Bulletin, 31*(10), 1315–1326.

Kashdan, T. B., Mishra, A., Breen, W. E., & Froh, J. J. (2009). Gender differences in gratitude: Examining appraisals, narratives, the willingness to express emotions, and changes in psychological needs. *Journal of Personality, 77*(3), 691–730.

Kelley, D. (1998). The communication of forgiveness. *Communication Studies, 49*, 255–271.

Kelley, D. L. (2017). *Just relationships*. New York, NY: Routledge.

Kelley, D. L., Waldron, V. R., & Kloeber, D. N. (2019). *A communicative approach to conflict, forgiveness, and reconciliation: Reimagining our relationships*. New York, NY: Routledge.

Kennedy, J. F. (1963). U.S. Proclamation 3560—Thanksgiving Day.

Kimball, S. W. (1969). *The miracle of forgiveness*. Salt Lake City, UT: Bookcraft Publishers.

Kini, P., Wong, J., McInnis, S., Gabana, N., & Brown, J. W. (2016). The effects of gratitude expression on neural activity. *Neuroimage, 128*, 1–10.

Ko, K., Margolis, S., Revord, J., & Lyubomirsky, S. (2021). Comparing the effects of performing and recalling acts of kindness. *The Journal of Positive Psychology, 16*(1), 73–81. DOI: 10.1080/17439760.2019.1663252

Kong, F., Zhao, J., You, X., & Xiang, Y. (2020). Gratitude and the brain: Trait gratitude mediates the association between structural variations in the medial prefrontal cortex and life satisfaction. *Emotion, 20*(6), 917.

Lambert, N. M., Graham, S. M., & Fincham, F. D. (2009). A prototype analysis of gratitude: Varieties of gratitude experiences. *Personality and Social Psychology Bulletin, 35*(9), 1193–1207.

Leong, J. L., Chen, S. X., Fung, H. H., Bond, M. H., Siu, N. Y., & Zhu, J. Y. (2020). Is gratitude always beneficial to interpersonal relationships? The interplay of grateful disposition, grateful mood, and grateful expression among married couples. *Personality and Social Psychology Bulletin, 46*(1), 64–78.

Lichtenfeld, S., Buechner, V. L., Maier, M. A., & Fernandez-Capo, M. (2015). Forgive and forget: Differences between decisional and emotional forgiveness. *PLoS One, 10*(5), e0125561. https://www.ncbi.nlm.nih.gov/pmc/articles/PMC4422736/#:~:text=However%2C%20one%20may%20grant%20decisional,a%20grudge%20against%20the%20transgressor.&text=Emotional%20forgiveness%20is%20the%20replacement,distinction%2C%20see%20%5B14%5D)

Maholmes, V. (2014). *Fostering resilience and well-being in children and families in poverty: Why hope still matters*. New York, NY: Oxford University Press.

Maio, G. R., Thomas, G., Fincham, F. D., & Carnelley, K. B. (2008). Unraveling the role of forgiveness in family relationships. *Journal of Personality and Social Psychology, 94*(2), 307–319.

Makridakis, S., & Moeskis, A. (2015). The costs and benefits of positive illusions. *Frontiers of Psychology, 6*, 859.

Malti, T. (2021). Kindness: A perspective from developmental psychology. *European Journal of Developmental Psychology, 18*(5), 629–657. DOI:10.1080/17405629.2020.1837617

McNeill, B. (2017). After four decades, Everett Worthington, leading expert on forgiveness, set to retire from VCU's Department of Psychology. *VCU News*. https://news.vcu.edu/article/After_four_decades_Everett_Worthington_leading_expert_on_forgiveness

Merolla, A. J. (2008). Communicating forgiveness in friendships and dating relationships. *Communication Studies*, *59*(2), 114–131.

Naito, T., & Washizu, N. (2019). Gratitude in life-span development: An overview of comparative studies between different age groups. *The Journal of Behavioral Science*, *14*(2), 80–93.

Nelson-Coffey, S. K., Fritz, M. M., & Lyubomirsky, S. (2017). Kindness in the blood: A randomized controlled trial of the gene regulatory impact of prosocial behavior. *Psychoneuroendocrinology*, *81*, 8–13.

O'Connell, B. H., O'Shea, D., & Gallagher, S. (2018). Examining psychosocial pathways underlying gratitude interventions: A randomized controlled trial. *Journal of Happiness Studies*, *19*(8), 2421–2444.

Otake, K., Shimai, S., Tanaka-Matsumi, J., Otsui, K., & Fredrickson, B. (2006). Happy people become happier through kindness: A counting kindnesses intervention. *Journal of Happiness Studies*, *7*(3), 361–375.

Park, Y., Impett, E. A., MacDonald, G., & Lemay, E. P. Jr (2019). Saying "thank you": Partners' expressions of gratitude protect relationship satisfaction and commitment from the harmful effects of attachment insecurity. *Journal of personality and social psychology*, *117*(4), 773.

Pervez, A. (2018). The concept of thankfulness in Islam. Why Islam: Facts about Islam. https://www.whyislam.org/on-faith/the-concept-of-gratitude-in-islam/

Raj, M., & Wiltermuth, S. S. (2016). Barriers to forgiveness. *Social and Personality Psychology Compass*, *10*(11), 679–690.

Richardson, D. S. (2014). Everyday aggression takes many forms. *Current Directions in Psychological Science*, *23*(3), 220–224.

Rothenberg, W. A., Hussong, A. M., Langley, H. A., Egerton, G. A., Halberstadt, A. G., Coffman, J. L. … Costanzo, P. R. (2017). Grateful parents raising grateful children: Niche selection and the socialization of child gratitude. *Applied developmental science*, *21*(2), 106–120.

Rowland, L., & Curry, O. S. (2019). A range of kindness activities boost happiness. *The Journal of Social Psychology*, *159*(3), 340–343. DOI: 10.1080/00224545.2018.1469461

Russell, V. M., Baker, L. R., McNulty, J. K., & Overall, N. C. (2018). "You're forgiven, but don't do it again!" Direct partner regulation buffers the costs of forgiveness. *Journal of Family Psychology*, *32*(4), 435–444.

Sansone, R. A., & Sansone, L. A. (2010). Gratitude and well-being: The benefits of appreciation. *Psychiatry (Edgmont)*, *7*(11), 18.

Seligman, M. E. P. (2006). *Learned optimism: How to change your mind and your life*. New York, NY: First Vintage Books.

Shah, S., & Sharma, A. (2018). Parents' forgiveness and coping styles as predictors of children's self-esteem. *Journal of Indian Association for Child & Adolescent Mental Health*, *14*(4), 109–124.

Sommers, S., & Kosmitski, C. (1988). Emotion and social context: An American-German comparison. *British Journal of Social Psychology*, *27*(1), 35–49.

Steger, M. F., Hicks, B. M., Kashdan, T. B., Krueger, R. F., & Bouchard, T. J. Jr (2007). Genetic and environmental influences on the positive traits of the values in action classification, and biometric covariance with normal personality. *Journal of Research in Personality*, *41*(3), 524–539.

Taylor, S. E., & Brown, J. D. (1994). Positive illusions and well-being revisited: Separating fact from fiction. *Psychological Bulletin*, *116*, 21–27.

Toussaint, L., Worthington, E. L. Jr, Cheadle, A., Marigoudar, S., Kamble, S., & Bussing, A. (2020). Efficacy of the REACH forgiveness intervention in Indian college students. *Frontiers in Psychology*, *11*, 671. https://www.frontiersin.org/articles/10.3389/fpsyg.2020.00671/full

Toussaint, L., Worthington, E. L. Jr, & Williams, D. (Eds.). (2015). *Forgiveness and health: Scientific evidence and theories relating forgiveness to better health*. New York, NY: Springer.

Tsang, J. A. (2006). BRIEF REPORT gratitude and prosocial behaviour: An experimental test of gratitude. *Cognition & Emotion*, *20*(1), 138–148.

Tudge, J. R., Freitas, L. B., O'Brien, L., & Mokrova, I. L. (2018). Methods for studying the virtue of gratitude cross-culturally. *Cross-Cultural Research*, *52*(1), 19–30.

Tuppance, J. (2009). A divine test. *Richmondmag*. https://richmondmagazine.com/news/a-divine-test-01-13-2009/

Viju, T. (2019). Why am I kinder to strangers than to my own family? *The Startup|Medium*. https://medium.com/swlh/why-am-i-kinder-to-strangers-than-to-my-own-family-ce678e4f7563

Wade, N. G., Cornish, M. A., Tucker, J. R., Worthington, E. L. Jr, Sandage, S. J., & Rye, M. S. (2018). Promoting forgiveness: Characteristics of the treatment, the clients, and their interaction. *Journal of Counseling Psychology, 65*(3), 358.

Wade, N. G., Hoyt, W. T., Kidwell, J. E. M., & Worthington, E. L. Jr. (2014). Efficacy of psychotherapeutic interventions to promote forgiveness: A meta-analysis. *Journal of Consulting and Clinical Psychology, 82*(1), 154–170.

Waldron, V. R., Braithwaite, D. O., Oliver, B. M., Kloeber, D. N., & Marsh, J. (2018). Discourses of forgiveness and resilience in stepchild–stepparent relationships. *Journal of Applied Communication Research, 46*(5), 561–582.

Waldron, V. R. & Kelley, D. I. (2008). *Communicating forgiveness*. Thousand Oaks, CA: Sage Publications.

Walsh, F. (2003). Family resilience: A framework for clinical practice. *Family Process, 42*(1), 1–18.

Walsh, F. (2020). Loss and resilience in the time of COVID-19: Meaning making, hope, and transcendence. *Family Process, 59*(3), 898–911.

Webb, J. I. (2020). The function of gratitude in marriage: Building ties that bind. *Family Perspectives, 2*(1), 2.

Weingarten, K. (2010). Reasonable hope: Construct, clinical applications, and supports. *Family Process, 49*, 5–25.

Weir, K. (2017). Forgiveness can improve mental and physical health. *CE Corner, 48*(2), 30. https://www.apa.org/monitor/2017/01/ce-corner#:~:text=Research%20has%20shown%20that%20forgiveness,symptoms%20and%20lower%20mortality%20rates

Welch, K. J. (2012). *Family life now* (2nd ed.). New York, NY: Allyn & Bacon.

Wiesel, E. (1986). *The Nobel Lecture; Hope, Despair, and Memory in The Nobel Peace Prize 1986*. New York, NY: Summit Books and Boston University.

Wood, A. M., Maltby, J., Stewart, N., Linley, P. A., & Joseph, S. (2008). A social-cognitive model of trait and state levels of gratitude. *Emotion, 8*(2), 281–290.

Woodyatt, L., Worthington, E. L. Jr, Wenzel, M., & Griffin, B. J. (2017). *Handbook of the psychology of self-forgiveness*. Cham, Switzerland: Springer International Publishing.

Worthington, E. L. Jr. (2003). *Forgiving and reconciling: Bridges to wholeness and hope*. Downers Grove, IL: InterVarsity Press.

Worthington, E. L. Jr. (2013). *Moving forward: Six steps to forgiving yourself and breaking free from the past*. Adapted as a Workbook by Brandon Griffin & Caroline Lovelock. Thttps://static1.squarespace.com/static/518a85e9e4b04323d507813b/t/5492ed7ee4b087ef8e051d78/1418915198400/moving-forward.pdf

Yeung, J. W., Chen, H. F., Lo, H. H., & Choi, A. W. (2017). Relative effects of parenting practices on child development in the context of family processes. *Revista de Psicodidáctica* (English ed.), *22*(2), 102–110.

Yu, H., Gao, X., Zhou, Y., & Zhou, X. (2018). Decomposing gratitude: Representation and integration of cognitive antecedents of gratitude in the brain. *Journal of Neuroscience, 38*(21), 4886–4898.

Zimet, D. M., & Jacob, T. (2001). Influences of marital conflict on child adjustment: Review of theory and research. *Clinical Child and Family Psychology Review, 4*(4), 319–335.

Other Resources

Photographs/Art Free use. Adult hug by Ketut Subiyanto; Father-child hug by August de Richelieu; Child helping brother with homework by Olia Danilevich.

Part IV

Change, Turbulence, Gains, and Losses

Change, Turbulence, Gains, and Losses

When we are no longer able to change a situation - we are challenged to change ourselves.

- Viktor E. Fankl

Our final section deals with the everchanging nature of family, challenging both our families and ourselves. What are the sources of change in family and how can families adjust to them? Why do some families seem to fall apart at the drop of a feather and other families remain strong and vital in the face of huge obstacles? It is here we more closely examine resilience. Finally, we reflect on our journey and the importance of understanding family through family processes.

CHAPTER 12

Families as Units of Change and Transition

CHAPTER PREVIEW

In this chapter, readers will learn:

- That individual family members are the bedrock of family and experience change that influences and is influenced by the family.
- How genetics plays a key role in contributing to our self-definition and how we respond to the world around us.
- That gender socialization occurs in families, with gendered parenting providing explicit, implicit, direct, and indirect messages related to gender.
- That understanding gender and gender roles helps us understand how home jobs, work outside the home, childcare, and decision-making get done in family life.
- Gender and power are strongly linked, and power imbalances can be a destructive force within family dynamics.
- Individual and family change are fundamental family processes.
- How life course theory is one way to describe the trajectories and changes that occur in families.
- How some events (like births and weddings) trigger long-term and complex changes. Other events (like illnesses and relatives moving in) create short-term and simple change processes.
- Changes in family life are both predictable and unpredictable.
- Anticipatory socialization, role strain, and transition procedures can make transitions easier.
- That morphogenesis (the pull toward change) and morphostasis (the pull toward sameness) are fundamental parts of family systems.
- How ambivalence and ambiguity are universal and inevitable in families.
- About the epigenesis principle and how it helps us understand family changes.

DOI: 10.4324/9781003128717-16

INTRODUCTION

The only constant in life is change – Heraclitus of Ephesus

Don't blink, just like that you're six years old
And you take a nap
And you wake up and you're twenty-five
And your high school sweetheart becomes your wife
Don't blink, you just might miss
Your babies growing like mine did
Turning into moms and dads
Next thing you know your better half
Of fifty years is there in bed
And you're praying God takes you instead
Trust me friend a hundred years
Goes faster than you think, so don't blink
            Chris Allen Wallin/Casey Michael Beathard

We would be sipping strawberry lemonade on a beach if we had a dollar for every parent looking at our newborns who said, "Watch out! They grow up so fast!" It's true. Don't blink! As we study family and family processes, we are constantly reminded (and repeating) that family systems are dynamic, especially since many of the concepts and constructs we discuss are considered almost in snapshot fashion.

The dynamism of family life is at once affirming and frustrating. The affirmation part is related to the knowledge that our families can grow, change, improve, even when faced with great difficulties. The frustrating part is trying to study deeply what is essentially a moving target!

In this chapter, we are going to try to capture some of these dynamics as we first examine the individual (on which the family system is built), and then the system itself in change and transition. Fasten your seatbelt…and don't blink.

INDIVIDUALS: THE BEDROCK OF FAMILY AND INTERLOCKING SOURCE OF CHANGE

Scholars in family systems theory sometimes overlook the importance of the individual family member, and overlooking the individual is just as "problematic as ignoring the system within which the individual lives and thrives" (Day, Gavazzi, Miller, & Van Langeveld, 2009, p. 121). Each family member brings "gender, genetics, personalities, quirks, preferences, beliefs and choices [that are] a bedrock, foundational force" to the family system. Within the contours and boundaries of family life, individuals undergo expected and unexpected changes, physically, emotionally, socially, spiritually, and cognitively. These changes are deeply intertwined with family and relationships. Take a moment to think about yourself and all the aspects that make you ★you★. Think about your likes and dislikes, your beliefs, your personality, your physical attributes, your strengths, and your weaknesses. If you have a sibling or a cousin, how similar and different are you? Now think of how you are now and how you were five years ago. Have you changed at all? How much of who you are is related to your genes? How much is related to your experience? How are your family relationships influenced by *you* and how are *you* influenced by your family relationships? Before jumping into family, let's consider two basic characteristics of the individual that may influence change, transition, and family relation-ships—genetics and gender.

Genetics

Biology was routinely ignored as a feature of family studies until the 1980s. It was during this time that bioscientists began unraveling the secrets of **genes** (**protein coding sequences** that provide the basic set of instructions to guide human development) in the **Human Genome Project** (https://www.genome.gov/human-genome-project). A **genome** is an organism's complete set of genetic material, mostly made up of DNA (deoxyribonucleic acid). The U.S. Human Genome Project was considered "one of the greatest feats of exploration in history," as international teams of scientists, from October 1990 to April 2003, mapped the entire blueprint for the human genome.

One surprising finding of the Human Genome Project (and the findings keep on coming in) was that humans did not have over 100,000 protein coding genes on their chromosomes as previously thought but only 19,000–20,000 (Piovesan et al., 2019). Compare that number to the 31,000 genes found in the water flea (NSF, 2011)! Another surprising finding was that only 1–2% of DNA is "**coding DNA**," with 98–99% of regions outside of genes (and some inside) being **noncoding DNA**. In the past, this was referred to as "junk" DNA. Now, it appears that not all non-coding DNA is junk; rather, parts play important roles in such areas as the expression of coding DNA. These discoveries have led to new areas of study: epig-enomics and epigenetics (Cheriyedath, 2019; NIH, 2020). In **epigenomics**, scientists chart the locations of chemical tags in the genome. In **epigenetics**, scientists study the chemical reactions that turn genes on and off and influence their expression without changing the actual DNA sequence.

Intriguingly, research has found that many factors can trigger epigenetic changes in people, including trauma (Curry, 2019). We have seen the cross generational physical and mental health effects of famine, war, the Holocaust, and other traumas experienced by people all over the world (Kiyimba, 2016; Krippner & Barrett, 2019). Originally, it was believed these negative effects were passed onto the victims' children as a result of psychological or social factors. Genetic research, however, has upended this idea and found that trauma may result in stress that influences the areas around the genes and shuts off or turns on certain genes (Youssef, Lockwood, Su, Hao, & Rutten, 2018). Thus, the genes themselves do not change but whether they are turned on or off does change and gets passed on to succeeding generations. For example, the children of people who had suffered during the 1944–1945 Dutch famine had a greater tendency toward obesity than the children whose parents had not suffered from famine. These changes in gene expression may be a way to insure survival of the species (Painter et al., 2008).

It is important to note that such findings, although provocative and exciting, are very pre-liminary and should be interpreted cautiously; many of the studies involved mice or rats and not humans (Krippner & Barrett, 2019). It should also be noted that our **genetic heritage** rarely determines what we will become. Instead, our genes push or influence us in certain directions. Likewise, the environments in which we are raised (e.g., single-parent home, rural farming community, or inner city) do not "determine" who we are in and of themselves. Instead, our genetic heritage and our environments—including our parents and where we grew up—and other situations contribute to who we are. Additionally, we make choices that might be quite independent of (albeit greatly influenced by) our genetic, familial, and community profiles. Social scientists have struggled for decades with the important philosophical question of how much of who we are is related to **nature** (genes) and how much is related to **nurture** (environment). This **nature–nurture controversy** has largely been replaced with the question of *how* nature and nurture *interact* to make us who we are.

The study of **behavioral genetics** (Baker, 2004; Booth, Carver, & Granger, 2000) examines the genetic influence on individual behavior vis-à-vis environmental influence. In a classic example of this type of research, a well-known family scientist examined antisocial behavior in twins (Reiss, 1995a, 1995b) and discovered that identical twins (who share 100% of their DNA code) were similar in their antisocial scores (0.81 correlation) and fraternal twins (who only share 50% of their DNA code) were not quite as similar (0.61 correlation). This relatively simple kind of research allows us to take a closer look at the influence of genetics and how it relates to environmental influence. Using a simple statistical procedure in this study, Reiss reasoned that about 60% of the influence to be antisocial (for the twins in this study) came from their genes, and 40% came from these children's close environments.

Other studies using similar approaches have examined such things as intelligence, memory ability, impulse control, and risk-taking behavior (for further reading in this area see Booth et al., 2000; Plomin, 1994; Reiss, 1995a, 1995b; Rowe, 1994). This line of research has long suggested that physiological processes are elemental, critical, and essential components of human interaction (Booth, Johnson, & Granger, 2005). One of the key problems of this research in the past has been that the physiological researchers only considered the impact of social influence as background noise and not really part of the total causal picture. However, some researchers (Booth et al., 2000, 2005; D'Onofrio et al., 2007) have led the way in the shifting worldview of the nature versus nurture controversy. A central idea of this shift is that biobehavioral relationship interactions can be greatly changed by our social environment.

For example, environment–genetics interactions were found by D'Onofrio et al. (2007) who conducted a landmark study in Australia with the offspring of identical twins. This three-generational study of family life is one of the few that have followed twins from an early age into the childbearing years. It began in 1980, when more than 8,000 twins were selected from the Australian National Twin Register. These twins were, at that time, entering young adulthood and responded to a self-report survey. The same twins were then contacted again in 1988 (with their spouses where possible) and they were again interviewed in 1992. By using twins (two people with the same genetic code, in this case) and by obtaining data about the twins' parents' marriages, these researchers could estimate the effects of social environment vis-à-vis genetic contribution to future divorce choices by this sample.

They found that these twin children raised with divorced parents were much more likely to divorce themselves when they got older and married. These researchers claimed that although environment and personal choice were all important contributors, something was passed along to the next generation that created potential problems with relationships. This type of research is not refined enough, as yet, to inform us about the mysterious "something" that gets passed on (Figure 12.1). Of course, it is not just one personality trait or one personal attribute that "makes" someone divorce. However, there is growing evidence that who we are and how we perform in relationships has a genetic component attached to it.

FIGURE 12.1 Identical twins separated at birth, with parents who are very different from another, grow up to be remarkably similar even though they have never met.

What should be the take-home message of genetics and its influence? One could read this information and develop an attitude of despair: Who I am is immutable and unchangeable, therefore why try? Another approach is one of realization. When we find an area in our personality, temperament, or makeup that is destructive to relationships, we can target that problem and work harder to strengthen that area. You certainly should not come away from this chapter thinking that if you or your spouse (or spouse to be) came from a divorced family that there is no hope for you. Instead, if you have relatives who struggle with relationship problems, it means you will have to be on a higher alert status. You will probably have to work harder to stay out of relationship distress. Principle 12.1 captures this idea and states that once we realize that much of who we are physically, emotionally, and mentally is tied to genetic predispositions, we can respond accordingly.

PRINCIPLE 12.1

GENETICS AND FAMILIES

Families are more effective and efficient when family members realize that individual family members have different talents, respond to stress differently, and have different abilities and skills that might be rooted in genetics. Individuals should pay close attention to traits and weaknesses they have inherited. By attending to those challenges, we can increase our chances of doing well in relationships.

Gender

Another essential aspect of the individual is **gender**. Gender, an important feature of daily living, is a combination of genetics and social construction. Understanding the texture that gender brings to relationships is central to understanding family processes. This discussion of gender, in turn, leads to a core message that individual differences often lead to power imbalances in relationships, and power imbalances are worth considering in times of family transition and change.

The terms *gender* and *sex* are often used interchangeably, and much controversy exists over this (Conger, 2017; Hyde, Bigler, Joel, Tate, & van Anders, 2019). For some scholars, sex and gender are separate constructs. Sex is a biological and genetically determined trait (though sometimes assigned) of male and female. Gender is, for the most part, learned and socially, culturally, and even personally defined. From this perspective, gender is not a single point on a line of opposites (masculine or feminine) but exists as a continuum, with a collection of various characteristics that have the potential to change throughout the lifespan (Castleberry, 2019). Other scholars insist that sex and gender are so intertwined that trying to differentiate between them is a fool's errand (Hyde et al., 2019). It is beyond the scope of this chapter to review the key literature on gender. Our discussion will be limited and focus on a few key points that can help direct our attention to this important element of family life.

Gender Socialization in Family

Even before a baby is born, the baby's gender appears to be important to its family, encompassing expectations, hopes, and dreams. Some parents see gender as fluid and engage in "Gender Creative Parenting" (Davies, 2020). They delight in raising "theybies," gender neutral children who will decide their own gender as they age. Most parents, however, still prefer traditional gender classifications (girl/boy), despite cultural trends toward valuing gender egalitarianism. A Gallup Poll found that American preference for boys (40%) over girls (28%) remained unchanged for 70 years, from 1941 to 2011, with men being particularly strong in their preference (Newport, 2011). Technology has allowed expectant parents to learn the sex of their child before birth, leading to the cultural phenomenon of "gender reveal parties." Those parents who choose not to learn their baby's sex may be met with resistance from friends and neighbors who use that information to provide gendered gifts (pink blankets and basketball onesies)!

It appears that we carry gendered beliefs and stereotypes that influence how we perceive infants. Research has found that parents of newborns perceive (and describe) their infants differently according to gender (Rubin, Provenzano, & Luria, 1974). Little girls were perceived as having finer features and being more delicate, softer, and inattentive than boys. Although such stereotypes appeared to decline over the two decades following the initial study, some persisted (Karraker, Vogel, & Lake, 1995). Similarly, Condry and Condry (1976) conducted an experiment that involved showing a videotape of a 9-month-old infant exposed to different stimuli (teddy bear, doll, jack-in-the-box, and buzzer) to a group of adults. On the video, the baby cries in response to the jack-in-the-box. Half of the adults were told the infant was female and the other half were told the infant was male. Remarkably, if the adults thought the baby was a boy, they saw the cry as a reflection of anger; if they thought the baby was a girl, they attributed the cry to fear. It is easy to imagine that an adult's response to the infant would vary depending on their perception of the infant's emotion of anger vs. fear. In simple and unnoticed ways, parents tell us when we are young what our crying means, how active

FIGURE 12.2 Researchers have often wondered if the environment (e.g., the kinds of toys children play with) have an influence on the development of gender.

we should be when we play, and how aggressively we should respond to stimulation. They tell us different things depending on whether we are male or female.

The messages and behaviors related to gender that we direct toward our children is referred to as **gendered parenting** (Mesman & Groeneveld, 2018). Decades of research in this area have yielded inconclusive results, not because gendered parenting might not truly exist but because most gendered parenting in families today occurs implicitly (Figure 12.2). These covert yet specific parenting practices can be direct or indirect. Directly, parents provide toys, clothing, and experiences that are gender specific. They verbally and nonverbally send messages of approval or disapproval regarding children's behaviors, choices, activities, and interactions (Mesman & Groeneveld, 2018). One young mother caught herself watching her 4-year-old son fearlessly jump from the top of a slide to another piece of nearby play equipment; however, when her 4-year-old daughter attempted the same feat, she was quick to jump in and suggest a different activity. Again, however, most parents are unaware that they respond to their children differently.

According to Mesman and Groeneveld (2018), parents' indirect gender messages to their children are done through such actions as modeling gender roles or making gender related comments about book characters engaging in stereotypical or non-stereotypical gender activities. Halpern and Perry-Jenkins (2016) found that mothers and fathers play unique roles in their children's knowledge of gender stereotypes, with parenting *behaviors* being stronger predictors of children's gender role attitudes than parent ideology. We will never forget the time we were driving, when a voice from the backseat of the car asked, "Why do daddies always get to do the driving?" Without saying a word, my husband pulled over and stopped the car. We both unbuckled our seatbelts and silently walked around to change drivers; I drove for the rest of the day. We always said, "Little pitchers have big ears," but that moment taught us they also have big eyes! What we do (often unconsciously) as we interact with our children is more important than what we say.

Recent research suggests that sociocultural pressures are not the only influences on gendered parenting. Babies' biological-hormonal states resulting from sex characteristics might push boys and girls to act differently when stimulated. This prompts the parents to then treat the baby more like a boy (or girl) and the cycle of socialization continues. (For a review of the literature on biosocial influences in family life across decades, see Booth et al., 2000 and D'Onofrio & Lahey, 2010).

Gender and Division of Household Labor

The result of how our parents socialize us, how we respond, and how they respond again is that men and women often develop characteristics that are gender specific, even defining roles and expectations in marriage and family, including the division of labor in a household. For over 50 years, scholars have studied gender divisions of time, tasks, and responsibilities finding that men's participation in household tasks and childcare do not usually match women's participation, although today's fathers in general tend to be increasing their participation (Doucet, 2013).

We know very little about how inner family bargains are struck and maintained related to household responsibilities or the ideological reasoning used by couples as they decide who does what and why; however, research has suggested several possible explanations, from economics to power and privilege. For example, in 1957, anthropologist and sociologist Elizabeth Bott tied the division of household labor to the organization of the family and social networks. In short, Bott's Hypothesis was that household labor was influenced by social network support. Using a large longitudinal data set, Rözer, Mollenhorst, and Volker (2018) found moderate support for Bott's classic hypothesis but found even stronger support for the *reverse* of the hypothesis; in other words, the division of labor affects social network patterns, especially for women. They conclude that for today's families, "Women who have more close contacts with colleagues tend to divide their tasks more equally with their spouse, while men who have more close contacts with colleagues tend to divide their tasks less equally with their spouse … But we also conclude that the influence of social contacts on the division of labor is remarkably weaker than Bott observed in the 1950s" (p. 3459).

If gender is somewhat related to division of household labor, how is such labor divided in same sex, transgender, or gender non-binary families? Previous research has found that same sex couples generally tend to be more equal in their division of household labor (Rothblum, 2017). Household tasks in these families tend to be assigned based on preference (and some people really do like cleaning!) and negotiation. Further, if the same sex couple had a biological child, the biological parent tended to do more childcare tasks. Similarly, Tornello (2020) found that her 163 transgender and nonbinary families reported their distribution of nonpaid labor was more egalitarian in nature. Tornello also found that how the couples divided household labor was unrelated to child behavior outcomes.

It may be significant that contemporary young adults appear to hold more flexible views on the division of household labor, although most prefer the "men as providers and women as homemakers" model (Dernberger & Pepin, 2020). Research in this area may indeed find continued changes in the distribution of unpaid household labor as these young people enter into family relationships.

Finally, the COVID-19 global pandemic has provided one additional insight of how unexpected life changes can influence such mundane tasks as housework (Shafer, Scheibling, & Milkie, 2020). For most of 2020, families were forced to stay home, as parents worked from home or lost jobs and children were kept out of school. Shafer and colleagues found that Canadian fathers took on a larger share of household labor during this time, but mothers continued to carry the lion's share of educational responsibilities. Some mothers even left employment to take care of children no longer attending school. According to these researchers, families "inched toward" more equitable distribution of household labor.

Gender and Power

When we speak of relationships and gender, we are often speaking of power relationships and gender inequality. Power is the ability to make other people do something you want them to do but they do not necessarily want to do of their own volition. An associated concept is control, which goes past the ability part of the equation into changing another's behavior.

We have power over another when the other person needs some resource we have, and we not only have some of that resource, but we have a way to transfer the resource to the other person. For example, Rob and Cindy are dating and thinking about getting married. He comes from a wealthy family who has given him large amounts of money to use in his personal account. Cindy comes from a poor family and has no money to add to the pot. We first must ascertain if Cindy needs the resource(s) Rob has or if she values the resources he has. In addition, we need to know if Cindy has any type of valuable resource to add to the exchange. According to Cook and Emerson (1978) and Molm (2003) the power in a relationship is unbalanced when the dependencies are unequal. The result is that the relationship will be imbalanced and will struggle. This idea is captured in Principle 12.2.

PRINCIPLE 12.2

WE HAVE POWER IN RELATIONSHIPS (AND THEREFORE ABILITY TO CONTROL ANOTHER'S BEHAVIOR) WHEN THE OTHER NEEDS SOMETHING WE HAVE AND WHEN WE NEED SOME RESOURCE THE OTHER PERSON HAS

Relationships suffer when there is a power imbalance that results from one person having fewer valued resources than the other. Imbalanced relationships are less effective in attaining desired goals.

The following ideas about power, gender, and family are based on the work of sociologist Karen Cook and her colleagues (e.g., Cook & Emerson, 1978; Cook & Rice, 2001). Many of these are, as of yet, untested in the family science literature but follow from theoretical suggestions applied to economic game theory and the social psychology of business management.

The first idea is that gendered relationships tend to be power imbalanced because men in Western cultures are physically stronger, have typically and historically controlled resources, and, in some cases, have relied on religious dogma to infer imbalanced relationship power.

When men take it on themselves to rule households through the process of domination, power imbalance, and control, they will actually have less ability to achieve the mutual well-being of all members of their families. And, because men are stronger, have typically controlled the wealth of family life, and have traditionally had exclusive access to education and the means to acquire social capital, there have been serious issues of power imbalance in family relationships for generations. It is only in recent years that women have been recognized as having a role of co-partnership with men in marriage.

Further, families are more effective and efficient when family members understand that the family environment is only one aspect of the decision-making process that influences the individual. In particular, as children get older, they make decisions that might be independent of ideology, training, and wishes of parents. When parents understand this principle, they will be more effective in providing support to children and other family members. Additionally, when family members realize that genetic predispositions and free will are in operation, even in younger children, parents are more likely to respond to family problems in effective ways.

When power imbalance is high, families are much less likely to be efficient in attaining desired goals. This type of efficiency is probably the result of many factors. One of them has to do with contention. When power imbalance is high, families are more likely to experience contention, unresolved conflict, and power-ridden competitive communication. When it is in a person's best interest to be kind, generous, and helpful (because being nasty could result in losing something valuable), the person is less likely to be contentious. In other words, if there is a power imbalance (meaning one person has fewer valuable resources to bring to the relationship) there are fewer barriers to prevent destructive power use.

When power imbalance is high, the satisfaction and well-being of close family relationships diminishes. As stated earlier, as power imbalance rises, contention, distancing, and disregard are also likely to rise. These conditions detract from the ability of a family to administer the nurturance and love needed. Additionally, when power imbalance is high, it is more likely that decisions will be made that favor the person with the most power. Obviously, when only one member of a group makes decisions for the rest, trouble is likely to follow. It should be obvious that input from all members of a group is likely to result in better decision making. In addition, when group members feel like their input is of no value, they will be less likely to endorse the decision.

These researchers have also noted that when power imbalance is high, it is more likely that divisions of labor, household routines, and the daily patterns of life will favor the person(s) with the most power. When people (male or female) have more power (and thus more control) they will (over time) most likely advantage themselves. That is, they will pick chores, jobs, and assignments that they like to do, leaving the worse jobs for those with less power.

Based on this information, one can conclude that when power imbalance is high, families will be less likely to do well at resolving crises or dealing with change and transition. Families within which one member has more power than another will be less likely to generate creative solutions and new resources in times of trouble. Power imbalance is usually a destructive force within family dynamics. Having balanced power in relationships means that all members have a more vested interest in outcomes.

Our discussion of genetics and gender are examples of just two individual characteristics that influence not only individual transition and change, but family transition and change. We cannot understand the family and how it experiences change and transitions across time without recognizing the individual and the individual's cognitive, social, spiritual, emotional, and physical development across the lifespan. Each member of the family is going through their own individual trajectories and changes in their life course. As explained by Carter and McGoldrick (1989), "The individual life course takes place within the family life course, which is the primary context of human development. We think this perspective is crucial to understanding the emotional problems that people develop as they move together through life" (p. 4). Thus, growth and development of the individual and family are mutually interdependent.

CHANGE AND TRANSITION IN THE FAMILY SYSTEM

Family change is an important part of family science. It is different from individual change in that it refers to the patterned changes that occur *in families* rather than changes in individuals. For example, newly formed families begin with a formative period. In some cultures, this first stage begins with courtship. In other cultures, it begins when the parents negotiate a marriage, and in still other cultures, it starts when couples begin to live together. During the formative stage, a family becomes more complex, more differentiated or separated from other family members, with the goal for family members to become increasingly more competent. This initial stage is a creative period because many new family rules or "understandings" are constructed. As you consider this family change, it is apparent that changes usually are not "events" (such as the wedding); rather they occur gradually over a period of time. They include both dramatic changes (e.g., divorce, death, birth), as well as small or minor changes (e.g., moving into a new house or starting school), but even these changes are not "one and done." In fact, much of family life involves change, transformations, evolution, instability, or an unfolding of potentials. These changes involve processes occurring over time that alter, convert, or modify what is happening in families. Changes in family life often involve changes in communication patterns, feelings of love and closeness, and family bonds.

PRINCIPLE 12.3

FAMILY CHANGE

Family change is different than individual change. Family change is about the change that happens to the system overall instead of a change in one's own life trajectory.

White (2005) suggested that the merging of family life course theory with family and human development theory be called **transition theory**. This is an attractive idea that informs much of this chapter section. As White aptly pointed out, the Roman philosopher Heraclitus (536–470 BC) argued that only change and transitions were real, per se, and that stability is only an illusion. That is a tempting idea: Is there anything that is not in flux? Let's have no sniveling as you consider this important question. The ball is in your court, so to speak. Can you think of anything that is actually unchanging? Aside from esoteric theological discussions that transcend this chapter, we are guessing you are having a difficult time thinking of something that is not changing or at least changeable. Scientists would probably argue that every particle of the universe is decaying or transforming in some way.

Before we get too abstract, let's back off from that extreme position for a minute and simply indicate that we use the concept of stability to denote rather ordinary observations of entities over time. For example, when we do research about marriage, we say a marriage is stable if there was no divorce reported from Time 1 to Time 2. But, as you can clearly imagine, the strength and veracity of a marriage could (and usually does) vary greatly from day to day. For the sake of reductionism and our attempts to take snapshots of entities like the family, however, we just say, "The marriage was stable for 20 years." It is much easier to consider stability if one simply looks at structure, such as divorce versus nondivorce or children versus no children. However, when we start to look at dynamic systems that are in flux and change, complete with life course issues of individuals with overlapping and interlocking trajectories, it becomes very dicey to glibly indicate that one system is stable and another is not.

Individuals occupy roles within the family entity. As those roles overlap and interlock, we begin to focus on the transitional nature of the individual and also on the collective group. Simply said, we want to know how effectively an individual or a group of individuals (a family in this case) makes the transition from one state to another, for example, from being married to being divorced, or from having no children to having several.

PRINCIPLE 12.4

INTERLOCKING TRAJECTORIES

Each family member has a life trajectory. The individual's trajectory is probably different (even slightly) than others in a family, but because they are bound together in a family system, the individual trajectories interlock and each one is influenced by the other's.

An important idea is that transitions are not simple. We do not just simply go from unmarried to married without a great deal of disruption. Not all disruption is bad, however, disruption and movement through time are inevitable. Elder (1985) commented on this notion and suggested that transitions are more like oscillations. That is, our well-being, functioning, ability to cope, and effectiveness during change oscillates. It is something of a rollercoaster. Change is inevitable, stability is probably a soothing illusion, and the job of life is to learn how to stay on the rollercoaster without getting too sick.

Predictable and Unpredictable Family Change

Families change in many ways, including size, sex composition, complexity of interrelationships, expectations, help patterns, and patterns of emotional distance and closeness. The generational alignments evolve in several predictable ways, and the ways the family system copes with the environment changes. Researchers commonly indicate that some of the changes that occur in families are expected, but sometimes they are a surprise. Sometimes the changes take family members away from us, and sometimes we gain new members. A key element of trajectories and transitions in families is that much of the change seems to be routine or patterned. Although the sequence is not always predictable, much of the time it is. Moreover, these changes occur both to the individuals in families and to the family itself.

PRINCIPLE 12.5

SOME CHANGES ARE PREDICTABLE AND OTHERS ARE NOT

It is important to know that some changes in families are predictable and expected, whereas other changes are much less predictable and are usually unexpected.

Recall in Chapter 2 Duvall's (1955) theory of the family life cycle. In the 1950s, family scientists assumed most families moved through a very predictable series of stages. One version of this cycle that has been widely used in recent years was suggested by Carter and McGoldrick (1989, p. 15) and includes the following stages:

Stage 1—Leaving home: Single young adults.
Stage 2—The joining of families through marriage: The new couple.
Stage 3—Families with young children.
Stage 4—Families with adolescents.
Stage 5—Launching children and moving on.
Stage 6—Families in later life.

Family scientists discovered, however, that very few families proceed in an orderly way through this series of stages. In fact, notice that this orientation focuses primarily on children and does not reflect the change sequence that many people actually go through. It is only a small minority of families who experience this cycle without any interruptions or without an unusual arrangement of the stages.

Despite such variations, some aspects of family life cycles are fairly predictable. The following examples illustrate the kinds of family patterns that are expected in modern Western family life. These patterns seem to be ubiquitous.

• Coping with aging and death
• Formation periods followed by family maintenance periods
• Moving from idealistic perceptions to more realistic perceptions of life
• Births
• Partings (children moving away from home)
• Long empty nest stages
• Living alone or single
• Living together before marriage

Although such changes are typical and predictable, even in their predictability we see variation. Many couples are surprised at the change in lifestyle necessitated with the coming of a baby, and families respond differently to the new addition. All people age but our response to aging differs, again influencing family life. When children grow and leave the family home, parents may engage in new and different pursuits, take on a new career, or move.

Variations also occur because of unexpected events that influence the family life cycle. These events can be both common and uncommon. Consider the following examples:

• Divorce and remarriage or remaining single
• Difficulty conceiving a child
• Early death of spouse or child
• Blended families
• "Boomerang" children returning to parent/s' home
• Being laid off or fired
• Unexpected pregnancy in and out of marriage

- Never marrying
- Disability of parent, child, grandparent
- Chronic illness
- Fostering/adoption

Such unexpected changes lead to several important insights about family life. First, they demonstrate there is great variability in the life course of families and individuals. Just as there are so many different types of families that we cannot talk about "the" American family or "the" Chinese family or "the" Kenyan family, there are so many variations in family life that we cannot talk about "the" life cycle of individuals or families. Second, even though there are great variations in the cycles of family life, there are also some aspects of these cycles that are fairly predictable. Courtship, living together, or both precede weddings, and births (or adoptions) usually precede child rearing. One's own aging tends to come late in the cycle of family life but coping with the aging parents and grandparents comes earlier. Midlife crises do not usually happen to people in their 20s or their 80s. They tend to come when people are between 40 and 50.

Some changes in family life mean that people and families become more complex, more differentiated, and more able to cope with their life situation. This is especially the case when families are in the formative stage of the family life cycle. For example, when children start to arrive, families usually become much more complex and differentiated and a number of other predictable changes occur.

All changes, however, do not lead to greater ability and complexity, and they are not all desirable. Although we don't like to think about it, life is a life-and-death cycle—again where nothing is static or stable. There are natural cycles for everything that is living, and these life courses all have ends as well as beginnings. Many of the change processes and transitions in family life have a bittersweet quality to them. Weddings, for example, are often a time of joy, but also a time of tears. The launching of children is a time of excitement and also loss. The coming of children is rewarding but also limiting and constraining. The natural movement from the excitement and euphoria of new love during engagement and the early months of marriage is both a loss and a relief to most couples. The couple feels the euphoria, but the bride's mother might feel great joy and deep sadness at the same time.

Taken together, we see a number of rhythms and patterns in the ebb and flow of family life, both predictable and unpredictable. The more we are aware of these patterns, the more we can help families prepare and cope with daily family life.

Transitions

The concept of **transitions** was created when scholars realized that living systems usually do not have a constant rate of change. They tend to have periods of rapid change followed by periods of relative stability. The periods of rapid or dramatic change are called **transitions** and the periods of stability are called **stages**. Most of the major transitions in families occur when there are changes in the membership of the family or in the way the family interacts with its environment. As we've seen, many of these transitions are fairly predictable and normal, and they can be anticipated. Some of them, however, are part of the unpredictable and variable parts of family life. Some examples of transitions that influence family life are engagements, starting to live together, weddings, birth of a first child, children starting school, children moving into adolescence, children leaving home, the death of a parent, retirement, the death of a spouse, and one's own death. Not all transitions in family life are routine.

Transitions are the result of a number of factors, both internal and external to the family. Teens go through puberty, grow in their ability to think abstractly (and thus create better arguments for parents!), develop new friendships and romances creating changes in family processes. Pregnancy and childbirth also result in transition. External factors leading to transition might be one's house burning to the ground in a wildfire or losing a job due to the pandemic.

Some transitions tend to be relatively easy and problem-free, yet others tend to be difficult. Also, some of them are easy for one family but difficult for another. For example, some families have a difficult time coping with children leaving home, but others find it an easy transition (Haley, 1987). Some families have a difficult time coping with retirement, but others find it easy. Some find the transition into parenthood easy, and others find it challenging.

Some changes result from a combination of factors. For example, the changes created by adolescence and midlife crisis are not caused by one event or process; rather, they are created by complex interactions of physiological, social, mental, economic, spatial, and emotional changes. These create sizable transitions in the individuals and family. One important challenge for family scientists is to find ways to help families cope with transitions so that there are healthy periods of growth rather than excessive difficulty.

Fortunately, in the late 1930s, sociologists such as Cottrell (1942) began trying to identify the principles that are involved in making transitions easy and difficult, and scholars have tried to use these principles to identify strategies that families, therapists, and educators can use to promote family health. The principles Cottrell identified are fairly specific, and they have since been revised and updated in light of subsequent research (Burr, Leigh, Day, & Constantine, 1979). The following three principles, **anticipatory socialization, role strain, and transition procedures**, are widely understood and utilized in many settings.

Anticipatory Socialization

The term *socialization* refers to the process of gradually learning the norms, scripts, attitudes, values, and subtle rules a person needs to know to be able to function effectively in society. **Anticipatory socialization** refers to learning that is done *before* people are in a role where they actually use what they have learned (Merton, 1968). Merton indicated that anticipatory socialization involved acquiring new abilities, skills, and, in some cases, changing one's reference or social group.

PRINCIPLE 12.6

ANTICIPATORY SOCIALIZATION

When one can anticipate a situation and learn from a previous experience (or an experience of someone else) then the next transition into a situation similar to the previous target experience will enhance the chances that the new transition will be smoother and more efficient.

Cottrell (1942) was the first scholar to develop the principle that anticipatory socialization helps people make transitions. Since then, other scholars such as Merton (1968), Burr (1973), and Bronfenbrenner (1979) have refined it. A study conducted in Norway illuminates this process. Waerdahl (2005) found that children making the transition from primary school into middle school at age 12 used symbolic objects and clothing that helped them practice and identify who they would become as they made this key transition. In Merton's study of soldiers making the transition back into civilian life, he noticed that they practiced being civilians by dressing in certain ways and using home-based language that replaced army clothes, hierarchies, and speech. In like manner, Norwegian children were more successful in transitioning into an advanced school when they were able to practice "being older" by dressing older and adopting the language and symbolic items of the older children. In Waerdahl's study, the key to success for these children was the ability to obtain the highly prized Levis jeans that signaled to others that they understood what was required to be a part of the older group.

In another study, Coleman and Hoffer (1987) found that students' successful transition into the workplace was guided by learning accurate information about working and work expectations. Parents were key facilitators of this pretraining, followed by friends and other family members. In all cases, the power of this principle is clear: Learning and practicing about a future role assists one in making the transition into that role. Although we know very little about how this process works for groups (as opposed to individuals), we can speculate that when families practice transitions before they occur (e.g., moving to a new school, getting divorced, having a new baby, etc.), the group will have an easier time making those transitions.

This principle helps us realize that *timing* is important in trying to help people learn what they need to do. There are moments of readiness or teachable moments when people are eager and motivated and other times when they are less interested in learning (Guerney & Guerney, 1981). As we begin to make transitions into difficult or even pleasant situations, it is critical to pre-arm family members about the nature of the transition. This strategy decreases role strain.

Role Strain

A second principle that helps people cope with transitions deals with role strain. **Role strain** refers to the felt difficulty people experience when they try to conform to the demands of a role (Figure 12.3). Many things can create role strain. For example, it can be introduced by ambiguity about what a person is supposed to do in a new situation, and by conflicting expectations about what should be done. It can also be caused by having too many roles that one is trying to perform simultaneously.

Some roles, such as caring for infants, are so demanding that there can be abundant role strain. When the parents both try to work full time and continue all the activities they were used to before the pregnancy, it can create one type of strain, an **overload** problem. To avoid this, couples need to learn that when they are expecting their first child, it usually helps to adjust and eliminate some of the competing roles they occupy. Frequently, at least one parent, and sometimes both parents, need to adjust the amount of time they spend on their careers, leisure activities, educational pursuits, and other activities.

Sometimes, anticipating does not help much. There might be other cultural factors that trump one's pre-learning. For example, a study by Baxter, Hewitt, and Haynes (2008) found that information about the transition from cohabitation to marriage yielded interesting results.

These researchers used data from the Australian panel survey called Negotiating the Life Course. They found that men were fairly constant in sharing household duties until the couple made the transition into parenthood. In Australia, about 75% of the couples cohabit before marriage. The question is this: Does this pretraining experience make a difference in who does which jobs in the household following marriage (when it occurs)? It turned out, in this case, that living together did not predict equality in marriage. Like many other studies, these researchers found that, over time, women were likely to do significantly more housework than were men. Further, over time, the amount of housework reported by husbands significantly decreased. This was magnified when a child was born. Even though there had been plenty of pretraining, the men in this study moved further away from household performance that resulted in increased role strain and tension.

PRINCIPLE 12.7

ROLE STRAIN

When role strain is high in a system or relationship, any transition into a new role or life course stage will be less efficient and more stressful.

Part of the role strain principle tells us that strain helps the transitions out of roles. For example, adolescence is usually a period of considerable role strain. The expectations for adolescents are ambiguous, and the important people in an adolescent's life do not agree on many of the expectations. Parents, teens, friends, and educators, for example, usually have different opinions. This makes the transition *into* adolescence difficult, but it usually makes the transition *out* of it much easier. In fact, most people are glad to have the teenage years behind them, and they are thrilled when they and others finally view them as adults, a stage of life where the expectations are clearer and there is less strain. Because the adolescent stage of the family life cycle also tends to be difficult for parents and siblings, they too, usually, find the transition out of the teen years a welcome breath of fresh air.

The main issues in applying this principle are knowing what role strain is, knowing the kinds of things that cause it, and finding ways to minimize or prevent it. Good anticipatory socialization often helps because it gives people clues about which roles are more and less demanding. It also frequently helps people learn that some roles are fairly incompatible with others. For example, it is helpful to know that roles such as dating, being engaged, and being married are fairly incompatible, and trying to do more than one of these at the same time can create more than a little strain.

Goode (1960) identified a number of other strategies that can help minimize strain. One of them is to talk extensively with others to try to clarify the expectations and get a clear understanding of what is expected. This also helps create agreement with others about these expectations. Role theorists have a term for each of these two processes: getting *role clarity* and *role consensus*. Trying to get clarity and consensus is a natural process in many situations. For example, most engaged couples find it natural to talk for hours and hours, almost endlessly, about what they want and do not want when they are married and how they want to act and not act.

Another of Goode's strategies for coping with role strain is to *compartmentalize* certain roles. When two roles, such as being an employee and lover, demand very different ways of

FIGURE 12.3 Sometimes life comes at you hard. Role strain occurs when parents have multiple tasks to complete and a new role demand occurs on the top of a previous one before the new one can be resolved.

acting, it is helpful to separate the situations and places where people are in these roles. Being an employee during working hours and a lover at other times helps the employee, employer, and lovers all minimize their strain. A different example is that the roles of caring for infants and having a career are fairly incompatible, so people usually separate them.

A third strategy is to periodically examine the role demands we have in our lives to determine if we are overcommitted. Most of us go through short periods of time, such as during final examinations, when we have an overload, but it is an acceptable part of the ebb and flow of demands. However, sometimes we gradually take on one more obligation, and then another, and then another until we have inadvertently overcommitted ourselves. In these situations, it is an effective strategy to reduce our obligations by eliminating some roles. If we do not want to eliminate any of our roles, we can lower our "standards" in some roles.

Transition Procedures

Another principle about transitions deals with the procedures that are used in making a transition. The principle is called the role transitions principle.

PRINCIPLE 12.8

ROLE TRANSITION PRINCIPLE

The clarity of the transition procedures helps the transition to be more efficient, smoother, and less stressful.

Imagine, for example, how difficult it would be if someone's wedding were spread out over several months. They would not know for sure when they were finally married. At what point would they have made the important commitments to each other, and when should their friends start thinking of them as a married couple? This type of ambiguity in the transition procedures would make the transition into marriage much more difficult than it usually is.

Morphogenesis and Morphostasis

Remember that family systems theory posits that families and family members are characterized by constant change and adaptation. They experience an ongoing dynamic tension between the desire for stability and sameness (morphostasis) and the desire for change (morphogenesis). These terms can be understood easily if they are divided into their two root words. First, let's examine **morphogenesis**. In Greek, *morpho* refers to the form or shape of something, and *genesis* means beginning or creating, and in this word, it also refers to changing or altering. Thus, family morphogenesis refers to changing or altering the shape or form of a family life. It means more than just changing the number or the ages of the people in the family, as it includes other things like changes in family dynamics, traditions, routines, emotional responses, rules, rituals, and other processes.

The main idea that family researchers have developed about morphogenesis can be called the **morphogenesis principle**: Some of the morphogenesis in families is routine and expected change as part of the lifespan or life cycle of individuals or families. Some morphogenesis is the result of the unexpected. For example, a member of a family might be paralyzed by an automobile accident, a family might win a large lottery prize, or someone in a family might go through a religious conversion. These and many other random and unforeseen events can create changes in the "form" of the families involved, but family scientists do not think of them as routine changes.

The concept of **morphostasis** is the opposite of morphogenesis, and it is also easily understood when we break it into its two parts. *Morpho* refers to form, and *stasis* refers to static or stable. Thus, family morphostasis is the process of maintaining the status quo or avoiding change in a family life. Family scientists also sometimes use the term **homeostasis** rather than morphostasis. These two words are synonymous and interchangeable. For ease, the word morphostasis is used in this book rather than homeostasis. The morphostasis principle was one of the first principles to be identified after scholars began thinking with a family process point of view (Jackson, 1957).

PRINCIPLE 12.9

MORPHOSTASIS PRINCIPLE

Organized systems tend to resist change. A system will usually go to great lengths to keep the system working like it has done in the past.

There are many reasons morphostasis is an inevitable and fundamental part of family systems. Three of these reasons are as follows:

1 Rules that are created in the early stages of a relationship become the first part of a complicated web or set of rules. Later on, if there are attempts to change the first rules it has implications for many parts of the web. One result of this pattern is that it creates some tendency to resist change.

2 A great deal of what happens in families is unconscious, or, using the iceberg analogy, it is beneath the surface and fairly invisible. Also, people have enough of a desire to control their lives that they like some degree of stability, security, and predictability. These tendencies lead to some resistance to change.

3 Family processes deal with many of the most fundamental and deeply experienced emotional processes that humans experience. For example, they deal with mating, reproduction, personal territory, intimacy, and belonging. People are highly motivated to arrange their life, so these deeply felt affective experiences are comfortable. One example of this is the unbelievable trials humans sometimes go through to find a mate. When people get these parts of their lives organized so the inner and core affective conditions are comfortable, they have very strong, affectively motivated reasons to resist attempts to change things. This is one reason divorce and death are resisted so much, and why they are such tremendously disruptive experiences when they cannot be avoided. They force us to reorganize some of the most fundamental parts of our lives.

When these ideas were being developed, the scholars who were creating them paid most of their attention to morphostasis, and they ignored morphogenesis (Jackson, 1963). This meant that during the 1950s and 1960s, family scholars who were developing these ideas assumed that family life was fairly stable and unchanging, and the primary tendency in family systems is to resist innovation and development. The current view in the field is that, on the one hand, there are always pressures, events, and processes that tend to create change in family life. At the same time, there are always pressures, events, and processes that tend to create stability and resist change. The two processes oppose each other and are incompatible, but both are inherent and unavoidable, and apparently, they are natural and inevitable parts of family life. Unfortunately, there is virtually no research that would tell us if families (or systems in general) resist change. This is a powerful theoretical idea that needs to be researched more.

Practical Implications of Morphogenesis and Morphostasis

When we understand the twin processes of morphogenesis and morphostasis in family life, it gives us ideas that have several implications. One implication is that it helps us be aware that families always experience **ambivalence** when they encounter significant change. Ambivalence is feeling two opposite affective states or desires at the same time. Even when families encounter desirable changes like weddings, births, graduations, children going out on their own, career opportunities, and other new challenges and opportunities, there is always ambivalence in the family about them. The ambivalence is frequently uneven. This means that sometimes one side of the feelings for or against something are stronger than the opposing feelings. Usually, when a change helps people attain important goals, the dominant feelings are in favor of the change.

When a change interferes with important goals or is threatening in other ways, the dominant feelings are against the change.

Sometimes perceptions determine the nature of the feelings, but perceptions are sometimes deceptive. Remembering the iceberg analogy, when a change has implications for the hidden parts of family life, people might not be aware of all of the pressures and processes. For example, a younger sibling might be relieved when an older sibling leaves home. They get a new bedroom. There is less hassle about the bathroom, no more getting picked on, and so on. The feelings of loss and emptiness can be very real and can have an effect on the child, but the child might not be aware of what is happening.

Another implication of these two ideas is that, because systems tend to become increasingly rigid as time passes, generally speaking, the earlier in the life of an individual or family system we try to influence the system, the greater the impact we will usually have. In family science, there are many ways this can be applied. For example, we can make more difference in the way a couple relates by helping them early in their marriage rather than later. We can have more impact on people's lives if we influence them early in life than if we influence them later (Bronfenbrenner, 1979). Additionally, it has become widely believed in our society that the first years of a child's life are the most important, and the principle of morphostasis is consistent with this idea. Family scientists, therefore, should do what they can to help parents find the resources they need to be able to exert the influence and care during this period that most parents want to have and children need.

When we try to apply these insights, we also need to be aware of the readiness of individuals and families for change. As discussed earlier, people are ready at certain times and not ready at others. For example, we would probably have little impact on a person's life by trying to teach him or her something about careers when he or she is three years old. They need to be more ready than most three year olds usually are.

A third implication of understanding morphogenesis and morphostasis is related to **timing of interventions**. Family scientists have discovered that periods of transition are a good time to try to influence family life (Klonsky & Bengston, 1996). Often it is most effective to try to create a change just before a transition or just after it. Some of the reasons transitions are a good time to try to make changes are because the morphogenetic processes are more powerful at transition points and systems are in a period of flux. After the transition, the family system tends to move into a new stage, the morphostatic processes take over and systems tend to resist change and promote stability.

An example of this idea is that just prior to the birth of the first child in a family is a good time for family scientists to help couples prepare to care for infants. The parents are thinking about the birth, anticipating it, and they are highly motivated by the emotions that surround birth and procreation. This is, therefore, a teachable moment or time of readiness for new ideas, skills, and ways of doing things. Attempts to help people learn how to cope with infants are not as effective before a couple is pregnant. Similarly, teaching parents of infants how to deal with the transition into the teen years will likely not be effective.

However, sometimes intervening at times of transition is not effective. Many other processes are always at work simultaneously in family systems, and we need to consider as much of the total system as possible. This is sometimes called having a *holistic* attitude or orientation. For example, if we just paid attention to the morphostasis and morphogenesis principles, we would conclude that the best time to help young couples prepare for marriage is just before the marriage. Experience in trying to help engaged couples, however, has revealed that the period just prior to a wedding is not a very good time to try to influence couples. Research about the effects of educational and counseling programs has revealed that they have very little impact when couples are in that transition (Druckman, 1979). Apparently, what is happening is that the period just prior to weddings is such an intensely emotional time that couples are not receptive to new ideas. They are so concerned about the relationship and the preparation for the wedding that intervention programs have little impact. Studies have found that premarital programs that have a follow-up phase about 6 months after the wedding are much more help-ful than programs that just work with couples before marriage (Bader, et al, 1980; Druckman, 1979). After couples have had time to settle into their marital relationship, they move into a period when they may be more ready to learn than they were just prior to the wedding.

A fourth implication for understanding morphogenesis and morphostasis is the insight it provides into **epigenesis**. Recall from Chapter 3 that the epigenesis principle includes three main ideas. One idea is that what is done during earlier stages of a life cycle sometimes limits future opportunities, and it can make later challenges more difficult. A second idea is that what is done during earlier stages of a life cycle also can expand future opportunities, and this can make later challenges easier to cope with. The third idea is that what is done during earlier stages of a life cycle tends to create habits or tendencies in family systems and in individuals' behaviors, and these tendencies are continued later even though the families or individuals have the capacity to do things differently. What this means is that such things as rituals, patterns, traditions, routines, themes, and mannerisms tend to be continued once they are established. Each of these elements of family processes is a vital aspect of family life.

Many situations illustrate this principle. One is that what couples do in the formative stages of their family life cycle can influence their options later. For example, assume a couple is beginning to get serious and they develop a pattern of talking openly and honestly about their feelings. In the process of developing this pattern, they create a complex set of rules about how they are going to interact in their relationship in their system. The rules are "understandings" about how they are going to act in relation to each other. Many of these rules are established without ever talking about them. They might develop rules such as agreeing they will try to take time to listen to the other one when there is an indication they have a strong emotion. They will try to understand, and they will try to avoid being demeaning or critical. They also will probably come to an "understanding" about such things as how hard they should try and what kinds of things, such as being "really tired," can interfere without it being a problem. In this example, we have only identified a few key "understandings" a couple could develop in this area, but if space were to allow, it would be possible to identify hundreds of these subtle rules about how a couple communicates about feelings.

The rules that are developed in the early stages of a relationship become the framework that is used to develop more elaborate and complicated rules and understandings. They also influence what can be done in the future. If a couple creates a pattern of being open and candid with their feelings, their system will then demand of them certain behaviors, and they will get certain things out of their system. The rules of openness demand that they take the time to listen to each other carefully and that they are patient and understanding whenever the other one wants to talk about feelings. They will get out of their system a certain degree of understanding, sense of belonging, closeness, and bondedness.

When people establish the "rules" they are going to have in their family, they are dealing with many of the most fundamental emotional aspects that we humans experience. Some of these basic affective states are desires for territory, belonging, establishing leaders and follow-ers, a sense of meaning and purpose, maintaining the species by reproducing, sexual arousal, and being connected to each other in ways that are at least minimally secure. Most of these emotional processes are so deeply experienced that we are not very aware of them. We do not have vocabularies to describe them well, and by and large, they are imperceptible. The result is that they cause vague emotional feelings, such as anger, attraction, love, and desire. This means that we do not have very good access to these affective experiences to know how to deal with them consciously or deliberately, yet they are so powerful that they exert tremendous effect on our lives.

In sum, once when we have established our "system," we find it a deeply disruptive emo-tional experience if we have to go back and renegotiate or change fundamental parts of it. The intensity of the affective aspects of these processes can be somewhat appreciated if we think about all of the elaborate human rituals, songs, dances, tokens, celebrations, covenants, and legal apparatus that are connected to the resolution of these processes.

Most of the discussion of this principle has focused on how it applies to family life, but it also applies to developmental processes in individuals. This means that what a person does in response to developmental changes and processes has important implications for what that person can and will tend to do later in his or her life. There are many examples of this process in individuals. If students do not apply themselves academically, they gradually eliminate future opportunities that demand educational excellence. If a person becomes proficient with a musi-cal instrument, that person has choices that a person without that proficiency does not have.

When people learn early in life how to express themselves orally and in writing, these skills open up many avenues that would otherwise be closed to them. When people learn social skills, or when they do not develop social skills, these characteristics influence what they can and cannot do the rest of their lives. This principle is a useful idea, but there are many aspects of it that we do not yet understand, and more research needs to be done on the subject. For example, some of the "rules" that are created early in relationships seem to change easily at later times, but some are very resistant to change. We do not yet know very much about which "rules" operate which way and why. These are some of the unknowns that future analysis, theorizing, and research can help address.

Discussions in Diversity: Adoption and Family Change

A True Story

The Gerritsens were already considered a fairly large family with their four chil-dren—3 boys (ages 5, 8, and 11) and a girl (3). They were a busy family; both parents worked full time and children participated in drum lessons, piano lessons, weekly church youth group activities, and an afterschool STEM program. The family enjoyed hiking, swimming, and *American Ninja Warrior*. In fact, the parents (Todd and Lucy) were busy preparing to run a Spartan together with some friends when their lives took an enormous and unexpected turn. At a Spartan group weightlifting session, Lucy was confronted with an opportunity and a challenge. One of her friends there mentioned that she knew two children, a five-year-old

FIGURE 12.4 Adding foster and adopted children to a family can result in numerous family changes and transitions that can be both challenging and uplifting.

girl and a three-year-old-boy, who were in foster care and would soon need an adoptive family. For reasons unknown to Lucy, she sent a text message to Todd that included a picture of the children and a message: "These kids are up for adoption. Want 2 more kids? 3 and 5?" Inexplicably, Todd, who had decided four children was enough, immediately responded, "Awwww. Who are they? How did you hear? Let's do it."

With that brief text exchange, the Gerritsens began the process of change and transition on many levels! Their **schedule and time commitments changed** as they attended 3-hour foster care training meetings each week, met with state and agency caseworkers, prepared for home inspections, scheduled inspections and interviews during lunch breaks when both parents could attend, and drove 1 hour each way to pick up and drop off the children for overnight weekend stays. As the kids spent more time with the Gerritsens and eventually moved in, the whole family had to adjust to sharing parent attention across six children. The Gerritsens also experienced **changes in privacy and boundaries** as children and parents were individually interviewed at the beginning of the foster care process and, later, as case workers checked on the well-being of children in the home regularly and required accident reports when children received even minor injuries. Further, each child experienced adjustments in their sleeping arrangements as they changed rooms and gained roommates.

Gender dynamics even changed. Not only did the gender ratio shift, but now a three-year-old girl (formerly the only girl) had an older sister who introduced her to dolls and Disney Princesses she had never been aware of. **Changes in finances** were negotiated as the Gerritsens purchased a new car, two sets of bunk beds, drank 5 gallons of milk every few days, put children into extracurricular activities, and began receiving a foster/adoption subsidy. **Responsibilities and relationships changed** for each member of the family as parental rights were severed, children learned to trust new parents (seeking a hug rather than running away when injured), an oldest brother helped oversee five younger siblings, children learned how to supportively talk to each other about families of origin and experiences, and parents juggled work and changing family expectations. As time went on, the entire **form of their family changed**. Todd and Lucy met the children's grandparents, aunts/uncles, cousins, foster parents, foster grandparents, and learned about previously unknown half-siblings, expanding their definition of family. In time, all 6 of Todd and Lucy's children would consider themselves to have 11 grandparents, along with a number of new aunts, uncles, and cousins. And then, there was **COVID-19**, which caused all-encompassing change, including closed schools, online learning, reduced opportunities for family excursions, disconnection from friends, and negotiating work from home. All of these transitions and changes were experienced over the course of 12 months! Ultimately, the adoption was finalized after an unceremonious Zoom meeting from their living room, with the judge pronouncing the Gerritsens a legal family of 8.

Looking back on the process, the Gerritsens marvel at the change, transitions, and, somehow, stability they experienced. Their transition from a family of 6 to a family of 8 and from a foster family to a permanent, legal family (now consisting of children ages 4, 4, 6, 6, 9, and 12) was challenging, as every family member experienced changes in trust, communication, scheduling, space, traditions, rituals, rules, and even roles (Todd and Lucy will always remember the feeling of moving from "Todd" and "Lucy" to "Dad" and "Mom"). Although it now feels natural to be a family of eight, the Gerritsens continue to confront change and transition as their children grow and develop and, relatedly, begin to ask new and more complicated questions. Yet, despite the changes, they found stability throughout the process in their commitment to support each other, talk openly, and shoulder each other's challenges (Figure 12.4). Today, the Gerritsens find it difficult to remember life without these six wonderful children, and they laugh at the days when they thought it would be impossible to go out in public with more than four!

Questions to Discuss:

- *How might genetics influence this family's experience?*
- *The Gerritsens already had a four-year-old girl and six-year-old boy when they adopted a four-year-old boy and six-year-old girl. How do you think having siblings the same age but opposite gender, might compare to having siblings the same age and same gender?*
- *Identify internal and external changes that confronted this family.*
- *Can you identify actions that made the transition to a family of six children smoother for this family?*
- *Speculate about potential examples of morphostasis and morphogenesis the family experienced.*

SUMMARY

In this chapter, we explored the interrelationship between individual change and family system change. Individual family members bring much to the table of "family" and routine family processes. Often, family members have certain unchangeable traits and genetic predispositions that can and do influence what happens in the family. Further, we discussed gender and how it is socialized within the family. Gender influences many family processes and is often related to power differences within the family structure. Some families learn early on to dampen the effects of naturally occurring power imbalance. It is clear that inequity in relationships creates disharmony. A mistaken idea is that inequity is the same as equality. Inequity is not about equality and perfect role sharing. Instead, inequity is about fairness of role distribution, resources, and interpersonal caring (meaning when there is equity, we care for one another in ways that are fair and well-distributed). When there is inequity, interpersonal care favors the one with the most power and demand capability. As we move toward gender equity, it would stand to reason that the inner life of families would strengthen, become enriched, and become a source of great power. For most of us, it takes significant effort to generate power equity—but with that equity comes relationship strength.

The second half of the chapter focused on family system change and transitions. Some changes are predictable, in which case families can anticipate them and prepare for them. Most families tend to be similar in these predictable processes. Many family processes, however, are not predictable. These unpredictable processes create great variability in family and individual development.

We discussed ways families can manage transitions so they are as manageable and growth-producing as possible. The processes of morphogenesis, morphostasis, and epigenesis were discussed and illustrated, as well as several strategies for using these concepts. One of the main ideas in the chapter is that those of us who want to understand families should always be sensitive to processes of change. We should never ignore them, even when we are concentrating on other parts of family processes or other things that are known in the field. Developmental ideas should be integrated with the ideas about the family realm, generational dimensions, and affect to form an increasingly comprehensive and helpful set of ideas.

In short, individual and family change are inevitable. One of the key jobs of all humans is to learn how to cope with change, learn from the past, and move into the next phase gracefully.

STUDY QUESTIONS

1   What do you think is meant by individual family members being the "bedrock" of family systems?
2   What is the Human Genome Project and why was it featured in this chapter?
3   Reread Principle 12.1 and restate this in your own words. What is the importance of knowing about genetics in family life?
4   What is meant by "gendered parenting?" How does gender socialization influence a child's life course?
5   How is gender related to power in families? What is the primary connection?
6   What are the key effects of power imbalance in family life?
7   List several "predictable" patterns of family life. Why do we pay attention to these?
8   Explain the concept of "anticipatory socialization."

9 What is the difference between morphostasis and morphogenesis?
10 How can the epigenesis principle be applied using the information from this chapter?
11 What is role strain?
12 How can you tell if a role you are in is stressful?

KEY TERMS

Genes
Genome
Coding DNA
Noncoding DNA
Epigenomics
Epigenetics
Nature/nurture controversy
Behavioral genetics
Gender
Gendered parenting
Theybies
Power
Transition theory
Transitions vs. stages
Anticipatory socialization
Role strain
Morphogenesis
Morphostasis
Ambivalence
Epigenesis

SUGGESTED READINGS

Aspinwall, L. G., & Staundinger, U. M. (2003). *A psychology of human strengths: Fundamental questions and future directions for a positive psychology.* Washington, DC: American Psychological Association.

Bianchi, S., Robinson, J., & Milkie, M. (2006). *Changing rhythms of American life.* New York, NY: Russell Sage Foundation.

Bush, K. R., & Price, C. A. (Eds.). (2020). *Families & change: Coping with stressful events and transitions* (6th ed.). Thousand Oaks, CA: Sage.

Conger, R., Lorenz, F., & Wickrama, K. A. S. (2004). *Continuity and change in family relations.* Mahwah, NJ: Lawrence Erlbaum Associates.

Cowan, P., & Hetherington, M. (1991). *Family transitions.* Hillsdale, NJ: Lawrence Erlbaum Associates.

Feller, B. (2020). *Life is in transitions: Mastering change at any age.* New York, NY: Penguin Press.

Glazer-Malbin, N., Waehrer, H., & Youngelson, Y. (Eds.). (1973). *Woman in a man-made world: A socioeconomic handbook.* New York, NY: Rand McNally.

Mikulinger, M., & Shaver, P. (2007). *Attachment in adulthood: Structure, dynamics, and change.* New York, NY: Guilford.

Noller, P., & Feeney, J. (2001). *Personal relationships across the lifespan.* London: Psychology Press.

Reiss, D., Neiderhiser, J., Hetherington, M., & Plomin, R. (2000). *The relationship code: Deciphering genetic and social influences on adolescent development.* Cambridge, MA: Harvard University Press.

REFERENCES

Bader, E., Microys, G., Sinclair, C., Willet, E., & Conway, B. (1980). Do marriage preparation programs really work? A Canadian experiment. *Journal of Marriage and Family Therapy, 6*, 171–179.

Baker, C. (2004). *Behavioral genetics.* New York, NY: The American Association for the Advancement of Science and Hastings Center. http://www.aaas.org/sites/default/files/Intro.pdf

Baxter, J., Hewitt, B., & Haynes, M. (2008). Life course transitions and housework: Marriage, parenthood, and time on housework. *Journal of Marriage and Family, 70*(2), 259–272.

Booth, A., Carver, K., & Granger, D. A. (2000). Biosocial perspectives on the family. *Journal of Marriage and the Family, 62*, 1018–1034.

Booth, A., Johnson, D., & Granger, D. (2005). Testosterone, marital quality, and role overload. *Journal of Marriage and the Family, 67*, 483–503.

Bronfenbrenner, U. (1979). *The ecology of human development.* Cambridge, MA: Harvard University Press.

Burr, W. R. (1973). *Theory construction and the sociology of the family.* New York, NY: Wiley.

Burr, W. R., Leigh, G. K., Day, R. D., & Constantine, J. (1979). Symbolic interaction and the family. In W. R. Burr, R. Hill, F. I. Nye, & I. L. Reiss (Eds.), *Contemporary theories about the family* (Vol. 2, pp. 42–111). New York, NY: Free Press.

Carter, B., & McGoldrick, M. (Eds.). (1989). *The changing family life cycle: A framework for family therapy* (2nd ed.). New York, NY: Allyn & Bacon.

Castleberry, J. (2019). Addressing the gender continuum: A content analysis. *Journal of Transcultural Nursing, 30*(4), 403–409.

Cheriyedath, S. (2019). Epigenetics and epigenomics. *News Medical.* https://www.news-medical.net/life-sciences/Epigenetics-and-Epigenomics.aspx

Coleman, J., & Hoffer, T. (1987). *Public and private high schools.* New York, NY: Basic Books.

Condry, J., & Condry, S. (1976). Sex differences: A study of the eye of the beholder. *Child Development, 47*, 812–819.

Conger, K. (2017). Of mice, men, and women: Making research more inclusive. *Stanford Medicine.* https://stanmed.stanford.edu/2017spring/how-sex-and-gender-which-are-not-the-same-thing-influence-our-health.html

Cook, K., & Emerson, R. M. (1978). Power, equity, and commitment in exchange networks. *American Sociological Review, 43*, 721–739.

Cook, K. S., & Rice, E. R. W. (2001). Exchange and power: Issues of structure and agency. In J. H. Turner (Ed.), *Handbook of sociological theory* (pp. 221–260). New York, NY: Kluwer.

Cottrell, L. S. Jr. (1942). The adjustment of the individual to his age and sex roles. *American Sociological Review, 7*, 617–620.

Curry, A. (2019). A painful legacy. *Science* (American Association for the Advancement of Science). https://www.sciencemag.org/news/2019/07/parents-emotional-trauma-may-change-their-children-s-biology-studies-mice-show-how

D'Onofrio, B. M., & Lahey, B. B. (2010). Biosocial influences on the family: A decade review. *Journal of Marriage and the Family, 72*(3), 762–782.

D'Onofrio, B. M., Turkheimer, E. N., Emery, R. E., Harden, K. P., Slutske, W., Heath, A. … Martin, N. G. (2007). A genetically informed study of the intergenerational transmission of marital instability. *Journal of Marriage and Family, 69*, 793–803.

Davies, M. (2020). Raising theybies: Navigating within a gendered world. Master's Thesis. https://www.researchgate.net/publication/342512893_Raising_Theybies_Navigating_within_a_Gendered_World

Day, R. D., Gavazzi, S., & Acock, A. (2009). Compelling family processes. In A. Thornton (Ed.), *The well-being of children and families: Research and data needs.* Ann Arbor, MI: University of Michigan Press.

Day, R. D., Gavazzi, S. M., Miller, R., & Van Langeveld, A. (2009). Compelling family processes. *Marriage & Family Review, 45*, 116–128.

Dernberger, B. N., & Pepin, J. R. (2020). Gender flexibility but not equality: Young adults' division of labor preferences. *Social Science.* https://www.sociologicalscience.com/download/vol-7/january/SocSci_v7_36to56.pdf

Doucet, A. (2013). Gender roles and fathering. In N. J. Cabrera, & C. S. Tamis-LeMonda (Eds.), *Handbook of father involvement: Multidisciplinary perspectives* (pp. 297–319). New York, NY: Routledge.

Druckman, J. M. (1979). *Effectiveness of five types of pre-marital preparations programs*. Grand Rapids, MI: Education for Marriage.

Duvall, E. (1955). *Family development*. New York, NY: Lippincott.

Elder, G. (1985). *Life course dynamics*. Ithaca, NY: Cornell.

Goode, W. J. (1960). A theory of role strain. *American Sociological Review, 35*, 483–496.

Guerney, B., & Guerney, L. (1981). Family life education as intervention. *Family Relations, 30*, 591–598.

Haley, J. (1987). *Reflections on therapy and other essays*. Washington, DC: The Family Therapy Institute.

Halpern, H. P., & Perry-Jenkins, M. (2016). Parents' gender ideology and gendered behavior as predictors of children's gender-role attitudes: A longitudinal exploration. *Sex roles, 74*(11–12), 527–542.

Hyde, J. S., Bigler, R. S., Joel, D., Tate, C. C., & van Anders, S. M. (2019). The future of sex and gender in psychology: Five challenges to the gender binary. *American Psychologist, 74*(2), 171–193.

Jackson, D. D. (1957). The question of family homeostasis. *Psychiatric Quarterly Supplement, 31*, 79–90.

Jackson, D. D. (1963). Suggestion for the technical handling of paranoid patients. *Psychiatry, 26*, 306–307.

Karraker, K. H., Vogel, D. A., & Lake, M. A. (1995). Parents' gender-stereotyped perceptions of newborns: The eye of the beholder revisited. *Sex Roles, 33*(9), 687–701.

Kiyimba, N. (2016). Developmental trauma and the role of epigenetics. *BACP Healthcare Counselling and Psychotherapy Journal*, October, 18–21.

Klonsky, J., & Bengston, V. L. (1996). Pulling together, drifting apart: A longitudinal case study of a four-generation family. *Journal of Aging Studies, 10*, 255–279.

Krippner, S., & Barrett, D. (2019). Transgenerational trauma: The role of epigenetics. *The Journal of Mind and Behavior, 40*(1), 53–62.

Merton, R. K. (1968). *Social theory and social structure*. Glencoe, IL: Free Press.

Mesman, J., & Groeneveld, M. G. (2018). Gendered parenting in early childhood: Subtle but unmistakable if you know where to look. *Child Development Perspectives, 12*(1), 22–27.

Molm, L. D. (2003). Theoretical comparisons of forms of exchange. *Sociological Theory, 21*, 1–17.

Newport, F. (2011). Men tend to want boys; women are divided in their gender preferences. *Gallup*. https://news.gallup.com/poll/148187/Americans-Prefer-Boys-Girls-1941.aspx

NIH (2020). *Epigenomics fact sheet*. National Human Genome Research Institute. https://www.genome.gov/about-genomics/fact-sheets/Epigenomics-Fact-Sheet

NSF (February 3, 2011). The most genes in any animal? Tiny crustacean holds the record. New Release. https://www.nsf.gov/news/news_summ.jsp?cntn_id=118530#:~:text=The%20tiny%20water%20flea%20Daphnia,of%20any%20animal%2C%20some%2031%2C000.&text=Scientists%20have%20discovered%20that%20the,Daphnia%20pulex%2C%20or%20water%20flea

Painter, R. C., Osmond, C., Gluckman, P., Hanson, M., Phillips, D. I., & Roseboom, T. J. (2008). Transgenerational effects of prenatal exposure to the Dutch famine on neonatal adiposity and health in later life. *British Journal of Obstetrics and Gynaecology, 115*, 1243–1249.

Piovesan, A., Antonaros, F., Vitale, L., Strippoli, P., Pelleri, M. C., & Caracausi, M. (2019). Human protein-coding genes and gene feature statistics in 2019. *BMC Research Notes, 12*, 315. DOI: 10.1186/s13104-019-4343-8

Plomin, R. (1994). *Genetics and experience: The interplay between nature and nurture*. Thousand Oaks, CA: Sage.

Reiss, D. (1995a). Genetic influence on family systems: Implications for development. *Journal of Marriage and the Family, 57*, 543–560.

Reiss, D. (1995b). Genetic questions for environmental studies: Differential parenting and psychopathology in adolescence. *Archives of General Psychiatry, 52*, 925–936.

Rothblum, E. D. (2017). Division of workforce and domestic labor among same-sex couples. In R. Connelly, & E. Kongar (Eds.), *Gender and time use in a global context* (pp. 283–303). New York, NY: Palgrave Macmillan.

Rowe, D. C. (1994). *The limits of family influence: Genes, experience, and behavior*. New York, NY: Guilford.

Rözer, J., Mollenhorst, G., & Volker, B. (2018). Families' division of labor and social networks in the 21st century: Revisiting Elizabeth Bott's classic hypotheses. *Journal of Family Issues, 39*(13), 3436–3462.

Rubin, J. Z., Provenzano, F. J., & Luria, Z. (1974). The eye of the beholder: Parents' views on sex of newborns. *American Journal of Orthopsychiatry, 44*(4), 512.

Shafer, K., Scheibling, C., & Milkie, M. A. (2020). The division of domestic labor before and during the COVID-19 pandemic in Canada: Stagnation versus shifts in fathers' contributions. *Canadian Review of Sociology/Revue canadienne de sociologie*, *57*(4), 523–549.

Tornello, S. L. (2020). Division of labor among transgender and gender non-binary parents: Association with individual, couple, and children's behavioral outcomes. *Frontiers in Psychology*, *11*, 15.

Waerdahl, R. (2005). Maybe I'll need a pair of Levi's before junior high? Child to youth trajectories and anticipatory socialization. *Childhood: A Global Journal of Child Research*, *12*, 201–222.

White, J. (2005). *Advancing family theories*. Thousand Oaks, CA: Sage.

Youssef, N. A., Lockwood, L., Su, S., Hao, G., & Rutten, B. P. F. (2018). The effects of trauma, with or without PTSD, on the transgenerational DNA methylation alterations in human offspring. *Brain Sciences*, *8*, 83–90.

CHAPTER 13

Family Stress and Resilience

CHAPTER PREVIEW

In this chapter, readers will learn:

- How considering a family strengths perspective provides a different view of family.
- Many processes influence family resilience.
- The difference between theories and models and how these relate to family stress.
- Many different "stressor events" can create stress in family life.
- Some stressor events are more serious than others. Also, some of them come from the environment, others come from inside the family, some are expected, and some are not.
- Family stress theory takes many forms. One of the most used is the ABC-X model of family crisis.
- Developmental processes and predictable patterns exist in the way family stress is managed. Recent research has identified five different ways families respond to stress.
- How research about families has begun to identify coping strategies that families can use to deal effectively with stressful situations.
- That some simple coping strategies seem to be helpful and several can be less effective in certain stressful situations.
- How recent research has begun to identify coping strategies that deal with more fundamental changes in family processes.
- How the Circumplex Model of Family Interaction can be used for research, therapy, and self-reflection.

INTRODUCTION

A fascinating saying is "May you live in interesting times!" Although it sounds like a blessing, it is considered a curse recognizing that change can be difficult. Challenges such as death in a family, loss of a home, or a serious injury can create stress in individuals and also in the entire family unit. Even positive life challenges, such as a new baby or a new job can create such stress. In some situations, stress can be severe, disabling, and enormously difficult. In other situations, the stress is more temporary, fleeting, and easy to cope with. An important concept in this chapter is that stress and crisis are common occurrences in families. Most families find

DOI: 10.4324/9781003128717-17

themselves coping with stress, and it is not uncommon for several stressors to occur at the same time. This chapter describes the various types of stressor events that families experience and the effects they have on family processes. It also summarizes what is known about enabling and disabling strategies that families tend to use. A central focus of this chapter is the ABC-X model of crisis. By understanding this theoretical idea, we can begin to not only understand crisis better, but understand how to better intervene as families experience crisis.

FAMILY STRESS AND FAMILY RESILIENCE THEORY

> If there is no struggle, there is no progress.
>
> Frederick Douglass (former slave, abolitionist, author)

Several theories and theoretical orientations have been presented throughout this text. The theory of **family stress and resiliency** explored here has been utilized by family researchers and practitioners for around 75 years and is a signature element of family process research. This research has an important characteristic. Instead of focusing on a *deficit* approach to family well-being, this theoretical orientation focuses on the *strengths and abilities* of families. A deficit approach is much more common in family research; for example, researchers focus on how children suffer during divorce. However, when we focus on what is strong in families and how they use **resources**, we gain a different view into the way most families approach daily life. We explore the idea of resources and protective mechanisms, such as life philosophy, problem solving ability, and communications skills, later. First, though, we need to start with definitions.

Family Resilience

The concept of resilience began when researchers focused on children who were experiencing adversity (Garmezy, 1991; Masten, 1994; Patterson, 2002). McCubbin et al. (1980) brought to light the idea of resilience and used the concept in their emerging research about military families. They noted that families undergoing harsh stressor events (e.g., the loss of a husband in combat) could adapt to the situation when they had a larger bank of resources from which to draw. Following that tradition, Patterson (2002) stated that resilience is "the phenomena of doing well in the face of adversity" (p. 350). Families that do well in the face of adversity are ones who have a strong resource base and protective mechanisms in place.

Patterson (2002) reminds us that there are several problems in understanding this concept, as it has been defined in various ways by researchers resulting in some confusion. First, the idea of resilience is sometimes used to denote an outcome. That is, we note that a family is doing well, and we code them as resilient. Second, when thinking about resilience, do we consider just the individual's well-being or the family collective? Third, some researchers think of resilience in terms of protective factors. These are resources or attributes a family (or individual) possesses that keeps them from experiencing the force of a power stressor event.

Froma Walsh is the leading authority on **family resilience**. She developed an empirically based framework that has been used to assist families dealing with adversity. According to Walsh (2016), "A basic premise in systems theory is that serious crises and persistent life challenges have an impact on the whole family, and in turn, key family processes mediate adaptation (or maladaptation) for all individual members, their relationships, and the family unit." Walsh posits

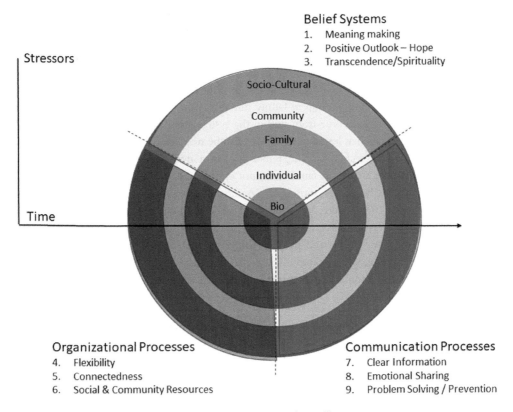

Belief Systems
1. Meaning making
2. Positive Outlook – Hope
3. Transcendence/Spirituality

Stressors

Socio-Cultural

Community

Family

Individual

Bio

Time

Organizational Processes
4. Flexibility
5. Connectedness
6. Social & Community Resources

Communication Processes
7. Clear Information
8. Emotional Sharing
9. Problem Solving / Prevention

FIGURE 13.1 Walsh's multilevel recursive processes in resilience.

Source: Adapted from Walsh (2016)

that resilience is more than successfully negotiating "stressful conditions, shouldering a burden, or surviving an ordeal"; rather, it provides the groundwork for personal and family growth and transformation. She mapped out nine key transactional processes in family resilience, attempting to capture the dynamism of families across time and within relationships (Figure 13.1). As seen on the figure, the nine key processes interact with the socio-cultural, community, family, individual, and biological systems.

Family Stress

The terms *theories* and *models* are often used interchangeably, but they are different (Wunsch, 1994). A theory is a generalized statement designed to explain particular phenomena. A model reflects reality and is often a schematic representation of reality. Models are used to describe applications of theories. So, theories are often expressed by models and models incorporate theories. As a result, you are likely to see these terms used interchangeably outside this text.

In the 1960s, psychologist Richard S. Lazarus developed the **transactional theory of stress** and coping. This theory has undergone significant revisions over the years, as is the case with most theories. It is based on the idea that stress does not lie within the person, nor within the environment; rather stress is in the transaction between the person and environment and the person's appraisal of the situation (Dewe, 2013). Thus, this theory focuses on the effects of stress on the individual.

Family stress theory, however, is an umbrella framework that examines the effects of stress on the entire family system and has been developing since the late 1940s. All families experience **family stress**, which we will define as a disturbance to the family system. Some stress is mild and barely causes a blip in family function, other stress results in severe crisis for the family. Family stress can come from within the system itself (such as a child becoming ill) or outside the system (such as losing a job). It can also be **normative** (something expected that most families face, such as a child entering puberty) or **non-normative** (something unexpected and specific to a family that most families do not experience, such as a parent dying in war). **Stressors** are the specific events, stimuli, or conditions that cause stress. The father of stress research, Hans Selye (1974) referred to stress that is seen as an opportunity for growth and has positive consequences as **eustress**; stress that has negative consequences is **distress**.

Stressors have been categorized in many different ways depending on who is creating the categories. Psychologists, sociologists, physicians, and counselors all have various ways of looking at stress and stressors. For our purposes, we'll consider three different levels of family stressors (Burr & Klein, 1994):

- **Level 1 stressors** are those events that are disruptive to the family but the change the family experiences is temporary. Families may need to temporarily change or rearrange family rules and responsibilities. For example, if Martiana forgot to take her signed field trip permission form to school, a family member may need to stop what they are doing and take the form to school. Other examples might be a refrigerator breaking or the dog escaping. Some of these stressors may be worse for some families than others. One family with plenty of money will hardly flinch at a refrigerator breaking but another family might have much greater difficulty.

- **Level 2 stressors** are those events that are not as easily solved and may even require some outside help. For these stressors, the normal way of handling things and interacting don't work, and the problems can't be resolved with the usual array of rules, rituals, patterns of daily living, or available resources. This type of stressor is not a missing permission slip; rather, it may be learning that your child has extreme ADHD or learning problems. Telling the child to do extra homework or stop playing video games is unlikely to help in this situation. The stressor may also result in additional stresses to the family, such as financial and emotional challenges.

- **Level 3 stressors** are those events that shake the family to its core. These are so serious that attempts to regroup are impossible and may push the family to high levels of disruption. Indeed, "the very fabric of the family is in trouble" (p. 49). Families experiencing Level 1 and 2 disruptions eventually return to their "normal" state of functioning. For Level 3, this is not the case and families may find themselves questioning the goals and beliefs they have mutually established. An example of this type of stressor might be coming home unexpectedly and finding your partner in bed with someone else. Such situations can be resolved but likely the family underpinnings will change dramatically.

Consider the dynamism of family, confronted daily with stressors at each level and even changing across time. For example, one family's son woke up with what appeared to be a cold (Level 1). Twenty-four hours later, his cold had become so severe that the son needed to be hospitalized

(Level 2). Within a few days, their active, healthy almost 15-year-old son was near death and quadriplegic (Level 3). It's not difficult to imagine the disruptions, changes, questioning of beliefs and actions that this family experienced! Today, with family and professional support, including intensive physical therapy, the young man is walking and attending college and the family is stronger than ever.

This case leads to the concept of **crisis**. Most people think of crisis as a calamity or something terrible happening. For our purposes, we will return to its original meaning: *krisis* is Greek for "decide"; *a decisive point in the progress of a disease* or *a vitally important state of things, point at which change must come, for better or worse* (etymonline.com). Thus, for us, crisis is when the old ways of doing things in the family don't work and decisions must be made as a result. Some family stressors are handled with minimal disruptions; other stressors, because of the number or severity or lack of family resources, can lead to crisis. For the family, crisis is a turning point where change must be made for better or worse.

ABC-X MODEL OF FAMILY STRESS

When reading the academic literature related to family stress, one rarely fails to come across the **ABC-X** model or some version of it (Figure 13.2). Researchers, scholars, and practitioners reference it for a variety of family experiences, including having children with autism, disaster stressors, cancer, divorce, neglect, developmental disabilities, and even work/family strategies during COVID-19. You will also find this model being used internationally, from Iran to Korea to Canada (see "Discussions in Diversity" below). Many iterations of family stress models have been created but almost all of them contain similar elements. So perhaps it helps to start with the founding father of family sociology and key family researcher, Reuben Hill (1912–1985).

Most family stress models stem from Hill's work (Olson & Boss, 1986). In 1949, Hill published his first book, *Families Under Stress*. This book was based on Hill's study of 135 military families from Iowa struggling after the fathers' separation and reunion in WWII. Hill found that families may experience a similar stressful event but the outcome of that event on the family varied, with some families doing better than others. As a result, he began crafting a theory for why this was so. Through diligent study and work, he found two factors that influenced the

FIGURE 13.2 The ABC-X model of crisis has been used in family research for almost 75 years.

outcome of stressful events on families. As a result, he developed the first family stress model, the ABC-X model. In this model, (A) is the stressful event (i.e., "stressor") and (X) is the outcome for the family. The B and C elements are the factors that influence that outcome, with (B) the resources the family has available and (C) how the family perceives the event (Hill, 1958).

> **PRINCIPLE 13.1**
>
> ## THE ABC-X MODEL OF CRISIS
>
> The ABC-X model of crisis helps us organize how we think about stressor events, available resources, and how the stressor event is defined by the family or individual. These elements mix and shape the X part of the process, which is how much disruption results from the stressor event(s). See Figure 13.4.

A—Stressor Events

> In our view family stress is often greatest at transition points from one stage to another of the family developmental process, and symptoms are most likely to appear when there is an interruption or dislocation in the unfolding family life cycle.
>
> (Carter & McGoldrick, 1989, pp. 4–5)

A stressor event is something that happens to a family that cannot be managed effectively within the family's normal ways of doing things (McCubbin & Patterson, 1982). Some stressor events tend to cause more disruption in family processes than others. Holmes and Rahe (1967) developed a method of ranking the relative magnitude of various stressor events (from disasters to having a baby). Their findings demonstrate the large number of stressors families encounter and show us that these events occur in many different times, transitions, and aspect of everyday life.

Stressors come in all shapes and sizes. Some stressors are single events, while others drag on. For example, stressors can be things we lose. We refer to this as **dismemberment** (Hill, 1958). Families may experience the loss of a child, a home, a parent, or a job. Some losses are **ambiguous losses** (Boss, 1999). In ambiguous losses, a person or family suffers from lack of closure related to a situation often surrounding the loss, physical or emotional, of a loved one; the person may be physically absent but still emotionally present or even physically present but emotionally absent. For example, a foster child may suffer grief at the ambiguous loss of her biological mother. She may talk about her and desire to return to her even while being loved and cared for by a foster parent. Similarly, a person might suffer an ambiguous loss related to a parent's dementia. The body of the parent is present, but the "person" part seems far away. Because of the lack of clarity in these situations, ambiguous loss is difficult to overcome and may influence the entire family system.

Not all stressors are negative. Sometimes we gain things that can result in family stress because our usual ways of adapting do not work very well. This is called **accession** (Hill, 1958). Getting married, having a baby, starting a job, and even winning the lottery result in disruption in family interactions. That newborn baby is adorable but new parents are often unprepared for the juggling of roles and physical demands created by this little creature.

FIGURE 13.3 Some crises are very devastating and create a multitude of cascading stressor events.

Many families experience stressors that are **demoralizing** to the family and result in difficulty coping. For example, suicide, having a child drop out of school, bankruptcy, or a parent who is an alcoholic can be demoralizing. These are things we rarely share with the outside world because of the stigma attached. Most demoralizing events are accompanied by gains and losses that challenge the family's normal ways of doing things.

When stressor events come one at a time, it is easier for families to cope with them. However, it is common for several stressor events to happen at the same time, and for new ones to occur while the family is still dealing with previous stressor events (Figure 13.3). When this happens, it increases the difficulty families have in coping effectively with the new inputs. McCubbin and Patterson (1982) used the term **stress pile-up** to refer to the stress that families experience from several changes occurring simultaneously, or several occurring in a short period of time before the initial stressor events are solved or resolved. Many of us have experienced "the straw that broke the camel's back" phenomenon, where a small stressor (added on top of many stressors) finally results in an eruption!

B—Resources Available

The B part of the ABC-X model of family stress focuses our attention on the resources families or family members can use when faced with stressors. **Resources** refer to the set of complex external and internal emotional, cognitive, physical, social, and material supports that families can draw upon when needed.

Resources that reside within the family's control may be scant or vast in their quantity. A family with a good sum of money in their checking account will have less trouble replacing a lawnmower destroyed in a garage fire or fixing their daughter's broken ankle. Families will also have less trouble if they have good insurance for the garage and for the broken ankle. Resources, however, are not just financial. Social capital, found in family, friends, and community, is one of the most powerful resources a family can tap into. The social capital we have in reserve resides within the relationships we nurture and maintain. For example, when a child is injured at home, a conversation with the neighbor, who happens to be a nurse, will be richer and perhaps more helpful/positive if we have invested in that relationship prior to the stressor event (or prior to the injury). Although stress sometimes brings us together with our neighbors, those relationships can be much more powerful (as a resource) if the building blocks of trust, reciprocal friendship, and mutual sharing have occurred before the need arises.

Internal resources include traits, characteristics, and abilities of family members that can be used to meet a demand. Previous experience handling similar demands builds problem solving capabilities. A sense of self-efficacy (the belief that "I can do it!"), high self-esteem, and sense of optimism developed within family members can help the entire family facing family stressors. Family characteristics can also help. Probably the most important family resources for managing stress are family **cohesion** (We stick together!) and **adaptation** (We can figure this out and adjust!). When families are faced with any level of disruption, family outcomes can be directly ameliorated by the bank of resources available.

C—Definition of the Situation

Hill's "C" variable is also known as the perception factor. Remember that symbolic interaction theory places a great deal of emphasis on how the person or family collectively defines the world and the daily events of life that surround them. Renowned sociologist and theorist, William Thomas wrote, "If people define situations as real, they are real in their consequences" (Thomas & Thomas, 1928, p. 594). How does the family perceive the stressor? Do they see it as a disaster or as an opportunity? For instance, some families perceived the loss of employment during the COVID-19 pandemic as a disaster; others (perhaps with more resources) perceived it as an opportunity to grow a new business, start a new hobby, or spend more time with family. In short, a family's response isn't to "what is" (objectively) but rather to what the family perceives it to be.

X—Outcomes

Families are faced with stressors ("A") that are influenced by the resources the family has ("B") and how the family perceives the situation ("C"). The "**X Factor**" refers to the outcomes or level of disruption and disorganization experienced by the family and depends on the family's resources and perceptions. Families usually experience disruptions but recover; however, this is not always the case, especially if the family experiences multiple or new stressors and are socially isolated or emotionally disconnected from each other. If families' old ways of solving problems don't seem to work in resolving new situations, the result may be family crisis and a need to change.

All kinds of stressor events necessitate changes in family life, but stressor events that the family does not know how to handle, with its available rules, traditions, and patterns of interaction, are particularly problematic to family members. They must rethink how they approach such situations and find new resources, learn new skills, and somehow adapt.

Imagine a family, for example, who has had no experience dealing with the juvenile courts. The family is sitting in front of the house when a police car drives up and an officer informs the family that he is there to arrest their 17-year-old daughter. The event is foreign to them (in this case), and they might not have the requisite variety of experience, problem-solving skills, or resources to know how to deal with the situation. For most, this situation would be a life-changing stressor event. If it were to happen again with another child, chances are they

FIGURE 13.4 Crisis can be like a rollercoaster. The downside of the rollercoaster is some-times used to depict the idea that as the stressor events occur, the family becomes more disorganized.

would not be nearly as disrupted as in the first case. With experience and learning, we adapt, grow, and are better able to deal with similar future events.

Patterns in Family Stress: Putting It All Together

When a stressor event occurs in a family, a number of processes can evolve. If the family is able to cope quickly, the normal family processes will not be as disrupted, and the family will be able to resume their normal routines and traditions. However, if the stressor event is serious enough that the family is not able to adjust quickly, other patterns will emerge.

Two kinds of patterns can emerge when a stressor event is so severe that the old ways of solving things do not work: an *acute phase* in which energy is directed toward minimiz-ing the impact of the stress, and a *reorganization phase* in which the new reality is faced and accepted (McCubbin & Dahl, 1985, p. 154). The acute stage of family stress is usually a short, disorganized period of time. During this time, families try to examine the breadth and width of the problem, they try to get routines back to "normal," and they might attempt breaking the situation into manageable parts, getting their emotions under control, and trying to get information about the problem.

During the reorganization stage, families are creating new rules, changing the ways they relate, gradually coming to terms with their emotions, getting help from others if they need it, trying to be adaptable, and learning how to accept the new realities. In this phase, the family gradually recovers, and in some situations, may end better off than they were before the stressor event. For example, it might be stressful to move, but if the economic condition of the family improves after the move, the "normal" level of organization for the family might be higher. In other situations, a family might never recover fully from a stressor event, and the new "normal" level might be lower than before the crisis. This often occurs with problems such as a child in a family running away, conflict that cannot be resolved, loss of trust in a relationship, alcoholism and other forms of substance abuse, and economic losses.

When family scientists first began to study family stress in the 1930s and 1940s, they assumed that all families went through this "rollercoaster" pattern of adjustment that was first described by Koos (1946). Recent research suggests that Koos's rollercoaster pattern is an accurate description of the developmental pattern for *some* but not *all* families. Burr and Klein (1994) interviewed families who had experienced six different types of stress, and they found the rollercoaster pattern was the response pattern only about half of the time. They found the five different developmental patterns. About 18% of their families experienced a pattern they called increased effectiveness, in which family life became better as a result of the stressful situation, and the families did not experience a period of disorganization. In 10% of the families the response pattern was no change; family life did not improve or get worse. About 5% of the families experienced decreased effectiveness, and 11% had a mixed pattern where they initially were better off and then experienced the rollercoaster pattern. The Harker and Taylor research helps us realize there are several different developmental patterns in the way families respond to stress.

There is a paradox in these insights. We usually do not think about stressful situations being desirable. We assume they bring pain, discomfort, anxiety, frustration, and anguish. Therefore, we usually assume it is better if we can avoid problems. Although it is true that life would be simpler and less painful, it also is apparently true that when we back off and take a long-term view of life, we realize that stressful situations also can have beneficial aspects. Ironically, when we look at the total life span and its experiences, we realize that some stress and problems help us grow, develop, learn, and become stronger.

One reason it is often "desirable" to encounter difficulties and stress is that sometimes when we experience pain, frustration, disappointment, tragedies, and other adversities we also may experience the deepest and most satisfying joy, happiness, and sense of accomplishment and fulfillment, such as the joy that comes from being needed and from nursing loved ones who are ill. For example, the challenge of caring for a child with a disability can bring bonds of closeness, learning about the richness of sacrificing, abilities to be patient and loving, and insights about the subtle beauties of the human spirit that can be deeply rewarding.

Expansion of ABC-X

Hill's ABC-X model has been studied and significantly expanded. McCubbin and Patterson (1982) proposed the **double ABC-X** model based on their longitudinal study of families. Their model tries to capture the dynamics of the family system, although even this model has been criticized as being ultimately static (Smith, 1984). These scholars also viewed the ABC-X model as a family's response to a stressor but not a crisis. You can compare the two models in Figure 13.5.

As you can see, the Double ABC-X model incorporates Hill's original model as well as post crisis variable (Rosino, 2016; Weber, 2013). In this model, family stress is defined as an imbalance between the demands (A) and the family's resources (B), with the (C) factor influencing the impact. If the imbalance is too great to overcome and the family defines it as a crisis, then more than likely the family will experience crisis. Notice the incorporation of **coping** into the process. The difference between resources (B) and coping is that resources are what a family has available to them and coping is what the family actually does. Sometimes, families may have resources available to them but not utilize them because they don't realize they are available, they don't know how to access them, or they chose not to utilize them.

Family Stress Theory and the ABC-X model have been elaborated on and expanded in unique ways. We recently became aware of a study in Korea using the "Triple ABC-X" model (Ju, Kweon, & Park, 2017) examining co-dependency in families. The use of Family Stress Theory and the ABC-X model have much empirical support, including application with diverse families, and remains a ripe area for continued study (Masarik & Conger, 2017).

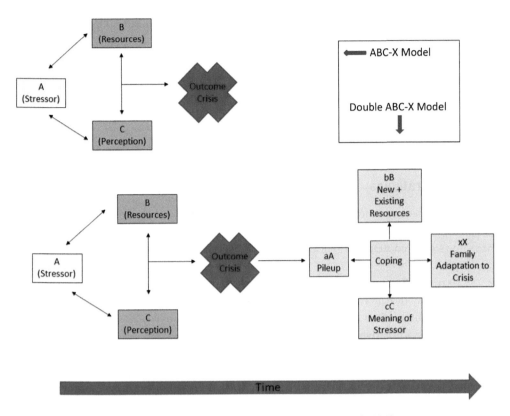

FIGURE 13.5 Illustration adapted from McCubbin and Patterson (1983).

COPING WITH THE X FACTOR: STRATEGIES FAMILIES USE

One of the goals of scientists who have studied family stress has been to identify **coping strategies** families find helpful in dealing with stressful situations. This research began in the 1930s (Angell, 1936), and there are now a large number of studies that have discovered many helpful strategies (Boss, 1987; McCubbin, Boss, Wilson & Lester, 1980; McCubbin, Balling, Possin, Frierdich & Bryne, 2002; Taylor & Conger, 2017).

Coping strategies are processes, behaviors, or patterns of behaviors that families go through to adapt to stress (McCubbin & Dahl, 1985). According to Pearlin and Schooler (1982), having a large repertoire of coping strategies is more important than using one or two strategies well. They stated:

> It is apparent from the foregoing analyses that the kinds of responses and resources people are able to bring to bear in coping with life-strains make a difference to their emotional well-being … (there is no magic wand). The magical wand does not appear in our results, and this suggests that having a particular weapon in one's arsenal is less important than having a variety of weapons.
>
> (Pearlin & Schooler, 1982, p. 127)

As you consider the following strategies, it is important to keep in mind that one of the first generalizations developed in family stress research is the idea that being flexible, pliable, or willing to change is helpful. Family scientists refer to this as **adaptability**. This idea goes back decades (e.g., Angell, 1936) and has been found again and again to be an important coping strategy (Boss, 1987; McCubbin et al., 1988). Adaptability is, in essence, the ability to be flexible and try something new. Families with this ability tend to be more accepting of change and therefore roll with the punches, so to speak. Families who are relatively adaptable are also more willing to try other coping strategies at all levels of change. In addition, this willingness to try more coping strategies will end up helping the family be more proficient at the use of a wider variety of coping strategies, which increases their requisite variety.

Enabling Strategies

Research has been conducted on various stressor events, and several strategies seem to be helpful in dealing with all of them and in all of the developmental stages of family stress. Following are some suggested strategies (but these aren't all inclusive):

- **Cognitive Strategies. Cognitive strategies** are approaches families take intellectually or mentally to help them cope with stress. Having an optimistic or positive attitude when faced with problems is an effective coping strategy (Innstrand, 2008). Practical methods of keeping a **positive attitude** include focusing on the positive aspects of life, visualizing a good outcome, and finding ways to help feel in control of the situation. When people have confidence in their ability to cope with a situation, they tend to have different "striving behaviors" than when they believe they are defeated. They invest more energy and try harder. They tend to focus on solutions rather than the overwhelming aspects of the problem situation, and this makes them more effective in finding and implementing solutions. These attitudes can be contagious, and others often work harder and more effectively when a positive attitude prevails. A positive attitude can simultaneously exist with realism, a good knowledge of the realities of situations, and efforts toward solving problems. What this idea means is that the definition of the situation tends to have a predictable influence on how seriously stressor events influence families and on how families tend to cope.

  Another cognitive strategy is **getting accurate information**. In their research about how families cope with serious illnesses, such as leukemia, Kaplan, Smith, Grobstien, and Fischman (1973) found that it helps families if they get accurate information as soon as possible. It seems as though this would be an obvious thing to do, but research about how families actually operate in stressful situations indicates a large number of families do not do this well. Their most common reaction is to deny the reality of the diagnosis. Such parents avoid those who refer to the illness as leukemia. They themselves use euphemisms (e.g., virus, anemia, blood disease) in speaking of the child's illness. They might even be fearful that the child will hear the news from someone outside the family (Kaplan et al., 1973). The Kaplan research team found that it is helpful if all the family members who are mature enough to understand are informed about the nature of the problem and the seriousness of it. Having accurate and prompt information allows the family to properly mourn if necessary, to face up to future consequences, to make plans, and to take realistic action (Kaplan et al., 1973).

  Another cognitive aspect of coping relates to the **perceived source of stressor events**. When stressor events are precipitated by events outside the family, families tend to deal with them more easily and effectively. This implies that, in the acute stage of coping, it can be helpful to externalize blame when possible. When it is not possible to attribute the blame outside the family, it is important for the family to deal with blame carefully. If someone in the family is blamed for the stressor event, the blaming itself tends to be another stressor event that can create a number of emotional, interpersonal, and perceptual reactions.

- **Communication Strategies.** A number of communication strategies help families dealing with stress. Just having someone to "listen" and "try to understand" can be enormously helpful. Trying to be honest and open in communication also tends to be helpful in most families. Two other communication strategies that tend to be helpful are to be **empathetic** and sensitive to nonverbal **messages** (McCubbin & Figley, 1983).

- **Emotional Strategies.** Research about family stress documents that stressor events tend to create strong emotional reactions. For example, when couples discover they are not able to bear children it usually takes years to adjust to the deeply felt emotional reactions (Snowden & Snowden, 1984). With some stressor events, such as chronic illnesses, families find themselves dealing with and managing painful emotions over and over again. They get their feelings resolved at one stage of the illness, but as the illness moves to a new stage or new experiences occur, the emotional reactions resurface, and they need to deal again and again with feelings such as helplessness, loss, and "why does this happen?"

According to McCubbin et al. (1988), the management of emotions involves two fairly different processes: (a) being aware of the emotions and fatigue, and (b) finding constructive ways to release or come to terms with the emotions. When emotions become intense, they tend to "take over," incapacitate a family, and interfere with the process of coping with the stressful event.

Families who are effective at coping with stress gradually learn that when emotions become intense, the attempts to "be sensible," "reasonable," and "get things done" need to be set aside temporarily while the emotional reactions are dealt with. To ignore the emotions, pretend they do not exist, or tell people they "shouldn't feel that way" does not eliminate them. It just forces the emotions into the part of the family iceberg that is below the surface, where family members are not aware of what is going on. Usually what happens in these situations is the emotions surface in other ways. Some examples of other ways emotions can surface are people getting angry at minor incidents, losing their temper often, developing physical illnesses such as having an upset stomach or always being tired or depressed, turning to excesses with alcohol or sex, and so on. Therefore, emotions that are involved in a stressful experience need to be dealt with, so they do not make coping more difficult. This can be facilitated by using the family as a collective support group, hugging, talking with others, being close, crying, reassuring, listening, getting feelings out, and being around loved ones.

- **System Strategies.** The various parts of family life tend to be intertwined. Therefore, changes in one part of the family tend to influence other parts. Kaplan et al. (1973) recognized this interdependence and suggested that it is helpful if the individuals in families can cope and mourn together when serious stressor events occur. A family can offer its individual members the potential for mutual support and access to its collective coping experience. According to Hill (1958), when helping an individual cope or handle stress, the individual should be treated as a family member not as an independent individual. Thus, the idea that the family realm has more impact than most people realize emerges again. The emotional, generational, and other ties to the family are so great that they are dealt with the most effectively when there is a network of family members who are involved. Families who can lean on each other have an advantage when dealing with life's problems. As McCubbin Thompson, Pirner, & McCubbin (1988) observed, maintaining family togetherness, even by taking the time to do little things with the children and plan family outings, is an effective coping strategy for dealing with family stress.

- **Spiritual Strategies.** Many families find it helpful to turn to spiritual sources for strength, meaning, and assistance when they are experiencing family stress, and research documents the benefits of spiritual resources (Walsh, 1999). Spiritual strategies can include praying, trying to have more faith, seeking help from one's God, accepting support from one's religious community, and becoming more involved in religious activities.

- **Environmental Strategies.** Families can do many things with their environment to help them cope with stress. When information is exchanged between the family and environment, it is called *social support* and provides families with (a) emotional support, leading recipients to believe they are cared for and loved, (b) self-esteem, leading them to believe they are valued, and (c) network support, which gives them a sense of belonging (Cobb, 1982). Support can come from family members, friends, work, clubs, police, churches, and so on. In addition to varying in *source*, social support also can vary in its *type*. It can be emotional, financial, physical, mental, and so forth. Many studies indicate that social support makes individuals and families less vulnerable when they experience such stressor events as losing a job or participating in a difficult line of work (Cobb, 1982; Gore, 1978; Maynard, Maynard, McCubbin, & Chao, 1980), raising a chronically ill child (Holroyd & Guthrie, 1986), recovering from a natural disaster (Scaramella, Sohr-Preston, Callahan, & Mirabile, 2008), or adjusting to war-induced separations (Campbell & Demi, 2000).

  Bronfenbrenner's (1979) review of the research in this area added an important new insight to the role of supportiveness inside families and in the amount of support families receive from the community and friends. When individuals and families are not coping with stressful events, it is growth producing to have considerable independence and autonomy and to have relatively little overt help, assistance, or support. However, when things are not going well, it then is helpful to have more supportiveness inside the family and between the family and the community. Another way of stating Bronfenbrenner's idea is that high supportiveness tends to be enabling when dealing with serious stressor events, but it can actually be disabling when things are going well.

- **Individual Strategies.** When it comes to coping with family stress, limited research suggests it can be helpful to focus on some aspects of individual development. Some of these strategies include promoting self-sufficiency (without overdoing it), working out to keep physically fit, developing a positive life outlook, and keeping up one's obligations to other organizations such as one's employment.

Disabling Strategies

Research also has identified ways of responding to stressor events that can have **disabling or destructive** effects. One of these is to react with violence. A number of research studies have found people tend to be more violent when experiencing stressful situations, such as undesirable behavior by a child, unemployment, unhappiness in their marriage or in their employment, or illnesses (McCubbin et al., 1988). The violence, however, tends to make the situations worse. It destroys positive emotional feelings toward the violent individuals and creates a number of negative emotions such as mistrust, anger, confusion, shame, and hate.

Other disabling strategies are denial, avoidance, rejection, increased use of alcohol, hostility, garbled and dishonest communication about the problem, preventing or limiting communication, prohibiting and interrupting individual and collective grieving within the family, and weakening family relationships precisely when they most need to be strengthened (Kaplan et al., 1973, p. 67; McCubbin et al., 1988). These strategies usually aggravate the original problem and create other problems, such as less connection to family members and decreases in problem solving effectiveness.

PRINCIPLE 13.2

THE STRATEGIES USED MATTER

The choice of strategies that families use in times of crisis matters greatly. Families who learn or can be taught to use more effective strategies in response to crisis will necessarily do better at recovering.

Boundary Ambiguity

Boss (2007) introduced another concept into the field that deals with coping strategies. The concept is **boundary ambiguity**. This occurs when families are uncertain in their perception of who is in or out of the family or who is performing what roles and tasks within the family. Her initial research was with military families and families who experience Alzheimer's disease. Military families find this problem especially severe when the father is listed as missing in action (MIA). The problem also occurs with families experiencing divorce, joint custody, desertion, and some chronic illnesses. When families, or professionals working with families, understand this concept, they can use it to help families cope because they can try to get the ambiguity within tolerable limits. Some strategies for helping families deal with their boundary ambiguity are to talk about who is in and out of the family, whether family members will be in or out for an identifiable period of time, and what the boundaries inside the family should be. Other strategies are to avoid keeping a physically absent family member psychologically present when it is disruptive for the family.

In some situations, families are not able to manage the new events with these strategies. When this occurs, the family gradually slips into a deeper and more serious crisis situation. When this happens, the very fabric of the family is in trouble, and the paradigmatic assumptions are called into question. The family's basic philosophy and orientations to life are examined, and these basic beliefs can evolve, change, be discarded, or be reconstructed. Examples of this would be changes in the way a family relates to its environment, changes in beliefs about who the family can "count on" when the chips are down, changes in beliefs about God and the role of the spiritual part of life, changes in beliefs about whether people are inherently good or bad, and differentiation from kin.

To illustrate, suppose a family did not believe in drug use yet found themselves with a teenage son who was adopting a lifestyle they did not understand; this could be a serious stressor event. The first strategies this family would tend to use involve trying to create simpler levels of change. For example, the parents could talk to the son about his life and why he is making these choices. If these simple methods do not work, the family might try enforcing rules about coming home earlier, grounding him, and taking away resources such as his access to money, and so on. If the simple rule changes do not work, the family would eventually resort to more fundamental changes. They might try to change their basic parenting methods, try to get professional assistance to make other changes, change where the child lives, or change the basic structure of the family.

If these methods do not work, the family will tend eventually to question some of their basic beliefs. For example, they might adopt a more fatalistic view of life and conclude that things will happen as they will, and they have less control over their world than they thought they had. They might rearrange their priorities in life and become more or less involved in trying to change their community values and structure. They might reevaluate their beliefs about the choices their children make try to understand them more fully.

PROFESSIONAL SUPPORT FOR FAMILIES IN STRESS

All families experience challenges (Figure 13.6). Occasionally, families may seek outside assistance in managing these challenges and the difficult internal issues families are experiencing. Family researchers are not only interested in how families work but also in how we can improve family functioning. Of course, this means we need ways to define and measure concepts in order to ensure effectiveness of treatment.

FIGURE 13.6 Sometimes stressor events come at very inconvenient times. This mother cannot really take time off to recover because many of her mothering duties and even work duties outside the home have to continue.

Family scientist David H. Olson, of the University of Minnesota, has received numerous awards for his excellent research contributions to our understanding of marriage and family. In 2000, he introduced the **Circumplex Model of Family Interaction** "specifically designed for clinical assessment, treatment planning, and research on outcome effectiveness of marital and family therapy" (p. 144).

A circumplex was originally a circular representation of variables (but has been updated to table form as seen in Figure 13.7); the closer the variables, the more similar they are. Such models are used in the social sciences, with specific measurements to determine the validity of the model. Olson based his model on the most basic and important dimensions related to family functioning:

1 Family cohesion—how emotionally bonded family members are, from disengage (low cohesion) to enmeshed (high cohesion).
2 Flexibility—also referred to as adaptability. This refers to the amount of change in leadership, role relationships, and relationship rules, from rigid (low flexibility) to chaotic (high flexibility).
3 Communication. Because Olson viewed communication as a facilitating dimension, it was not included graphically in the model.

As you examine Olson's model (Figure 13.7), you will notice that the dimensions of family flexibility and family cohesion each have five levels. The items on the similarly colored areas are more closely related. The nine boxes in the center grid represent balanced families, as well as the

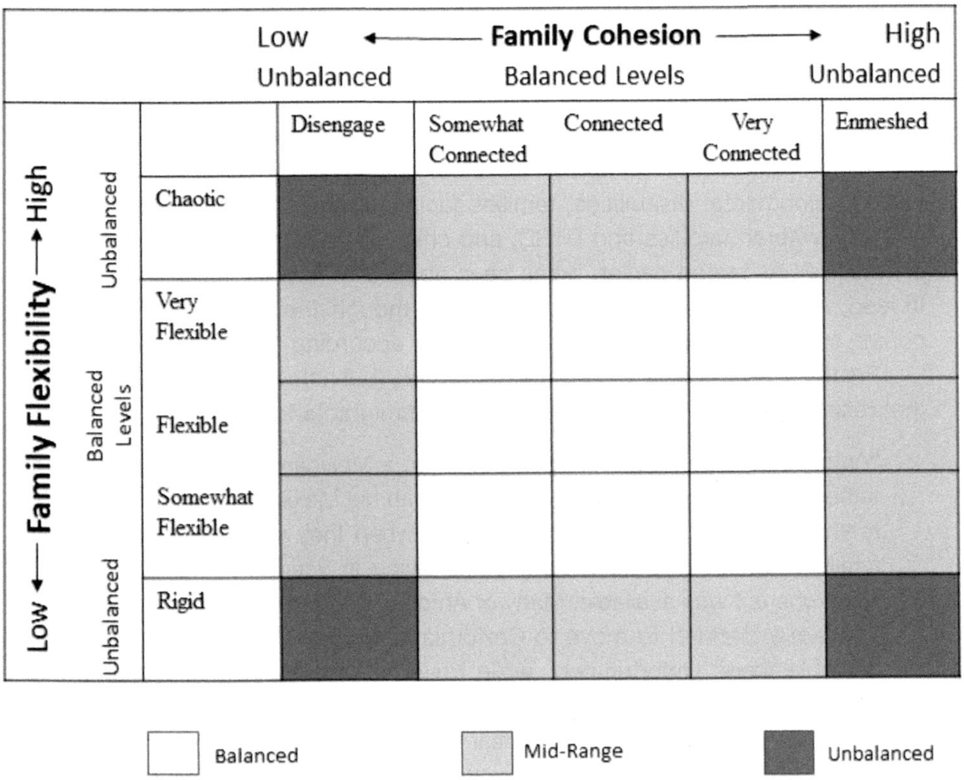

| | | Low ←——— Family Cohesion ———→ High | | | | |
		Unbalanced	Balanced Levels			Unbalanced
		Disengage	Somewhat Connected	Connected	Very Connected	Enmeshed
Family Flexibility →High / Unbalanced	Chaotic					
Balanced Levels	Very Flexible					
	Flexible					
	Somewhat Flexible					
Low← / Unbalanced	Rigid					

☐ Balanced   ▨ Mid-Range   ■ Unbalanced

FIGURE 13.7 Family Circumplex Model.

Source: Adapted from Olson, Waldvogel, and Schlieff (2019)

variations that can exist within these families. These families are more likely to be happy and successful in their relationships. The mid-range boxes represent families that may benefit from outside assistance in improving their family relationships, and the extreme corners of the figure represent families that are likely highly dysfunctional. Olson acknowledges that not all families in the "unbalanced" areas are dysfunctional. For families from certain religious or cultural groups, these relationships are considered normative and "work" within that cultural context.

This model recognizes how dynamic families are and assumes that families change family type in response to changes in the lifecycle or family stressors. Thus, the model can be used for plotting changes in a family's cohesion and flexibility across time. Olson's family Circumplex Model has been well-studied and used extensively by family therapists and other family professionals for helping families under stress (Olson et al., 2019). In addition, the model has been applied to non-family systems and contexts, such as classrooms, leadership styles, and parenting. Families also can measure their own "placement" on the chart and consider what ways can improve the functioning of their relationship.

Discussions in Diversity

Application of ABC-X across Contexts: A Case Study

The ABC-X model has been utilized successfully in numerous contexts (Figure 13.8). A quick search of the publications between 2017 and 2020* finds its application for: loss of a parent in adolescence, African-American families coping with COVID-19, families with children with autism spectrum disorder, adoptive parenting during the pandemic, same sex parenting, family finances, psychiatric nurses and workplace violence, ageing family caregivers of adults with developmental disabilities, families facing disaster, chronic illness within a family, veteran families and PTSD, and children of clergy (and this list is not exhaustive)! As stated earlier, it has been applied to families across the globe. Indeed, all families experience stress, even though the stressors, resources, coping strategies, and perceptions may differ according to culture and family.

For this discussion, let's consider a true story (but names have been changed) that reflects the lives of many refugees and immigrants today:

> "Antonio" was born near El Paso, Texas, to a Mexican mother and American father (who was raised mostly in Mexico with his Mexican parents). Antonio's mother had 15 children, although 3 died when they were quite young. The family crossed the border many times, living in various towns and finding work where it was available. Many of Antonio's siblings were born in Mexico. The family decided to move to California in 1955 and follow the crop work available there. Unfortunately, while traveling across Arizona, 6-month-old Antonio, became dangerously ill and needed to be hospitalized. The family put down roots in a rural community near Phoenix to wait for Antonio's recovery. They lived in various housing, some without running water or windows or air conditioning in a climate that reached over 110 degrees in the summer and under freezing in the winter. When Antonio was a teen, a government program

FIGURE 13.8 Can you apply the ABC-X model to a family struggling during the COVID 19 epidemic?

provided the family with a home that they built themselves. Staunch Catholics, they had a few family members living nearby; relatives from Mexico, California, and elsewhere in Arizona were frequent visitors. Antonio did not speak English when he entered kindergarten and was held back. Antonio's family was marked by poverty, domestic violence, substance abuse, and many moves. Despite these difficulties, Antonio has positive memories of taking lunch his mother had made to his father working in the field and eating with him, family gatherings that might include a watermelon cooled in the irrigation ditch, ranch owners who allowed Antonio to swim in their pools and ride their horses, trips to the lake, surprises from their neighbors (such as a large homemade gingerbread house cooked by a former German baker), and roaming free on the ranch. He recalls he didn't even know he was poor until he read a letter of recommendation a neighbor had written for him to obtain a job; interestingly, he recalls standing in food lines and feeling sorry for all the poor people in the line. Until the death of his parents (in their 80s), Antonio's family remained close.

Questions to Discuss:

- *Place information from the case into the ABC-X components (i.e., what might be an "A," "B," or "C"?). Speculate about potential family outcomes.*
- *What strengths might one see in this family?*
- *What stressors did this family encounter?*
- *Why might Antonio not see the family as poor?*
- *How might an understanding of Family Stress Theory and ABC-X models assist professionals in working with families and building family resilience? Note: "Professionals" could be teachers, doctors, policy makers, disaster preparedness specialists, public information officers.*

*See below for sample articles.

SUMMARY

Numerous events create stress in families, with some stressor events more serious than others. Some family stressors come from the environment, and others come from inside the family. How families define the stressors and what resources they have available to them to meet the challenge determine the potential outcomes.

The process of family stress has phases, and there seem to be five different patterns in the way families respond to stress: a rollercoaster pattern where some families experience disorganization followed by reorganization, a descending pattern where some families become disorganized and stay there, an ascending pattern where some families get better off in a stressful situation and stay there, a no-change pattern, and a mixed pattern where some families are better off and then have the rollercoaster experience.

Research about families has begun to identify coping strategies that families can use to deal effectively with stressful situations. Some families require professional help and may seek family therapy. The Circumplex Model of Family Interactions, based on family flexibility, cohesion, and communication, was created for clinical assessment, treatment planning, and research on the effectiveness of therapy and has been successfully applied to these settings and more. A main point of this chapter is that families can show resilience and, with effective coping strategies, bounce back from even significant stressors stronger than ever.

STUDY QUESTIONS

1   What is meant by family resilience?
2   Is ABC-X a theory or a model? Explain.
3   Give an example of each level of family stressors.
4   Name two stressful events that can originate outside the family and two that can originate from inside the family.
5   What is the difference between normative and non-normative family stressors?
6   What are the primary elements of the stress process?
7   Give an example of a serious stressor event and then tell how a family could generate a coping strategy to match.
8   Describe the five patterns of adjustment to stress found by Burr et al. (1994).
9   Why would the suicide of a family member be so devastating? Use the information in this chapter to explain your answer.
10 Using the Circumplex Model of Family Relationships, speculate the movement across the grid of a newlywed couple through their first five years of marriage.

KEY TERMS

Resources
Resilience
Transactional theory of stress
Family stress theory
Normative vs. non normative

Stressors

Eustress

Distress

Level 1/Level 2/Level 3 stressors

Crisis

ABC-X

Double ABC-X

Dismemberment

Accession

Ambiguous loss

Demoralizing

Stress pile-up

Cohesion

Adaptation

Coping and coping strategies

Boundary ambiguity

Circumplex Model of Family Interaction

SUGGESTED READINGS

Boss, P. (1999). *Ambiguous loss*. Cambridge, MA: Harvard University Press.

Cherlin, A. J. (1992). *Marriage, divorce, and remarriage*. Cambridge, MA: Harvard University Press.

Duncan, G., & Brooks-Gunn, J. (1997). *Consequences of growing up poor*. New York, NY: Russell Sage Foundation.

Henick, M. (2021). *So-called normal: A memoir of family, depression, and resilience*. New York, NY: HarperCollins Publishers.

L'Abate, L. (1990). *Building family competence*. Newbury Park, CA: Sage.

Masten, A. S. (2015). *Ordinary magic: Resilience in development*. New York, NY: Guilford.

Walsh, F. (2016). *Strengthening family resilience* (3rd ed.). New York, NY: Guilford.

*ABC-X Sample Articles (2017–2020)

• Apelian, E., & Nesteruk, O. (2017). Reflections of young adults on the loss of a parent in adolescence. *International Journal of Child, Youth and Family Studies, 8*(3/4), 79–100.

• Chaney, C. (2020). Family stress and coping among African Americans in the age of COVID-19. *Journal of Comparative Family Studies, 51*(3–4), 254–273.

• Enea, V., & Rusu, D. M. (2020). Raising a child with autism spectrum disorder: A systematic review of the literature investigating parenting stress. *Journal of Mental Health Research in Intellectual Disabilities, 13*(4), 283–321.

• Goldberg, A. E., McCormick, N., & Virginia, H. (2020). Parenting in a pandemic: Work–Family arrangements, well-being, and intimate relationships among adoptive parents. *Family Relations, 70*, 7–25.

• Heo, W., Lee, J. M., & Rabbani, A. G. (2020). Mediation effect of financial education between financial stress and use of financial technology. *Journal of Family and Economic Issues, 42*, 413–428. DOI: 10.1007/s10834-020-09720-w

• Hill, E. J., Allsop, D. B., LeBaron, A. B., & Bean, R. A. (2017). How do money, sex, and stress influence marital instability?. *Journal of Financial Therapy, 8*, 21–42. DOI: 10.4148/1944-9771.1135

• Hsieh, H. F., Wang, H. H., Shen, S. H., & Li, Y. C. (2018). Predictors of depressive symptoms among psychiatric nurses who suffered from workplace violence. *Journal of Advanced Nursing, 74*(2), 425–432.

- McCallion, P., & Ferretti, L. A. (2021). Psychosocial concerns among ageing family caregivers. In V. P. Prasher, P. W. Davidson, & F. H. Santos (Eds.), *Mental health, intellectual and developmental disabilities and the ageing process* (pp. 249–259). Cham: Springer.
- Silao, L. J. (2020). Physical development and disaster preparedness in children. In C. J. Goodhue, & N. Blake (Eds.), *Nursing management of pediatric disaster* (pp. 209–222). Cham: Springer.
- Soonthorndhada, A., Bwesigye, D. A., Hongthong, J., & Hutaphat, W. (2020). Situational stressors among caregivers of older persons in Thailand. In J. Poot, & M. Roskruge (Eds.), *Population change and impacts in Asia and the Pacific* (pp. 341–358). Singapore: Springer.
- Treder-Rochna, N. (2020). Adaptation to the disease—the psychological resources of families struggling with multiple sclerosis. *Health Psychology Report, 8*(2), 136–144.
- Weisenhorn, D. A., Frey, L. M., van de Venne, J., & Cerel, J. (2017). Suicide exposure and posttraumatic stress disorder: Is marriage a protective factor for veterans? *Journal of Child and Family Studies, 26*(1), 161–167.
- Wilson, C. B., & Darling, C. A. (2017). Understanding stress and life satisfaction for children of clergy: A retrospective study. *Pastoral Psychology, 66*(1), 129–142.
- Wu, Q., & Xu, Y. (2020). Parenting stress and risk of ch9ild maltreatment during the COVID-19 pandemic: A family stress theory-informed perspective. *Developmental Child Welfare, 2*(3), 180–196.

REFERENCES

Angell, R. C. (1936). *The family encounters the depression*. New York, NY: Scribner.

Boss, P. (1987). Family stress. In M. B. Sussman, & S. K. Steinmetz (Eds.), *Handbook of marriage and the family* (pp. 22–42). New York, NY: Plenum.

Boss, P. (1999). *Ambiguous loss: Learning to live with unresolved grief*. Cambridge, MA: Harvard University Press.

Boss, P. (2007). Ambiguous loss theory: Challenges for scholars and practitioners. *Family Relations, 56*, 105–112.

Bronfenbrenner, U. (1979). *The ecology of human development*. Cambridge, MA: Harvard University Press.

Burr, W. R., & Klein, S. (1994). *Reexamining family stress: New theory and research*. Thousand Oaks, CA: Sage Publications.

Campbell, C., & Demi, A. (2000). Adult children of father missing in action: An examination of emotional distress, grief, and family hardiness. *Family Relations, 49*, 267–277.

Carter, B., & McGoldrick, M. (Eds.). (1989). *The changing family life cycle: A framework for family therapy* (2nd ed.). New York, NY: Allyn & Bacon.

Cobb, S. (1982). Social support and health through the life course. In H. I. McCubbin, A. E. Cauble, & J. M. Patterson (Eds.), *Family stress, coping and social support* (pp. 351–372). Thousand Oaks, CA: Sage.

Dewe, P. (2013). The transactional model of stress: Some implications for stress management programs. *Asia Pacific Journal of Human Resources, 35*(2), 41–51.

Garmezy, N. (1991). Resilience and vulnerability to adverse developmental outcomes associated with poverty. *American Behavioral Scientist, 34*, 416–430.

Gore, S. (1978). The effect of social support in moderating the health consequences of unemployment. *Journal of Health and Social Behavior, 19*, 157–165.

Hill, R. (1949). *Families under stress: Adjustment to the crises of war separation and reunion*. New York, NY: Harper & Brothers.

Hill, R. (1958). 1. Generic features of families under stress. *Social casework, 39*(2–3), 139–150.

Holmes, T. H., & Rahe, R. R. (1967). The social readjustment rating scale. *Journal of Psychosomatic Research, 11*, 213–218.

Holroyd, J., & Guthrie, D. (1986). Family stress with chronic childhood illness. *Journal of Clinical Psychology, 42*, 552–568.

Innstrand, S. (2008). Positive and negative work—family interaction and burnout. *Work & Stress, 22*(1), 1–15.

Ju, S., Kweon, S. O., & Park, H. (2017). A study on the predictive causal model of codependency for introducing implications in family welfare policy-basing on the application of triple ABC-X model. *Journal of the Korea Society of Computer and Information, 22*(3), 139–145.

Kaplan, D. M., Smith, A., Grobstien, R., & Fischman, S. E. (1973). Family mediation of stress. *Social Work*, *18*, 60–69.

Koos, E. (1946). *Families in trouble*. New York, NY: King's Crown Press.

Manzi, C., Vignoles, V., Rgalia, C., & Scabini, E. (2006). Cohesion and enmeshment revisited: Differentiation, identity, and well-being in two European cultures. *Journal of Marriage and Family*, *68*(3), 673–689.

Masarik, A. S., & Conger, R. D. (2017). Stress and child development: A review of the family stress model. *Current Opinion in Psychology*, *13*, 85–90.

Masten, A. (1994). Resilience in individual development: Successful adaptation despite risk and adversity. In M. Wang, & E. Gordon (Eds.), *Educational resilience in inner-city America: Challenges and prospects* (pp. 3–25). Hillsdale, NJ: Lawrence Erlbaum Associates.

Maynard, P., Maynard, N., McCubbin, H. I., & Chao, D. (1980). Family life and the police profession: Coping patterns wives employ in managing job stress and the family environment. *Family Relations*, *29*(4), 495–501.

McCubbin, M., Balling, K., Possin, P., Frierdich, S., & Bryne, B. (2002). Family resiliency in childhood cancer. *Family Relations*, *51*, 103–111.

McCubbin, H., Boss, P., Wilson, L., & Lester, G. (1980). Developing family vulnerability to stress: Coping patterns and strategies wives employ. In J. Trost (Ed.), *The family and change* (pp. 89–103). Sweden: International Library.

McCubbin, H. I., & Dahl, B. (1985). *Marriage and family*. New York, NY: Wiley.

McCubbin, H. I., & Figley, C. (1983). *Stress and the family: Vol. 1. Coping with normative transitions*. New York, NY: Brunner & Mazel.

McCubbin, H., & Patterson, J. (1982). Family adaptation to crises. In H. McCubbin, A. Cauble, & J. Patterson (Eds.), *Family stress, coping and social support* (pp. 26–47). Springfield, IL: Thomas.

McCubbin, H. I., & Patterson, J. M. (1983). The family stress process: The double ABC-X model of family adjustment and adaptation. In H. I. McCubbin, M. Sussman, & J. M. Patterson (Eds.), *Social stress and the family: Advances and developments in family stress theory and research* (pp. 7–37). New York, NY: The Haworth Press, Inc.

McCubbin, H. I., Thompson, A. I., Pirner, P. A., & McCubbin, M. A. (1988). *Family types and strengths: A life cycle and ecological perspective*. Edina, MN: Burgess International Group.

Olson, D. H. (2000). Circumplex model of marital and family systems. *Journal of Family Therapy*, *22*, 144–167.

Olson, D. H., & Boss, P. (1986). Reuben l. Hill: A memorium: 1912–1985. *Family Process*, 25(1), 1–3. DOI: 10.1111/j.1545-5300.1986.00001.x

Olson, D. H., Waldvogel, L., & Schlieff, M. (2019). Circumplex model of marital and family systems: An update. *Journal of Family Theory & Review*, *11*, 199–211.

Patterson, J. (2002). Integrating family resilience and family stress theory. *Journal of Marriage and Family*, *64*, 349–360.

Pearlin, L., & Schooler, C. (1982). The structure of coping. *Journal of Health and Social Behavior*, *19*, 2–21.

Rosino, M. (2016). ABC-X model of family stress and coping. In C. L. Shehan & M. Duncan (Eds.), *The Wiley Blackwell encyclopedia of family studies*. Malden, MA: Wiley Blackwell. Retrieved from https://www.researchgate.net/profile/Michael_Rosino/publication/314932267_ABC-X_Model_of_Family_Stress_and_Coping/links/59e39b490f7e9b97fbeb0005/ABC-X-Model-of-Family-Stress-and-Coping.pdf

Scaramella, L. V., Sohr-Preston, S. L., Callahan, K. L., & Mirabile, S. P. (2008). A test of the family stress model on toddler-aged children's adjustment among hurricane Katrina impacted and nonimpacted low-income families. *Journal of Clinical Child & Adolescent Psychology*, *37*, 530–542.

Selye, H. (1974). *Stress without distress*. Philadelphia, PA: J.B. Lippincott Company.

Smith, S. D. (1984). Family stress theory: Review and critique. Paper presented at the annual meeting of the National Council on Family Relations, San Francisco, October 16–20, 1984.

Snowden, R., & Snowden, E. (1984). *The gift of a child*. London: George Allen & Unwin.

Taylor, Z. E., & Conger, R. D. (2017). Promoting strengths and resilience in single-mother families. *Child Development*, *88*(2), 350–358.

Thomas, W. I., & Thomas, D. S. (1928). *The child in America*. Oxford, UK: Knopf.

Walsh, F. (1999). *Spiritual resources in family therapy*. New York, NY: Guilford Press.

Walsh, F. (2016). Family resilience: A developmental systems framework. *European Journal of Developmental Psychology, 13*(3), 313–324.

Weber, J. G. (2011/2013). The ABCX formula and the double ABCX model. In J. G. Weber (Ed.), *Individual and family stress and crises* (pp. 82–96, Chapter 4). Thousand Oaks, CA: Sage Publications.

Wunsch, G. (1994). Theories, models, and data. *Demografie, 36*(1), 20–29.

CHAPTER **14**

Epilogue

We began our study of family and family processes with philosopher George Santayana's quote, "Family is one of nature's masterpieces." As with exploring nature's other masterpieces, such as the Grand Canyon in Arizona, we discovered through our journey unimagined depth and complexity with its layers, twists, and turns, finding beautiful vistas and unexpected surprises (Figure 14.1).

For family scholars, family, in all its forms, is important, and we care about our study of the internal workings of family. Why?

1 **Families Are a Fundamental Unit of Society.** This idea reflects a belief that people everywhere in virtually every society have selected family life as the preferred way of joining for survival and strength. Somewhere in our prehistorical past, individuals found that they could do better if they formed small, intimate family groups. Society seems to begin when individuals claim a family group. We have all seen pictures and movies of animals that begin their lives and must be quite independent from the beginning. You might have seen documentaries about animals such as baby wildebeest that can be up and running from a hunting lion within a few hours of birth. Contrast that image to the helplessness of a human infant. A newborn baby is very reliant on a caregiver for several months and is quite dependent on sustained family life for several years. Therefore, the family unit is fundamental to society because it helps the human race survive to the next generations.

2 **The Best Way to Rear Children Is in Families.** Family researchers and family observers believe that the most effective forum for raising children is the family. A child's parents are more likely to take a special and attentive interest in the well-being of their children. That is not to say that they always do a good job. Rather, overall, the job they do is usually better than that of a disinterested third party. Parents are more likely to make better decisions about their children than would someone else. Family processes are of great interest to a wide number of people for whom these close relationships are of high importance. The well-being of individuals is affected by what goes on in close family relationships.

3 **Family Problems Are Costly (Dalaker, 2001).** Those costs are incurred not only by the individuals involved but the community at large. For example, divorce incurs high costs (financial, emotional, social, etc.) for the individual, but it also costs employers, causes disruption in the lives of children, and may result in intervention of costly government programs (such as Temporary Assistance to Needy Families [TANF]).

4 **Better Family Life Means Stronger Community Well-Being.** Noted professor, intellectual, and former president of the American Sociological Association, Amitai Etzioni (1993), has created an intellectual movement in which he suggests that strength in family life creates community strength. He suggests that when children perform better in school, are arrested less, are more responsible to civic law, and experience less violence in homes, each of us in a community of families benefits. That is, the social and economic standard for all increases and each individual is better able to reach his or her desired life goals.

DOI: 10.4324/9781003128717-18

FIGURE 14.1 Grand Canyon, Arizona.

Source: Photo by Alan Carrillo, free use

It is in the interest of all community members that we find ways of rearing and caring for children in ways that create the best outcomes for those children. In general, when children are emotionally, socially, spiritually, and economically stronger, the larger community does better.

PRINCIPLE 14.1

FAMILIES ARE IMPORTANT

We care about families because of the value they have to individuals, society, and the economy.

As we study and discuss family, we are often struck by the number of people who point out that what constitutes a family is changing, as well as the context of family life itself. Consider:

- A rise in divorce rates
- More women working outside the home and becoming professionals
- Increased numbers of veterans competing for jobs
- Widespread prosperity, with the United States, having 2/5 of the world's wealth
- More people linked through mass communication than ever before
- New technologies, new science, new wealth

- Increased racial and religious diversity, mixed with immigration issues
- Bounce back from a world-wide pandemic
- Fear the family will go extinct

Current day issues? No, the 1920s (Braughman, Bondi, Layman, McConnell, & Tompkins, 2001)! Further, author/historian/scholar Stephanie Coontz (1995/2005) tells us that diversity in family form has always existed and the "traditional" family form found in the 1950s was actually an aberration, a blip, a myth. What families do (e.g., have and rear children, solve problems, take care of each other) has remained relatively unchanged for centuries. However, how those activities are performed and who is present (i.e., the composition of family life) is ever changing over time and varies from family to family and culture to culture.

Should you explore your own family history, you are likely to find it changing in a protean manner, with divorce, desertion, extended family, diversity, immigration, language differences, poverty, religion changes, widowhood, many children, and few children from generation to generation. Yet, still, much of its essence has been passed to you. A key idea of this book is that families must meet the challenges before them, even though our idea of what constitutes a family might be changing, and even though family life might or might not be the same as it was in times past. They engage in rituals and routines and draw on family beliefs and philosophies, all culturally and personally influenced. They use strategies to solve problems, make decisions, and allocate resources. Our study of family processes is the study of those strategies families use to maximize the goals they set out to achieve. We encourage you to think past the clichés of our family existence and to begin thinking more analytically and specifically about what happens in families on a daily basis as they try to solve problems, make decisions, allocate resources, and make sense out of a very complicated world.

It is safe to say that we understand *studying* family life is not the same as *living* family life. Unlike other academic pursuits (e.g., chemistry, math, or music), nearly everyone experiences family life firsthand. Although more general life experience can be helpful in understanding larger principles of inner family life, our personal unique perspective can sometimes get in the way of objectivity. Think of how many times you have been in a bank. It might have been dozens or even hundreds of times. Just because you have been there and have borrowed money for a car, paid a loan, or deposited or cashed a check does not necessarily mean that you know how to run the bank. Biochemistry provides another example of this principle. Most of us know very little about the chemistry of life even though we use chemicals and our bodies certainly perform complicated chemical reactions every second of life. Some of us might have a superficial understanding of simple chemical interactions, but the point is that having food transformed into energy within your body is not the same as understanding how that happens. We live daily family life without really thinking about it, knowing how, or having to understand how it all works. In this regard, we understand that family scientists have something important to contribute, and we have tried to present information in a way that gives you a clearer understanding of the inner workings of family.

Our study of family processes can help families successfully reach their goals, whether your own family or families you might work with in a variety of capacities. As family scientists learn about the insides and outsides of family, they hope to influence more than individual families, however; they also hope to influence policy, politics, and future research. Families all over the world face many important issues, from economics to pandemics, from health to education, from family structure to racial inequality, and most people believe that families should be supported and strengthened. How that should be done (who should pay for it) is a matter of great debate, but policies and politics should be informed by the best research related to family. These issues raise key questions, such as: What is family? What family forms should our legal and financial systems attend to? Who should have the ultimate say about individual matters? Who should have the ultimate say in matters that may influence children? And, does a government have the right (or responsibility) to dictate moral direction? If the government does have the right or responsibility to promote a particular ethical or moral view, which of the myriad of competing moral views should they adopt? These highly charged political issues find their way into elections, public debate, and legislative bodies, and even courts, leading to small- and large-scale public policy shifts. Family life researchers have made important contributions to the safety and well-being of families so far, and it is hoped their research will continue to do so.

Finally, it goes without saying that most people realize family life is a double-edged sword; it can be a source of love, compassion, and fulfillment, but it can also be a harbor of destruction, oppression, and violence. Either condition is possible; however, we believe it is the responsibility of each family member to learn how to make family life better for all involved. Therefore, another goal of this text was to convince you that by understanding the processes that occur in daily family life, one can change the quality of family life. In other words, a primary assumption of this text is the idea that family members can make a difference in the quality of their family life. Related to this idea is hope. Even if your family has experienced or will experience difficult times or even the usual stresses of daily living, you can make your family experience one that helps you cope and even survive.

Our journey into family processes (the inside of the elephant) has come to an end. We hope that the principles and ideas presented in this textbook can be of assistance to you. We hope you gained a new appreciation about the complexity of family and family life. We also hope you learned not only about family but also about yourself. We celebrate our diversity as we simultaneously recognize our similarities. As poet laureate Maya Angelou penned in the *Human Family*:

> I note the obvious differences
> between each sort and type,
> but we are more alike, my friends,
> than we are unalike.
> We are more alike, my friends,
> than we are unalike.
> We are more alike, my friends,
> than we are unalike.

SUGGESTED READINGS

Bogenschneider, K. (2014). *Family policy matters: How policymaking affects families and what professionals can do*. New York, NY: Routledge.

Coontz, S. (1995, July). The way we weren't: the myth and reality of the "traditional" family. *National Forum*, *75*(3), 11. https://link.gale.com/apps/doc/A17476379/AONE?u=anon~7dc15a21&sid=googleScholar&xid=ed0c9e16

Karpowitz, C. F., & Pope, J. C. (2020). *American Family Survey Summary Report: Family Life During a Pandemic*. The American Family Survey. Center for the Study of Elections and Democracy, Deseret News, and YouGov. http://csed.byu.edu/american-family-survey/ NOTE: This survey is conducted yearly, beginning in 2015, with results for each survey available, including policies and trends.

Kolker, R. (2020). *Hidden Valley Road: Inside the mind of an American family*. New York, NY: Doubleday.

Parr, T. (2010). *The family book*. New York, NY: Little, Brown, & Company (a picture book).

REFERENCES

Braughman, J. S., Bondi, V., Layman, R., McConnell, T., & Tompkins, V. (Eds.). (2001). *The 1920s: Lifestyles and social trends: Overview. American Decades* (Vol. 3, 1920–1929). Detroit, MI: Gale. Retrieved from https://wjccschools.org/wp-content/uploads/sites/2/2016/05/The-1920s-Lifestyles-and-Trends-Overview.pdf

Coontz, S. (1995, July). The way we weren't: the myth and reality of the "traditional" family. *National Forum*, *75*(3), 11. https://link.gale.com/apps/doc/A17476379/AONE?u=anon~7dc15a21&sid=googleScholar&xid=ed0c9e16

Dalaker, J. (2001). *Current population report*. Washington, DC: U.S. Census Bureau.

Etizoni, A. (1993). *The spirit of community*. New York, NY: Crown Publishers.

Subject Index

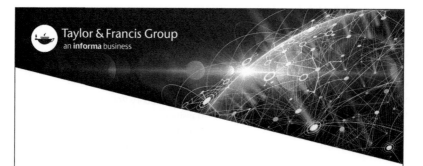